Church of England

Day-hours of the Church of England

Church of England

Day-hours of the Church of England

ISBN/EAN: 9783337849344

Printed in Europe, USA, Canada, Australia, Japan

Cover: Foto ©Lupo / pixelio.de

More available books at **www.hansebooks.com**

The Day-Hours of the Church of England

The Day-Hours of the Church of England

THE DAY-HOURS

OF

THE CHURCH OF ENGLAND

NEWLY REVISED

ACCORDING TO THE PRAYER-BOOK AND THE AUTHORISED
TRANSLATION OF THE BIBLE.

TWENTY-SEVENTH THOUSAND.

"Thou shalt talk of them when thou sittest in thine house, and when thou walkest by the way, and when thou liest down, and when thou risest up."—*Deut.* vi. 7.

LONDON:
J. MASTERS AND CO., 78, NEW BOND STREET.
1891.

"He made the Moon also to serve in Her Season for a declaration of times, and a sign of the world. From the Moon is the sign of feasts."—*Ecclus.* xliii. 6, 7.

FORMER Editions of this Book have been valued and used by many who desire to emulate the practice of the Psalmist in his religious observance of the hours of the day. The structure of our Book of Common Prayer has made us familiar with the methods, on which the Law and the Prophets are here, as of old, interwoven with the framework of devotion proper to the Seasons of our Christian Year. Its aim is to form and guide the mind of the worshipper by a constant and orderly use of the Treasures of Devotion contained in Holy Scripture, rather than by the modern plan of making prayer and praise exclusively a reflection of his own accidental mode of feeling.

In this view of it I desire heartily to commend the New Edition of these Offices to my brethren, acknowledging the care with which they have been Edited, and praying that God may bless the use of them to the growth in spiritual attainments of all who are able to follow their rule.

J. F. OXON.

CUDDESDEN PALACE,
Sept. 12, 1876.

THE CONTENTS OF THIS BOOK.

	PAGE
Plain Directions for using this Book	vii
Patris Sapientia	x
The Kalendar	xi
Tables and Rules for the Feasts and Fasts throughout the Year	xxiii
The PROPER SERVICES for the Seasons of the Christian Year, i.e. (Advent, Christmas, Epiphany, Lent, Easter, Whitsuntide, and Trinity)	1
The PSALTER:	
Lauds—Sunday	139
—— Monday	147
—— Tuesday	151
—— Wednesday	153
—— Thursday	156
—— Friday	159
—— Saturday	162
Prime—Sunday	166
—— On Festivals	171
—— On week-days	171
Terce	179
Sext	183
None	186
Vespers—Sunday	190
—— Monday	196
—— Tuesday	199
—— Wednesday	201
—— Thursday	204
—— Friday	207
—— Saturday	211
Compline	215
The Penitential Psalms	226
The SERVICE COMMON of Saints:	
For the Feasts of the Blessed Virgin Mary	231
For the Feast of an Apostle or Apostles	235
The SERVICE PROPER of Holy-Days	240
Appendix to the Service Proper of Holy-Days	293
Table of Psalms	300
—— Canticles	300
—— Latin Hymns	301
—— English Translations of Latin Hymns	302

PLAIN DIRECTIONS FOR USING THIS BOOK.

THIS Book consists of three parts: (A) the Proper Service for the Seasons; (B) the Psalter, or Daily Service; (C) the Common and Proper Service for Holy-Days.

A. THE PROPER SERVICE FOR THE SEASONS, as the name implies, contains those portions of the Service which follow the changing course of the Christian year: such are the "Antiphons" (or "Anthems") to the Psalms, the "Chapters," "Responses," "Hymns," "Antiphons" to *Benedictus* and *Magnificat;* also the "Collects," and occasionally the "Memorials." Each of these will find its own place in the Psalter.

B. THE PSALTER, consisting of the Seven Hours of Prayer, viz., Lauds, Prime, Terce, Sext, None, Vespers, and Compline, may be described as a framework to receive the changing treasures of the Proper Services.

C. THE COMMON AND PROPER SERVICE FOR HOLY-DAYS comprehends the variations of the service for those immovable Festivals whereon are commemorated the Saints of God.

The Service of LAUDS begins with the Invocation of the Holy Trinity, and the Lord's Prayer, followed by a Verse (or V.,) with its Response (or R.:) this V. and R. vary according to the Sunday, Season, or Holy-Day; and afterwards is said the V. *O God, make speed, &c.*, with the R. *O Lord, make haste, &c.* Then follows *Glory be to the Father, &c.*, with its R.; after which is said *Alleluia*, for which, however, from Septuagesima till Easter is substituted,

> *Praise to Thee, O Lord, we sing,*
> *Of Glory the Eternal King.*

Five Psalms, or combinations of Psalms, or Canticles, are always said at Lauds, partly varied on each day of the week, and Holy-Days; the last group being invariably Ps. cxlviii., cxlix., cl., which confer upon the Service its name of "Lauds," or "Praise." Each Psalm, or group, is followed by an "Antiphon," the first words of which are always said before the Psalm or Canticle, to which it belongs. Then follows the "Chapter," to which is made the "Response," *Thanks be to God.* The Chapter varies according to the Sunday, Season, or Holy-Day. The "Hymn," which succeeds, is varied according to the day of the week, or Holy-Day, during the weeks after Epiphany, but at other times by the Season or Holy-Day. A V. and R. are attached to the Hymn at Lauds, so that when a Hymn is ordered to be said, the V. and R. belonging to it are always included in such order. [It should be observed that from Maundy Thursday to Low Sunday no Hymn is said.] *Benedictus*, the Song of Zachariah, which Christians have always delighted to apply to the Incarnation of their Lord and the Redemption of His people, is then said with its Antiphon, which during Epiphany and Trinity will be found in its place in the "Psalter" on each day of the week; at other times, and on Sundays and Feast-days, in the "Proper Services." The Antiphon for an Immovable Feast (except those immediately following Christmas-Day) will be found in the Proper Service for Holy-Days. On all days which have a Collect, Epistle, and Gospel, in the Book of Common Prayer, the whole Antiphon is said before as well as after *Benedictus*. On Sundays and Holy-Days the Collect immediately follows, but on week-days the "Week-day Prayers" are inserted before it. Certain "Memorials" (consisting of an Antiphon, V. and R., and Collect) are then said, usually three in number; but at various seasons; and when one Festival clashes with another, or with a Sunday, additions are sometimes made. The Service concludes with a short form of intercession "for the peace of the Church."

PRIME begins with the Invocation of the Holy Trinity and the Lord's Prayer, followed by *O God, make speed, &c.*, as at Lauds. [In the same manner are begun Terce, Sext, None, and Vespers.] Prime then proceeds, except from Maundy Thursday to Low Sunday, with the Hymn, *Jam lucis orto sidere*; the Doxology, or last verse, being varied at certain seasons and feasts. After the first words of the Antiphon, which varies with the Sunday, Season, or Holy-Day, *Deus in nomine*, Psalm liv., is said, followed (except on Saturdays) by a Psalm which varies on each day of the week; to this are added the first thirty-two verses of *Beati immaculati*, Ps. cxix., and on Sundays the Creed of St. Athanasius also. The Chapter, varied on Sundays and Holy-Days, is completed by a Response, in which, during some great Festivals, a slight change occurs. A few Prayers conclude this Service on Sundays, and Holy-Days, but on week-days a longer form is used, containing a short Confession, &c., (and in Lent *Miserere*, Psalm li.) The Service ends with the customary commemoration of the dead in Christ.

TERCE, SEXT, and NONE begin as does Prime (*vide ante*.) Each has its own Hymn, the Doxology being variable. In each forty-eight verses of Ps. cxix. are said, with an Antiphon, varied with the Sunday, Season, or Holy-Day. Then follows a Chapter, completed with a Response: these also vary with the Antiphon to the Psalm. These three Services end as does that of Lauds, with the Collect for the week, preceded on week-days by the Week-day Prayers. Neither Memorials, however, nor the form for the Peace of the Church, are said at Prime, Terce, Sext, or None.

VESPERS.—This Service is the counterpart of Lauds, like which, it has its Five Psalms, Chapter, and Hymn; *Magnificat* being made to answer to *Benedictus*. It is to be observed, that all Sundays and Feast-days, except those of St. Stephen, St. John, and Holy Innocents, have two Vespers, those of the day next before being reckoned as of the

Feast. Vespers begin as do Prime, &c.; but after the Alleluia proceed with the first words of the Antiphon to the first of the five Psalms. Each Psalm has its own Antiphon, except on certain Feast-days and Sundays, when all the Psalms are said under one Antiphon. Then is said the Chapter, which is varied according to the Season or Festival, and is completed by the Response, *Thanks be to God*, for which, at certain Festivals and Seasons, a special Response is substituted: these will be found in the Proper Services. The Hymn is then said, followed by its ℣. and ℟. and *Magnificat*, with its Antiphon, which, together with the Hymn, is found during Epiphany and Trinity in the Psalter; at other Seasons, and on Festivals, in the Proper Services. On all days which have a Collect, Epistle and Gospel in the Book of Common Prayer, the whole Antiphon is said before as well as after *Magnificat*, at the Second Vespers. The whole Antiphon is also said before as well as after *Magnificat*, at the First Vespers of Christmas Day, the Circumcision, the Epiphany, the Purification, the Annunciation, Easter Day, Ascension Day, Whitsun Day, Trinity Sunday, and All Saints. On Sundays and Holy-Days the Collect immediately follows, but on week-days the Week-day Prayers are inserted before it. Certain Memorials are then said, usually three in number, but additions are sometimes made.

COMPLINE begins with the invocation of the Holy Trinity, and proceeds with a ℣. and ℟., followed by *O God, make speed, &c.*, as at Lauds. Four Psalms are said at Compline under one Antiphon; this latter varied according to the Season. The Chapter, which follows, is never varied, but said without change throughout the year (except that it is omitted altogether from Maundy Thursday to Low Sunday,) and is completed by the ℟. *Thanks be to God*, for which is substituted, during Lent till Maundy Thursday, a special ℟. Then is said a Hymn, varied according to the Seasons and Feasts, and concluded by the ℣. and ℟. *Keep me as the apple of an eye, &c. Nunc Dimittis* follows, with its Antiphon, which on Feast-days is said before as well as after the Canticle; the Antiphon varies with the Season, and on Feast-days. Then are said the "Prayers," including the form of Confession said at Lauds, and on week-days Psalm li. is inserted. The "Prayers" and the Intercession for the Peace of the Church, which immediately follows, are omitted on certain days and seasons.

The Seven PENITENTIAL PSALMS, one of which is said at each Hour in Lent, complete the "PSALTER."

Some latitude was frequently allowed as to the precise time at which these Services were said, but the original design was, that LAUDS were to be said at daybreak; followed by PRIME, as its name implies, at the first hour, i.e., six o'clock a.m.; TERCE, at the third hour, or nine a.m.; SEXT, at the sixth hour, or noon; NONE, at the ninth hour, i.e. three p.m.; VESPERS, at six p.m., and COMPLINE at nightfall, or nine p.m. Thus according to the example of the Psalmist of Israel, praising our Lord seven times in the day, "because of His righteous judgments."

PATRIS SAPIENTIA.

Circled by His enemies,
　By His own forsaken,
God made Man, at time of Lauds,
　For our sakes was taken:
Very Wisdom, Very Light,
　Monarch long expected,
In the garden by the Jews
　Bought, betrayed, afflicted.

See them, at the hour of Prime,
　Unto Pilate leading
Him 'gainst Whom with lying tongues
　Witnesses are pleading;
There with spitting and with shame
　Ill for good they render,
Marring of That Face which gives
　Heaven Eternal splendour.

"Crucify Him!" for His love
　Is their bitter payment,
When they lead Him forth at Terce,
　Clad in purple raiment;
And a Crown of woven thorns
　On His Head He weareth,
And the Cross of Calvary
　On His Shoulders beareth.

He upon the Cross at Sext
　For man's sake was mounted,
By the passers-by reviled,
　With transgressors counted:
Mocking, vinegar, and gall
　To His thirst they proffer:
To the Holy Lamb of God
　Such the taunts they offer.

At the hour of None the strife
　Long and sharp was ended,
Gently to His Father's Hands
　He His soul commended:
And a soldier pierced His Side
　With a spear unbidden,
While earth quaked exceedingly,
　And the sun was hidden.

When it came to Vesper-time,
　From the Cross they take Him,
Whose great Love to bear such woes
　For our sakes could make Him:
Such a death He underwent,
　Our alone Physician,
That of everlasting Life
　We might have fruition.

At the holy Compline-tide,
　Holy hands array Him
In the garments of the grave,
　Where the mourners lay Him:
Myrrh and spices have they brought,
　Scripture is completed;
And by death, the Prince of Life
　Death and hell defeated.

Therefore these Canonical
　Hours my tongue shall ever
In Thy praise, O Christ, recite
　With my heart's endeavour:
That the Love, Which for my sake
　Bore such tribulation,
In mine own Death-agony
　May be my Salvation.

THE KALENDAR.

JANUARY hath XXXI. DAYS.

1	A	Kalendæ.	Circumcision of our Lord Jesus Christ.	Holy-Day.
2	b	4 Nonas.		
3	c	3 Non.		
4	d	Prid. Non.		
5	e	Nonæ.		
6	f	8 Idus.	Epiphany of our Lord. Holy-Day.	
7	g	7 Id.		
8	A	6 Id.	Lucian, Priest and Martyr.	
9	b	5 Id.		
10	c	4 Id.		
11	d	3 Id.	*David, King.*	
12	e	Prid. Id.		
13	f	Idus.	Hilary, Bishop and Confessor.	
14	g	19 Kal. Feb.		
15	A	18 Kal.		
16	b	17 Kal.		
17	c	16 Kal.		
18	d	15 Kal.	Prisca, Rom. Virgin and Martyr.—*Mungo, Bishop.*	
19	e	14 Kal.		
20	f	13 Kal.	Fabian, Bishop of Rome and Martyr.	
21	g	12 Kal.	Agnes, Rom. Virgin and Martyr.	
22	A	11 Kal.	Vincent, Span. Deacon and Martyr.	
23	b	10 Kal.		
24	c	9 Kal.		
25	d	8 Kal.	Conversion of St. Paul. Holy-Day.	
26	e	7 Kal.		
27	f	6 Kal.		
28	g	5 Kal.		
29	A	4 Kal.		
30	b	3 Kal.	Martyrdom of Charles I., 1648—9.	
31	c	Prid. Kal.		

FEBRUARY HATH XXVIII. DAYS.

1	d	Kalendæ.	*Fast.*
2	e	4 Nonas.	**Purification of the B. Virgin Mary. Holy-Day.**
3	f	3 Non.	Blasius, an Armenian Bishop and Martyr.
4	g	Prid. Non.	
5	A	Nonæ.	Agatha, a Sicilian Virgin and Martyr.
6	b	8 Idus.	
7	c	7 Id.	
8	d	6 Id.	
9	e	5 Id.	
10	f	4 Id.	
11	g	3 Id.	
12	A	Prid. Id.	
13	b	Idus.	
14	c	16 Kal. Mart.	Valentine, Bishop and Martyr.
15	d	15 Kal.	
16	e	14 Kal.	
17	f	13 Kal.	
18	g	12 Kal.	*Colman, Bishop and Confessor.*
19	A	11 Kal.	
20	b	10 Kal.	
21	c	9 Kal.	
22	d	8 Kal.	
23	e	7 Kal.	*Fast.*
24	f	6 Kal.	**Matthias, Apostle and Martyr. Holy-Day.**
25	g	5 Kal.	
26	A	4 Kal.	
27	b	3 Kal.	
28	c	Prid. Kal.	
29			

MARCH HATH XXXI. DAYS.

	1	d	Kalendæ.	David, Bishop of Menevia.
	2	e	6 Nonas.	Cedde, or Chad, Bishop of Lichfield.
	3	f	5 Non.	
	4	g	4 Non.	
	5	A	3 Non.	
	6	b	Prid. Non.	
	7	c	Nonæ.	Perpetua, Mauritan. Martyr.
	8	d	8 Idus.	
	9	e	7 Id.	
	10	f	6 Id.	
	11	g	5 Id.	*Constantine, King.*
	12	A	4 Id.	Gregory the Great, Bishop of Rome and Con-
	13	b	3 Id.	[fessor.
	14	c	Prid. Id.	
	15	d	Idus.	
	16	e	17 Kal. Apr.	
	17	f	16 Kal.	*Patrick, Bishop and Confessor.*
	18	g	15 Kal.	Edward, King of the West Saxons.—*Cyril,*
	19	A	14 Kal.	[*Bishop.*
	20	b	13 Kal.	*Cuthbert, Bishop.*
14	21	c	12 Kal.	Benedict, Abbot.
3	22	d	11 Kal.	
	23	e	10 Kal.	
11	24	f	9 Kal.	*Fast.*
	25	g	8 Kal.	𝕬nnunciation of the 𝕭. 𝖁. 𝕸ary. 𝕳oly=𝕯ay.
19	26	A	7 Kal.	
8	27	b	6 Kal.	
	28	c	5 Kal.	
16	29	d	4 Kal.	
5	30	e	3 Kal.	
	31	f	Prid. Kal.	

APRIL hath XXX. DAYS.

13	1	g	Kalendæ.	
2	2	A	4 Nonas.	
	3	b	3 Non.	Richard, Bishop of Chichester.
10	4	c	Prid. Non.	St. Ambrose, Bishop of Milan.
	5	d	Nonæ.	
18	6	e	8 Idus.	
7	7	f	7 Id.	
	8	g	6 Id.	
15	9	A	5 Id.	
4	10	b	4 Id.	
	11	c	3 Id.	
12	12	d	Prid. Id.	
1	13	e	Idus.	
	14	f	18 Kal. Maij.	
9	15	g	17 Kal.	
	16	A	16 Kal.	
17	17	b	15 Kal.	
6	18	c	14 Kal.	
	19	d	13 Kal.	Alphege, Archbishop of Canterbury.
	20	e	12 Kal.	*Serf, Bishop.*
	21	f	11 Kal.	
	22	g	10 Kal.	
	23	A	9 Kal.	St. George, Martyr.
	24	b	8 Kal.	
	25	c	7 Kal.	𝕾t. 𝕸ark, 𝕰vangelist and 𝕸artyr. 𝕳oly= [Day.
	26	d	6 Kal.	
	27	e	5 Kal.	
	28	f	4 Kal.	
	29	g	3 Kal.	
	30	A	Prid. Kal.	

MAY HATH XXXI. DAYS.

1	b	Kalendæ.	SS. Philip and James, Apostles and Martyrs.
2	c	6 Nonas.	[Holy=Day.
3	d	5 Non.	Invention of the Cross.
4	e	4 Non.	
5	f	3 Non.	
6	g	Prid. Non.	St. John Evangelist, ante Portam Latinam.
7	A	Nonæ.	
8	b	8 Id.	
9	c	7 Id.	
10	d	6 Id.	
11	e	5 Id.	
12	f	4 Id.	
13	g	3 Id.	
14	A	Prid. Id.	
15	b	Idus.	
16	c	17 Kal. Junij.	
17	d	16 Kal.	
18	e	15 Kal.	
19	f	14 Kal.	Dunstan, Archbishop of Canterbury.
20	g	13 Kal.	
21	A	12 Kal.	
22	b	11 Kal.	
23	c	10 Kal.	
24	d	9 Kal.	
25	e	8 Kal.	
26	f	7 Kal.	Augustin, First Archbishop of Canterbury.
27	g	6 Kal.	Venerable Bede, Priest.
28	A	5 Kal.	
29	b	4 Kal.	King Charles II. Nativ. and Restor.
30	c	3 Kal.	
31	d	Prid. Kal.	

JUNE HATH XXX. DAYS.

1	c	Kalendæ.	Nicomede, Roman Priest and Martyr.
2	f	4 Nonas.	
3	g	3 Non.	
4	A	Prid. Non.	
5	b	Nonæ.	Boniface, Bishop of Mentz and Martyr.
6	c	8 Idus.	
7	d	7 Id.	
8	e	6 Id.	
9	f	5 Id.	*Columba, Abbot.*
10	g	4 Id.	
11	A	3 Id.	**St. Barnabas, Apostle and Martyr. Holy-Day.**
12	b	Prid. Id.	
13	c	Idus.	
14	d	18 Kal. Julij.	
15	e	17 Kal.	
16	f	16 Kal.	
17	g	15 Kal.	St. Alban, Martyr.
18	A	14 Kal.	
19	b	13 Kal.	
20	c	12 Kal.	Translation of Edward, King of the West Saxons.
21	d	11 Kal.	
22	e	10 Kal.	
23	f	9 Kal.	*Fast.*
24	g	8 Kal.	**Nativity of St. John Baptist. Holy-Day.**
25	A	7 Kal.	
26	b	6 Kal.	
27	c	5 Kal.	
28	d	4 Kal.	*Fast.*
29	e	3 Kal.	**St. Peter, Apostle and Martyr. Holy-Day.**
30	f	Prid. Kal.	

JULY HATH XXXI. DAYS.

1	g	Kalendæ.	
2	A	6 Nonas.	Visitation of the Blessed Virgin Mary.
3	b	5 Non.	
4	c	4 Non.	Translation of St. Martin, Bishop and Confessor.
5	d	3 Non.	
6	e	Prid. Non.	*Palladius, Bishop.*
7	f	Nonæ.	
8	g	8 Idus.	
9	A	7 Id.	
10	b	6 Id.	
11	c	5 Id.	
12	d	4 Id.	
13	e	3 Id.	
14	f	Prid. Id.	
15	g	Idus.	Translation of St. Swithun, Bishop of Winchester.
16	A	17 Kal. Aug.	
17	b	16 Kal.	
18	c	15 Kal.	
19	d	14 Kal.	
20	e	13 Kal.	Margaret, Virgin and Martyr, at Antioch.
21	f	12 Kal.	
22	g	11 Kal.	St. Mary Magdalene.
23	A	10 Kal.	
24	b	9 Kal.	*Fast.*
25	c	8 Kal.	**St. James, Apostle and Martyr. Holy-Day.**
26	d	7 Kal.	St. Anne, Mother of the Blessed Virgin.
27	e	6 Kal.	
28	f	5 Kal.	
29	g	4 Kal.	
30	A	3 Kal.	
31	b	Prid. Kal.	

AUGUST HATH XXXI. DAYS.

1	c	Kalendæ.	Lammas Day.
2	d	4 Nonas.	
3	e	3 Non.	
4	f	Prid. Non.	
5	g	Nonæ.	
6	A	8 Idus.	Transfiguration of our Lord.
7	b	7 Id.	Name of Jesus.
8	c	6 Id.	
9	d	5 Id.	
10	e	4 Id.	St. Lawrence, Archdeacon of Rome and Martyr.
11	f	3 Id.	
12	g	Prid. Id.	
13	A	Idus.	
14	b	19 Kal. Sept.	
15	c	18 Kal.	
16	d	17 Kal.	
17	e	16 Kal.	
18	f	15 Kal.	
19	g	14 Kal.	
20	A	13 Kal.	
21	b	12 Kal.	
22	c	11 Kal.	
23	d	10 Kal.	*Fast.*
24	e	9 Kal.	𝔖𝔱. 𝔅𝔞𝔯𝔱𝔥𝔬𝔩𝔬𝔪𝔢𝔴, 𝔄𝔭𝔬𝔰𝔱𝔩𝔢 𝔞𝔫𝔡 𝔐𝔞𝔯𝔱𝔶𝔯. 𝔥𝔬𝔩𝔶=𝔇𝔞𝔶.
25	f	8 Kal.	
26	g	7 Kal.	
27	A	6 Kal.	[tor.
28	b	5 Kal.	St. Augustine, Bishop of Hippo, Confessor and Doc-
29	c	4 Kal.	Beheading of St. John Baptist.
30	d	3 Kal.	
31	e	Prid. Kal.	

SEPTEMBER HATH XXX. DAYS.

1	f	Kalendæ.	Giles, Abbot and Confessor.
2	g	4 Nonas.	
3	A	3 Non.	
4	b	Prid. Non.	
5	c	Nonæ.	
6	d	8 Idus.	
7	e	7 Id.	Enurchus, Bishop of Orleans.
8	f	6 Id.	Nativity of the Blessed Virgin Mary.
9	g	5 Id.	
10	A	4 Id.	
11	b	3 Id.	
12	c	Prid. Id.	
13	d	Idus.	
14	e	18 Kal. Oct.	Exaltation of the Holy Cross.
15	f	17 Kal.	
16	g	16 Kal.	*Ninian, Bishop.*
17	A	15 Kal.	Lambert, Bishop and Martyr.
18	b	14 Kal.	
19	c	13 Kal.	
20	d	12 Kal.	*Fast.*
21	e	11 Kal.	**St. Matthew, Apostle, Evangelist, and Martyr.** [Holy-Day.
22	f	10 Kal.	
23	g	9 Kal.	*Adamnan, Abbot.*
24	A	8 Kal.	
25	b	7 Kal.	
26	c	6 Kal.	St. Cyprian, Archbishop of Carthage, and Martyr.
27	d	5 Kal.	
28	e	4 Kal.	
29	f	3 Kal.	**St. Michael and All Angels.** Holy-Day.
30	g	Prid. Kal.	St. Jerome, Priest, Confessor, and Doctor.

OCTOBER HATH XXXI. DAYS.

1	A	Kalendæ.	Remigius, Bishop of Rheims.
2	b	6 Nonas.	
3	c	5 Non.	
4	d	4 Non.	
5	e	3 Non.	
6	f	Prid. Non.	Faith, Virgin and Martyr.
7	g	Nonæ.	
8	A	8 Idus.	
9	b	7 Id.	St. Denys, Areopagite, Bishop and Martyr.
10	c	6 Id.	
11	d	5 Id.	
12	e	4 Id.	
13	f	3 Id.	Translation of King Edward the Confessor.
14	g	Prid. Id.	
15	A	Idus.	
16	b	17 Kal. Nov.	
17	c	16 Kal.	Etheldreda, Virgin, Queen, and Abbess of Ely.
18	d	15 Kal.	**St. Luke, Evangelist. Holy-Day.**
19	e	14 Kal.	
20	f	13 Kal.	
21	g	12 Kal.	
22	A	11 Kal.	
23	b	10 Kal.	
24	c	9 Kal.	
25	d	8 Kal.	Crispin, Martyr.
26	e	7 Kal.	
27	f	6 Kal.	*Fast.*
28	g	5 Kal.	**SS. Simon and Jude, Apostles and Martyrs.** [**Holy-Day.**
29	A	4 Kal.	
30	b	3 Kal.	
31	c	Prid. Kal.	*Fast.*

NOVEMBER HATH XXX. DAYS.

1	d	Kalendæ.	**All Saints' Day. Holy-Day.**
2	e	4 Nonas.	
3	f	3 Non.	
4	g	Prid. Non.	
5	A	Nonæ.	Gunpowder Conspiracy.
6	b	8 Idus.	Leonard, Confessor.
7	c	7 Id.	
8	d	6 Id.	
9	e	5 Id.	
10	f	4 Id.	
11	g	3 Id.	St. Martin, Bishop and Confessor.
12	A	Prid. Id.	
13	b	Idus.	Britius, Bishop.
14	c	18 Kal. Dec.	
15	d	17 Kal.	Machutus, Bishop.
16	e	16 Kal.	*Margaret, Queen.*
17	f	15 Kal.	Hugh, Bishop of Lincoln.
18	g	14 Kal.	
19	A	13 Kal.	
20	b	12 Kal.	Edmund, King and Martyr.
21	c	11 Kal.	
22	d	10 Kal.	Cecilia, Virgin and Martyr.
23	e	9 Kal.	St. Clement, first Bishop of Rome and Martyr.
24	f	8 Kal.	
25	g	7 Kal.	Catherine, Virgin and Martyr.
26	A	6 Kal.	
27	b	5 Kal.	*Ode, Virgin.*
28	c	4 Kal.	
29	d	3 Kal.	Fast.
30	e	Prid. Kal.	**St. Andrew, Apostle and Martyr. Holy-Day.**

DECEMBER hath XXXI. DAYS.

1	f	Kalendæ.	
2	g	4 Nonas.	
3	A	3 Non.	
4	b	Prid. Non.	*Drostane, Abbot.*
5	c	Nonæ.	
6	d	8 Idus.	Nicolas, Bishop of Myra in Lycia.
7	e	7 Id.	
8	f	6 Id.	Conception of the Blessed Virgin Mary.
9	g	5 Id.	
10	A	4 Id.	
11	b	3 Id.	
12	c	Prid. Id.	
13	d	Idus.	Lucy, Virgin and Martyr.
14	e	19 Kal. Jan.	
15	f	18 Kal.	
16	g	17 Kal.	O Sapientia.
17	A	16 Kal.	
18	b	15 Kal.	
19	c	14 Kal.	
20	d	13 Kal.	*Fast.*
21	e	12 Kal.	𝔖𝔱. 𝔗𝔥𝔬𝔪𝔞𝔰, 𝔄𝔭𝔬𝔰𝔱𝔩𝔢 𝔞𝔫𝔡 𝔐𝔞𝔯𝔱𝔶𝔯. 𝔥𝔬𝔩𝔶=𝔇𝔞𝔶.
22	f	11 Kal.	
23	g	10 Kal.	
24	A	9 Kal.	*Fast.*
25	b	8 Kal.	𝔈𝔥𝔯𝔦𝔰𝔱𝔪𝔞𝔰 𝔇𝔞𝔶. 𝔥𝔬𝔩𝔶=𝔇𝔞𝔶.
26	c	7 Kal.	𝔖𝔱. 𝔖𝔱𝔢𝔭𝔥𝔢𝔫, 𝔱𝔥𝔢 𝔉𝔦𝔯𝔰𝔱 𝔐𝔞𝔯𝔱𝔶𝔯. 𝔥𝔬𝔩𝔶=𝔇𝔞𝔶.
27	d	6 Kal.	𝔖𝔱. 𝔍𝔬𝔥𝔫, 𝔈𝔳𝔞𝔫𝔤𝔢𝔩𝔦𝔰𝔱 𝔞𝔫𝔡 𝔐𝔞𝔯𝔱𝔶𝔯. 𝔥𝔬𝔩𝔶=𝔇𝔞𝔶.
28	e	5 Kal.	𝔗𝔥𝔢 𝔥𝔬𝔩𝔶 𝔈𝔫𝔫𝔬𝔠𝔢𝔫𝔱𝔰. 𝔥𝔬𝔩𝔶=𝔇𝔞𝔶.
29	f	4 Kal.	
30	g	3 Kal.	
31	A	Prid. Kal.	Silvester, Bishop of Rome.

A TABLE

Of all the Feasts that are to be observed in the Church of England throughout the Year.

All Sundays in the Year.

The Days of the Feasts of
- *The Circumcision of our Lord Jesus Christ.
- *The Epiphany.
- The Conversion of St. Paul.
- *The Purification of the Blessed Virgin.
- St. Matthias, the Apostle.
- *The Annunciation of the Blessed Virgin.
- St. Mark, the Evangelist.
- St. Philip and St. James, the Apostles.
- *The Ascension of our Lord Jesus Christ.
- St. Barnabas.
- The Nativity of St. John Baptist.

The Days of the Feasts of
- St. Peter, the Apostle.
- St. James, the Apostle.
- St. Bartholomew, the Apostle.
- St. Matthew, the Apostle.
- St. Michael and All Angels.
- St. Luke, the Evangelist.
- St. Simon and St. Jude, the Apostles.
- *All Saints.
- St. Andrew, the Apostle.
- St. Thomas, the Apostle.
- *The Nativity of our Lord Jesus Christ.
- St. Stephen, the Martyr.
- St. John, the Evangelist.
- The Holy Innocents.

Monday and Tuesday in Easter Week.
Monday and Tuesday in Whitsun Week.

[On all these days the Antiphon to *Benedictus* (at Lauds,) to *Magnificat* (at the Second Vespers,) is said all through, before as well as after the Canticle, and on the days marked (*) at the First Vespers also; to which must be added Easter Day, Whitsun Day, and Trinity Sunday. The Antiphon to *Nunc Dimittis* (at Compline) follows the same rule.]

A TABLE

Of the Vigils, Fasts, and Days of Abstinence to be observed in the Year.

The Evens or Vigils before
- The Nativity of our Lord.
- The Purification of the Blessed Virgin Mary.
- The Annunciation of the Blessed Virgin.
- Easter Day.
- Ascension Day.
- Pentecost.
- St. Matthias.

The Evens or Vigils before
- St. John Baptist.
- St. Peter.
- St. James.
- St. Bartholomew.
- St. Matthew.
- St. Simon and St. Jude.
- St. Andrew.
- St. Thomas.
- All Saints.

Note, that if any of these Feast days fall upon a Monday, then the Vigil or Fast-day shall be kept upon the Saturday, and not upon the Sunday next before it.

Days of Fasting, or Abstinence.

I. The Forty Days of Lent.

II. The Ember Days at the Four Seasons, being the Wednesday, Friday and Saturday after
- The First Sunday in Lent.
- The Feast of Pentecost.
- September 14.
- December 13.

III. The Three Rogation Days, being the Monday, Tuesday, and Wednesday before Holy Thursday, or the Ascension of our Lord.

IV. All the Fridays in the Year, except CHRISTMAS DAY.

A TABLE

Of the Moveable Feasts for Forty Years.

Year of our Lord.	The Golden Number.	The Epact.	Sunday Letter.	Sundays after Epiphany.	Septuagesima Sunday.	The First Day of Lent.	Easter Day.	Rogation Sunday.	Ascension Day.	Whitsun Day.	Sundays after Trinity.	Advent Sunday.
1881	1	0	B	5	Feb. 13	Mar. 2	April 17	May 22	May 26	June 5	23	Nov. 27
1882	2	11	A	4	— 5	Feb. 22	— 9	— 14	— 18	May 28	25	Dec. 3
1883	3	22	G	2	Jan. 21	— 7	Mar. 25	April 29	— 3	— 13	27	— 2
1884	4	3	FE	4	Feb. 10	— 27	April 13	May 18	— 22	June 1	24	Nov. 30
1885	5	14	D	3	— 1	— 18	— 5	— 10	— 14	May 24	25	— 29
1886	6	25	C	6	— 21	Mar. 10	— 25	— 30	June 3	June 13	22	— 28
1887	7	6	B	4	— 6	Feb. 23	— 10	— 15	May 19	May 29	24	— 27
1888	8	17	AG	3	Jan. 29	— 15	— 1	— 6	— 10	— 20	26	Dec. 2
1889	9	28	F	5	Feb. 17	Mar. 6	— 21	— 26	— 30	June 9	23	— 1
1890	10	9	E	3	— 2	Feb. 19	— 6	— 11	— 15	May 25	25	Nov. 30
1891	11	20	D	2	Jan. 25	— 11	Mar. 29	— 3	— 7	— 17	26	— 29
1892	12	1	CB	5	Feb. 14	Mar. 2	April 17	— 22	— 26	June 5	23	— 27
1893	13	12	A	3	Jan. 29	Feb. 15	— 2	— 7	— 11	May 21	26	Dec. 3
1894	14	23	G	2	— 21	— 7	Mar. 25	April 29	— 3	— 13	27	— 2
1895	15	4	F	4	Feb. 10	— 27	April 14	May 19	— 23	June 2	24	— 1
1896	16	15	ED	5	— 2	— 19	— 5	— 10	— 14	May 24	25	Nov. 29
1897	17	26	C	5	— 14	Mar. 3	— 18	— 23	— 27	June 6	23	— 28
1898	18	7	B	4	— 6	Feb. 23	— 10	— 15	— 19	May 29	24	— 27
1899	19	18	A	3	Jan. 29	— 15	— 2	— 7	— 11	— 21	26	Dec. 3
1900	1	29	G	5	Feb. 11	— 28	— 15	— 20	— 24	June 3	24	— 2
1901	2	10	F	3	— 3	— 20	— 7	— 12	— 16	May 26	25	— 1
1902	3	21	E	4	Jan. 26	— 12	Mar. 30	— 4	— 8	— 18	26	Nov. 30
1903	4	2	D	4	Feb. 8	— 25	April 12	— 17	— 21	— 31	24	— 29
1904	5	13	CB	3	Jan. 31	— 17	— 3	— 8	— 12	— 22	25	— 27
1905	6	24	A	6	Feb. 19	Mar. 8	— 23	— 28	June 1	June 11	23	Dec. 3
1906	7	5	G	5	— 11	Feb. 28	— 15	— 20	May 24	— 3	24	— 2
1907	8	16	F	2	Jan. 27	— 13	Mar. 31	— 5	— 9	May 19	26	— 1
1908	9	27	ED	5	Feb. 16	Mar. 4	April 19	— 24	— 28	June 7	23	Nov. 29
1909	10	8	C	4	— 7	Feb. 24	— 11	— 16	— 20	May 30	24	— 28
1910	11	19	B	2	Jan. 23	— 9	Mar. 27	— 1	— 5	— 15	26	— 27
1911	12	30	A	5	Feb. 12	Mar. 1	April 16	— 21	— 25	June 4	24	Dec. 3
1912	13	11	GF	4	— 4	Feb. 21	— 7	— 12	— 16	May 26	25	— 1
1913	14	22	E	1	Jan. 19	— 5	Mar. 23	April 27	— 1	— 11	27	Nov. 30
1914	15	3	D	4	Feb. 8	— 25	April 12	May 17	— 21	— 31	24	— 29
1915	16	14	C	3	Jan. 31	— 17	— 4	— 9	— 13	— 23	25	— 28
1916	17	26	BA	6	Feb. 20	Mar. 8	— 23	— 28	June 1	June 11	23	Dec. 3
1917	18	6	G	4	— 4	Feb. 21	— 8	— 13	May 17	May 27	25	— 2
1918	19	17	F	2	Jan. 27	— 13	Mar. 31	— 5	— 9	— 19	26	— 1
1919	1	29	E	5	Feb. 16	Mar. 5	April 20	— 25	— 29	June 8	23	Nov. 30
1920	2	10	DC	3	— 1	Feb. 18	— 4	— 9	— 13	May 23	25	— 28

RULES to know when the Moveable Feasts and Holy-Days begin.

EASTER DAY (on which the rest depend) is always the First Sunday after the Full Moon which happens upon or next after the Twenty-first day of March; and if the Full Moon happens upon a Sunday, Easter Day is the Sunday after.

Advent Sunday is always the nearest Sunday to the Feast of St. Andrew, whether before or after.

Septuagesima
Sexagesima
Quinquagesima
Quadragesima
} Sunday is { Nine / Eight / Seven / Six } Weeks before Easter.

Rogation Sunday
Ascension Day
Whitsun Day
Trinity Sunday
} is { Five Weeks / Forty Days / Seven Weeks / Eight Weeks } after Easter.

THE SERVICE PROPER FOR THE SEASONS.

The First Sunday in Advent.

AT THE FIRST VESPERS.

Antiphons and Psalms as in the Psalter.

The Chapter, Isa. ii. 2.

And it shall come to pass in the last days, that the mountain of the Lord's House shall be established in the top of the mountains, and shall be exalted above the hills; and all nations shall flow unto it.

R. Behold, the days come, saith the Lord, that I will raise unto David a righteous Branch, and

B

a King shall reign and prosper, and shall execute judgment and justice in the earth. And this is His Name whereby He shall be called, The Lord our Righteousness. ℣. In His days Judah shall be saved, and Israel shall dwell safely. ℟. And this is His Name whereby He shall be called, The Lord our Righteousness. ℣. Glory be to the Father, and to the Son: and to the Holy Ghost. ℟. The Lord our Righteousness, (*and the first* ℟. Behold, &c., *is repeated down to* ℣.)

Hymn. Conditor alme siderum.

Creator of the stars of night,
Thy people's everlasting Light,
Jesu, Redeemer, save us all,
And hear Thy servants when they call.

Thou, grieving that the ancient curse
Should doom to death an universe,
Hast found a med'cine full of grace,
To heal and save Thy ruined race.

Thou cam'st the Bridegroom of the Bride,
As drew the world to evening-tide;
Proceeding from a Virgin shrine,
The spotless Victim all divine.

At Whose dread Name, Majestic now,
All knees must bend, all hearts must bow;
And things celestial Thee shall own,
And things terrestrial, Lord alone.

O Thou Whose coming is with dread
To judge and doom the quick and dead,
Preserve us, while we dwell below,
From every insult of the foe.

To Him Who comes the world to free,
To God the Son, all glory be:
To God the Father, as is meet,
To God the blessed Paraclete. Amen.

℣. Drop down, ye heavens, from above.

℟. And let the skies pour down righteousness: let the earth open, and let them bring forth Salvation.

Antiphon to Magnificat.
Behold, the Name of the Lord: cometh from far.

Magnificat, St. Luke i.

The Collect.

ALMIGHTY God, give us grace that we may cast away the works of darkness, and put upon us the armour of light, now in the time of this mortal life, in which Thy Son Jesus Christ came to visit us in great humility; that in the Last Day, when He shall come again in His glorious Majesty to judge both the quick and dead, we may rise to the life immortal, through Him Who liveth and reigneth with Thee and the Holy Ghost, now and ever. Amen.

AT LAUDS.

Instead of the ℣. *and* ℟., The Lord is high, &c.,

℣. Send, O Lord, the Lamb to the Ruler of the land.

℟. From Sela to the wilderness, unto the mount of the daughter of Sion. *This* ℣. *and* ℟. *are said till Christmas Eve.*

℣. O God, make speed, &c., (*as in the Psalter.*)

Antiphons at Lauds.

(1.) In that day: the mountains shall drop down new wine, and the hills shall flow with milk. Alleluia.

Psalms as in the Psalter.

(2.) Rejoice greatly: O daughter of Sion; shout, O daughter of Jerusalem. Alleluia.

(3.) The Lord my God: shall come, and all His Saints with Him. And it shall come to pass in that day, that the light shall not be clear, nor dark; but at evening time it shall be light.

(4.) Ho, every one that thirsteth : come ye to the waters. Seek ye the Lord, while He may be found.

(5.) Shiloh shall come : and unto Him shall the gathering of the people be. He washed His garments in wine, and His clothes in the blood of grapes.

The Chapter, Rom. xiii. 11.

Now it is high time to awake out of sleep : for now is our Salvation nearer than when we believed.

R⁊. Thanks be to God.

Hymn. Vox clara ecce intonat.

Lo! now a thrilling voice sounds forth,
And chides the darken'd shades of earth :
Away, pale dreams, dim shadows, fly,
Christ in His might doth shine on high.

Now let the sluggard soul arise,
Which stained by sin and wounded lies :
All ill and harm dispelling far,
Rises the new-born Morning Star.

The Lamb of God is sent below,
Himself to pay the debt we owe;
Oh! for this gift let every voice
With heart-felt songs and tears rejoice.

That when again His light shines clear,
And wraps the world in sudden fear,
His utmost wrath He may not wreak,
But shield us for His mercy's sake.

To Him Who comes the world to free,
To God the Son, all glory be :
To God the Father, as is meet,
To God the blessed Paraclete. Amen.

℣. The voice of him that crieth in the wilderness.

R⁊. Prepare ye the way of the Lord : make straight in the desert a highway for our God.

In the Service of the Season this Hymn, ℣. and R⁊. are said at Lauds daily throughout Advent.

Antiphon. The Holy Ghost shall come upon thee, Mary : fear not ; thou shalt conceive in thy womb the Son of God. Alleluia.

Benedictus, St. Luke i., *as in the Psalter.*

The Antiphon is repeated.

The Collect.

ALMIGHTY God, give us grace, &c.

AT PRIME.

Antiphon (1.) In that day : the mountains shall drop down new wine, and the hills shall flow with milk. Alleluia.

Psalms as in the Psalter.

AT TERCE.

Antiphon (2.) Rejoice greatly : O daughter of Sion ; shout, O daughter of Jerusalem.

Psalms as in the Psalter.

The Chapter, Rom. xiii. 11.

Now it is high time to awake out of sleep : for now is our Salvation nearer than when we believed.

R. Come and save us, O Lord God of Hosts. ℣. Show the light of Thy Countenance, and we shall be whole. R⁊. O Lord God of Hosts. ℣. Glory be to the Father, and to the Son : and to the Holy Ghost. R⁊. Come and save us, O Lord God of Hosts.

℣. The heathen shall fear Thy Name, O Lord.

R⁊. And all the kings of the earth Thy Majesty.

Collect as at the First Vespers.

AT SEXT.

Antiphon (3.) The Lord my God : shall come, and all His Saints with Him. And it shall come to pass in that day, that the light shall not be clear nor dark; but at evening time it shall be light.

Psalms as in the Psalter.

The Chapter, Rom. xiii. 12.

The night is far spent, the day is at hand; let us therefore cast off the works of darkness, and let us put on the armour of light.

R. O Lord, show Thy Mercy upon us. ℣. And grant us Thy Salvation. ℟. Thy Mercy upon us. ℣. Glory be to the Father, and to the Son : and to the Holy Ghost. ℟. O Lord, show Thy Mercy upon us.

℣. Remember me, O Lord, according to the favour that Thou bearest unto Thy people.

℟. O visit me with Thy Salvation.

Collect as at the First Vespers.

AT NONE.

Antiphon (5.) Shiloh shall come: and unto Him shall the gathering of the people be. He washed His garments in wine, and His clothes in the blood of grapes.

Psalms as in the Psalter.

The Chapter, Rom. xiii. 13, 14.

Let us walk honestly as in the day; not in rioting and drunkenness, not in chambering and wantonness, not in strife and envying. But put ye on the Lord Jesus Christ.

R. The Lord shall arise upon thee, O Jerusalem. ℣. And His Glory shall be seen upon thee. ℟. O Jerusalem. ℣. Glory be to the Father, and to the Son : and to the Holy Ghost. ℟. The Lord shall arise upon thee, O Jerusalem.

℣. Turn us again, O Lord God of Hosts.

℟. Show the light of Thy Countenance, and we shall be whole.

Collect as at the First Vespers.

AT THE SECOND VESPERS.

Antiphons and Psalms as in the Psalter.

The Chapter, Rom. xiii. 11.

Now it is high time to awake out of sleep: for now is our Salvation nearer than when we believed.

R. Thou shalt arise, O Lord, and have mercy upon Sion. ℣. For it is time that Thou have mercy upon her, yea, the time is come. ℟. Have mercy upon Sion. ℣. Glory be to the Father, and to the Son : and to the Holy Ghost. ℟. Thou shalt arise, O Lord, and have mercy upon Sion.

This Respond is said at Vespers daily till O Sapientia.

Hymn, ℣. and ℟., as at the First Vespers, p. 2.

Antiphon. Fear not, Mary; for thou hast found favour with God : and behold, thou shalt conceive, and bring forth a Son. Alleluia.

Magnificat.

The Antiphon is repeated.

Collect as at the First Vespers.

MONDAY. AT LAUDS.

℣. Send, O Lord, &c., *as on Sunday.*

Everything else as in the Psalter, till

The Chapter, Jer. xxiii. 5.

Behold, the days come, saith the Lord, that I will raise unto David a righteous Branch, and a King shall reign and prosper, and shall execute judgment and justice in the earth.

℟. Thanks be to God.

Hymn, ℣. and ℟., as on Advent Sunday, at Lauds, p. 3.

Antiphon to Benedictus.

The Angel of the Lord: appeared unto Mary; and she conceived by the Holy Ghost. Alleluia.

The week-day Prayers as usual.

Collect as on Sunday.

AT PRIME.

Antiphon. Come, and deliver us : O our God.

This Antiphon is said at Prime on all week-days in Advent.

Psalms, and everything, as in the Psalter.

AT TERCE.

Antiphon. O Lord, raise up Thy Power : and come and save us.

Psalms as in the Psalter.

The Chapter, Heb. x. 37.

For yet a little while, and He that shall come will come, and will not tarry.

R. Come, and save us, O Lord God of Hosts. ℣. Show the light of Thy countenance, and we shall be whole. ℟. O Lord God of Hosts. ℣. Glory be to the Father, and to the Son : and to the Holy Ghost. ℟. Come, and save us, O Lord God of Hosts.

℣. The heathen shall fear Thy Name, O Lord.

℟. And all the kings of the earth Thy Majesty.

Collect as on Sunday.

This Antiphon, Chapter, Respond, ℣. and ℟., are said at Terce on all week-days in Advent.

AT SEXT.

Antiphon. When Thou comest : deliver us, O Lord.

Psalms as in the Psalter.

The Chapter, Isa. xiii. 22, xiv. 1.

Her time is near to come, and her days shall not be prolonged. For the Lord will have mercy on Jacob, and will yet choose Israel.

R. O Lord, show Thy Mercy upon us. ℣. And grant us Thy Salvation. ℟. Thy Mercy upon us. ℣. Glory be to the Father, and to the Son : and to the Holy Ghost. ℟. O Lord, show Thy Mercy upon us.

℣. Remember me, O Lord, according to the favour that Thou bearest unto Thy people.

℟. O visit me with Thy Salvation.

Collect as on Sunday.

This Antiphon, Chapter, Respond, ℣. and ℟., are said at Sext on all week-days in Advent.

AT NONE.

Antiphon. Come, O Lord : and tarry not; do away the offences of Thy people Israel.

Psalms as in the Psalter.

The Chapter, Micah iv. 2.

Come, and let us go up to the mountain of the Lord, and to the house of the God of Jacob; and He will teach us of His ways, and we will walk in His paths: for the law shall go forth of Sion, and the Word of the Lord from Jerusalem.

R. The Lord shall arise upon thee, O Jerusalem. ℣. And His glory shall be seen upon thee. ℟. O Jerusalem. ℣. Glory be to the Father, and to the Son: and to the Holy Ghost. ℟. The Lord shall arise upon thee, O Jerusalem.

℣. Turn us again, O Lord God of Hosts.

℟. Show the light of Thy Countenance, and we shall be whole.

Collect as on Sunday.

This Antiphon, Chapter, Respond, ℣. and ℟., are said at None on all week-days in Advent.

AT VESPERS.

Everything as in the Psalter, till

The Chapter, Jer. xxiii. 6.

In His days Judah shall be saved, and Israel shall dwell safely: and this is His Name whereby He shall be called, THE LORD OUR RIGHTEOUSNESS.

R. Thou shalt arise, O Lord, and have mercy upon Sion. ℣. For it is time that Thou have mercy upon her, yea, the time is come. ℟. Have mercy upon Sion. ℣. Glory be to the Father, and to the Son: and to the Holy Ghost. ℟. Thou shalt arise, O Lord, and have mercy upon Sion.

This Chapter and Respond are said at Vespers in Advent until O Sapientia daily, except on Saturdays and Sundays.

Hymn, ℣. and ℟., p. 2.

Antiphon to Magnificat.

O Jerusalem, look about thee: toward the east, and behold the Joy that cometh unto thee from God. Alleluia.

The week-day Prayers as usual.

Collect as on Sunday.

On all week-days in the First and Second weeks of Advent, at all the Hours, everything as on this Monday, except the daily Psalms at Lauds and Vespers, which shall be as in the Psalter, and the Antiphons to Benedictus and Magnificat *as below.*

TUESDAY.

Antiphon to Benedictus.

O Jerusalem, lift up thine eyes: and behold the might of thy King. Lo, thy Saviour cometh to cure thee of thy wound.

Antiphon to Magnificat.

Seek ye the Lord: while He may be found, call ye upon Him while He is near.

WEDNESDAY.

Antiphon to Benedictus.

The law shall go forth: of Sion, and the Word of the Lord from Jerusalem.

Antiphon to Magnificat.

One mightier than I cometh:

the latchet of whose shoes I am not worthy to unloose. Alleluia.

THURSDAY.

Antiphon to Benedictus.

Blessed art thou : among women, and Blessed is the Fruit of thy womb.

Antiphon to Magnificat.

I will wait : upon the Lord; and I will look for Him. Alleluia.

FRIDAY.

Antiphon to Benedictus.

Behold, He that is God and Man : shall come forth from the house of David, to sit upon His throne. Alleluia.

Antiphon to Magnificat.

Out of Egypt : have I called My Son, for He shall save His people from their sins.

SATURDAY.

Antiphon to Benedictus.

Fear not, daughter of Sion : behold thy King cometh.

The Second Sunday in Advent.

AT THE FIRST VESPERS.

The Chapter, Isa. iv. 2.

In that day shall the Branch of the Lord be beautiful and glorious, and the Fruit of the earth shall be excellent and comely, for them that are escaped out of Israel.

R. The Lord shall teach us His ways, and we will walk in His paths. ℣. For the law shall go forth of Sion, and the Word of the Lord from Jerusalem. ℟. And we will walk in His paths. ℣. Glory be to the Father, and to the Son : and to the Holy Ghost. ℟. The Lord shall teach us His ways, and we will walk in His paths.

Hymn, ℣. *and* ℟., *p.* 2.

Antiphon to Magnificat.

The Saviour of the world : the Sun of Righteousness, shall arise, and come down into the Virgin's womb, as the showers upon the grass.

The Collect.

BLESSED Lord, Who hast caused all Holy Scriptures to be written for our learning; Grant that we may in such wise hear them, read, mark, learn, and inwardly digest them, that by patience, and comfort of Thy Holy Word, we may embrace, and ever hold fast the blessed hope of everlasting life, which Thou hast given us in our Saviour Jesus Christ. *Amen.*

AT LAUDS.

Antiphons. (1.) Behold, the Son of Man : shall come in the clouds of heaven with power and great glory. Alleluia.

Psalms as in the Psalter.

(2.) We have a strong city : Salvation will God appoint for walls and bulwarks. Open ye the gates. Alleluia.

(3.) For the Vision : though It tarry, wait for It; because It will surely come, It will not tarry. Alleluia.

(4.) The mountains and the hills: shall break forth before Him into singing, and all the trees of the field shall clap their hands, for the Lord God shall come unto His Everlasting Kingdom. Alleluia, Alleluia.

(5.) Behold, our Lord shall come: with power, to enlighten the eyes of His servants. Alleluia.

The Chapter, Rom. xv. 4.

Whatsoever things were written aforetime, were written for our learning; that we through patience, and comfort of the Scriptures, might have hope.

R̲. Thanks be to God.

Hymn, V̄. and R̲., p. 2.

Antiphon. Upon the throne: of David, and upon his Kingdom, shall He sit for ever and ever. Alleluia.

Benedictus.

The Antiphon is repeated.

Collect as at the First Vespers.

AT PRIME.

Antiphon (1.) Behold, the Son of Man: shall come in the clouds of heaven with power and great glory. Alleluia.

AT TERCE.

Antiphon (2.) We have a strong city: Salvation will God appoint for walls and bulwarks. Open ye the gates. Alleluia.

The Chapter, Rom. xv. 4.

Whatsoever things were written aforetime, were written for our learning; that we through patience, and comfort of the Scriptures, might have hope.

R. *as at Terce on the First Sunday in Advent, p. 3.*

Collect as at the First Vespers.

AT SEXT.

Antiphon (3.) For the Vision: though It tarry, wait for It; because It will surely come, It will not tarry. Alleluia.

The Chapter, Rom. xv. 5.

Now the God of patience and consolation grant you to be likeminded one towards another, according to Christ Jesus: that ye may with one mind and one mouth glorify God, even the Father of our Lord Jesus Christ.

R. *as at Sext on the First Sunday in Advent, p. 4.*

Collect as at the First Vespers.

AT NONE.

Antiphon (5.) Behold, our Lord shall come: with power, to enlighten the eyes of His servants.

The Chapter, Rom. xv. 13.

Now the God of hope fill you with all joy and peace in believing, that ye may abound in hope, through the power of the Holy Ghost.

R. *as at None on the First Sunday in Advent, p. 4.*

Collect as at the First Vespers.

AT THE SECOND VESPERS.

Everything as in the Psalter, till

The Chapter, Rom. xv. 4.

Whatsoever things were written aforetime, were written for our learning; that we through patience, and comfort of the Scriptures, might have hope.

℟. as at the Second Vespers of the First Sunday in Advent, p. 4.

Antiphon. Blessed art thou: Mary, that believedst; for there shall be a performance of those things which were told thee from the Lord.

Magnificat.
The Antiphon is repeated.
Collect as at the First Vespers.

MONDAY.

Antiphon to Benedictus.

From heaven: shall the mighty Lord come; and in His Hand is power and might.

Antiphon to Magnificat.

Behold, our King cometh: the Lord of the whole earth, and He shall take away the yoke of our captivity.

TUESDAY.

Antiphon to Benedictus.

The Lord shall arise upon thee: O Jerusalem, and His glory shall be seen upon thee.

Antiphon to Magnificat.

The voice of one crying in the wilderness: Prepare ye the way of the Lord; make His paths straight.

WEDNESDAY.

Antiphon to Benedictus.

Behold, I will send My Messenger: and he shall prepare the way before Me.

Antiphon to Magnificat.

O Sion, thou shalt renew thy strength: and see thy Righteousness, Who cometh unto thee.

THURSDAY.

Antiphon to Benedictus.

Thou art He that should come: for Whom we look, to save Thy people.

Antiphon to Magnificat.

He that cometh after me: is preferred before me; Whose shoe's latchet I am not worthy to unloose.

FRIDAY.

Antiphon to Benedictus.

Say to them that are of a fearful heart: Be strong, fear not; behold, your God will come.

Antiphon to Magnificat.

Sing unto the Lord a new song: and His praise from the end of the earth.

SATURDAY.

Antiphon to Benedictus.

He shall set up an ensign: for the nations, and shall assemble the outcasts of Israel.

The Third Sunday in Advent.

AT THE FIRST VESPERS.

The Chapter, Gen. xlix. 10.

The sceptre shall not depart from Judah, nor a lawgiver from between his feet, until Shiloh come; and unto Him shall the gathering of the people be.

℟. He that shall come will come, and will not tarry. Now shall there be no more fear in thy borders. ℣. For He is our Saviour. ℟. Now shall there be no more fear in thy borders. ℣. Glory be to the Father, and to the

THE THIRD SUNDAY IN ADVENT.

Son : and to the Holy Ghost. R⁊. He that shall come will come, and will not tarry. Now shall there be no more fear in thy borders.

Hymn, ℣. *and* R⁊., *p.* 2.

Antiphon to Magnificat.

Before Me there was no God : formed, neither shall there be after Me; for to Me every knee shall bow, and Me every tongue confess.

The Collect.

O LORD Jesu Christ, Who at Thy first coming didst send Thy Messenger to prepare Thy way before Thee; Grant that the ministers and stewards of Thy Mysteries may likewise so prepare and make ready Thy way, by turning the hearts of the disobedient to the wisdom of the just, that at Thy Second Coming to judge the world we may be found an acceptable people in Thy sight, Who livest and reignest with the Father and the Holy Spirit, ever One God, world without end. *Amen.*

AT LAUDS.

Antiphons. (1.) The Lord will surely come : He will not tarry; and will bring to light the hidden things of darkness, and reveal Himself to all people. Alleluia.

(2.) Rejoice greatly : O daughter of Sion; behold thy King cometh unto thee. Alleluia.

(3.) I will place Salvation : in Sion, for Israel My glory. Alleluia.

(4.) Every mountain and hill shall be made low : and the crooked shall be made straight, and the rough places plain. Come, O Lord, and tarry not. Alleluia.

(5.) Let us live soberly, righteously, and godly : in this present world; looking for that blessed Hope, and the glorious Appearing of the Great God, and our Saviour Jesus Christ.

The Chapter, 1 Cor. iv. 1.

Let a man so account of us, as of the ministers of Christ, and stewards of the Mysteries of God. Moreover, it is required in stewards, that a man be found faithful.

R⁊. Thanks be to God.

Hymn, ℣. *and* R⁊., *p.* 3.

Antiphon. When John had heard : in the prison the works of Christ, he sent two of his disciples, and said unto Him, Art Thou He that should come, or do we look for another?

Benedictus.

Collect as at the First Vespers.

AT PRIME.

Antiphon (1.) The Lord will surely come : He will not tarry; and will bring to light the hidden things of darkness, and reveal Himself to all people. Alleluia.

AT TERCE.

Antiphon (2.) Rejoice greatly : O daughter of Sion; behold thy King cometh unto thee. Alleluia.

The Chapter, 1 Cor. iv. 1.

Let a man so account of us, as of the ministers of Christ, and stewards of the Mysteries of God. Moreover, it is required in stewards, that a man be found faithful.

R. *as at Terce on the First Sunday in Advent, p.* 3.

Collect as at the First Vespers.

THE THIRD SUNDAY IN ADVENT.

AT SEXT.

Antiphon (3.) I will place Salvation : in Sion, for Israel My glory. Alleluia.

The Chapter, 1 Cor. iv. 3.

But with me it is a very small thing that I should be judged of you, or of man's judgment; yea, I judge not mine own self.

R. *as at Sext on the First Sunday in Advent, p. 4.*

Collect as at the First Vespers.

AT NONE.

Antiphon (5.) Let us live soberly, righteously, and godly : in this present world; looking for that blessed Hope, and the glorious Appearing of the Great God, and our Saviour Jesus Christ.

The Chapter, 1 Cor. iv. 5.

Therefore judge nothing before the time, until the Lord come, Who both will bring to light the hidden things of darkness, and will make manifest the counsels of the hearts; and then shall every man have praise of God.

R. *as at None on the First Sunday in Advent, p. 4.*

Collect as at the First Vespers.

AT THE SECOND VESPERS.

Everything as in the Psalter till

The Chapter, 1 Cor. iv. 1.

Let a man so account of us, as of the ministers of Christ, and stewards of the Mysteries of God. Moreover, it is required in stewards, that a man be found faithful.

R. *if before* O Sapientia, *as at the Second Vespers of the First Sunday in Advent, p. 4.*

But on or after O Sapientia, *this* R., *which shall be said daily, except at the First Vespers of the Fourth Sunday in Advent.*

R. Make no long tarrying, O my God. ℣. Come, O Lord, tarry not, do away the offences of Thy people Israel. R. O my God. ℣. Glory be to the Father, and to the Son : and to the Holy Ghost. R. Make no long tarrying, O my God.

Hymn, ℣. *and* R., *p. 2.*

Antiphon.

If not O Sapientia, *or one of the other Great Antiphons.*

Go and show John again those things which ye do hear and see; the blind receive their sight, and the lame walk, the lepers are cleansed, and the deaf hear.

Magnificat.

Collect as at the First Vespers.

The following Great Antiphons to Magnificat *supersede others, and are to be said at Vespers always on their own days.*

DECEMBER 16.

O Sapientia.

O Wisdom : Which camest forth out of the mouth of the Most High, and reachest from one end to the other, mightily and sweetly ordering all things : Come and teach us the way of prudence.

DECEMBER 17.

O Adonai.

O Lord and Ruler of the House of Israel : Who appearedst unto Moses in a flame of fire in the bush, and gavest unto him the Law in Sinai : Come and redeem us with an outstretched Arm.

THE THIRD WEEK IN ADVENT.

DECEMBER 18.
O Radix Jesse.

O Root of Jesse : Who standest for an ensign of the people, at Whom Kings shall shut their mouths, unto Whom the Gentiles shall pray : Come and deliver us, and tarry not.

DECEMBER 19.
O Clavis David.

O Key of David : and Sceptre of the house of Israel, Thou that openest and no man shutteth, and shuttest and no man openeth : Come, and loose the prisoner from the prison-house, and him that sitteth in darkness, from the shadow of death.

DECEMBER 20.
O Oriens.

O Orient : Brightness of the Eternal Light, and Sun of Righteousness : Come, and lighten them that sit in darkness, and in the shadow of death.

DECEMBER 21.
O Rex Gentium.

O King of the Gentiles : and their Desire, the Corner-stone, Who madest both one : Come and save man, whom Thou hast made out of the dust of the earth.

DECEMBER 22.
O Emmanuel.

O Emmanuel : our King and Lawgiver, the Desire of all Nations, and their Saviour : Come and save us, O Lord our God.

DECEMBER 23.
O Virgo Virginum.

O Virgin of Virgins : how shall this be? For neither before thee was any like thee, nor shall there be after.—Daughters of Jerusalem, why marvel ye at me? The thing which ye behold is a divine mystery.

MONDAY. AT LAUDS.

Everything on the remaining weekdays in Advent as before, except that each Psalm at Lauds has its proper Antiphon.

Antiphons. (1.) Behold, the Lord : shall come, the Prince of the Princes of the earth ; blessed are they that are ready and go out to meet Him.

Psalms as in the Psalter.

(2.) When the Son of Man : cometh, shall He find faith on the earth?

(3.) Behold, the fulness of the time : is come, and God hath sent forth His Son.

(4.) With joy : shall ye draw water out of the wells of salvation.

(5.) The Lord cometh forth : out of His Place.

Antiphon to Benedictus.

There shall come forth a Rod : out of the stem of Jesse, and all the earth shall be filled with the knowledge of the glory of the Lord : and all flesh shall see the Salvation of God.

AT VESPERS.

Antiphon to Magnificat, *if not a Great Antiphon.*

Awake, awake : stand up, O Jerusalem ; loose thyself from the bands of thy neck, O captive daughter of Sion.

TUESDAY. AT LAUDS.

Antiphons. (1.) Behold, our Lord : shall come with power, and

Himself shall break the yoke of our burden.

Psalms as in the Psalter.

(2.) Send, O Lord, the Lamb : to the Ruler of the Land from Sela to the wilderness, unto the mount of the daughter of Sion.

(3.) That Thy way, O Lord : may be known upon earth; Thy Saving Health among all nations.

(4.) Reward them : O Lord, that wait for Thee; and let Thy prophets be found faithful.

(5.) The law was given by Moses : but Grace and Truth came by Jesus Christ.

Antiphon to Benedictus.

And thou, Bethlehem : in the land of Juda, art not the least among the princes of Juda; for out of thee shall come a Governor, that shall rule my people Israel.

AT VESPERS.

Antiphon to Magnificat, *if not a Great Antiphon.*

Let the mountains break forth : into singing, and the hills with righteousness; for the Lord, the Light of the world, cometh with power.

WEDNESDAY. AT LAUDS.

Antiphons. (1.) Drop down, ye heavens : from above, and let the skies pour down Righteousness; let the earth open, and let them bring forth Salvation.

Psalms as in the Psalter.

(2.) The prophets did foretell : that Messiah should be born of Mary.

(3.) The Spirit of the Lord : is upon Me; He hath anointed Me to preach the Gospel to the poor.

(4.) Behold, the Lord : shall come; that He may sit among princes, and inherit the throne of His glory.

(5.) Tell it out among the nations : and say ye; Behold, God our Saviour cometh.

Antiphon to Benedictus.

The Angel Gabriel : was sent from God to a Virgin espoused to a man whose name was Joseph, and the Virgin's name was Mary.

AT VESPERS.

Antiphon to Magnificat, *if not a Great Antiphon.*

How shall this be : seeing I know not a man? The Holy Ghost shall come upon thee, and the power of the Highest shall overshadow thee.

THURSDAY. AT LAUDS.

Antiphons. (1.) Out of Sion : shall come forth the Lord Almighty, to save His people.

Psalms as in the Psalter.

(2.) Turn Thee again, O Lord : a little while; and delay not to come unto Thy servants.

(3.) Out of Sion : shall come He that shall reign; He is our Lord Immanuel; great is His Name.

(4.) Behold, He is my God : and I will prepare Him an habitation; my Father's God, and I will exalt Him.

(5.) The Lord is our Judge : the Lord is our Lawgiver, the Lord is our King; He will come and save us.

Antiphon to Benedictus.

The Lord our God : is at hand ; watch ye therefore in your hearts.

AT VESPERS.

Antiphon to Magnificat, *if not a Great Antiphon.*

Rejoice ye with Jerusalem : and be glad with her, all ye that love her for ever.

FRIDAY. AT LAUDS.

Antiphons. (1.) Stand ye still : and see the Salvation of the Lord with you.

Psalms as in the Psalter.

(2.) Unto Thee, O Lord : do I lift up my soul ; come and deliver me, for unto Thee, O Lord, have I fled.

(3.) Come, O Lord, and tarry not : do away the offences of Thy people Israel.

(4.) God shall come from Teman : and the Holy One from Mount Paran ; His brightness shall be as the light.

(5.) Therefore I will look unto the Lord : I will wait for the God of my salvation.

Antiphon to Benedictus.

As soon as the voice of thy salutation : sounded in mine ears, the babe leaped in my womb for joy. Alleluia.

AT VESPERS.

Antiphon to Magnificat, *one of the Great Antiphons, according to the day of the month.*

SATURDAY. AT LAUDS.

Antiphons. (1.) The Lord shall come : with great power ; and all flesh shall see the Salvation of God.

Psalms as in the Psalter.

(2.) Now consider how great this Man is : Who entereth in to save His people to the uttermost.

(3.) Thy messenger shall come again : O Lord, and shall prepare Thy ways.

(4.) The Doctrine of the Lord : shall drop as the rain, and our God shall distil upon us as the dew.

(5.) Prepare to meet thy God : O Israel, for He cometh.

Antiphon to Benedictus.

Every valley shall be exalted : and every mountain and hill shall be made low ; and all flesh shall see the salvation of God.

The Fourth Sunday in Advent.

AT THE FIRST VESPERS.

The Chapter, Isa. xxviii. 16 ; Rom. ix. 33.

Behold, I lay in Sion for a foundation a Stone, a tried Stone, a precious Corner-stone, a sure foundation : and whosoever believeth on Him shall not be ashamed.

℞. The sceptre shall not depart from Judah, nor a lawgiver from between his feet. ℣. Until Shiloh come. ℞. Nor a lawgiver from between his feet. ℣. Glory be to the Father, and to the Son : and to the Holy Ghost. ℞. The sceptre shall not depart from Judah, nor a lawgiver from between his feet.

Hymn, ℣. *and* ℞., *p.* 2.

Antiphon to Magnificat, *one of the Great Antiphons, according to the day of the month.*

THE FOURTH SUNDAY IN ADVENT.

The Collect.

O LORD, raise up (we pray Thee) Thy power, and come among us, and with great might succour us; that whereas, through our sins and wickedness, we are sore let and hindered in running the race that is set before us, Thy bountiful Grace and Mercy may speedily help and deliver us; through the satisfaction of Thy Son our Lord, to Whom with Thee and the Holy Ghost be honour and glory, world without end. *Amen.*

AT LAUDS.

Antiphons. (1.) Blow ye the trumpet : in Sion; for the day of the Lord cometh, for it is nigh at hand; behold, He cometh to save us. Alleluia, Alleluia.

(2.) Behold, the Desire of all nations : shall come; and the House of the Lord shall be filled with glory. Alleluia.

(3.) The crooked shall be made straight : and the rough places plain; Come, O Lord, and tarry not. Alleluia.

(4.) The Bridegroom cometh : go ye out to meet Him; and say ye, Great is His Dominion, and of His Kingdom there shall be no end; the Mighty God, the Everlasting Father, the Prince of Peace. Alleluia, Alleluia.

(5.) Thine Almighty Word, O Lord : leaped down from Heaven, out of Thy royal throne. Alleluia.

The Chapter, Phil. iv. 4.

Rejoice in the Lord alway, and again I say, Rejoice. Let your moderation be known unto all men. The Lord is at hand.

R̊. Thanks be to God.

Hymn, V̊. *and* R̊., *p.* 3.

Antiphon. I am the voice of one crying in the wilderness, Make straight the way of the Lord, as said the prophet Esaias.

Benedictus.

Collect as at the First Vespers.

AT PRIME.

Antiphon (1.) Blow ye the trumpet : in Sion; for the day of the Lord cometh, for it is nigh at hand; behold, He cometh to save us. Alleluia, Alleluia.

AT TERCE.

Antiphon (2.) Behold, the Desire of all nations : shall come; and the House of the Lord shall be filled with glory. Alleluia.

The Chapter, Phil. iv. 4.

Rejoice in the Lord alway, and again I say, Rejoice. Let your moderation be known unto all men. The Lord is at hand.

R. *as at Terce on the First Sunday in Advent, p.* 3.

Collect as at the First Vespers.

AT SEXT.

Antiphon (3.) The crooked shall be made straight : and the rough places plain; Come, O Lord, and tarry not. Alleluia.

The Chapter, Phil. iv. 6.

Be careful for nothing; but in everything by prayer and supplication with thanksgiving, let your requests be made known unto God.

R. *as at Sext on the First Sunday in Advent, p.* 4.

Collect as at the First Vespers.

AT NONE.

Antiphon (5.) Thine Almighty Word, O Lord : leaped down from heaven out of Thy royal throne. Alleluia.

The Chapter, Phil. iv. 7.

And the peace of God, which passeth all understanding, shall keep your hearts and minds through Christ Jesus.

R. *as at None on the First Sunday in Advent, p.* 4.

Collect as at the First Vespers.

AT THE SECOND VESPERS.

Everything as in the Psalter, till

The Chapter, Phil. iv. 4.

Rejoice in the Lord alway, and again I say, Rejoice. Let your moderation be known unto all men. The Lord is at hand.

R. Make no long tarrying, *as at the Second Vespers of the Third Sunday in Advent, p.* 11.

Hymn, ℣. and ℟., p. 2.

Antiphon to Magnificat, *one of the Great Antiphons according to the day of the month.*

Collect as at the First Vespers.

MONDAY. AT LAUDS, (*if it be not Christmas Eve.*)

Antiphons to Psalms as at Lauds on the third Monday in Advent, p. 12.

Antiphon to Benedictus.

The Lord saith, Repent ye : for the Kingdom of Heaven is at hand. Alleluia.

TUESDAY. AT LAUDS, (*if it be not Christmas Eve.*)

Antiphons to Psalms as at Lauds on the third Tuesday in Advent, p. 12.

Antiphon to Benedictus.

Awake, awake : put on strength, O Arm of the Lord.

WEDNESDAY. AT LAUDS, (*if it be not Christmas Eve.*)

Antiphons to Psalms as at Lauds on the third Wednesday in Advent, p. 13.

Antiphon to Benedictus.

Let them give glory unto the Lord : and declare His praise in the Islands; for behold, He cometh, and will not tarry.

THURSDAY. AT LAUDS, (*if it be not Christmas Eve.*)

Antiphons to Psalms as at Lauds on the third Thursday in Advent, p. 13.

Antiphon to Benedictus.

Comfort ye : comfort ye My people, saith your God.

FRIDAY. AT LAUDS, (*if it be not Christmas Eve.*)

Antiphons to Psalms as at Lauds on the third Friday in Advent, p. 14.

Antiphon to Benedictus.

The day of the Lord cometh : as a thief in the night; be ye therefore also ready, for at such an hour as ye think not, the Son of Man cometh.

Christmas Eve.

AT LAUDS.

Instead of ℣. *and* ℟., The Lord is high, *shall be said*,

℣. To-morrow shall the wickedness of the earth be done away.

℟. And the Saviour of the world shall be King over us.

℣. O God, make speed, *and the rest as in the Psalter.*

Antiphons. (1.) O Judah and Jerusalem : fear not, nor be dismayed; to-morrow go ye forth; for the Lord will be with you.

Psalms of that day in the week on which Christmas Eve may fall.

(2.) Ye shall know this day : that the Lord will come; and in the morning, then shall ye see His glory.

(3.) To-morrow : shall the wickedness of the earth be done away; and the Saviour of the world shall be King over us.

(4.) The Doctrine of the Lord : shall drop as the rain, and our God shall distil upon us as the dew, and as the showers upon the grass.

(5.) To-morrow : ye shall have Help, saith the Lord God of Hosts.

The Chapter, Isa. lxii. 1.

For Sion's sake will I not hold my peace, and for Jerusalem's sake I will not rest, until the Righteousness thereof go forth as brightness, and the Salvation thereof as a lamp that burneth.

℟. Thanks be to God.

Hymn, p. 3.

℣. Ye shall know this day that the Lord will come.

℟. And in the morning, then shall ye see His glory.

Antiphon to Benedictus.

When Mary the mother of Jesus : was espoused unto Joseph, before they came together she was found with Child; for that Which was conceived in her, was of the Holy Ghost. Alleluia.

Collect as on Sunday.

The week-day Prayers are not said. If a week-day no Memorial is said save that of All Saints.

The Psalm Ad Te levavi, *and the Prayers "for the peace of the Church" are omitted from now till the First Sunday after Epiphany.*

AT PRIME.

Antiphon (1.) O Judah and Jerusalem : fear not, nor be dismayed; to-morrow go ye forth; for the Lord will be with you.

The Chapter, 1 Tim. i. 17.

Now unto the King Eternal, Immortal, Invisible, the only wise God, be honour and glory for ever and ever. Amen.

R. Jesu Christ, Son of the Living God, have mercy upon us. Alleluia, Alleluia. ℣. Thou that sittest at the Right Hand of the Father. Alleluia. ℟. Have mercy upon us. Alleluia, Alleluia. ℣. Glory be to the Father, and to the Son : and to the Holy Ghost. ℟. Jesu Christ, Son of the Living God, have mercy upon us. Alleluia, Alleluia.

AT TERCE.

Antiphon (2.) Ye shall know

this day: that the Lord will come; and in the morning, then shall ye see His Glory.

The Chapter, Isa. lxii. 1.

For Sion's sake will I not hold my peace, and for Jerusalem's sake I will not rest, until the Righteousness thereof go forth as brightness, and the Salvation thereof as a lamp that burneth.

R. Stand ye still. Alleluia, Alleluia. ℣. And see the Salvation of the Lord with you. ℟. Alleluia, Alleluia. ℣. Glory be to the Father, and to the Son: and to the Holy Ghost. ℟. Stand ye still. Alleluia, Alleluia.

℣. To-morrow ye shall have Help.

℟. Saith the Lord God of Hosts.

AT SEXT.

Antiphon (3.) To-morrow: shall the wickedness of the earth be done away; and the Saviour of the world shall be King over us.

The Chapter, Isa. lxii. 2.

The Gentiles shall see thy Righteousness, and all kings thy Glory: and thou shalt be called by a new name, which the mouth of the Lord shall name.

R. To-morrow ye shall have Help. Alleluia, Alleluia. ℣. Saith the Lord God of Hosts. ℟. Alleluia, Alleluia. ℣. Glory be to the Father, and to the Son: and to the Holy Ghost. ℟. To-morrow ye shall have Help. Alleluia, Alleluia.

℣. Ye shall know this day that the Lord will come.

℟. And in the morning, then shall ye see His Glory.

AT NONE.

Antiphon (5.) To-morrow: ye shall have Help, saith the Lord God of Hosts.

The Chapter, Isa. lxii. 4.

Thou shalt no more be termed Forsaken; neither shall thy land any more be termed Desolate: but thou shalt be called Hephzi-bah, and thy land Beulah: for the Lord delighteth in thee, and thy land shall be married.

R. Ye shall know this day that the Lord will come. Alleluia, Alleluia. ℣. And in the morning, then shall ye see His glory. ℟. Alleluia, Alleluia. ℣. Glory be to the Father, and to the Son: and to the Holy Ghost. ℟. Ye shall know this day that the Lord will come. Alleluia, Alleluia.

℣. Stand ye still.

℟. And see the Salvation of the Lord with you.

CHRISTMAS DAY.

The Nativity of our Lord, or the Birthday of CHRIST, commonly called

CHRISTMAS DAY.

AT THE FIRST VESPERS.

Antiphon (1.) The King of peace.

Laudate, pueri. Ps. cxiii.

1 Praise the Lord, ye servants : O praise the Name of the Lord.

2 Blessed be the Name of the Lord : from this time forth for evermore.

3 The Lord's Name is praised : from the rising up of the sun unto the going down of the same.

4 The Lord is high above all heathen : and His glory above the heavens.

5 Who is like unto the Lord our God, that hath His dwelling so high : and yet humbleth Himself to behold the things that are in heaven and earth?

6 He taketh up the simple out of the dust : and lifteth the poor out of the mire ;

7 That He may set him with the princes : even with the princes of His people.

8 He maketh the barren woman

to keep house : and to be a joyful mother of children.

Glory be to the Father, &c.

Antiphon (1.) The King of peace: is exalted, Whom the whole earth seeketh.

(2.) The King of peace.

Laudate Dominum, omnes gentes. Ps. cxvii.

1 O praise the Lord, all ye heathen : praise Him, all ye nations.

2 For His merciful kindness is ever more and more towards us : and the truth of the Lord endureth for ever. Praise the Lord.

Glory be to the Father, &c.

(2.) The King of peace : is exalted, higher than the kings of the earth.

(3.) Know ye that the Kingdom of God is nigh at hand.

Lauda anima mea. Ps. cxlvi.

1 Praise the Lord, O my soul; while I live will I praise the Lord : yea, as long as I have any being I will sing praises unto my God.

2 O put not your trust in princes, nor in any child of man : for there is no help in them.

3 For when the breath of man goeth forth he shall turn again to his earth : and then all his thoughts perish.

4 Blessed is he that hath the God of Jacob for his help : and whose hope is in the Lord his God;

5 Who made heaven and earth, the sea, and all that therein is : Who keepeth His promise for ever;

6 Who helpeth them to right that suffer wrong : Who feedeth the hungry.

7 The Lord looseth men out of prison : the Lord giveth sight to the blind.

8 The Lord helpeth them that are fallen : the Lord careth for the righteous.

9 The Lord careth for the strangers; He defendeth the fatherless and widow : as for the way of the ungodly, He turneth it upside down.

10 The Lord thy God, O Sion, shall be King for evermore : and throughout all generations.

Glory be to the Father, &c.

(3.) Know ye that the Kingdom of God is nigh at hand : Verily I say unto you, it shall not tarry.

(4.) Lift up your heads.

Laudate Dominum quoniam. Ps. cxlvii. 1—11.

1 O praise the Lord, for it is a good thing to sing praises unto our God : yea, a joyful and pleasant thing it is to be thankful.

2 The Lord doth build up Jerusalem : and gather together the out-casts of Israel.

3 He healeth those that are broken in heart : and giveth medicine to heal their sickness.

4 He telleth the number of the stars : and calleth them all by their names.

5 Great is our Lord, and great is His power : yea, and His wisdom is infinite.

6 The Lord setteth up the meek : and bringeth the ungodly down to the ground.

7 O sing unto the Lord with thanksgiving : sing praises upon the harp unto our God;

8 Who covereth the heaven with clouds, and prepareth rain for the earth : and maketh the grass to grow upon the mountains, and herb for the use of men.

9 Who giveth fodder unto the

cattle : and feedeth the young ravens that call upon Him.

10 He hath no pleasure in the strength of an horse : neither delighteth He in any man's legs.

11 But the Lord's delight is in them that fear Him : and put their trust in His mercy.

Glory be to the Father, &c.

(4.) Lift up your heads : for your Redemption draweth nigh.

(5.) The days of Mary were accomplished.

Lauda Hierusalem. Ps. cxlvii. 12.

12 Praise the Lord, O Jerusalem : praise thy God, O Sion.

13 For He hath made fast the bars of thy gates : and hath blessed thy children within thee.

14 He maketh peace in thy borders : and filleth thee with the flour of wheat.

15 He sendeth forth His commandment upon earth : and His word runneth very swiftly.

16 He giveth snow like wool : and scattereth the hoar-frost like ashes.

17 He casteth forth His ice like morsels : who is able to abide His frost?

18 He sendeth out His word, and melteth them : He bloweth with His wind, and the waters flow.

19 He showeth His word unto Jacob : His statutes and ordinances unto Israel.

20 He hath not dealt so with any nation : neither have the heathen knowledge of His laws.

Glory be to the Father, &c.

(5.) The days of Mary were accomplished : that she should bring forth her first-born Son.

The Chapter, Isa. ix. 2.

The people that walked in darkness have seen a great Light : they that dwell in the land of the shadow of death, upon them hath the Light shined.

℟. O Judah and Jerusalem, fear not, nor be dismayed : To-morrow go ye forth. ℣. For the Lord will be with you. ℟. To-morrow go ye forth. ℣. Glory be to the Father, and to the Son : and to the Holy Ghost. ℟. O Judah and Jerusalem, fear not, nor be dismayed : To-morrow go ye forth.

℣. Stand ye still.

℟. And see the Salvation of the Lord with you.

Hymn. Veni Redemptor gentium.

Come, Thou Redeemer of the earth,
Come, testify Thy Virgin birth :
All lands admire,—all times applaud :
Such is the birth that fits a God.

Begotten of no human will,
But of the Spirit, mystic still,
The Word of God in flesh arrayed,
The promised fruit to man displayed.

The Virgin womb that burden gained
With Virgin honour all unstained :
The banners there of virtue glow :
God in His temple dwells below.

Proceeding from His chamber free,
The royal hall of chastity,
Giant of twofold substance, straight
His destined way He runs elate.

From God the Father He proceeds :
To God the Father back He speeds :
Proceeds,—as far as very hell ;
Speeds back,—to light ineffable.

O Equal to Thy Father, Thou,
Gird on Thy fleshly mantle now :
The weakness of our mortal state
With deathless might invigorate.

Thy cradle here shall glitter bright,
And darkness breathe a newer light :
Where endless faith shall shine serene,
And twilight never intervene.

All honour, laud, and glory be,
O Jesu, Virgin-born, to Thee !
All glory, as is ever meet,
To Father and to Paraclete. Amen.

℣. As a Bridegroom out of His chamber.

℞. The Lord cometh forth to run His course.

Antiphon. At sunrise ye shall behold the King of kings from heaven, as a Bridegroom out of His chamber proceeding from God the Father.

Magnificat.

The Antiphon is repeated.

The Collect.

ALMIGHTY God, Who hast given us Thy Only-begotten Son to take our nature upon Him, and as at this time to be born of a pure Virgin; Grant that we, being regenerate and made Thy children by adoption and grace, may daily be renewed by Thy Holy Spirit; through the same our Lord Jesus Christ, Who liveth and reigneth with Thee and the same Spirit, ever one God, world without end. *Amen.*

AT LAUDS.

℣. The Word was made flesh. Alleluia.

℞. And dwelt among us. Alleluia.

℣. O God, make speed, &c.

Antiphons. (1.) Whom saw ye, O shepherds: Say ye, tell us Who hath appeared upon earth? We beheld The Child and a Choir of Angels singing unto our Lord and Saviour. Alleluia, Alleluia.

Psalms as on Sundays and Feast-days.

(2.) A maiden hath borne the King Whose Name is everlasting: she hath the joy of a mother, and likewise the honour of Virginity; none hath been seen like unto her, neither shall there be any such. Alleluia.

(3.) The Angel said unto the shepherds: Behold, I bring you good tidings of great joy; for unto you is born this day in the city of David a Saviour. Alleluia, Alleluia.

(4.) And suddenly: there was with the Angel a multitude of the Heavenly Host, praising God, and saying, Glory to God in the highest, and on earth peace, good-will towards men. Alleluia.

(5.) Unto us a Child is Born: this day; and His Name shall be called the Mighty God. Alleluia, Alleluia.

The Chapter, Titus ii. 11.

The Grace of God that bringeth Salvation hath appeared to all men, teaching us that, denying ungodliness and worldly lusts, we should live soberly, righteously, and godly in this present world.

℞. Thanks be to God.

Hymn. A solis ortus cardine.

From lands that see the sun arise,
To earth's remotest boundaries,
The Virgin-born to-day we sing,
The Son of Mary, Christ the King.

Blest Author of this earthly frame,
To take a servant's form He came,
That liberating flesh by flesh,
Whom He had made might live afresh.

In that chaste parent's holy womb
Celestial grace hath found its home:
And she, as earthly bride unknown,
Yet calls that Offspring blest her own.

The mansion of the modest breast
Becomes a shrine where God shall rest:
The pure and undefiled one
Conceived in her womb the Son.

That Son, that Royal Son, she bore,
Whom Gabriel's voice had told afore;
Whom, in His Mother yet conceal'd,
The Infant Baptist had reveal'd.

The manger and the straw He bore,
The cradle did He not abhor:

CHRISTMAS DAY.

By milk in infant portions fed,
Who gives e'en fowls their daily bread.

The heavenly chorus fill'd the sky,
The Angels sang to God on high,
What time to shepherds, watching lone,
They made Creation's Shepherd known.

For that Thine Advent glory be,
O Jesu, Virgin-born, to Thee!
With Father, and with Holy Ghost,
From men and from the Heavenly Host.
Amen.

℣. Blessed be He that cometh in the Name of the Lord.

℟. God is the Lord, Who hath showed us Light.

Antiphon. Glory to God in the highest, and on earth peace, goodwill towards men. Alleluia, Alleluia.

Benedictus.
The Antiphon is repeated.
Collect as at the First Vespers.

Memorial of ST. MARY *to commemorate the completion of the Mystery of the Incarnation.*

Antiphon. All things are fulfilled which were spoken by the Angel of the Virgin Mary.

℣. After her Child-bearing she abode Ever-Virgin.

℟. Blessed among women.

Let us pray.
The Collect.

WE beseech Thee, O Lord, pour Thy grace into our hearts; that as we have known the Incarnation of Thy Son Jesus Christ by the message of an Angel, so by His Cross and Passion we may be brought unto the glory of His Resurrection; through the same Jesus Christ our Lord. Amen.

This Memorial shall be said at these Lauds only.

AT PRIME.

The last verse of the Hymn Jam lucis *is sung thus.*

All honour, laud, and glory be,
O Jesu, Virgin-born, to Thee!
All glory, as is ever meet,
To Father and to Paraclete. Amen.

So end the Hymns at Terce, Sext, and None, till the Purification, except on the Epiphany.

Antiphon (1.) Whom saw ye, O shepherds: Say ye, tell us Who hath appeared upon earth? We beheld The Child and a Choir of Angels singing unto our Lord and Saviour. Alleluia, Alleluia.

The Chapter, 1 Tim. i. 17.

Now unto the King Eternal, Immortal, Invisible, the only Wise God, be honour and glory for ever and ever. Amen.

R. Jesu Christ, Son of the living God, have mercy upon us. Alleluia, Alleluia. ℣. Thou that didst not abhor the Virgin's womb. ℟. Have mercy upon us. Alleluia, Alleluia. ℣. Glory be to the Father, and to the Son: and to the Holy Ghost. ℟. Jesu Christ, Son of the living God, have mercy upon us. Alleluia, Alleluia.

℣. O Lord, arise, help us.

℟. And deliver us for Thy Name's sake.

This R. *is said at Prime daily, till the Purification, except on the Epiphany.*

AT TERCE.

Antiphon (2.) A maiden hath borne the King: Whose Name is everlasting; she hath the joy of a mother, and likewise the honour of Virginity; none hath been seen like unto her, neither shall there be any such. Alleluia.

The Chapter, Titus ii. 11.

The Grace of God that bringeth Salvation hath appeared unto all men, teaching us that, denying ungodliness and worldly lusts, we should live soberly, righteously, and godly in this present world.

R. The Word was made Flesh. Alleluia, Alleluia. ℣. And dwelt among us. ℟. Alleluia, Alleluia. ℣. Glory be to the Father, and to the Son: and to the Holy Ghost. ℟. The Word was made Flesh. Alleluia, Alleluia.

℣. He shall call Me.

℟. Thou art My Father.

Collect as at the First Vespers.

AT SEXT.

Antiphon (3.) The Angel said unto the shepherds: Behold, I bring you good tidings of great joy; for unto you is born this day in the city of David, a Saviour. Alleluia.

The Chapter, Titus iii. 4, 5.

After that the kindness and love of God our Saviour toward man appeared, not by works of righteousness which we have done, but according to His mercy He saved us.

R. He shall call Me. Alleluia, Alleluia. ℣. Thou art My Father. ℟. Alleluia, Alleluia. ℣. Glory be to the Father, and to the Son: and to the Holy Ghost. ℟. He shall call Me. Alleluia, Alleluia.

℣. The Lord declared.

℟. His salvation.

Collect as at the First Vespers.

AT NONE.

Antiphon (5.) Unto us a Child is born: this day; and His Name shall be called the Mighty God. Alleluia, Alleluia.

The Chapter, Heb. i. 1.

God, Who at sundry times and in divers manners spake in time past unto the fathers by the prophets, hath in these last days spoken unto us by His Son.

R. The Lord declared. Alleluia, Alleluia. ℣. His salvation. ℟. Alleluia, Alleluia. ℣. Glory be to the Father, and to the Son: and to the Holy Ghost. ℟. The Lord declared. Alleluia, Alleluia.

℣. Blessed be He that cometh in the Name of the Lord.

℟. God is the Lord Who hath showed us light.

Collect as at the First Vespers.

AT THE SECOND VESPERS.

These Antiphons and Psalms are said at Vespers daily, till the First Sunday after the Epiphany.

Antiphon (1.) In the day of Thy power.

Dixit Dominus. Ps. cx.

1 The Lord said unto my Lord: Sit Thou on My right hand, until I make Thine enemies Thy footstool.

2 The Lord shall send the rod of Thy power out of Sion: be

Thou ruler even in the midst among Thine enemies.

3 In the day of Thy power shall the people offer Thee free-will offerings with an holy worship : the dew of Thy birth is of the womb of the morning.

4 The Lord sware, and will not repent : Thou art a Priest for ever after the order of Melchisedech.

5 The Lord upon Thy right hand : shall wound even kings in the day of His wrath.

6 He shall judge among the heathen ; He shall fill the places with the dead bodies : and smite in sunder the heads over divers countries.

7 He shall drink of the brook in the way : therefore shall He lift up His head.

Glory be to the Father, &c.

Antiphon (1.) In the day of Thy power : shall the people offer Thee free-will offerings with an holy worship; the dew of Thy birth is of the womb of the morning.

(2.) He sent Redemption unto His people.

Confitebor Tibi. Ps. cxi.

1 I will give thanks unto the Lord with my whole heart : secretly among the faithful, and in the congregation.

2 The works of the Lord are great : sought out of all them that have pleasure therein.

3 His work is worthy to be praised, and had in honour : and His righteousness endureth for ever.

4 The merciful and gracious Lord hath so done His marvellous works : that they ought to be had in remembrance.

5 He hath given meat unto them that fear Him : He shall ever be mindful of His covenant.

6 He hath showed His people the power of His works : that He may give them the heritage of the heathen.

7 The works of His hands are verity and judgment : all His commandments are true.

8 They stand fast for ever and ever : and are done in truth and equity.

9 He sent redemption unto His people : He hath commanded His covenant for ever; holy and reverend is His Name.

10 The fear of the Lord is the beginning of wisdom : a good understanding have all they that do thereafter; the praise of it endureth for ever.

Glory be to the Father, &c.

(2.) He sent Redemption unto His people : He hath commanded His covenant for ever.

(3.) Unto the godly there ariseth up Light in the darkness.

Beatus vir. Ps. cxii.

1 Blessed is the man that feareth the Lord : he hath great delight in His commandments.

2 His seed shall be mighty upon earth : the generation of the faithful shall be blessed.

3 Riches and plenteousness shall be in his house : and his righteousness endureth for ever.

4 Unto the godly there ariseth up light in the darkness : he is merciful, loving, and righteous.

5 A good man is merciful, and lendeth : and will guide his words with discretion.

6 For he shall never be moved : and the righteous shall be had in everlasting remembrance.

7 He will not be afraid of any evil tidings : for his heart standeth fast, and believeth in the Lord.

8 His heart is established, and will not shrink : until he see his desire upon his enemies.

9 He hath dispersed abroad, and given to the poor : and his righteousness remaineth for ever; his horn shall be exalted with honour.

10 The ungodly shall see it, and it shall grieve him : he shall gnash with his teeth, and consume away; the desire of the ungodly shall perish.

Glory be to the Father, &c.

(3.) Unto the godly there ariseth up Light in the darkness : the Lord is merciful, loving, and righteous.

(4.) With the Lord there is Mercy.

De profundis. Ps. cxxx.

1 Out of the deep have I called unto Thee, O Lord : Lord, hear my voice.

2 O let Thine ears consider well : the voice of my complaint.

3 If Thou, Lord, wilt be extreme to mark what is done amiss : O Lord, who may abide it?

4 For there is mercy with Thee : therefore shalt Thou be feared.

5 I look for the Lord; my soul doth wait for Him : in His word is my trust.

6 My soul fleeth unto the Lord : before the morning watch, I say, before the morning watch.

7 O Israel, trust in the Lord, for with the Lord there is mercy : and with Him is plenteous redemption.

8 And He shall redeem Israel : from all his sins.

Glory be to the Father, &c.

(4.) With the Lord there is Mercy : and with Him is plenteous Redemption.

(5) Of the Fruit of thy body.

Memento, Domine. Ps. cxxxii.

1 Lord, remember David : and all his trouble.

2 How he sware unto the Lord : and vowed a vow unto the Almighty God of Jacob;

3 I will not come within the tabernacle of mine house : nor climb up into my bed;

4 I will not suffer mine eyes to sleep, nor mine eyelids to slumber : neither the temples of my head to take any rest;

5 Until I find out a place for the temple of the Lord : an habitation for the mighty God of Jacob.

6 Lo, we heard of the same at Ephrata : and found it in the wood.

7 We will go into His tabernacle : and fall low on our knees before His footstool.

8 Arise, O Lord, into Thy resting place : Thou, and the ark of Thy strength.

9 Let Thy priests be clothed with righteousness : and let Thy saints sing with joyfulness.

10 For Thy servant David's sake : turn not away the presence of Thine Anointed.

11 The Lord hath made a faithful oath unto David : and He shall not shrink from it.

12 Of the Fruit of thy body : shall I set upon thy seat.

13 If thy children will keep My covenant, and My testimonies that

ST. STEPHEN'S DAY.

I shall learn them: their children also shall sit upon thy seat for evermore.

14 For the Lord hath chosen Sion to be an habitation for Himself: He hath longed for her.

15 This shall be My Rest for ever: here will I dwell, for I have a delight therein.

16 I will bless her victuals with increase: and will satisfy her poor with bread.

17 I will deck her priests with health: and her saints shall rejoice and sing.

18 There shall I make the horn of David to flourish: I have ordained a lantern for Mine Annointed.

19 As for his enemies, I shall clothe them with shame: but upon himself shall his crown flourish.

Glory be to the Father, &c.

(5.) Of the Fruit of thy body: shall I set upon thy seat.

The Chapter, Heb. i. 1.

God, Who at sundry times and in divers manners spake in time past unto the fathers by the prophets, hath in these last days spoken unto us by His Son.

R. The Word was made Flesh. Alleluia, Alleluia. ℣. And dwelt among us. ℟. Alleluia, Alleluia. ℣. Glory be to the Father, and to the Son: and to the Holy Ghost. ℟. The Word was made Flesh. Alleluia, Alleluia.

℣. He shall call Me.

℟. Thou art My Father.

Hymn with ℣. *and* ℟., *p.* 21.

Antiphon. To-day Christ is born, to-day our Saviour appeared; to-day Angels sing upon earth, and Archangels rejoice; to-day the Righteous are merry and say, Glory be to God on high. Alleluia.

Magnificat.

The Antiphon is repeated.

Collect as at the First Vespers.

Memorial of St. Stephen.

Antiphon. Thou art Chief in the Choir of Martyrs, like unto an Angel. O blessed Stephen, thou didst entreat God for them that stoned thee.

℣. Thou hast crowned him with glory and worship.

℟. Thou makest him to have dominion of the works of Thy Hands.

Let us pray.

The Collect.

GRANT, O Lord, that in all our sufferings here upon earth for the testimony of Thy Truth, we may steadfastly look up to heaven, and by faith behold the glory that shall be revealed; and being filled with the Holy Ghost, may learn to love and bless our persecutors by the example of Thy first Martyr Saint Stephen, who prayed for his murderers to Thee, O blessed Jesus, Who standest at the Right Hand of God to succour all those that suffer for Thee, our only Mediator and Advocate. *Amen.*

St. Stephen's Day.

AT LAUDS.

℣. The Righteous shall flourish like a palm tree.

ST. STEPHEN'S DAY.

℟. And shall spread abroad like a cedar in Libanus.

℣. O God, make speed, &c.

Antiphons. (1.) And they stoned Stephen: calling upon God, saying, Lord, lay not this sin to their charge.

Psalms as on Sundays and Feast-days.

(2.) The shower of stones was lovely unto Stephen: him doth every soul of the righteous follow.

(3.) My soul hangeth upon Thee: O God; for Thy sake hath my body been stoned.

(4.) Stephen saw the heavens opened; he saw and entered in: blessed is he unto whom the heavens shall lie open.

(5.) Behold, I see the heavens opened: and the Son of Man standing on the Right Hand of God.

The Chapter, Acts vi. 8.

And Stephen, full of faith and power, did great wonders and miracles among the people.

℟. Thanks be to God.

Hymn. Sancte Dei pretiose.

Saint of God, elect and precious,
  Protomartyr Stephen, bright
With thy love, of amplest measure,
  Shining round thee like a light,
Who to God commendedst, dying,
  Them that did thee all despite:

Glitters now the Crown above thee,
  Figured in thy sacred name:
Oh! that we, who truly love thee,
  May have portion in the same;
In the dreadful Day of Judgment
  Fearing neither sin nor shame.

Laud to God, and might and honour,
  Who with flowers of rosy dye
Crowned thy forehead, and hath placed thee
  In the starry throne on high:
He direct us, He protect us
  From death's sting eternally. Amen.

℣. The Righteous shall grow as a lily.

℟. He shall flourish for ever before the Lord.

Antiphon. The wicked thrust sore at him to give him over unto death, but he endured the stones, rejoicing that he was counted worthy to receive the crown of glory. Alleluia.

Benedictus.

The Collect.

GRANT, O Lord, &c.

Memorial of the NATIVITY OF OUR LORD.

Antiphon. Now hath a pure Virgin brought forth the Incarnate Word: and yet after child-bearing doth she abide Ever-Virgin; Behold, from henceforth all generations shall call her Blessed.

℣. Blessed be He that cometh in the Name of the Lord.

℟. God is the Lord, Who hath showed us Light.

The Collect for Christmas Day, p. 22.

AT PRIME.

Antiphon (1.) And they stoned Stephen: calling upon God, saying, Lord, lay not this sin to their charge.

R. *as on Christmas Day, p. 23.*

AT TERCE.

Antiphon (2.) The shower of stones was lovely unto Stephen: him doth every soul of the righteous follow.

ST. STEPHEN'S DAY.

The Chapter, Acts vi. 8.

And Stephen, full of faith and power, did great wonders and miracles among the people.

R. Thou hast crowned him with glory and worship. Alleluia, Alleluia. ℣. Thou makest him to have dominion of the works of Thy Hands. ℟. Alleluia, Alleluia. ℣. Glory be to the Father, and to the Son : and to the Holy Ghost. ℟. Thou hast crowned him with glory and worship. Alleluia, Alleluia.

℣. Thou hast set upon his head, O Lord.

℟. A crown of pure gold.

Collect as at Lauds.

AT SEXT.

Antiphon (3.) My soul hangeth upon Thee : O God ; for Thy sake hath my body been stoned.

The Chapter, Acts vii. 55, 56.

Stephen, being full of the Holy Ghost, looked up steadfastly into heaven, and saw the glory of God, and Jesus standing on the Right Hand of God, and said, Behold, I see the heavens opened, and the Son of Man standing on the Right Hand of God.

R. Thou hast set upon his head, O Lord. Alleluia, Alleluia. ℣. A crown of pure gold. ℟. Alleluia, Alleluia. ℣. Glory be to the Father, and to the Son : and to the Holy Ghost. ℟. Thou hast set upon his head, O Lord. Alleluia, Alleluia.

℣. The Righteous shall flourish like a palm-tree.

℟. And shall spread abroad like a cedar in Libanus.

Collect as at Lauds.

AT NONE.

Antiphon (5.) Behold, I see the heavens opened : and the Son of Man standing on the Right Hand of God.

The Chapter, Acts vii. 60.

And he kneeled down, and cried with a loud voice, Lord, lay not this sin to their charge. And when he had said this, he fell asleep.

R. The Righteous shall flourish like a palm-tree. Alleluia, Alleluia. ℣. And shall spread abroad like a cedar in Libanus. ℟. Alleluia, Alleluia. ℣. Glory be to the Father, and to the Son : and to the Holy Ghost. ℟. The Righteous shall flourish like a palm-tree. Alleluia, Alleluia.

℣. The Righteous shall grow as the lily.

℟. He shall flourish for ever before the Lord.

Collect as at Lauds.

AT VESPERS.

The Antiphons and Psalms as on Christmas Day, p. 24.

The Chapter, Acts vi. 8.

And Stephen, full of faith and power, did great wonders and miracles among the people.

R. They ran upon him with one accord, and cast him out of the city. Alleluia, Alleluia. ℣. Calling upon God, and saying, Lord Jesus, receive my spirit. ℟. Alleluia, Alleluia. ℣. Glory be to the Father, and to the Son : and to the Holy Ghost. ℟. They ran upon him with one accord, and cast him out of the city. Alleluia, Alleluia.

℣. Glory be to God the Father, and His Only-begotten Son, our King.

℟. And to the Holy Ghost, from Both proceeding, now and for ever. Amen.

Hymn, Sancte Dei pretiose, *as at Lauds, p.* 28.

Antiphon to Magnificat.

The doors of heaven are laid open to the Blessed Stephen, Martyr of Christ, who was first to be numbered among the Saints, and is therefore triumphantly crowned in heaven.

Collect as at Lauds.

Memorial of the NATIVITY.

Antiphon. Upon us hath the light shined; for unto us is Born this day a Saviour. Alleluia.

℣. The Word was made Flesh. Alleluia.

℟. And dwelt among us. Alleluia.

The Collect for Christmas Day, p. 22.

Memorial of ST. JOHN THE EVANGELIST.

Antiphon. Greatly is Blessed John to be had in honour, for he leant on Jesu's bosom at the Last Supper.

℣. Their sound is gone out into all lands. Alleluia.

℟. And their words into the ends of the world. Alleluia.

Let us pray.
The Collect.

MERCIFUL Lord, we beseech Thee to cast Thy bright beams of light upon Thy Church, that it being enlightened by the doctrine of Thy blessed Apostle and Evangelist Saint John, may so walk in the light of Thy Truth, that it may at length attain to the light of everlasting life; through Jesus Christ our Lord. *Amen.*

𝔖𝔱. 𝔍𝔬𝔥𝔫 𝔱𝔥𝔢 𝔈𝔳𝔞𝔫𝔤𝔢𝔩𝔦𝔰𝔱'𝔰 𝔇𝔞𝔶.

AT LAUDS.

℣. Greatly is Blessed John to be had in honour.

℟. For he leant on Jesu's bosom at the Last Supper.

℣. O God, make speed, &c.

Antiphons. (1.) This is the disciple : which did testify and write ; and we know that his testimony is true.

Psalms as on Sundays and Feastdays.

(2.) This is My disciple : and if I will that he tarry till I come, what is that to thee ?

(3.) Behold My servant : whom I uphold ; Mine elect in whom My Soul delighteth ; I have put My Spirit upon him.

(4.) There be some of them that stand here : which shall not taste of death, till they have seen the Kingdom of God.

(5.) If I will that he tarry till I come : what is that to thee ? follow thou Me.

The Chapter, Ecclus. xv. 1, 2.

He that feareth the Lord will do good : and he that hath knowledge of the Law shall obtain Wisdom. And as a mother shall she

ST. JOHN THE EVANGELIST'S DAY.

meet him, and receive him as a wife married of a Virgin.

℞. Thanks be to God.

Hymn, Æterna Christi munera, *as at Lauds in the Common of Apostles, with the Doxology of Christmas, as at p. 23.*

℣. They have declared His honour unto the heathen.

℞. And His wonders unto all people.

Antiphon to Benedictus.

This is that John who leant on Jesu's bosom at the Last Supper: blessed is the Apostle to whom were made known the secrets of heaven.

The Collect for St. John's Day, Merciful Lord, &c.

Memorial of the Nativity of our Lord, as at Lauds on St. Stephen's Day, p. 28.

AT PRIME.

Antiphon (1.) This is the disciple: which did testify and write; and we know that his testimony is true.

R. *as on Christmas Day, p. 23.*

AT TERCE.

Antiphon (2.) This is My disciple: and if I will that he tarry till I come, what is that to thee?

The Chapter, Ecclus. xv. 1, 2.

He that feareth the Lord will do good: and he that hath knowledge of the Law shall obtain Wisdom. And as a mother shall she meet him, and receive him as a wife married of a Virgin.

R. Their sound is gone out into all lands. Alleluia, Alleluia. ℣. And their words into the ends of the world. ℞. Alleluia, Alleluia. ℣. Glory be to the Father, and to the Son: and to the Holy Ghost. ℞. Their sound is gone out into all lands. Alleluia, Alleluia.

℣. Thou shalt make them princes in all lands.

℞. They shall remember Thy Name, O Lord.

Collect as at Lauds.

AT SEXT.

Antiphon (3.) Behold My servant: whom I uphold; Mine elect in whom My Soul delighteth; I have put My Spirit upon him.

The Chapter, Ecclus. xv. 3—5.

With the bread of understanding shall she feed him, and give him the water of wisdom to drink. He shall be stayed upon her, and shall not be moved; and shall rely upon her, and shall not be confounded. She shall exalt him above his neighbours.

R. Thou shalt make them princes in all lands. Alleluia, Alleluia. ℣. They shall remember Thy Name, O Lord. ℞. Alleluia, Alleluia. ℣. Glory be to the Father, and to the Son: and to the Holy Ghost. ℞. Thou shalt make them princes in all lands. Alleluia, Alleluia.

℣. How dear are Thy counsels unto me, O God.

℞. O how great is the sum of them.

Collect as at Lauds.

AT NONE.

Antiphon (5.) If I will that he tarry till I come: what is that to thee? follow thou Me.

The Chapter, Ecclus. xv. 5, 6.

In the midst of the Congregation shall Wisdom open his mouth; he shall find joy and a crown of gladness, and she shall cause him to inherit an everlasting name.

R. How dear are Thy counsels unto me, O God. Alleluia, Alleluia. ℣. O how great is the sum of them. ℞. Alleluia, Alleluia. ℣. Glory be to the Father, and to the Son : and to the Holy Ghost. ℞. How dear are Thy counsels unto me, O God. Alleluia, Alleluia.

℣. They have declared His honour unto the heathen.

℞. And His wonders unto all people.

Collect as at Lauds.

AT VESPERS.

The Antiphons and Psalms as on Christmas Day, p. 24.

The Chapter, Ecclus. xv. 1, 2.

He that feareth the Lord will do good; and he that hath knowledge of the Law shall obtain Wisdom. And as a mother shall she meet him, and receive him as a wife married of a Virgin.

R. This is that John who leant on Jesu's bosom at the Last Supper. Alleluia, Alleluia. ℣. Blessed is the Apostle to whom were made known the secrets of heaven. ℞. Alleluia, Alleluia. ℣. Glory be to the Father, and to the Son : and to the Holy Ghost. ℞. This is that John who leant on Jesu's bosom at the Last Supper. Alleluia, Alleluia.

℣. Glory be to God the Father, and His Only-begotten Son, our King.

℞. And to the Holy Ghost, from Both proceeding, now and for ever. Amen.

Hymn, Annue Christe, *as in the Common of Apostles.*

℣. They have declared His honour unto the heathen.

℞. And His wonders unto all people.

Antiphon to Magnificat.

In the midst of the Congregation shall Wisdom open his mouth; he shall find joy and a crown of gladness, and she shall cause him to inherit an everlasting name. Alleluia, Alleluia, Alleluia.

Collect as at Lauds.

Memorial of the Nativity of our Lord, as on St. Stephen's Day, p. 30.

Memorial of the HOLY INNOCENTS.

Antiphon. Innocent children by cruel Herod were slain for Christ, even children at the breast. These are they which follow the Lamb whithersoever He goeth.

℣. Be glad, O ye Righteous, and rejoice in the Lord.

℞. And be joyful, all ye that are true of heart.

Let us pray.

The Collect.

O ALMIGHTY God, Who out of the mouths of Babes and Sucklings hast ordained strength, and madest Infants to glorify Thee by their deaths; Mortify and kill all vices in us, and so strengthen us by Thy Grace, that by the innocency of our lives and constancy of our faith, even unto death, we may glorify Thy holy Name; through Jesus Christ our Lord. *Amen.*

The Innocents' Day.

AT LAUDS.

℣. The Righteous live for evermore.

℟. Their reward also is with the Lord.

℣. O God, make speed, &c.

Antiphons. (1.) Herod being exceeding wroth : sent forth and slew all the children that were in Bethlehem.

Psalms as on Sundays and Feast-days.

(2.) From two years old and under : did Herod slay many children for the Lord's sake.

(3.) A voice was heard in Ramah : lamentation and bitter weeping ; Rachel weeping for her children.

(4.) From under the Altar : the souls of them that were slain do cry with a loud voice, saying, How long, O Lord, Holy and True, dost Thou not judge and avenge our blood?

(5.) Let children praise Thee : O Lord of Hosts, for by the victory Thou hast won they rejoice in their innocence.

The Chapter, Rev. xiv. 1.

I looked, and lo, a Lamb stood on the Mount Sion, and with Him an hundred forty and four thousand, having His Father's Name written in their foreheads.

℟. Thanks be to God.

Hymn. Rex gloriose Martyrum.

All-glorious King of Martyrs Thou,
Crown of Confessors here below ;
Thou guidest to celestial day,
Those who for Thee cast earth away.

Do Thou vouchsafe with gracious ear
To listen to our humble prayer ;
And, while their triumphs blest we chant,
Forgiveness to our errors grant.

All honour, laud, and glory be,
O Jesu, Virgin-born, to Thee !
All glory, as is ever meet,
To Father and to Paraclete. Amen.

℣. The Righteous Lord loveth Righteousness.

℟. His Countenance will behold the thing that is Just.

Antiphon to Benedictus.

Be of good comfort, O my children, and cry unto God ; for ye shall be remembered of Him.

The Collect for the Innocents' Day,
O Almighty God, &c.

Memorial of the Nativity of our Lord, as at Lauds on St. Stephen's Day, p. 28.

AT PRIME.

Antiphon (1.) Herod being exceeding wroth : sent forth and slew all the children that were in Bethlehem.

R. *as on Christmas Day,* p. 23.

AT TERCE.

Antiphon (2.) From two years old and under : did Herod slay many children for the Lord's sake.

The Chapter, Rev. xiv. 1.

I looked, and lo, a Lamb stood on the Mount Sion, and with Him an hundred forty and four thousand, having His Father's Name written in their foreheads.

R. Be glad, O ye Righteous, and rejoice in the Lord. Alleluia, Alleluia. ℣. And be joyful, all ye that are true of heart. ℟.

Alleluia, Alleluia. ℣. Glory be to the Father, and to the Son : and to the Holy Ghost. ℟. Be glad, O ye Righteous, and rejoice in the Lord. Alleluia, Alleluia.

℣. Let the Righteous be glad, and rejoice before God.

℟. Let them also be merry and joyful.

Collect as at Lauds.

AT SEXT.

Antiphon (3.) A voice was heard in Ramah : lamentation and bitter weeping ; Rachel weeping for her children.

The Chapter, Rev. xiv. 4.

These are they which were not defiled with women ; for they are virgins. These are they which follow the Lamb whithersoever He goeth.

℟. Let the Righteous be glad, and rejoice before God. Alleluia, Alleluia. ℣. Let them also be merry and joyful. ℟. Alleluia, Alleluia. ℣. Glory be to the Father, and to the Son : and to the Holy Ghost. ℟. Let the Righteous be glad, and rejoice before God. Alleluia, Alleluia.

℣. The souls of the Righteous are in the Hand of God.

℟. And there shall no torment touch them.

Collect as at Lauds.

AT NONE.

Antiphon (4.) From under the Altar : the souls of them that were slain do cry with a loud voice, saying, How long, O Lord, Holy and True, dost Thou not judge and avenge our blood ?

The Chapter, Rev. xiv. 4, 5.

These were redeemed from among men, being the first-fruits unto God, and to the Lamb. And in their mouth was found no guile.

℟. The souls of the Righteous are in the Hand of God. Alleluia, Alleluia. ℣. And there shall no torment touch them. ℟. Alleluia, Alleluia. ℣. Glory be to the Father, and to the Son : and to the Holy Ghost. ℟. The souls of the Righteous are in the Hand of God. Alleluia, Alleluia.

℣. The Righteous Lord loveth Righteousness.

℟. His Countenance will behold the thing that is Just.

Collect as at Lauds.

AT VESPERS.

The Antiphons and Psalms as on Christmas Day, p. 24.

The Chapter, Rev. xiv. 1.

I looked, and lo, a Lamb stood on the Mount Sion, and with Him an hundred forty and four thousand, having His Father's Name written in their foreheads.

℟. The hundred and forty and four thousand which were redeemed from the earth. These are they which were not defiled with women. Alleluia, Alleluia. ℣. For they are virgins. ℟. Alleluia, Alleluia. ℣. Glory be to the Father, and to the Son : and to the Holy Ghost. ℟. The hundred and forty and four thousand, which were redeemed from the earth. These are they which were not defiled with women. Alleluia, Alleluia.

℣. The Righteous Lord loveth Righteousness.

℟. His Countenance will behold the thing that is Just.

Hymn, Rex gloriose Martyrum, ℣. *and* ℟., *as at Lauds, p.* 33.

Antiphon to Magnificat.

These are they which were not defiled with women; for they are virgins. These are they which follow the Lamb whithersoever He goeth.

Collect as at Lauds.

Memorial of the Nativity of our Lord, as at Vespers on St. Stephen's Day, p. 30.

THE TWENTY-NINTH, THIRTIETH, AND THIRTY-FIRST OF DECEMBER.

AT LAUDS.

℣. The Word was made Flesh. Alleluia.

℟. And dwelt among us. Alleluia.

℣. O God, make speed, &c.

Antiphon. Whom saw ye, O shepherds: Say ye, tell us Who hath appeared upon earth? We beheld The Child, and a Choir of Angels singing unto our Lord and Saviour. Alleluia, Alleluia.

The Psalms are all said to this one Antiphon.

Psalms as on Sundays and Feastdays.

The Chapter, Gal. iv. 1, 2.

Now I say, that the Heir, as long as He is a Child, differeth nothing from a servant, though He be Lord of all; but is under tutors and governors, until the time appointed of the Father.

℟. Thanks be to God.

Hymn, A solis ortus cardine, *p.* 22.

℣. Blessed be He that cometh in the Name of the Lord.

℟. God is the Lord Who hath showed us Light.

Antiphon to Benedictus.

While all things were in quiet silence, and night was in the midst of her swift course, Thine Almighty Word, O Lord, leaped down from heaven out of Thy royal throne.

The Collect for Christmas Day.

Prime, Terce, Sext, None, and Vespers, as on Christmas Day, pp. 23, 24.

The Circumcision of Christ.

AT THE FIRST VESPERS.

Antiphons and Psalms as on Christmas Day, p. 24.

The Chapter, Titus ii. 11, 12.

The Grace of God that bringeth Salvation hath appeared to all men, teaching us that, denying ungodliness and worldly lusts, we should live soberly, righteously, and godly in this present world.

R. The Word was made Flesh. Alleluia, Alleluia. ℣. And dwelt among us. ℟. Alleluia, Alleluia. ℣. Glory be to the Father, and to the Son: and to the Holy Ghost. ℟. The Word was made Flesh. Alleluia, Alleluia.

℣. He shall call Me.

℟. Thou art my Father.

THE CIRCUMCISION OF CHRIST.

Hymn, A solis ortus cardine, *p*. 22.

℣. As a Bridegroom out of His Chamber.

℟. The Lord cometh forth to run His course.

Antiphon to Magnificat.

He that is of the earth is earthly, and speaketh of the earth: He that cometh from heaven is above all. And what He hath seen and heard, that He testifieth; and no man receiveth His testimony. He that hath received His testimony hath set to his seal that God is true.

The Collect.

ALMIGHTY God, Who madest Thy blessed Son to be Circumcised, and obedient to the law for man; Grant us the true Circumcision of the Spirit; that, our hearts, and all our members, being mortified from all worldly and carnal lusts, we may in all things obey Thy blessed will; through the Same Thy Son Jesus Christ our Lord. *Amen.*

At these Vespers shall there be no Memorial.

AT LAUDS.

℣. The Word was made Flesh. Alleluia.

℟. And dwelt among us. Alleluia.

℣. O God, make speed, &c.

Antiphons. (1.) O wonderful condescension: the Creator of mankind hath taken to Himself a living Body, and vouchsafed to be born of a Virgin. He, Very Man, yet begotten after no carnal manner, hath made us co-heirs of His Godhead.

Psalms as on Sundays and Feast-days.

(2.) When Thou wast Born of a Virgin: all ineffably, then was the Scripture fulfilled, He shall come down like the rain into a fleece of wool, to save mankind. We praise Thee, O our God.

(3.) In the Burning Bush: which Moses saw unconsumed, we acknowledge the preservation of the glorious Virginity of the Mother of God.

(4.) The Root of Jesse: hath sprung up; the Star hath come out of Jacob; a Virgin hath brought forth a Saviour. We praise Thee, O our God.

(5.) Lo! Mary hath brought forth the Saviour: of Whom, when John saw Him, he said, Behold the Lamb of God, Which taketh away the sin of the world. Alleluia.

The Chapter, Titus ii. 11, 12.

The Grace of God that bringeth Salvation hath appeared to all men, teaching us that, denying ungodliness and worldly lusts, we should live soberly, righteously, and godly in this present world.

℟. Thanks be to God.

Hymn, A solis ortus cardine, *p*. 22.

℣. Blessed be He that cometh in the Name of the Lord.

℟. God is the Lord Who hath showed us Light.

Antiphon to Benedictus.

A wonderful mystery is made known. To-day is nature to do a new thing. God is made Man. That which was still abideth, and that which was not, that He taketh into Himself without confusion or division.

Collect as at the First Vespers.

At these Lauds shall there be no Memorial.

AT PRIME.

Antiphon (1.) O wonderful condescension : the Creator of mankind hath taken to Himself a living Body, and vouchsafed to be born of a Virgin. He, Very Man, yet begotten after no carnal manner, hath made us co-heirs of His Godhead.

Everything else shall be said as at Prime on Christmas Day, p. 23.

AT TERCE.

Antiphon (2.) When Thou wast Born of a Virgin : all ineffably, then was the Scripture fulfilled, He shall come down like the rain into a fleece of wool, to save mankind. We praise Thee, O our God.

Everything else here and at Sext and at None, except the Antiphons, is said as on Christmas Day, but the Collect for the Circumcision is said instead of that for Christmas Day.

AT SEXT.

Antiphon (3.) In the Burning Bush : which Moses saw unconsumed, we acknowledge the preservation of the glorious Virginity of the Mother of God.

AT NONE.

Antiphon (4.) The Root of Jesse : hath sprung up; the Star hath come out of Jacob; a Virgin hath brought forth a Saviour. We praise Thee, O our God.

AT VESPERS.

Antiphons and Psalms as on Christmas Day.

The Chapter, Titus ii. 11, 12.

The Grace of God that bringeth Salvation hath appeared to all men, teaching us that, denying ungodliness and worldly lusts, we should live soberly, righteously, and godly in this present world.

R. The heart of the Virgin is established and will not shrink, in which she received the divine mysteries at the message of the Angel. Alleluia, Alleluia. ℣. Who, fairer than the children of men, conceived with a chaste womb. ℟. Alleluia, Alleluia. ℣. Glory be to the Father, and to the Son : and to the Holy Ghost. ℟. The heart of the Virgin is established and will not shrink, in which she received the divine mysteries at the message of the Angel. Alleluia, Alleluia.

℣. The mansion of the modest breast Becomes a shrine where God shall rest.
℟. The pure and undefiled one Conceived in her womb the Son.

Hymn, A solis ortus cardine, *p.* 22.

℣. Blessed be He that cometh in the Name of the Lord.

℟. God is the Lord, Who hath showed us Light.

Antiphon to Magnificat.

O marvellous mystery ! The womb of a Virgin who knew not man is become the unspotted temple of God. Of her He taketh Flesh, and to Him shall all nations come, saying, Glory be to Thee, O Lord.

Collect as at the First Vespers.

At these Vespers there shall be no Memorial.

The Second, Third, Fourth, and Fifth Day of January.

AT LAUDS.

℣. The Word was made Flesh. Alleluia.

℟. And dwelt among us. Alleluia.

℣. O God, make speed, &c.

Antiphon. Whom saw ye, O shepherds : Say ye, tell us Who hath appeared upon earth ? We beheld The Child, and a Choir of Angels singing unto our Lord and Saviour. Alleluia, Alleluia.

The Psalms are all said to this one Antiphon.

Psalms as on Sundays and Feast-days.

The Chapter, Gal. iv. 1.

Now I say, that the Heir, as long as He is a Child, differeth nothing from a servant, though He be Lord of all; but is under tutors and governors, until the time appointed of the Father.

℟. Thanks be to God.

Hymn, A solis ortus cardine, *p.* 22.

℣. Blessed be He that cometh in the Name of the Lord.

℟. God is the Lord Who hath showed us Light.

Antiphon to Benedictus.

While all things were in quiet silence : and night was in the midst of her swift course, Thine Almighty Word, O Lord, leaped down from heaven out of Thy royal throne.

Memorial of the Nativity of our Lord.

Antiphon. Shepherds, what saw ye : tell us. We came with haste, and found Mary, and Joseph, and the Babe lying in a manger, wrapped in swaddling clothes.

℣. He shall call Me. Alleluia.

℟. Thou art My Father. Alleluia.

The Collect for the Annunciation.

Prime, Terce, Sext, None, and Vespers, as on the Circumcision, p. 37.

THE EPIPHANY.

come, and the Glory of the Lord is risen upon thee.

℟. The kings of Tharsis and of the Isles shall give presents. Alleluia, Alleluia. ℣. The kings of Arabia and Saba shall bring gifts. ℟. Alleluia, Alleluia. ℣. Glory be to the Father, and to the Son: and to the Holy Ghost. ℟. The kings of Tharsis and of the Isles shall give presents. Alleluia, Alleluia.

℣. All kings shall fall down before Him.

℟. All nations shall do Him service.

The Epiphany,

Or, the Manifestation of Christ to the Gentiles.

AT THE FIRST VESPERS.

Antiphons and Psalms as on Christmas Day, p. 24.

The Chapter, Isa. lx. 1.

Arise, shine; for thy Light is

Hymn. Hostis Herodes impie.

Why, impious Herod, vainly fear,
That Christ the Saviour cometh here?
He takes not earthly realms away,
Who gives the crown that lasts for aye.

To greet His birth the Wise Men went,
Led by the Star before them sent:
Called on by light, toward Light they pressed,
And by their gifts their God confessed.

In holy Jordan's purest wave
The heavenly Lamb vouchsafed to lave:
That He, to Whom was sin unknown,
Might cleanse His people from their own.

New miracle of Power Divine!
The water reddens into wine:
He spake the word; and poured the wave
In other streams than Nature gave.

All glory, Lord, to Thee we pay
For Thine Epiphany to-day:
All glory, as is ever meet,
To Father and to Paraclete. Amen.

℣. All they from Sheba shall come.

℟. They shall bring gold and incense, and they shall show forth the praises of the Lord.

Antiphon to Magnificat.

When the Wise Men saw the Star : they said one to another, This is the sign of the Great King, come let us seek Him and present unto Him gifts; gold, and frankincense, and myrrh.

The Collect.

O GOD, Who by the leading of a Star didst Manifest Thine Only-begotten Son to the Gentiles; Mercifully grant, that we, which know Thee now by faith, may after this life have the fruition of Thy glorious Godhead; through Jesus Christ our Lord. *Amen.*

AT LAUDS.

℣. All they from Sheba shall come.

℟. They shall bring gold and incense, and they shall show forth the praises of the Lord.

℣. O God, make speed, &c.

Antiphons. (1.) He that is Begotten before all worlds : the Lord our Saviour, hath to-day appeared to the world.

Psalms as on Sundays and Feast-days.

(2.) Thy Light, O Jerusalem : is come, and the Glory of the Lord is risen upon thee; and the Gentiles shall come to thy Light. Alleluia.

(3.) When they had opened their treasures : they presented unto Him gifts; gold, and frankincense, and myrrh. Alleluia.

(4.) O ye Seas and Floods, bless ye the Lord : praise Him and magnify Him for ever.

(5.) Three are the gifts : which the Wise Men presented unto the Lord; gold, and frankincense, and myrrh, to the King, the Son of God. Alleluia.

The Chapter, Isa. lx. 1.

Arise, shine; for thy Light is come, and the Glory of the Lord is risen upon thee.

℟. Thanks be to God.

Hymn. A Patre Unigenitus.

From God the Father, Virgin-born
To us the Only Son came down;
By death the Font to consecrate,
The faithful to regenerate.

From highest heaven His course began,
He took the form of mortal man;
Creation by His death restored,
And shed new joys of life abroad.

We pray Thee, Saviour, of Thy love,
To hear us from Thy throne above:
Enlighten Thou our clouded sense,
Fresh beams of light to us dispense.

Abide with us, O Lord, we pray,
The gloom of night remove away;
Thy work of healing, Lord, begin,
And wash away the stain of sin.

Thou Who we know hast come to men,
And we believe shalt come again,
Do Thou Thy guardian shield extend,
Thine own dear sheepfold to defend.

All glory, Lord, to Thee we pay,
For Thine Epiphany to-day;
All glory, as is ever meet,
To Father, and to Paraclete. Amen.

So end the Hymns at Prime, Terce, Sext, and None until Sunday.

℣. It is the Lord that commandeth the waters : it is the glorious God that maketh the thunder.

℟. The Voice of the Lord is mighty in operation : the Voice of the Lord is a glorious voice.

Antiphon to Benedictus.

To-day is the Church joined to her heavenly Bridegroom ; in Jordan is Christ baptized ; the Wise Men bring gifts to the Royal marriage ; and by water made wine are the guests rejoiced.

The Collect.

O GOD, Who by the leading of a Star didst Manifest Thy Onlybegotten Son to the Gentiles ; Mercifully grant that we, which know Thee now by faith, may after this life have the fruition of Thy glorious Godhead; through Jesus Christ our Lord. *Amen.*

AT PRIME.

Antiphon (1.) He that is Begotten before all worlds : the Lord our Saviour, hath to-day appeared to the world.

The Chapter, 1 Tim. i. 17.

Now unto the King Eternal, Immortal, Invisible, the only Wise God, be honour and glory for ever and ever. Amen.

R. Jesu Christ, Son of the Living God, have mercy upon us. Alleluia, Alleluia. ℣. Thou Who on this Day didst appear to the world. ℟. Have mercy upon us. Alleluia, Alleluia. ℣. Glory be to the Father, and to the Son : and to the Holy Ghost. ℟. Jesu Christ, Son of the Living God, have mercy upon us. Alleluia, Alleluia.

℣. O Lord, arise, help us.

℟. And deliver us for Thy Name's sake.

AT TERCE.

Antiphon (2.) Thy Light, O Jerusalem : is come, and the Glory of the Lord is risen upon thee ; and the Gentiles shall come to thy Light. Alleluia.

The Chapter, Isa. lx. 1.

Arise, shine ; for thy Light is come, and the Glory of the Lord is risen upon thee.

R. All they from Sheba shall come. Alleluia, Alleluia. ℣. They shall bring gold and incense, and they shall show forth the praises of the Lord. ℟. Alleluia, Alleluia. ℣. Glory be to the Father, and to the Son : and to the Holy Ghost. ℟. All they from Sheba shall come. Alleluia, Alleluia.

℣. The kings of Tharsis and of the Isles shall give presents.

℟. The kings of Arabia and Saba shall bring gifts.

Collect as at Lauds.

AT SEXT.

Antiphon (3.) When they had opened their treasures : they presented unto Him gifts ; gold, and frankincense, and myrrh. Alleluia.

The Chapter, Isa. lx. 2, 3.

The Lord shall arise upon thee, O Jerusalem, and His Glory shall be seen upon thee. And the Gentiles shall come to thy Light, and kings to the brightness of thy rising.

℟. The kings of Tharsis and of the Isles shall give presents. Alleluia, Alleluia. ℣. The kings of Arabia and Saba shall bring gifts. ℟. Alleluia, Alleluia. ℣. Glory be to the Father, and to the Son: and to the Holy Ghost. ℟. The kings of Tharsis and of the Isles shall give presents. Alleluia, Alleluia.

℣. O worship the Lord.

℟. In the beauty of holiness.

Collect as at Lauds.

AT NONE.

Antiphon (5.) Three are the gifts: which the Wise Men presented unto the Lord; gold, and frankincense, and myrrh, to the King, the Son of God. Alleluia.

The Chapter, Isa. xl. 6.

All they from Sheba shall come; they shall bring gold and incense, and they shall show forth the praises of the Lord.

℟. O worship the Lord. Alleluia, Alleluia. ℣. In the beauty of holiness. ℟. Alleluia, Alleluia. ℣. Glory be to the Father, and to the Son: and to the Holy Ghost. ℟. O worship the Lord. Alleluia, Alleluia.

℣. Worship the Lord.

℟. All ye Angels of His.

Collect as at Lauds.

AT THE SECOND VESPERS.

The Antiphons and Psalms as on Christmas Day, p. 24.

The Chapter, Isa. lx. 1.

Arise, shine; for thy Light is come, and the Glory of the Lord is risen upon thee.

℟. Three are the gifts which the Wise Men presented unto the Lord. Alleluia, Alleluia. ℣. Gold, and frankincense, and myrrh, to the King, the Son of God. ℟. Alleluia, Alleluia. ℣. Glory be to the Father, and to the Son: and to the Holy Ghost. ℟. Three are the gifts which the Wise Men presented unto the Lord. Alleluia, Alleluia.

℣. All kings shall fall down before Him.

℟. All nations shall do Him service.

The Hymn, Hostis Herodes impie, ℣. *and* ℟., *as at the First Vespers, p.* 39.

Antiphon to Magnificat.

There came Wise Men from the East to Bethlehem to worship the Lord, and when they had opened their treasures they presented unto Him precious gifts: gold as to the Great King; frankincense as to the true God; and myrrh for His Burial. Alleluia.

Collect as at Lauds.

From the Feast of the Epiphany till the First Sunday after the Epiphany.

AT LAUDS.

℣. All they from Sheba shall come.

℟. They shall bring gold and incense, and they shall show forth the praises of the Lord.

℣. O God, make speed, &c.

Antiphon. He that is Begotten

before all worlds : the Lord our Saviour, hath to-day appeared to the world.

Psalms as on Sundays and Feast-days, but said under this one Antiphon.

The Chapter, Hymn, ℣. and ℟., as on the Day of the Epiphany, p. 40.

The following Antiphons are said at Lauds and Vespers to Benedictus *and* Magnificat.

a. The Star in the East : shone like a flame, and showed where God the King of kings was. The Wise Men saw it, and brought gifts to Christ the King.

b. When the Wise Men saw the Star : they rejoiced with exceeding great joy. And when they were come into the house, they presented unto Him gifts ; gold, frankincense, and myrrh.

c. Lo ! a Voice from heaven : saying, This is My beloved Son, in Whom I am well pleased.

d. The Wise Men : being warned of God in a dream, departed into their own country another way.

Collect as on the Day of the Epiphany.

The other Hours as on the Day of the Epiphany, except that one of the four Antiphons above is said at Vespers to Magnificat.

The First Sunday after the Epiphany.

AT THE FIRST VESPERS.

Everything as in the Psalter for Saturday at Vespers.

Antiphon to Magnificat.

My sins, O Lord, are stuck fast in me like arrows : but do Thou heal me by the remedies of penitence, before the wounds become corrupt.

This Antiphon is said at the Saturday Vespers till Septuagesima.

The Collect.

O LORD, we beseech Thee mercifully to receive the prayers of Thy people which call upon Thee ; and grant that they may both perceive and know what things they ought to do, and also may have grace and power faithfully to fulfil the same ; through Jesus Christ our Lord. *Amen.*

AT LAUDS.

Everything as in the Psalter.

Antiphon to Benedictus.

Son, why hast Thou thus dealt with us ? behold Thy father and I have sought Thee sorrowing. And He said unto them, How is it that ye sought Me ? wist ye not that I must be about My Father's business ?

Collect as at the First Vespers.

AT PRIME.

Everything as in the Psalter, except that till the Purification the R. *to the Chapter is said as on Christmas Day, p. 23.*

Terce, Sext, and None, as in the Psalter, with the Collect of the Day.

AT THE SECOND VESPERS.

Everything as in the Psalter.

Antiphon to Magnificat.

And Jesus increased in wisdom and stature, and in favour with God and man.

The Collect of the Day.

Throughout the Week everything as in the Psalter, except on Holydays.

The Second Sunday after the Epiphany.

AT THE FIRST VESPERS.

Antiphon to Magnificat *as on the preceding Sunday.*

The Collect.

ALMIGHTY and Everlasting God, Who dost govern all things in heaven and earth; Mercifully hear the supplications of Thy people, and grant us Thy peace all the days of our life; through Jesus Christ our Lord. *Amen.*

AT LAUDS.

Antiphon to Benedictus.

There was a marriage at Cana of Galilee, and the Mother of Jesus was there. And Jesus also was called.

The Collect as above.

AT THE SECOND VESPERS.

Antiphon to Magnificat.

And when they wanted wine, Jesus saith unto them, Fill the waterpots with water; and it was made wine.

The Third Sunday after the Epiphany.

AT THE FIRST VESPERS.

Antiphon to Magnificat *as on the First Sunday after the Epiphany.*

The Collect.

ALMIGHTY and Everlasting God, mercifully look upon our infirmities, and in all our dangers and necessities stretch forth Thy Right Hand to help and defend us; through Jesus Christ our Lord. *Amen.*

AT LAUDS.

Antiphon to Benedictus.

When He was come down from the mountain, great multitudes followed Him. And behold, there came a leper and worshipped Him, saying, Lord, if Thou wilt, Thou canst make me clean. And Jesus put forth His Hand, and touched him, saying, I will; be thou clean.

The Collect as above.

AT THE SECOND VESPERS.

Antiphon to Magnificat.

Lord, my servant lieth at home sick of the palsy, grievously tormented. And Jesus saith unto him, I will come and heal him.

The Collect as above.

The Fourth Sunday after the Epiphany.

AT THE FIRST VESPERS.

Antiphon to Magnificat *as on the First Sunday after the Epiphany, p. 43.*

The Collect.

O GOD, Who knowest us to be set in the midst of so many and great dangers, that by reason of the frailty of our nature we cannot always stand upright; Grant to us such strength and protection, as may support us in all dangers, and carry us through all temptations; through Jesus Christ our Lord. *Amen.*

AT LAUDS.

Antiphon to Benedictus.

And when He was entered into a ship, His disciples followed Him. And behold, there arose a great tempest in the sea, insomuch that the ship was covered with the waves: but He was asleep. And His disciples came to Him, and awoke Him, saying, Lord, save us: we perish.

The Collect as above.

AT THE SECOND VESPERS.

Antiphon to Magnificat.

He arose, and rebuked the winds and the sea, and there was a great calm.

The Fifth Sunday after the Epiphany.

AT THE FIRST VESPERS.

Antiphon to Magnificat *as on the First Sunday after the Epiphany.*

The Collect.

O LORD, we beseech Thee to keep Thy Church and household continually in Thy true Religion; that they who do lean only upon the hope of Thy heavenly grace may evermore be defended by Thy mighty power; through Jesus Christ our Lord. *Amen.*

AT LAUDS.

Antiphon to Benedictus.

Sir, didst not Thou sow good seed in Thy field? from whence then hath it tares? He said unto them, An enemy hath done this.

The Collect as above.

AT THE SECOND VESPERS.

Antiphon to Magnificat.

Gather ye together first the tares, and bind them in bundles to burn them: but gather the wheat into My barn.

The Collect as above.

The Sixth Sunday after the Epiphany.

AT THE FIRST VESPERS.

Antiphon to Magnificat *as on the First Sunday after the Epiphany, p. 43.*

The Collect.

O GOD, Whose blessed Son was manifested that He might destroy the works of the devil, and make us the sons of God, and heirs of eternal life; Grant us, we beseech Thee, that, having this hope, we may purify ourselves, even as He is pure; that, when He shall appear again with power and great glory, we may be made like unto Him in His eternal and glorious kingdom; where with Thee, O Father, and Thee, O Holy Ghost, He liveth and reigneth, ever one God, world without end. *Amen.*

AT LAUDS.

Antiphon to Benedictus.

Immediately after the tribulation of those days shall the sun be darkened, and the moon shall not give her light, and the stars shall fall from heaven, and the powers of the heaven shall be shaken.

The Collect as above.

AT THE SECOND VESPERS.

Antiphon to Magnificat.

Then shall appear the Sign of the Son of Man in heaven : and then shall all the tribes of the earth mourn.

The Collect as above.

The Sunday called Septuagesima, or the Third Sunday before Lent.

AT THE FIRST VESPERS.

Instead of Alleluia *at the beginning of each Hour, is now said,—*

Praise to Thee, O Lord, we sing ;
Of glory the Eternal King.

The Chapter, 1 Cor. ix. 24.

Know ye not, that they which run in a race run all, but one receiveth the prize? So run that ye may obtain.

R. Thus the heavens and the earth were finished, and all the host of them. ℣. And on the seventh day God ended all His work which He had made. ℞. And all the host of them. ℣. Glory be to the Father, and to the Son : and to the Holy Ghost. ℞. Thus the heavens and the earth were finished, and all the host of them.

℣. And God saw every thing that He had made. ℞. And, behold, it was very good.

Hymn, ℣. *and* ℞., *as in the Psalter.*

Antiphon to Magnificat.

And the Lord God planted a garden eastward in Eden : and there He put the man whom He had formed.

The Collect.

O LORD, we beseech Thee favourably to hear the prayers of Thy people; that we, who are justly punished for our offences, may be mercifully delivered by Thy goodness, for the glory of Thy Name ; through Jesus Christ our Saviour, Who liveth and reigneth with Thee and the Holy Ghost, ever one God, world without end. Amen.

AT LAUDS.

Antiphon (1.) Have mercy upon me, O God.

Miserere mei, Deus. Ps. li.

1 Have mercy upon me, O God, after Thy great goodness : according to the multitude of Thy mercies do away mine offences.

2 Wash me throughly from my wickedness : and cleanse me from my sin.

3 For I acknowledge my faults : and my sin is ever before me.

4 Against Thee only have I sinned, and done this evil in Thy sight : that Thou mightest be justified in Thy saying, and clear when Thou art judged.

5 Behold, I was shapen in wickedness : and in sin hath my mother conceived me.

6 But lo, Thou requirest truth

'd parts : and shalt
understand wisdom

alt purge me with
I shall be clean :
ash me, and I shall
.n snow.

alt make me hear of
less : that the bones
last broken may re-

y face from my sins :
ll my misdeeds.

le a clean heart, O
enew a right spirit

: not away from Thy
l take not Thy Holy
le.

me the comfort of
in : and stablish me
: Spirit.

all I teach Thy ways
cked : and sinners
erted unto Thee.

me from blood-guil-
l, Thou that art the
alth : and my tongue
Thy righteousness.

talt open my lips, O
y mouth shall show

ou desirest no sacri-
ild I give it Thee :
ightest not in burnt-

crifice of God is a
t : a broken and con-
God, shalt Thou not

avourable and gra-
on : build Thou the
salem.

talt Thou be pleased
fice of righteousness,
t-offerings and obla-
all they offer young
1 Thine altar.
) the Father, &c.

Antiphon (1.) Have mercy upon me, O God : wash me throughly from my wickedness, for against Thee only have I sinned.

(2.) I will thank Thee.

Confitemini Domino. Ps. cxviii.

1 O give thanks unto the Lord, for He is gracious : because His mercy endureth for ever.

2 Let Israel now confess that He is gracious : and that His mercy endureth for ever.

3 Let the house of Aaron now confess : that His mercy endureth for ever.

4 Yea, let them now that fear the Lord confess : that His mercy endureth for ever.

5 I called upon the Lord in trouble : and the Lord heard me at large.

6 The Lord is on my side : I will not fear what man doeth unto me.

7 The Lord taketh my part with them that help me : therefore shall I see my desire upon mine enemies.

8 It is better to trust in the Lord : than to put any confidence in man.

9 It is better to trust in the Lord : than to put any confidence in princes.

10 All nations compassed me round about : but in the Name of the Lord will I destroy them.

11 They kept me in on every side, they kept me in, I say, on every side : but in the Name of the Lord will I destroy them.

12 They came about me like bees, and are extinct even as the fire among the thorns : for in the Name of the Lord I will destroy them.

13 Thou hast thrust sore at me,

that I might fall : but the Lord was my help.

14 The Lord is my strength, and my song : and is become my salvation.

15 The voice of joy and health is in the dwellings of the righteous : the Right Hand of the Lord bringeth mighty things to pass.

16 The Right Hand of the Lord hath the pre-eminence : the Right Hand of the Lord bringeth mighty things to pass.

17 I shall not die, but live : and declare the works of the Lord.

18 The Lord hath chastened and corrected me : but He hath not given me over unto death.

19 Open me the gates of righteousness : that I may go into them, and give thanks unto the Lord.

20 This is the gate of the Lord : the righteous shall enter into it.

21 I will thank Thee, for Thou hast heard me : and art become my salvation.

22 The same stone which the builders refused : is become the head-stone in the corner.

23 This is the Lord's doing : and it is marvellous in our eyes.

24 This is the day which the Lord hath made : we will rejoice and be glad in it.

25 Help me now, O Lord : O Lord, send us now prosperity.

26 Blessed be he that cometh in the Name of the Lord : we have wished you good luck, ye that are of the house of the Lord.

27 God is the Lord Who hath showed us light : bind the sacrifice with cords, yea, even unto the horns of the altar.

28 Thou art my God, and I will thank Thee : Thou art my God, and I will praise Thee.

29 O give thanks unto the Lord, for He is gracious : and His mercy endureth for ever.

Glory be to the Father, &c.

(2.) I will thank Thee : for Thou hast heard me.

(3.) O God, my God.

Deus, Deus meus. Ps. lxiii.

1 O God, Thou art my God : early will I seek Thee.

2 My soul thirsteth for Thee, my flesh also longeth after Thee : in a barren and dry land, where no water is.

3 Thus have I looked for Thee in holiness : that I might behold Thy power and glory.

4 For Thy loving-kindness is better than the life itself : my lips shall praise Thee.

5 As long as I live will I magnify Thee on this manner : and lift up my hands in Thy Name.

6 My soul shall be satisfied, even as it were with marrow and fatness : when my mouth praiseth Thee with joyful lips.

7 Have I not remembered Thee in my bed : and thought upon Thee when I was waking?

8 Because Thou hast been my helper : therefore under the shadow of Thy wings will I rejoice.

9 My soul hangeth upon Thee : Thy Right Hand hath upholden me.

10 These also that seek the hurt of my soul : they shall go under the earth.

11 Let them fall upon the edge of the sword : that they may be a portion for foxes.

12 But the King shall rejoice in God ; all they also that swear by Him shall be commended : for the mouth of them that speak lies shall be stopped.

Deus misereatur. Ps. lxvii.

1 God be merciful unto us, and bless us : and show us the light of His countenance, and be merciful unto us;

2 That Thy way may be known upon earth : Thy saving health among all nations.

3 Let the people praise Thee, O God : yea, let all the people praise Thee.

4 O let the nations rejoice and be glad : for Thou shalt judge the folk righteously, and govern the nations upon earth.

5 Let the people praise Thee, O God : let all the people praise Thee.

6 Then shall the earth bring forth her increase : and God, even our own God, shall give us His blessing.

7 God shall bless us : and all the ends of the world shall fear Him.

Glory be to the Father, &c.

(3.) O God, my God : early will I seek Thee, because Thou hast been my helper.

(4.) Blessed art Thou, O God, in the firmament of heaven.

Benedicite, omnia opera.

O all ye Works of the Lord, bless ye the Lord : praise Him, and magnify Him for ever.

O ye Angels of the Lord, bless ye the Lord : praise Him, and magnify Him for ever.

O ye Heavens, bless ye the Lord : praise Him, and magnify Him for ever.

O ye Waters that be above the Firmament, bless ye the Lord : praise Him and magnify Him for ever.

O all ye Powers of the Lord, bless ye the Lord : praise Him, and magnify Him for ever.

O ye Sun and Moon, bless ye the Lord : praise Him, and magnify Him for ever.

O ye Stars of Heaven, bless ye the Lord : praise Him, and magnify Him for ever.

O ye Showers and Dew, bless ye the Lord : praise Him and magnify Him for ever.

O ye Winds of God, bless ye the Lord : praise Him, and magnify Him for ever.

O ye Fire and Heat, bless ye the Lord : praise Him, and magnify Him for ever.

O ye Winter and Summer, bless ye the Lord : praise Him, and magnify Him for ever.

O ye Dews and Frosts, bless ye the Lord : praise Him, and magnify Him for ever.

O ye Frost and Cold, bless ye the Lord : praise Him, and magnify Him for ever.

O ye Ice and Snow, bless ye the Lord : praise Him, and magnify Him for ever.

O ye Nights and Days, bless ye the Lord : praise Him, and magnify Him for ever.

O ye Light and Darkness, bless ye the Lord : praise Him, and magnify Him for ever.

O ye Lightnings and Clouds, bless ye the Lord : praise Him, and magnify Him for ever.

O let the Earth bless the Lord : yea, let it praise Him, and magnify Him for ever.

O ye Mountains and Hills, bless ye the Lord : praise Him, and magnify Him for ever.

O all ye Green Things upon the earth, bless ye the Lord : praise Him, and magnify Him for ever.

O ye Wells, bless ye the Lord :

praise Him, and magnify Him for ever.

O ye Seas and Floods, bless ye the Lord : praise Him and magnify Him for ever.

O ye Whales, and all that move in the waters, bless ye the Lord : praise Him, and magnify Him for ever.

O all ye Fowls of the Air, bless ye the Lord : praise Him, and magnify Him for ever.

O all ye Beasts and Cattle, bless ye the Lord : praise Him, and magnify Him for ever.

O ye Children of Men, bless ye the Lord : praise Him, and magnify Him for ever.

O let Israel bless the Lord : praise Him, and magnify Him for ever.

O ye Priests of the Lord, bless ye the Lord : praise Him, and magnify Him for ever.

O ye Servants of the Lord, bless ye the Lord : praise Him, and magnify Him for ever.

O ye Spirits and Souls of the Righteous, bless ye the Lord : praise Him, and magnify Him for ever.

O ye holy and humble Men of heart, bless ye the Lord : praise Him, and magnify Him for ever.

O Ananias, Azarias, and Misael, bless ye the Lord : praise Him, and magnify Him for ever.

Glory be to the Father, &c.

(4.) Blessed art Thou, O God, in the firmament of heaven : and above all to be praised and glorified for ever.

(5.) O praise.

Laudate Dominum. Ps. cxlviii.

1 O praise the Lord of heaven : praise Him in the height.

2 Praise Him, all ye Angels of His : praise Him, all His host.

3 Praise Him, sun and moon : praise Him, all ye stars and light.

4 Praise Him, all ye heavens : and ye waters that are above the heavens.

5 Let them praise the Name of the Lord : for He spake the word, and they were made; He commanded, and they were created.

6 He hath made them fast for ever and ever : He hath given them a law which shall not be broken.

7 Praise the Lord upon earth : ye dragons and all deeps;

8 Fire and hail, snow and vapours : wind and storm, fulfilling His word;

9 Mountains and all hills : fruitful trees and all cedars;

10 Beasts and all cattle : worms and feathered fowls;

11 Kings of the earth and all people : princes and all judges of the world;

12 Young men and maidens, old men and children, praise the Name of the Lord : for His Name only is excellent, and His praise above heaven and earth.

13 He shall exalt the horn of His people; all His saints shall praise Him : even the children of Israel, even the people that serveth Him.

Cantate Domino. Ps. cxlix.

1 O sing unto the Lord a new song : let the congregation of saints praise Him.

2 Let Israel rejoice in Him that made him : and let the children of Sion be joyful in their King.

3 Let them praise His Name in the dance : let them sing praises unto Him with tabret and harp.

4 For the Lord hath pleasure in His people : and helpeth the meek-hearted.
5 Let the saints be joyful with glory : let them rejoice in their beds.
6 Let the praises of God be in their mouth : and a two-edged sword in their hands ;
7 To be avenged of the heathen : and to rebuke the people ;
8 To bind their kings in chains : and their nobles with links of iron.
9 That they may be avenged of them, as it is written : Such honour have all His saints.

Laudate Dominum. Ps. cl.

1 O praise God in His holiness : praise Him in the firmament of His power.
2 Praise Him in His noble acts : praise Him according to His excellent greatness.
3 Praise Him in the sound of the trumpet : praise Him upon the lute and harp.
4 Praise Him in the cymbals and dances : praise Him upon the strings and pipe.
5 Praise Him upon the well-tuned cymbals : praise Him upon the loud cymbals.
6 Let every thing that hath breath : praise the Lord.
Glory be to the Father, &c.

(5.) O praise : the Lord of heaven.

These Psalms are thus said on all Sundays till Easter.

The Chapter, 1 Cor. ix. 24.

Know ye not that they which run in a race run all, but one receiveth the prize? So run that ye may obtain.

℟. Thanks be to God.

Hymn. Æterne rerum Conditor.

Creator Blest, Eternal King,
Who day and night about dost bring,
Who weary mortals to relieve
Dost in their times the seasons give.

Now the shrill cock proclaims it day,
And calls the sun's awakening ray,
The wandering pilgrim's guiding light,
That marks the watches night by night.

Roused at the note the morning star
Heaven's dusky veil uplifts afar ;
Night's wicked bands no longer roam,
But from their dark ways hie them home.

The encouraged sailor's fears are o'er,
The foaming waters rage no more ;
Repentance once the crowing cock
Brought to the Church's promised Rock.

O let us then like men arise ;
The cock rebukes our slumbering eyes ;
Bestirs who still in sleep would lie,
And shames who would their Lord deny ;

Revives once more hope's fading fires,
Through the sick frame new health inspires ;
Sheathes the wild robber's weapon dark,
Lights in the fall'n faith's dying spark.

Look on us, Jesu, when we fall,
And with that look our souls recall ;
If Thou but look, our stains are gone,
And with due tears our pardon won.

Shed through our souls Thy piercing ray,
Our souls' dull slumber drive away :—
Thy Name be first on every tongue,
To Thee our earliest praises sung.

All praise to God the Father be,
All praise, Eternal Son, to Thee ;
All praise for ever, as is meet,
To God the Holy Paraclete. Amen.

℣. Lord, Thou hast been our Refuge.

℟. From one generation to another.

Antiphon to Benedictus.

The kingdom of heaven is like unto a man that is an Householder, Which went out early in the morning to hire labourers into His vineyard.

Collect as at the First Vespers.

AT PRIME.

Antiphon. And when He had agreed with the labourers : for a penny a day, He sent them into His vineyard.

In place of Confitemini Domino, Ps. cxviii., *is said* Dominus regnavit, Ps. xciii., *and this is done till Easter.*

AT TERCE.

Antiphon. And He went out about the third hour : and saw others standing idle in the market-place, and said unto them, Go ye also into the vineyard, and whatsoever is right I will give you.

The Chapter, 1 Cor. ix. 24.

Know ye not, that they which run in a race run all, but one receiveth the prize? So run that ye may obtain.

R. Thou hast been my Succour, leave me not. ℣. Neither forsake me, O God of my Salvation. ℟. Leave me not. ℣. Glory be to the Father, and to the Son : and to the Holy Ghost. ℟. Thou hast been my Succour, leave me not.

℣. I said, Lord, be merciful unto me.

℟. Heal my soul, for I have sinned against Thee.

Collect as at the First Vespers.

AT SEXT.

Antiphon. Why stand ye here : all the day idle? They say unto Him, Because no man hath hired us.

The Chapter, 1 Cor. ix. 25.

And every man that striveth for the mastery is temperate in all things : now they do it to obtain a corruptible crown; but we an incorruptible.

R. Thou wast my Hope, when I hanged yet upon my mother's breasts. ℣. I have been left unto Thee ever since I was born : Thou art my God even from my mother's womb. ℟. When I hanged yet upon my mother's breasts. ℣. Glory be to the Father, and to the Son : and to the Holy Ghost. ℟. Thou wast my Hope, when I hanged yet upon my mother's breasts.

℣. The Lord is my Shepherd, therefore can I lack nothing.

℟. He shall feed me in a green pasture.

Collect as at the First Vespers.

AT NONE.

Antiphon. And He went out and found others : standing idle, and saith unto them, Why stand ye here all the day idle? They say unto Him, Because no man hath hired us. He saith unto them, Go ye also into the vineyard ; and whatsoever is right, that shall ye receive.

The Chapter, 1 Cor. ix. 26, 27.

I therefore so run, not as uncertainly; so fight I, not as one that beateth the air: but I keep under my body, and bring it into subjection.

R. O cleanse Thou me from my secret faults. ℣. Keep Thy servant also from presumptuous sins. ℟. From my secret faults. ℣. Glory be to the Father, and to the Son : and to the Holy Ghost. ℟. O cleanse Thou me from my secret faults.

℣. Thou hast been my Succour.

℟. Leave me not, neither forsake me, O God of my salvation.

Collect as at the First Vespers.

AT THE SECOND VESPERS.

The Chapter, 1 Cor. ix. 24.

Know ye not that they which run in a race run all, but one receiveth the prize? So run that ye may obtain.

℟. Thanks be to God.

Hymn, ℣. and ℟., as in the Psalter.

Antiphon to Magnificat.

So when even was come, the Lord of the vineyard saith unto His steward, Call the labourers, and give them their hire.

Collect as at the First Vespers.

The following Antiphons are said at Lauds and Vespers of this week, to Benedictus *and* Magnificat.

a. Call the labourers : and give them their hire, saith the Lord.

b. But the Lord of the vineyard : answered one of them and said, Friend, I do thee no wrong, didst thou not agree with Me for a penny? Take that thine is, and go thy way.

c. I will give unto this last : even as unto thee.

d. Is it not lawful for Me : to do what I will with Mine own? Is thine eye evil, because I am good?

e. So the last shall be first : and the first last; for many are called, but few chosen.

The Sunday called Sexagesima, or the Second Sunday before Lent.

AT THE FIRST VESPERS.

The Chapter, 2 Cor. xi. 19, 20.

Ye suffer fools gladly, seeing ye yourselves are wise. For ye suffer if a man bring you into bondage, if a man devour you, if a man take of you, if a man exalt himself, if a man smite you on the face.

R. And the Lord God said unto the serpent, I will put enmity between thee and the woman, and between thy seed and her Seed. ℣. It shall bruise thy head, and thou shalt bruise His heel. ℟. Between thy seed and her Seed. ℣. Glory be to the Father, and to the Son : and to the Holy Ghost. ℟. And the Lord God said unto the serpent, I will put enmity between thee and the woman, and between thy seed and her Seed.

℣. Dust thou art.

℟. And unto dust shalt thou return.

THE SUNDAY CALLED SEXAGESIMA.

Antiphon to Magnificat.

My Spirit shall not always strive with man: for that he also is flesh.

The Collect.

O LORD God, Who seest that we put not our trust in any thing that we do; Mercifully grant that by Thy power we may be defended against all adversity; through Jesus Christ our Lord. *Amen.*

AT LAUDS.

Antiphons. (1.) According to the multitude of Thy mercies: do away mine offences.

Psalms as on Septuagesima, p. 46.

(2.) Thou art my God: and I will thank Thee; Thou art my God, and I will praise Thee.

(3.) Early will I seek Thee: that I might behold Thy power and glory.

(4.) Praise Him: and magnify Him for ever.

(5.) O praise the Lord of Heaven: praise Him, all ye Angels of His.

The Chapter, 2 Cor. xi. 19, 20.

Ye suffer fools gladly, seeing ye yourselves are wise. For ye suffer if a man bring you into bondage, if a man devour you, if a man take of you, if a man exalt himself, if a man smite you on the face.

℟. Thanks be to God.

Hymn as in the Psalter, and at p. 51.

℣. Lord, Thou hast been our Refuge.

℟. From one generation to another.

Antiphon to Benedictus.

When much people were gathered together, and were come to Him out of every city, He spake by a parable; A Sower went out to sow His seed.

Collect as at the First Vespers.

AT PRIME.

Antiphon. And other fell on good ground: and sprang up and bare fruit an hundred-fold.

AT TERCE.

Antiphon. That on the good ground are they, which in an honest and good heart: having heard the word keep it, and bring forth fruit with patience.

The Chapter, 2 Cor. xi. 19, 20.

Ye suffer fools gladly, seeing ye yourselves are wise. For ye suffer if a man bring you into bondage, if a man devour you, if a man take of you, if a man exalt himself, if a man smite you on the face.

℟. *as at Terce on Septuagesima Sunday, p.* 52.

Collect as at the First Vespers.

AT SEXT.

Antiphon. When Jesus had said these things: He cried, He that hath ears to hear, let him hear.

The Chapter, 2 Cor. xii. 2.

I knew a man in Christ, above fourteen years ago, (whether in the body I cannot tell: or whether out of the body I cannot tell:

God knoweth;) such an one caught up to the third heaven.

R. *as at Sext on Septuagesima Sunday, p. 52.*

Collect as at the First Vespers.

AT NONE.

Antiphon. Unto you it is given to know : the mysteries of the kingdom of God; but to others in parables.

The Chapter, 2 Cor. xii. 3, 4.

And I knew such a man, (whether in the body or out of the body I cannot tell: God knoweth;) how that he was caught up into paradise, and heard unspeakable words, which it is not lawful for a man to utter.

R. *as at None on Septuagesima Sunday, p. 53.*

Collect as at the First Vespers.

AT THE SECOND VESPERS.

The Chapter, 2 Cor. xi. 19, 20.

Ye suffer fools gladly, seeing ye yourselves are wise. For ye suffer if a man bring you into bondage, if a man devour you, if a man take of you, if a man exalt himself, if a man smite you on the face.

R̷. Thanks be to God.

Hymn, V̷. and R̷., as in the Psalter.

Antiphon to Magnificat.

But that on the good ground are they, which in an honest and good heart, having heard the word, keep it, and bring forth fruit with patience.

Collect as at the First Vespers.

The following Antiphons are said during the week at Lauds and Vespers to Benedictus *and* Magnificat.

a. The seed is the word of God : but the Sower is Christ; he that heareth Him abideth for ever.

b. But that on the good ground are they, which in an honest and good heart : having heard the word, keep it, and bring forth fruit with patience.

c. If ye would be My disciples : have root in yourselves, lest in time of temptation ye fall away.

d. If ye would bring fruit to perfection : be not choked with cares and riches and pleasures of this life.

𝔗𝔥𝔢 𝔖𝔲𝔫𝔡𝔞𝔶 𝔠𝔞𝔩𝔩𝔢𝔡 𝔔𝔲𝔦𝔫𝔮𝔲𝔞𝔤𝔢𝔰𝔦𝔪𝔞, 𝔬𝔯 𝔱𝔥𝔢 𝔫𝔢𝔵𝔱 𝔖𝔲𝔫𝔡𝔞𝔶 𝔟𝔢𝔣𝔬𝔯𝔢 𝔏𝔢𝔫𝔱.

AT THE FIRST VESPERS.

The Chapter, 1 Cor. xiii. 1.

Though I speak with the tongues of men and of angels, and have not Charity, I am become as sounding brass, or a tinkling cymbal.

R̷. And the Lord said in His heart, I will not again curse the ground any more for man's sake; for the imagination of man's heart is evil from his youth. V̷. Neither will I again smite any more every thing living. R̷. For the imagination of man's heart is evil from his youth. V̷. Glory be to the Father, and to the Son : and to the Holy Ghost. R̷. And the

Lord said in His heart, I will not again curse the ground any more for man's sake, for the imagination of man's heart is evil from his youth.

℣. This is the token of the covenant which I make between Me and you.

℟. I do set My bow in the cloud.

Antiphon to Magnificat.

And God said, I do set My bow in the cloud : and it shall be for a token of a covenant between Me and the earth.

The Collect.

O LORD, Who hast taught us that all our doings without charity are nothing worth ; Send Thy Holy Ghost, and pour into our hearts that most excellent gift of charity, the very bond of peace and of all virtues, without which whosoever liveth is counted dead before Thee : Grant this for Thine only Son Jesus Christ's sake. *Amen.*

AT LAUDS.

Antiphons. (1.) Turn Thy Face from my sins : and put out all my misdeeds.

Psalms as on Septuagesima, p. 46.

(2.) The Lord is my Strength : and my Song : and is become my Salvation.

(3.) Have I not thought upon Thee : when I was waking ? because Thou hast been my Helper.

(4.) Praise and magnify for ever : the Father, the Son, and the Holy Ghost.

(5.) Young men and maidens, old men and children : praise the Name of the Lord.

The Chapter, 1 Cor. xiii. 1.

Though I speak with the tongues of men and of angels, and have not Charity, I am become as sounding brass, or a tinkling cymbal.

℟. Thanks be to God.

Hymn, ℣. and ℟., as in the Psalter, and at p. 51.

Antiphon to Benedictus.

Behold, we go up to Jerusalem, and all things that are written by the Prophets concerning the Son of Man shall be accomplished.

Collect as at the First Vespers.

AT PRIME.

Antiphon. As Jesus was come nigh unto Jericho : a certain blind man sat by the wayside begging.

AT TERCE.

Antiphon. And the blind man cried : saying, Jesus, Thou Son of David, have mercy on me.

The Chapter, 1 Cor. xiii. 1.

Though I speak with the tongues of men and of angels, and have not Charity, I am become as sounding brass, or a tinkling cymbal.

R. *as at Terce on Septuagesima Sunday, p.* 52.

Collect as at the First Vespers.

AT SEXT.

Antiphon. And they which went before, rebuked the blind man ; that he should hold his peace : but he cried so much the more, Thou Son of David, have mercy on me.

The Chapter, 1 Cor. xiii. 4, 5.

Charity suffereth long, and is kind; Charity envieth not; Charity vaunteth not itself, is not puffed up, doth not behave itself unseemly, seeketh not her own.

R. *as at Sext on Septuagesima Sunday, p. 52.*

Collect as at the First Vespers.

AT NONE.

Antiphon. And Jesus stood: and commanded the blind man to be brought unto Him.

The Chapter, 1 Cor. xiii. 5, 6.

Charity is not easily provoked, thinketh no evil; rejoiceth not in iniquity, but rejoiceth in the Truth.

R. *as at None on Septuagesima Sunday, p. 53.*

Collect as at the First Vespers.

AT THE SECOND VESPERS.

The Chapter, 1 Cor. xiii. 1.

Though I speak with the tongues of men and of angels, and have not Charity, I am become as sounding brass, or a tinkling cymbal.

R̷. Thanks be to God.

Hymn, V̷. and R̷., as in the Psalter.

Antiphon to Magnificat.

And when he was come near, Jesus asked him, saying, What wilt thou that I should do unto thee? And he said, Lord, that I may receive my sight. And Jesus said unto him, Receive thy sight; thy faith hath saved thee. And immediately he received his sight, and followed Him, glorifying God.

Collect as at the First Vespers.

The following Antiphons are said on Monday and Tuesday at Lauds and Vespers to Benedictus *and* Magnificat.

a. All the people when they saw it: gave praise unto God.

b. Jesus, Thou Son of David: have mercy on me.

c. Lord: that I may receive my sight.

d. Receive thy sight: thy faith hath saved thee.

The First Day of Lent, commonly called

Ash-Wednesday.

AT LAUDS.

The Antiphons and Psalms of Wednesday.

The Chapter, Joel ii. 12, 13.

Turn ye even unto Me, saith the Lord, with all your heart, and with fasting, and with weeping, and with mourning: and rend your heart, and not your garments, and turn unto the Lord your God.

R̷. Thanks be to God.

This Chapter is said daily, on week-days, at Lauds of the week-day, until the Fifth Sunday in Lent.

Hymn, V̷. and R̷., as in the Psalter.

Antiphon to Benedictus.

When ye fast: be not as the hypocrites, of a sad countenance.

The Collect.

ALMIGHTY and Everlasting God, Who hatest nothing that Thou hast made, and dost forgive the sins of all them that are penitent; Create and make in us new and contrite hearts, that we worthily lamenting our sins, and acknowledging our wretchedness, may obtain of Thee, the God of all mercy, perfect remission and forgiveness; through Jesus Christ our Lord. *Amen.*

This Collect is also said at all the Hours every day in Lent, till Wednesday in Holy Week inclusive, after the Collect appointed for the day.

Memorial of penitent sinners, to be said at Lauds, on all weekdays till Wednesday in Holy Week inclusive.

Antiphon. Turn ye even unto Me, saith the Lord, with all your heart, and with fasting, and with weeping, and with mourning.

℣. We have sinned with our fathers.

℟. We have done amiss, and dealt wickedly.

Let us pray.

O LORD, we beseech Thee, mercifully hear our prayers, and spare all those who confess their sins unto Thee; that they, whose consciences by sin are accused, by Thy merciful pardon may be absolved; through Christ our Lord. *Amen.*

Prime and the other Hours as usual, except that the Collect for the day is "Almighty and Everlasting God," as at Lauds. The Hours are thus said till the First Sunday in Lent.

AT VESPERS.

Antiphon to Magnificat.

Lay up for yourselves treasures in heaven : where neither moth nor rust doth corrupt.

Memorial of penitent sinners, to be said at Vespers on all weekdays (except Saturdays) till Wednesday in Holy Week, inclusive.

Antiphon. Who knoweth if the Lord will return and repent, and leave a blessing behind Him?

℣. O Lord, deal not with us after our sins.

℟. Neither reward us after our iniquities.

Let us pray.

O LORD, we beseech Thee, mercifully hear our prayers, and spare all those who confess their sins unto Thee; that they, whose consciences by sin are accused, by Thy merciful pardon may be absolved; through Christ our Lord. *Amen.*

Thursday, Friday, and Saturday, the Chapter at Lauds and the Antiphons to Benedictus *and* Magnificat, *as on Ash-Wednesday.*

The First Sunday in Lent.

AT THE FIRST VESPERS.

The Chapter, 2 Cor. vi. 1, 2.

We then, as workers together with Him, beseech you also that ye receive not the grace of God in vain. (For He saith, I have heard thee in a time accepted, and in the day of Salvation have I succoured thee.)

R. Let us amend our evil ways, lest we be prevented with death. ℣. And find no place for repentance, though we seek it carefully with tears. ℟. Lest we be prevented with death. ℣. Glory be to the Father, and to the Son : and to the Holy Ghost. ℟. Let us amend our evil ways, lest we be prevented with death.

℣. We have sinned with our fathers.

℟. We have done amiss, and dealt wickedly.

Hymn. Ex more docti mystico.

This Hymn is said at Vespers daily, till the Third Sunday in Lent.

The fast, as taught by holy lore,
We keep in solemn course once more :
The fast to all men known, and bound
In forty days of yearly round.

The law and seers that were of old
In divers ways this Lent foretold,
Which Christ, all seasons' King and Guide,
In after ages sanctified.

More sparing therefore let us make
The words we speak, the food we take,
Our sleep and mirth,—and closer barred
Be every sense in holy guard.

In prayer together let us fall,
And cry for mercy one and all,
And weep before the Judge's feet,
And His avenging wrath entreat.

Thy grace have we offended sore
By sins, O God, which we deplore,
But pour upon us from on high,
O pardoning One, Thy clemency !

Remember Thou, though frail we be,
That yet Thine handiwork are we ;
Nor let the honour of Thy Name
Be by another put to shame.

Forgive the sin that we have wrought ;
Increase the good that we have sought ;
That we at length, our wanderings o'er,
May please Thee here and evermore.

Grant, O Thou Blessed Trinity,
Grant, O Essential Unity,
That this our fast of forty days
May work our profit and Thy praise.
      Amen.

℣. He shall give His Angels charge over Thee.

℟. To keep Thee in all Thy ways.

Antiphon to Magnificat.

Behold, now is the accepted time : behold, now is the day of Salvation. Let us then in all things approve ourselves as the servants of God, in much patience, in watchings, in fastings ; by love unfeigned.

The Collect.

O LORD, Who for our sake didst fast forty days and forty nights ; Give us grace to use such abstinence, that, our flesh being subdued to the Spirit, we may ever obey Thy godly motions in righteousness, and true holiness, to Thy honour and glory, Who livest and reignest with the Father and the Holy Ghost, one God, world without end. *Amen.*

The Collect for Ash-Wednesday.

AT LAUDS.

℣. He shall deliver Thee from the snare of the hunter.

℟. And from the noisome pestilence.

℣. O God, make speed, &c.

Antiphons. (1.) Make me a clean heart : O God ; and renew a right spirit within me.

Psalms as on Septuagesima, p. 46.

(2.) Help me now, O Lord : O Lord, send us now prosperity.

(3.) As long as I live will I magnify Thee : on this manner ; and lift up my hands in Thy Name.

(4.) In a contrite heart and an humble spirit : let us be accepted by Thee, O Lord, and so let our sacrifice be in Thy sight this day.

(5.) Praise Him, all ye heavens: and ye waters that are above the heavens.

The Chapter, 2 Cor. vi. 1, 2.

We then, as workers together with Him, beseech you also that ye receive not the grace of God in vain. (For He saith, I have heard thee in a time accepted, and in the day of Salvation have I succoured thee.)

℟. Thanks be to God.

Hymn. Audi benigne Conditor.

This Hymn is said at Lauds daily until the Third Sunday in Lent.

O Maker of the world, give ear!
Accept the prayer, and own the tear,
Towards Thy seat of mercy sent
In this most holy fast of Lent.

Each heart is manifest to Thee:
Thou knowest our infirmity;
Forgive Thou then each soul that fain
Would seek to Thee, and turn again.

Our sins are manifold and sore;
But pardon them that sin deplore;
And, for Thy Name's sake, make each soul
That feels and owns its languor whole.

So mortify we every sense
By grace of outward abstinence,
That from each stain and spot of sin
The soul may keep her fast within.

Grant, O Thou Blessed Trinity,
Grant, O Essential Unity,
That this our fast of forty days
May work our profit and Thy praise.
      Amen.

℣. His faithfulness and truth shall be thy shield and buckler.

℟. Thou shalt not be afraid for any terror by night.

Antiphon to Benedictus.

Then was Jesus led up of the Spirit into the wilderness to be tempted of the devil. And when He had fasted forty days and forty nights, He was afterwards an hungred.

Collects as at the First Vespers.

AT PRIME.

Antiphon. Man shall not live by bread alone : but by every word that proceedeth out of the Mouth of God.

AT TERCE.

Antiphon. Then the devil taketh Him up : into the Holy City, and setteth Him on a pinnacle of the Temple, and saith unto Him, If Thou be the Son of God, cast Thyself down.

The Chapter, 2 Cor. vi. 1, 2.

We then, as workers together with Him, beseech you also that ye receive not the grace of God in vain. (For He saith, I have heard thee in a time accepted, and in the day of Salvation have I succoured thee.)

R. Make me a companion of all them that fear Thee, and keep Thy commandments. ℣. O look Thou upon me, and be merciful unto me : as Thou usest to do unto those that love Thy Name. ℟. And keep Thy commandments. ℣. Glory be to the Father, and to the Son : and to the Holy Ghost. ℟. Make me a companion of all them that fear Thee, and keep Thy commandments.

℣. I will say unto the Lord, Thou art my Hope, and my strong hold.

℞. My God, in Him will I trust.

Collects as at the First Vespers.

AT SEXT.

Antiphon. Thou shalt not tempt: the Lord thy God.

The Chapter, 2 Cor. vi. 2, 3.

Behold, now is the accepted time; behold, now is the day of Salvation. Giving no offence in any thing, that the ministry be not blamed.

R. Refrain my feet from every evil way, that I may keep Thy Word. ℣. I have not shrunk from Thy Judgments, for Thou teachest me. ℞. That I may keep Thy Word. ℣. Glory be to the Father, and to the Son : and to the Holy Ghost. ℞. Refrain my feet from every evil way, that I may keep Thy Word.

℣. He shall deliver Thee from the snare of the hunter.

℞. And from the noisome pestilence.

Collects as at the First Vespers.

AT NONE.

Antiphon. Again, the devil taketh Him up : into an exceeding high mountain, and showeth Him all the kingdoms of the world, and the glory of them; and saith unto Him, All these things will I give Thee, if Thou wilt fall down and worship me.

The Chapter, 2 Cor. vi. 4.

In all things approving ourselves as the ministers of God in much patience, in fastings, by the armour of righteousness.

R. Let Thy loving mercy come also unto me, O Lord. ℣. When Thy Word goeth forth, it giveth understanding. ℞. Unto me, O Lord. ℣. Glory be to the Father, and to the Son : and to the Holy Ghost. ℞. Let Thy loving mercy come also unto me, O Lord.

℣. He shall defend Thee under His wings.

℞. And Thou shalt be safe under His feathers.

Collects as at the First Vespers.

AT THE SECOND VESPERS.

The Chapter, 2 Cor. vi. 1, 2.

We then, as workers together with Him, beseech you also that ye receive not the grace of God in vain. (For He saith, I have heard thee in a time accepted, and in the day of Salvation have I succoured thee.)

R. Be Thou for us, O Lord, a strong tower. ℣. Against the enemy. ℞. A strong tower. ℣. Glory be to the Father, and to the Son : and to the Holy Ghost. ℞. Be Thou for us, O Lord, a strong tower.

This R. *is said at Vespers daily, till the Third Sunday in Lent, except on Saturdays and Saints' days.*

Hymn, Ex more docti mystico, *as at the First Vespers, p.* 59.

℣. He shall give His Angels charge over Thee.

℞. To keep Thee in all Thy ways.

Antiphon. Get thee hence, Satan; for it is written, Thou shalt worship the Lord thy God, and Him only shalt thou serve. Then the devil leaveth Him, and behold, Angels came and ministered unto Him.

Collects as at the First Vespers.

All the ℣s. and ℟s. from Psalm xci. appointed to be said on this day, at each Hour, shall be said daily (when the service is not that of a Saint's day) till the Fifth Sunday in Lent.

MONDAY. AT LAUDS.

℣. He shall deliver Thee from the snare of the hunter.

℟. And from the noisome pestilence.

℣. O God, make speed, &c.

This ℣. and ℟. are said daily at Lauds of the week-day.

Antiphons and Psalms as in the Psalter.

The Chapter, Joel ii. 12, 13.

Turn ye even unto Me, saith the Lord, with all your heart, and with fasting, and with weeping, and with mourning. And rend your heart, and not your garments, and turn unto the Lord your God.

This Chapter shall be daily said at Lauds of the week-day till the Fifth Sunday in Lent.

℟. Thanks be to God.

Hymn, Audi benigne Conditor, ℣. *and* ℟., *p.* 60.

Antiphon to Benedictus.

Come, ye blessed of My Father: inherit the kingdom prepared for you from the foundation of the world.

After the Psalm, Miserere mei Deus, *in the week-day Prayers at Lauds, shall be added* Domine, ne in furore, *Psalm* vi., *daily, till Wednesday in Holy Week, inclusive.*

The Collects as on Sunday.

AT PRIME.

Antiphon. As I live, saith the Lord God : I have no pleasure in the death of the wicked; but that the wicked turn from his way and live.

This Antiphon shall be daily said at Prime of the week-day till the Fifth Sunday in Lent.

After the Psalm, Miserere mei Deus, *in the week-day Prayers at Prime, shall be added* Beati quorum, *Psalm* xxxii., *daily, till Wednesday in Holy Week, inclusive.*

AT TERCE.

Antiphon. Let us chasten ourselves : in much patience, by the armour of the righteousness of God.

These Antiphons and Chapters at Terce, Sext, and None, shall be said on week-days until the Fifth Sunday in Lent.

The Chapter, Joel ii. 13.

Turn unto the Lord your God; for He is gracious and merciful; slow to anger, and of great kindness, and repenteth Him of the evil.

THE FIRST WEEK IN LENT.

℟. Make me a companion of all them that fear Thee, and keep Thy Commandments. ℣. O look Thou upon me, and be merciful unto me, as Thou usest to do unto those that love Thy Name. ℟. And keep Thy Commandments. ℣. Glory be to the Father, and to the Son : and to the Holy Ghost. ℟. Make me a companion of all them that fear Thee, and keep Thy Commandments.

These ℟s. *to the Chapters at Terce, Sext, and None shall be daily said on week-days till the Third Sunday in Lent.*

℣. I will say unto the Lord, Thou art my Hope, and my Strong Hold.

℟. My God, in Him will I trust.

After the Psalm, Miserere mei Deus, *in the week-day Prayers at Terce, shall be added* Domine, ne in furore, *Psalm* xxxviii., *daily, till Wednesday in Holy Week, inclusive.*

The Collects as on Sunday.

AT SEXT.

Antiphon. Let us chasten ourselves : in much patience and fastings, by the armour of righteousness.

The Chapter, Isa. lv. 7.

Let the wicked forsake his way, and the unrighteous man his thoughts : and let him return unto the Lord, and He will have mercy upon him, and to our God, for He will abundantly pardon.

℟. Refrain my feet from every evil way, that I may keep Thy Word. ℣. I have not shrunk from Thy judgments, for Thou teachest me. ℟. That I may keep Thy Word. ℣. Glory be to the Father, and to the Son : and to the Holy Ghost. ℟. Refrain my feet from every evil way, that I may keep Thy Word.

℣. He shall deliver Thee from the snare of the hunter.

℟. And from the noisome pestilence.

Before the Psalm, Miserere mei Deus, *in the week-day Prayers at Sext, shall be said* Deus misereatur, *Psalm* lxvii., *daily, till Wednesday in Holy Week, inclusive.*

The Collects as on Sunday.

AT NONE.

Antiphon. The days of repentance : have come unto us, to break off our sins and iniquities.

The Chapter, Isa. lviii. 6, 7.

Is not this the fast that I have chosen? saith the Lord. To deal thy bread to the hungry, and that thou bring the poor that are cast out to thy house? when thou seest the naked, that thou cover him; and that thou hide not thyself from thine own flesh?

℟. Let Thy loving mercy come also unto me, O Lord. ℣. When Thy Word goeth forth, it giveth understanding. ℟. Unto me, O Lord. ℣. Glory be to the Father, and to the Son : and to the Holy Ghost. ℟. Let Thy loving mercy come also unto me, O Lord.

℣. He shall defend Thee under His wings.

℟. And Thou shalt be safe under His feathers.

After the Psalm, Miserere mei Deus, *in the week-day Prayers at None, shall be added* Domine exaudi, *Psalm* cii., *daily till Wednesday in Holy Week, inclusive.*

The Collects as on Sunday.

AT VESPERS.

Antiphons and Psalms of Monday.

The Chapter, Ezek. xviii. 20.

The soul that sinneth, it shall die. The son shall not bear the iniquity of the father, neither shall the father bear the iniquity of the son.

This Chapter shall be said at Vespers of the week-day till the Fifth Sunday in Lent.

R. Be Thou for us, O Lord : a strong Tower. ℣. Against the enemy. ℟. A strong Tower. ℣. Glory be to the Father, and to the Son : and to the Holy Ghost. ℟. Be Thou for us, O Lord, a strong Tower.

Hymn, ℣. *and* ℟., *as at Vespers on the First Sunday in Lent, p.* 59.

Antiphon to Magnificat.

Inasmuch as ye have done it unto one of the least of these : My brethren, ye have done it unto Me.

After the Psalm, Miserere mei Deus, *in the week-day Prayers at Vespers, shall be added* De profundis, *Psalm* cxxx., *daily, till Wednesday in Holy Week, inclusive.*

The Collects as on Sunday.

Lauds, *Prime, Terce, Sext, None, and Vespers, shall be thus said on week-days until the Third Sunday in Lent.*

TUESDAY.

Antiphon to Benedictus.

And Jesus went into the temple : and began to cast out them that sold and bought in the temple, and overthrew the tables of the money-changers, and the seats of them that sold doves.

Antiphon to Magnificat.

And He went out of the city : to Bethany, and there He taught them the things concerning the Kingdom of God.

WEDNESDAY.

Antiphon to Benedictus.

An evil and adulterous generation : seeketh after a sign; and there shall no sign be given to it, but the sign of the prophet Jonas.

Antiphon to Magnificat.

For as Jonas : was three days and three nights in the whale's belly; so shall the Son of Man be three days and three nights in the heart of the earth.

THURSDAY.

Antiphon to Benedictus.

If ye continue in My Word : then are ye My disciples indeed; and ye shall know the truth, and the truth shall make you free.

Antiphon to Magnificat.

I proceeded forth : and came

from God; neither came I of Myself, but He sent Me.

FRIDAY.

Antiphon to Benedictus.

An Angel went down at a certain season : into the pool, and troubled the water; whosoever then first after the troubling of the water stepped in was made whole.

Antiphon to Magnificat.

He that made me whole : the Same said unto me, Take up thy bed, and walk.

SATURDAY.

Antiphon to Benedictus.

Jesus taketh Peter, and James, and John : his brother, and bringeth them up into an high mountain apart, and was Transfigured before them.

The Second Sunday in Lent.

AT THE FIRST VESPERS.

The Chapter, 1 Thess. iv. 1.

We beseech you, brethren, and exhort you by the Lord Jesus, that as ye have received of us how ye ought to walk, and to please God, so ye would abound more and more.

R. God give thee of the dew of heaven, and the fatness of the earth, and plenty of corn and wine. ℣. Let people serve thee, and nations bow down to thee. ℟. Plenty of corn and wine. ℣. Glory be to the Father, and to the Son : and to the Holy Ghost. ℟. God give thee of the dew of heaven, and the fatness of the earth, and plenty of corn and wine.

℣. Be lord over thy brethren.

℟. And let thy mother's sons bow down to thee.

Hymn, Ex more docti mystico, ℣. *and* ℟., *p.* 59.

Antiphon to Magnificat.

Lord, it is good for us to be here : if Thou wilt, let us make here three tabernacles; one for Thee, and one for Moses, and one for Elias.

The Collect.

ALMIGHTY God, Who seest that we have no power of ourselves to help ourselves ; Keep us both outwardly in our bodies, and inwardly in our souls ; that we may be defended from all adversities which may happen to the body, and from all evil thoughts which may assault and hurt the soul; through Jesus Christ our Lord. Amen.

The Collect for Ash-Wednesday.

AT LAUDS.

℣. He shall deliver Thee, &c.

Antiphons. (1.) Thou shalt open my lips : O Lord; and my mouth shall show Thy praise.

Psalms as on Septuagesima, p. 46.

(2.) The Right Hand of the Lord hath the pre-eminence : the Right Hand of the Lord bringeth mighty things to pass.

(3.) Thou hast been my helper.

(4.) Let us sing the Song of the Three : Holy Children, which they sang as they walked in the midst of the fire, praising God and blessing the Lord.

(5.) He hath made them fast for ever and ever : He hath given them a law which shall not be broken.

The Chapter, 1 Thess. iv. 1.

We beseech you, brethren, and exhort you by the Lord Jesus, that as ye have received of us how ye ought to walk, and to please God, so ye would abound more and more.

℟. Thanks be to God.

Hymn, Audi benigne Conditor, *and ℟., as at Lauds on the First Sunday in Lent, p.* 60.

Antiphon to Benedictus.

Jesus went thence, and departed into the coasts of Tyre and Sidon. And behold, a woman of Canaan came out of the same coasts, and cried unto Him, saying, Have mercy on me, O Lord, Thou Son of David.

Collects as at the First Vespers.

AT PRIME.

Antiphon. And His disciples : came and besought Him, saying, Send her away; for she crieth after us.

AT TERCE.

Antiphon. Jesus answered and said : I am not sent but unto the lost sheep of the house of Israel.

The Chapter, 1 Thess. iv. 1.

We beseech you, brethren, and exhort you by the Lord Jesus, that as ye have received of us how ye ought to walk, and to please God, so ye would abound more and more.

℟. *as at Terce on the First Sunday in Lent, p.* 60.

Collects as at the First Vespers.

AT SEXT.

Antiphon. O woman, great is thy faith : be it unto thee even as thou wilt.

The Chapter, 1 Thess. iv. 3, 4.

For this is the will of God, even your sanctification, that ye should abstain from fornication; that every one of you should know how to possess his vessel in sanctification and honour.

℟. *as at Sext on the First Sunday in Lent, p.* 61.

Collects as at the First Vespers.

AT NONE.

Antiphon. Said I not unto thee, that, if thou wouldest believe : thou shouldest see greater things than these?

The Chapter, 1 Thess. iv. 6.

This is the will of God : that no man go beyond and defraud his brother in any matter; because that the Lord is the Avenger of all such, as we have also forewarned you, and testified.

℟. *as at None on the First Sunday in Lent, p.* 61.

Collects as at the First Vespers.

AT THE SECOND VESPERS.

The Chapter, 1 Thess. iv. 1.

We beseech you, brethren, and exhort you by the Lord Jesus, that as ye have received of us how ye ought to walk, and to please

God, so ye would abound more and more.

R. *as on the First Sunday in Lent, p.* 61.

Hymn, Ex more docti mystico, ℣. *and* ℟., *as on the First Sunday in Lent, p.* 59.

Antiphon to Magnificat.

Jesus said unto the woman of Canaan, It is not meet to take the children's bread, and to cast it to dogs. And she said, Truth, Lord; yet the dogs eat of the crumbs which fall from their master's table. Then Jesus answered and said unto her, O woman, great is thy faith : be it unto thee even as thou wilt.

Collects as at the First Vespers.

MONDAY.

Antiphon to Benedictus.

I am the Same : that I said unto you from the beginning.

Antiphon to Magnificat.

He that sent Me is with Me : the Father hath not left Me alone; for I do always those things that please Him.

TUESDAY.

Antiphon to Benedictus.

One is your Master : Which is in heaven.

Antiphon to Magnificat.

He that is greatest among you shall be your servant : and whosoever shall exalt himself shall be abased.

WEDNESDAY.

Antiphon to Benedictus.

Behold, we go up to Jerusalem : and the Son of Man shall be betrayed to be crucified.

Antiphon to Magnificat.

To sit on My right Hand, and on My left, is not Mine to give : but it shall be given to them for whom it is prepared of My Father.

THURSDAY.

Antiphon to Benedictus.

I receive not testimony from man : but these things I say, that ye might be saved.

Antiphon to Magnificat.

The same works that I do, bear witness of Me : that the Father hath sent Me.

FRIDAY.

Antiphon to Benedictus.

He will miserably destroy those wicked men : and will let out His vineyard to other husbandmen, which shall render Him the fruits in their seasons.

Antiphon to Magnificat.

When they sought to lay hands on Him : they feared the multitude, because they took Him for a Prophet.

SATURDAY.

Antiphon to Benedictus.

I will arise, and go to my Father : and will say unto Him, Father, I have sinned against heaven and before Thee, and am no more worthy to be called Thy son; make me as one of Thy hired servants.

The Third Sunday in Lent.

AT THE FIRST VESPERS.

The Chapter, Ephes. v. 1.

Be ye therefore followers of God, as dear children; and walk in love, as Christ also hath loved us, and hath given Himself for us, an Offering and a Sacrifice to God for a sweet-smelling savour.

R. And Joseph was brought down to Egypt, and the Lord was with Joseph. ℣. And he was a prosperous man. ℟. And the Lord was with Joseph. ℣. Glory be to the Father, and to the Son: and to the Holy Ghost. ℟. And Joseph was brought down to Egypt, and the Lord was with Joseph.

℣. And the Lord showed him mercy.

℟. And that which he did, the Lord made it to prosper.

Hymn. Ecce tempus idoneum.

This Hymn is said at Vespers daily till the Fifth Sunday in Lent.

Lo! now is our accepted day,
The med'cine purging sin away;
Where'er our lives have wrought offence,
By thought and word, by deed and sense!

For God, the merciful and true,
Hath spared His people hitherto;
Nor us and ours, with searching eyes,
Destroyed for our iniquities.

Him therefore now, with earnest care,
And contrite fast, and tear and prayer,
And works of mercy and of love,
We pray for pardon from above:

That from pollution making whole,
With virtues He may deck each soul,
And join us in the Heavenly Place,
To Angel cohorts by His grace.

O Father, that we ask be done,
Through Jesus Christ, Thine only Son;
Who, with the Holy Ghost and Thee,
Shall live and reign eternally. Amen.

℣. He shall give His Angels charge over Thee.

℟. To keep Thee in all Thy ways.

Antiphon to Magnificat.

The Father gave to his prodigal son: when he repented, the best robe, and a ring, and put shoes on his feet, and they began to be merry: we, too, have in Baptism our best robe, and for a ring the sign of the Faith.

The Collect.

WE beseech Thee, Almighty God, look upon the hearty desires of Thy humble servants, and stretch forth the Right Hand of Thy Majesty, to be our defence against all our enemies; through Jesus Christ our Lord. Amen.

The Collect for Ash-Wednesday.

AT LAUDS.

℣. He shall deliver Thee, &c.

Antiphons. (1.) O be favourable and gracious unto Sion: build Thou the walls of Jerusalem.

Psalms as on Septuagesima, p. 46.

(2.) The Lord is on my side: I will not fear what man doeth unto me.

(3.) God be merciful unto us: and bless us.

THE THIRD SUNDAY IN LENT. 69

(4.) The fire forgat his own virtue: the flames wasted not the flesh of the corruptible living things, though they walked therein.

(5.) Praise Him, sun and moon: for His Name only is excellent.

The Chapter, Ephes. v. 1.

Be ye therefore followers of God, as dear children; and walk in love, as Christ also hath loved us, and hath given Himself for us, an Offering and a Sacrifice to God for a sweet-smelling savour.

℟. Thanks be to God.

Hymn. Jesu quadragenariæ.

This Hymn is said at Lauds daily till the Fifth Sunday in Lent.

Jesu, the Law and Pattern, whence
Our forty days of abstinence,
Who souls to save, that else had died,
This sacred fast hast ratified;

That so to Paradise once more
Might abstinence preserved restore
Them that had lost its fields of light
Through crafty wiles of appetite:

Be present now, be present here,
And mark Thy Church's falling tear,
And own the grief that fills her eyes
In mourning her iniquities.

Oh by Thy Grace be pardon won
For sins that former years have done;
And let Thy mercy guard us still
From crimes that threaten future ill.

That by the Fast we offer here,
Our annual sacrifice sincere,
To Paschal gladness at the end,
Set free from guilt, our souls may tend.

O Father, that we ask be done,
Through Jesus Christ, Thine only Son;
Who, with the Holy Ghost and Thee,
Shall live and reign eternally. Amen.

℣. His faithfulness and truth shall be Thy shield and buckler.

℟. Thou shalt not be afraid for any terror by night.

Antiphon to Benedictus.

Jesus was casting out a devil, and it was dumb. And it came to pass, when the devil was gone out, the dumb spake; and the people wondered.

Collects as at the First Vespers.

AT PRIME.

Antiphon. If I, by the Finger of God, cast out devils: no doubt the kingdom of God is come upon you.

AT TERCE.

Antiphon. When a strong man armed keepeth his Palace: his goods are in peace.

The Chapter, Ephes. v. 1.

Be ye therefore followers of God, as dear children; and walk in love, as Christ also hath loved us, and hath given Himself for us, an Offering and a Sacrifice to God for a sweet-smelling savour.

R. It is good for me that I have been in trouble; the law of Thy Mouth is dearer unto me than thousands of gold and silver. ℣. Thy hands have made me, and fashioned me: O give me understanding, that I may learn Thy Commandments. ℟. The law of Thy Mouth is dearer unto me than thousands of gold and silver. ℣. Glory be to the Father, and to the Son: and to the Holy Ghost. ℟. It is good for me that I have been in trouble; the law of Thy Mouth is dearer unto me than thousands of gold and silver.

℣. I will say unto the Lord, Thou art my hope and my strong hold.

THE THIRD SUNDAY IN LENT.

℟. My God, in Him will I trust.

Collects as at the First Vespers.

AT SEXT.

Antiphon. He that is not with Me is against Me : and he that gathereth not with Me scattereth.

The Chapter, Ephes. v. 3.

But fornication, and all uncleanness or covetousness, let it not be once named amongst you, as becometh saints.

R. I am Thy servant, O grant me understanding. ℣. That I may know Thy testimonies. ℟. O grant me understanding. ℣. Glory be to the Father, and to the Son : and to the Holy Ghost. ℟. I am Thy servant, O grant me understanding.

℣. He shall deliver Thee from the snare of the hunter.

℟. And from the noisome pestilence.

Collects as at the First Vespers.

AT NONE.

Antiphon. When the unclean spirit is gone out of a man : he walketh through dry places, seeking rest and finding none.

The Chapter, Ephes. v. 5.

For this ye know, that no whoremonger, nor unclean person, nor covetous man, who is an idolater, hath any inheritance in the kingdom of Christ, and of God.

R. Seven times a day do I praise Thee ; because of Thy righteous judgments. ℣. I have gone astray like a sheep that is lost ; O seek Thy servant, for I do not forget Thy commandments. ℟. Because of Thy righteous judgments. ℣. Glory be to the Father, and to the Son : and to the Holy Ghost. ℟. Seven times a day do I praise Thee ; because of Thy righteous judgments.

℣. He shall defend Thee under His wings.

℟. And Thou shalt be safe under His feathers.

Collects as at the First Vespers.

AT THE SECOND VESPERS.

The Chapter, Ephes. v. 1.

Be ye therefore followers of God, as dear children ; and walk in love, as Christ also hath loved us, and hath given Himself for us, an Offering and a Sacrifice to God for a sweet-smelling savour.

R. Bring my soul out of prison, that I may give thanks unto Thy Name. ℣. I had no place to flee unto, and no man cared for my soul. ℟. That I may give thanks unto Thy Name. ℣. Glory be to the Father, and to the Son : and to the Holy Ghost. ℟. Bring my soul out of prison, that I may give thanks unto Thy Name.

Hymn, Ecce tempus idoneum, ℣. *and* ℟., *as at the First Vespers, p.* 68.

Antiphon to Magnificat.

And it came to pass, as He spake these things, a certain woman of the company lifted up her voice, and said unto Him, Blessed is the womb that bare Thee, and the paps which Thou hast sucked. But He said, Yea rather, blessed are they that hear the Word of God, and keep it.

Collects as at the First Vespers.

MONDAY. AT LAUDS.

℣. He shall deliver Thee from the snare of the hunter.

℟. And from the noisome pestilence.

℣. O God, make speed, &c.

This ℣. and ℟. are said daily at Lauds of the week-day until the Fifth Sunday in Lent.

Antiphons and Psalms as in the Psalter.

The Chapter, Joel ii. 12, 13.

Turn ye even unto Me, saith the Lord, with all your heart, and with fasting, and with weeping, and with mourning. And rend your heart, and not your garments, and turn unto the Lord your God.

This Chapter is said daily at Lauds of the week-day until the Fifth Sunday in Lent.

℟. Thanks be to God.

Hymn, Jesu quadragenariæ, ℣. and ℟., p. 69.

Antiphon to Benedictus.

Verily I say unto you, No prophet is accepted in his own country.

AT PRIME.

Antiphon. As I live, saith the Lord God : I have no pleasure in the death of the wicked ; but that the wicked turn from his way and live.

AT TERCE.

Antiphon. Let us chasten ourselves : in much patience, by the armour of the righteousness of God.

The Chapter, Joel ii. 13.

Turn unto the Lord your God ; for He is gracious and merciful ; slow to anger, and of great kindness, and repenteth Him of the evil.

R. It is good for me that I have been in trouble ; the law of Thy Mouth is dearer unto me than thousands of gold and silver. ℣. Thy Hands have made me, and fashioned me ; O give me understanding, that I may learn Thy Commandments. ℟. The law of Thy Mouth is dearer unto me than thousands of gold and silver. ℣. Glory be to the Father, and to the Son : and to the Holy Ghost. ℟. It is good for me that I have been in trouble ; the law of Thy Mouth is dearer unto me than thousands of gold and silver.

℣. I will say unto the Lord, Thou art my hope and my strong hold.

℟. My God, in Him will I trust.

The Collects as on Sunday.

AT SEXT.

Antiphon. Let us chasten ourselves : in much patience and fastings, by the armour of righteousness.

THE THIRD WEEK IN LENT.

The Chapter, Isa. lv. 7.

Let the wicked forsake his way, and the unrighteous man his thoughts : and let him return unto the Lord, and He will have mercy upon him, and to our God, for He will abundantly pardon.

R. I am Thy servant, O grant me understanding. ℣. That I may know Thy testimonies. ℟. O grant me understanding. ℣. Glory be to the Father, and to the Son : and to the Holy Ghost. ℟. I am Thy servant, O grant me understanding.

℣. He shall deliver Thee from the snare of the hunter.

℟. And from the noisome pestilence.

The Collects as on Sunday.

AT NONE.

Antiphon. The days of repentance : have come unto us, to break off our sins and iniquities.

The Chapter, Isa. lviii. 6, 7.

Is not this the fast that I have chosen ? saith the Lord. To deal thy bread to the hungry, and that thou bring the poor that are cast out to thy house ? when thou seest the naked, that thou cover him ; and that thou hide not thyself from thine own flesh ?

R. Seven times a day do I praise Thee ; because of Thy righteous judgments. ℣. I have gone astray like a sheep that is lost ; O seek Thy servant, for I do not forget Thy commandments. ℟. Because of Thy righteous judgments. ℣. Glory be to the Father, and to the Son : and to the Holy Ghost. ℟. Seven times a day do I praise Thee ; because of Thy righteous judgments.

℣. He shall defend Thee under His wings.

℟. And Thou shalt be safe under His feathers.

The Collects as on Sunday.

AT VESPERS.

Antiphons and Psalms of Monday.

The Chapter, Ezek. xviii. 20.

The soul that sinneth, it shall die. The son shall not bear the iniquity of the father, neither shall the father bear the iniquity of the son.

This Chapter is said at week-day Vespers till the Fifth Sunday in Lent.

R. Bring my soul out of prison, that I may give thanks unto Thy Name. ℣. I had no place to flee unto, and no man cared for my soul. ℟. That I may give thanks unto Thy Name. ℣. Glory be to the Father, and to the Son : and to the Holy Ghost. ℟. Bring my soul out of prison, that I may give thanks unto Thy Name.

This R. *is said daily at Vespers of the week-day till the Fourth Sunday in Lent.*

Hymn, ℣. *and* ℟., *as at Vespers on the Third Sunday in Lent, p. 68.*

Antiphon to Magnificat.

But Jesus passing through the midst of them : went His way.

Lauds, Prime, Terce, Sext, None, and Vespers are thus said on week-days until the Fifth Sunday in Lent, except the R. *at week-day Vespers.*

TUESDAY.

Antiphon to Benedictus.

If two of you shall agree on earth : as touching anything that they shall ask, it shall be done for them of My Father Which is in heaven.

Antiphon to Magnificat.

Where two or three are gathered together : in My Name, there am I in the midst of them.

WEDNESDAY.

Antiphon to Benedictus.

Hear : and understand.

Antiphon to Magnificat.

To eat with unwashen hands defileth not : a man.

THURSDAY.

Antiphon to Benedictus.

Labour not for the meat which perisheth : but for that Meat which endureth unto everlasting life.

Antiphon to Magnificat.

The Bread of God : is He Which cometh down from heaven, and giveth life unto the world.

FRIDAY.

Antiphon to Benedictus.

Sir, I perceive that Thou art a prophet : Our fathers worshipped in this mountain.

Antiphon to Magnificat.

True worshippers shall worship : the Father in spirit and in truth.

SATURDAY.

Antiphon to Benedictus.

Jesus stooped down and wrote : on the ground, He that is without sin among you, let him first cast a stone at her.

The Fourth Sunday in Lent.

AT THE FIRST VESPERS.

The Chapter, Gal. iv. 22, 23.

It is written, that Abraham had two sons, the one by a bond-maid, the other by a free-woman. But he who was of the bond-woman was born after the flesh; but he of the free-woman was by promise.

R. And Joseph said unto his brethren, I am Joseph ; doth my father yet live ? Be not grieved nor angry with yourselves that ye sold me hither. ℣. For God did send me before you to preserve life. R℣. Be not grieved nor angry with yourselves that ye sold me hither. ℣. Glory be to the Father, and to the Son : and to the Holy Ghost. R℣. And Joseph said unto his brethren, I am Joseph ; doth my father yet live ? Be not grieved nor angry with yourselves that ye sold me hither.

℣. And Israel said, It is enough : Joseph my son is yet alive.

R℣. I will go and see him before I die.

Hymn, Ecce tempus idoneum, ℣. and ℟., *p.* 68.

Antiphon to Magnificat.

Neither do I condemn thee : go, and sin no more.

The Collect.

GRANT, we beseech Thee, Almighty God, that we, who for our evil deeds do worthily deserve to be punished, by the comfort of Thy grace may mercifully be relieved; through our Lord and Saviour Jesus Christ. Amen.

The Collect for Ash-Wednesday.

AT LAUDS.

℣. He shall deliver Thee, &c.

Antiphons. (1.) Then shalt Thou be pleased : with the sacrifice of righteousness : if Thou wilt turn Thy Face from my sins.

Psalms as on Septuagesima, p. 46.

(2.) It is better to trust in the Lord : than to put any confidence in princes.

(3.) God, even our own God : shall give us His blessing.

(4.) The Lord hath saved us : from the hand of death ; even out of the midst of the fire hath He delivered us.

(5.) Kings of the earth, and all people : praise the Name of the Lord.

The Chapter, Gal. iv. 22, 23.

It is written, that Abraham had two sons, the one by a bond-maid, the other by a free-woman. But he who was of the bond-woman was born after the flesh ; but he of the free-woman was by promise.

℟. Thanks be to God.

Hymn, Jesu quadragenariæ, ℣. and ℟., *p.* 69, *as at Lauds on the Third Sunday.*

Antiphon to Benedictus.

Jesus went over the sea of Galilee, which is the sea of Tiberias. And a great multitude followed Him, because they saw His miracles which He did on them that were diseased.

Collects as at the First Vespers.

AT PRIME.

Antiphon. And Jesus went up into a mountain : and there He sat with His disciples. And the Passover, a feast of the Jews, was nigh.

AT TERCE.

Antiphon. And Jesus took the loaves : and when He had given thanks He distributed to the disciples, and the disciples to them that were set down ; and likewise of the fishes as much as they would.

The Chapter, Gal. iv. 22, 23.

It is written, that Abraham had two sons, the one by a bond-maid, the other by a free-woman. But he who was of the bond-woman was born after the flesh ; but he of the free-woman was by promise.

℟. *as at Terce on the Third Sunday in Lent, p.* 69.

Collects as at the First Vespers.

AT SEXT.

Antiphon. With five barley loaves and two small fishes : did the Lord feed men in number about five thousand.

The Chapter, Gal. iv. 27; Isa. liv. 1.

Rejoice, thou barren that bearest not; break forth and cry, thou that travailest not; for the desolate hath many more children than she which hath an husband.

R. *as at Sext on the Third Sunday in Lent, p. 70.*

Collects as at the First Vespers.

AT NONE.

Antiphon. Gather up the fragments : that remain, that nothing be lost.

The Chapter, Gal. iv. 28—30.

Now we, brethren, as Isaac was, are the children of promise. But as then he that was born after the flesh persecuted him that was born after the Spirit; even so it is now. Nevertheless, what saith the Scripture? Cast out the bond-woman and her son.

R. *as at None on the Third Sunday in Lent, p. 70.*

Collects as at the First Vespers.

AT THE SECOND VESPERS.

The Chapter, Gal. iv. 22, 23.

It is written, that Abraham had two sons, the one by a bond-maid, the other by a free-woman. But he who was of the bond-woman was born after the flesh; but he of the free-woman was by promise.

R. The Lord made him eat the increase of the fields, to suck Honey out of the Rock, and Oil out of the flinty rock. ℣. He fed them also with the finest Wheat-Flour : and with Honey out of the stony rock did He satisfy them. ℟. Honey out of the Rock, and Oil out of the flinty rock. ℣. Glory be to the Father, and to the Son : and to the Holy Ghost. ℟. The Lord made him eat the increase of the fields, and to suck Honey out of the Rock, and Oil out of the flinty rock.

This R. *is daily said at Vespers of the week-day till the Fifth Sunday in Lent.*

Hymn, Ecce tempus idoneum, ℣. *and* ℟., *as on the Third Sunday in Lent, p. 68.*

Antiphon to Magnificat.

Then those men, when they had seen the miracle that Jesus did, said, This is of a truth that Prophet that should come into the world.

Collects as at the First Vespers.

MONDAY.

Antiphon to Benedictus.

Take these things hence : make not My Father's House an house of merchandise.

AT VESPERS.

The Chapter, Ezek. xviii. 20.

The soul that sinneth it shall die. The son shall not bear the iniquity of the father, neither shall the father bear the iniquity of the son.

R. *as on the Fourth Sunday in Lent.*

Antiphon to Magnificat.

Destroy this Temple : and in three days I will raise it up; but He spake of the Temple of His Body.

TUESDAY.

Antiphon to Benedictus.

Ye seek to kill Me : a Man that hath told you the truth.

Antiphon to Magnificat.

Are ye angry at Me : because I have made a man every whit whole on the Sabbath day?

WEDNESDAY.

Antiphon to Benedictus.

Master, who did sin : this man, or his parents, that he was born blind? Jesus answered, Neither hath this man sinned, nor his parents : but that the works of God should be made manifest in him.

Antiphon to Magnificat.

A Man that is called Jesus : put clay upon mine eyes, and I washed, and do see.

THURSDAY.

Antiphon to Benedictus.

The Father loveth the Son : and showeth Him all things that Himself doeth.

Antiphon to Magnificat.

As the Father raiseth up the dead : and quickeneth them ; even so the Son quickeneth whom He will.

FRIDAY.

Antiphon to Benedictus.

Our friend Lazarus sleepeth : but I go that I may awake him out of sleep.

Antiphon to Magnificat.

Lord, if Thou hadst been here : my brother had not died. By this time he stinketh : for he hath been dead four days.

SATURDAY.

Antiphon to Benedictus.

Then spake Jesus, I am the Light of the world : he that followeth Me shall not walk in darkness, but shall have the Light of life.

The Fifth Sunday in Lent, sometimes called Passion Sunday.

AT THE FIRST VESPERS.

The Chapter, Lament. iii. 58.

O Lord, Thou hast pleaded the causes of My Soul ; Thou hast Redeemed My Life.

R. The ungodly compassed Me about, and scourged Me without a cause, but Thou, O Lord, art My defender. ℣. For trouble is hard at hand : and there is none to help Me. ℟. But Thou, O Lord, art My defender. The ungodly compassed Me about, and scourged Me without a cause, but Thou, O Lord, art My defender.

Hymn. Vexilla Regis prodeunt.

This Hymn is said at Vespers daily, till Wednesday in Holy Week, inclusive.

The Royal Banners forward go ;
The Cross shines forth in mystic glow ;
Where He in flesh, our flesh Who made,
Our sentence bore, our ransom paid.

THE FIFTH SUNDAY IN LENT.

Where deep for us the spear was dyed,
Life's torrent rushing from His side,
To wash us in that precious flood
Where mingled Water flowed, and Blood.

Fulfilled is all that David told
In true prophetic song of old ;
Amidst the nations God, saith he,
Hath reigned and triumphed from the Tree.

O Tree of beauty, Tree of light ;
O Tree with royal purple bright !
Elect on whose triumphal breast
Those holy Limbs should find their rest :

On whose dear arms, so widely flung,
The weight of this world's Ransom hung :
The price of human kind to pay,
And spoil the spoiler of his prey.

To Thee, Eternal Three in One,
Let homage meet by all be done :
Whom by the Cross Thou dost restore,
Preserve and govern evermore ! Amen.

℣. They gave Me gall to eat.

℞. And when I was thirsty they gave Me vinegar to drink.

Antiphon to Magnificat.

I am one that bear witness of Myself : and the Father that sent Me beareth witness of Me.

The Collect.

WE beseech Thee, Almighty God, mercifully to look upon Thy people; that by Thy great goodness they may be governed and preserved evermore both in body and soul; through Jesus Christ our Lord. *Amen.*

The Collect for Ash-Wednesday.

AT LAUDS.

℣. Draw nigh unto My soul and save It.

℞. O deliver Me because of Mine enemies.

This ℣. and ℞. shall be daily said at Lauds of the week-day till Wednesday in Holy Week, inclusive.

℣. O God, make speed, &c.

Antiphons. (1.) O Lord, behold My affliction : for the enemy hath magnified himself.

Psalms as on Septuagesima, p. 46.

(2.) I called upon the Lord in trouble : and the Lord heard Me at large.

(3.) O Lord, Thou hast pleaded : the causes of My Soul ; Thou hast Redeemed My Life.

(4.) O My people, what have I done unto thee ; and wherein have I wearied thee ? testify against Me.

(5.) Shall evil be recompensed for good ? for they have digged a pit for My Soul.

The Chapter, Heb. ix. 11, 12.

Christ being come an High Priest of good things to come, by a greater and more perfect tabernacle, not made with hands, that is to say, not of this building ; neither by the blood of goats and calves, but by His Own Blood He entered in once into the holy place, having obtained eternal Redemption for us.

℞. Thanks be to God.

Hymn. Pange lingua gloriosi.

This Hymn is said at Lauds daily, till Wednesday in Holy Week, inclusive.

This Hymn, if too long, may be begun at the verse "Thirty years among us dwelling."

Sing, my tongue, the glorious battle
With completed victory rife ;
And above the Cross's trophy
Tell the triumph of the strife :
How the world's Redeemer conquered
By surrendering of His Life.

God his Maker, sorely grieving
  That the first-made Adam fell,
When he ate the fruit of sorrow,
  Whose reward was death and hell,
Noted then this wood, the ruin
  Of the ancient wood to quell.

For the work of our Salvation
  Needs would have his order so,
And the multiform deceiver's
  Art by art would overthrow,
And from thence would bring the Med'cine
  Whence the insult of the foe.

Wherefore, when the sacred fulness
  Of th' appointed time was come,
This world's Maker left His Father,
  Sent the Heavenly Mansion from,
And proceeded, God Incarnate,
  Of the Virgin's Holy Womb.

THIRTY years among us dwelling,
  His appointed time fulfilled,
Born for this, He meets His Passion,
  For that this He freely willed:
On the Cross the Lamb is lifted,
  Where His life-blood shall be spilled.

He endured the nails, the spitting,
  Vinegar, and spear, and reed;
From that Holy Body broken
  Blood and Water forth proceed:
Earth and stars, and sky, and ocean,
  By that flood from stain are freed.

Faithful Cross! above all other
  One and only noble Tree!
None in foliage, none in blossom,
  None in fruit thy peer may be:
Sweetest wood and sweetest iron!
  Sweetest Weight is hung on thee.

Bend Thy boughs, O Tree of Glory!
  Thy relaxing sinews bend;
For awhile the ancient rigour,
  That thy birth bestowed, suspend;
And the King of Heavenly Beauty
  On thy bosom gently tend!

Thou alone wast counted worthy
  This world's Ransom to uphold;
For a shipwrecked race preparing
  Harbour, like the Ark of old;
With the sacred Blood anointed
  From the smitten Lamb that roll'd.

To the Trinity be glory
  Everlasting, as is meet;
Equal to the Father, equal
  To the Son and Paraclete;
Trinal Unity, Whose praises
  All created things repeat. Amen.

℣. Deliver Me from Mine enemies, O God.

℞. Defend Me from them that rise up against Me.

Antiphon to Benedictus.

Jesus saith, Which of you convinceth Me of sin? and if I say the truth, why do ye not believe Me? He that is of God heareth God's words; ye therefore hear them not, because ye are not of God.

Collects as at the First Vespers.

AT PRIME.

Antiphon. I have not a devil: but I honour My Father, and ye do dishonour Me.

From this day to Low Sunday is not said the R. *to the Chapter at Prime, but till Wednesday in Holy Week, inclusive, in its place is said,*

℣. O Lord, arise and help us.

℞. And deliver us for Thy Name's sake.

AT TERCE.

Antiphon. I seek not Mine own glory: there is One that seeketh, and judgeth.

The Chapter, Heb. ix. 11, 12.

Christ being come an High Priest of good things to come, by a greater and more perfect tabernacle, not made with hands, that is to say, not of this building; neither by the blood of goats and calves, but by His own Blood He entered in once into the holy place, having obtained eternal Redemption for us.

R. Deliver My Soul from the sword: My Darling from the power of the dog. ℣. Deliver Me, O Lord, from the evil man : and preserve Me from the wicked man. ℟. My Darling from the power of the dog. Deliver My Soul from the sword, My Darling from the power of the dog.

These ℟s. to the Chapters at Terce, Sext, None, and Vespers are said daily on week-days till the Wednesday in Holy Week inclusive.

℣. Save Me from the lion's mouth.

℟. Thou hast heard Me also from among the horns of the unicorns.

Collects as at the First Vespers.

AT SEXT.

Antiphon. Verily, verily, I say unto you : if a man keep My saying, he shall never see death.

The Chapter, Heb. ix. 13, 14.

For if the blood of bulls and of goats, and the ashes of an heifer sprinkling the unclean, sanctifieth to the purifying of the flesh ; how much more shall the Blood of Christ, Who, through the eternal Spirit, offered Himself without spot to God, purge your conscience from dead works to serve the living God ?

R. Save Me from the lion's mouth ; Thou hast heard Me also from among the horns of the unicorns. ℣. Deliver My Soul from the sword, My Darling from the power of the dog. ℟. Thou hast heard Me also from among the horns of the unicorns. Save Me from the lion's mouth ; Thou hast heard Me also from among the horns of the unicorns.

℣. O shut not up My soul with the sinners.

℟. Nor My life with the bloodthirsty.

Collects as at the First Vespers.

AT NONE.

Antiphon. Your father Abraham : rejoiced to see My day, and he saw it, and was glad.

The Chapter, Heb. ix. 15.

And for this cause He is the Mediator of the new testament, that by means of death, for the redemption of the transgressions that were under the first testament, they which are called might receive the promise of eternal inheritance.

R. Princes have persecuted Me without a cause, but My heart standeth in awe of Thy Word. I am as glad of Thy Word. ℣. As one that findeth great spoils. ℟. I am as glad of Thy Word. Princes have persecuted Me without a cause, but My heart standeth in awe of Thy Word. I am as glad of Thy Word.

℣. Deliver Me, O Lord, from the evil man.

℟. And preserve Me from the wicked man.

Collects as at the First Vespers.

AT THE SECOND VESPERS.

The Chapter, Heb. ix. 11, 12.

Christ being come an High Priest of good things to come, by a greater and more perfect tabernacle, not made with hands, that is to say, not of this building ; neither by the blood of goats and calves, but by His own Blood He entered in once into the holy place, having obtained eternal Redemption for us.

R. How long shall Mine enemies triumph over Me? consider and hear Me, O Lord My God. V. For if I be cast down, they that trouble Me will rejoice at it. R. Consider and hear Me, O Lord My God. How long shall Mine enemies triumph over Me? consider and hear Me, O Lord My God.

Hymn, Vexilla Regis prodeunt, *p.* 76.

V. They gave Me gall to eat.

R. And when I was thirsty they gave Me vinegar to drink.

Antiphon to Magnificat.

Verily, verily, I say unto you, Before Abraham was, I am. Then took they up stones to cast at Him; but Jesus hid Himself, and went out of the temple.

Collects as at the First Vespers.

MONDAY. AT LAUDS.

V. *and* R. *as at p.* 77.

Antiphons and Psalms as in the Psalter.

The Chapter, Jer. xi. 18, 19.

The Lord hath given Me knowledge of it, and I know it: then Thou showedst Me their doings. But I was like a Lamb or an ox that is brought to the slaughter.

R. Thanks be to God.

Hymn, Pange lingua gloriosi, V. *and* R., *p.* 77.

Antiphon to Benedictus.

In the last day, that great day of the Feast: Jesus stood and cried, saying, If any man thirst, let him come unto Me and drink.

Lauds are thus said daily till the end of the week, except the Antiphon to Benedictus, *which is daily changed.*

The Collects as on Sunday.

AT PRIME.

Antiphon. The ungodly are minded: to do Me some mischief, and My Heart is disquieted within Me.

AT TERCE.

Antiphon. O Lord, Thou hast pleaded: the causes of My Soul; Thou hast Redeemed My Life.

The Chapter, Isa l. 6, 7.

I gave My Back to the smiters, and My Cheeks to them that plucked off the hair: I hid not My Face from shame and spitting. For the Lord God will help Me; therefore shall I not be confounded.

R. *as at Terce on Sunday, p.* 78.

The Collects as on Sunday.

AT SEXT.

Antiphon. O My people, what have I done unto thee: and wherein have I wearied thee? testify against Me.

The Chapter, Isa. l. 7.

For the Lord God will help Me; therefore shall I not be confounded: therefore have I set My Face like a flint, and I know that I shall not be ashamed.

R. *as at Sext on Sunday, p.* 79.

The Collects as on Sunday.

AT NONE.

Antiphon. Shall evil be recompensed for good : for they have digged a pit for My Soul.

The Chapter, Jer. xvii. 18.

Let them be confounded that persecute Me, but let not Me be confounded; let them be dismayed, but let not Me be dismayed : bring upon them the day of evil, and destroy them with double destruction.

R. *as at None on Sunday, p.* 79.

The Collects as on Sunday.

Prime, Terce, Sext, and None are thus said daily, with the change of the Collect for the week, till Wednesday in Holy Week inclusive, except on Palm Sunday.

AT VESPERS.

Antiphons and Psalms as in the Psalter.

The Chapter, Lament. iii. 58.

O Lord, Thou hast pleaded the causes of My Soul; Thou hast redeemed My Life.

R. How long shall Mine enemies triumph over Me? consider and hear Me. O Lord My God. ℣. For if I be cast down, they that trouble Me will rejoice at it. ℟. Consider and hear Me, O Lord My God. How long shall Mine enemies triumph over Me? Consider and hear Me, O Lord My God.

Hymn, Vexilla Regis prodeunt, ℣. *and* ℟., *p.* 76.

Antiphon to Magnificat.

If any man thirst: let him come unto Me, and drink, and out of his belly shall flow rivers of living water.

The Collects as on Sunday.

Vespers are thus said daily till the end of the week, except the Antiphon to Magnificat, *which is daily changed.*

TUESDAY.

Antiphon to Benedictus.

My time is not yet come : but your time is alway ready.

Antiphon to Magnificat.

Go ye up unto this feast : I go not up yet unto this feast, for My time is not yet full come.

WEDNESDAY.

Antiphon to Benedictus.

My sheep hear My voice : and I know them.

Antiphon to Magnificat.

Many good works have I showed you : from My Father; for which of those works do ye stone Me?

THURSDAY.

Antiphon to Benedictus.

Why trouble ye the woman : for she hath wrought a good work upon Me.

Antiphon to Magnificat.

In that she hath poured this ointment : on My Body, she did it for My Burial.

FRIDAY.

Antiphon to Benedictus.

Now the feast of unleavened bread drew nigh : which is called the Passover, and the chief priests and scribes sought how they might kill Him; for they feared the people.

Antiphon to Magnificat.

The chief priests and the scribes: sought how they might take Him by craft, and put Him to death. But they said, Not on the feast day, lest there be an uproar of the people.

SATURDAY.

Antiphon to Benedictus.

With desire : have I desired to eat this Passover with you, before I suffer.

The Sunday next before Easter, commonly called Palm Sunday.

AT THE FIRST VESPERS.

Antiphons and Psalms as in the Psalter.

The Chapter, Phil. ii. 5—7.

Let this mind be in you, which was also in Christ Jesus: Who, being in the form of God, thought it not robbery to be equal with God; but made Himself of no reputation, and took upon Him the form of a servant.

R. *as at the First Vespers of the Fifth Sunday in Lent, p.* 76.

Hymn, Vexilla Regis prodeunt, V̄. and R̄. *p.* 76.

THE SUNDAY NEXT BEFORE EASTER.

Antiphon to Magnificat.

And now, O Father; glorify Thou Me with Thine Own Self with the glory which I had with Thee before the world was.

The Collect.

ALMIGHTY and everlasting God, Who, of Thy tender love towards mankind, hast sent Thy Son, our Saviour Jesus Christ, to take upon Him our flesh, and to suffer death upon the Cross, that all mankind should follow the example of His great humility; Mercifully grant that we may both follow the example of His patience, and also be made partakers of His Resurrection; through the Same Jesus Christ our Lord. Amen.

The Collect for Ash Wednesday.

AT LAUDS.

This ℣. and ℟. said till Thursday.

℣. Draw nigh unto My Soul, and save It.

℟. O deliver Me because of Mine enemies.

Antiphons. (1.) The Lord God will help Me: therefore shall I not be confounded.

Psalms as on Septuagesima, p. 46.

(2.) They kept Me in: on every side; they kept Me in, I say, on every side; but in the Name of the Lord will I destroy them.

(3.) Give sentence with Me: O God, and defend My cause.

(4.) Let them be confounded: that persecute Me; but let not Me be confounded.

(5.) With Angels and holy children: may we be found faithful to the Conqueror of death, and sing Hosanna in the highest.

The Chapter, Phil. ii. 5—7.

Let this mind be in you, which was also in Christ Jesus: Who being in the form of God, thought it not robbery to be equal with God; but made Himself of no reputation, and took upon Him the form of a servant.

℟. Thanks be to God.

Hymn, Pange lingua gloriosi, ℣. *and* ℟., *as at p.* 77.

Antiphon to Benedictus.

And the multitudes that went before, and that followed, cried, saying, Hosanna to the Son of David; Blessed is He that cometh in the Name of the Lord; Hosanna in the highest.

Collects as at the First Vespers.

AT PRIME.

Antiphon. Hosanna: Blessed is the King of Israel that cometh in the Name of the Lord.

AT TERCE.

Antiphon. And a very great multitude: spread their garments in the way, others cut down branches from the trees, and strawed them in the way, saying, Hosanna to the Son of David; Blessed is He that cometh in the Name of the Lord; Hosanna in the highest.

The Chapter, Phil. ii. 5—7.

Let this mind be in you, which was also in Christ Jesus: Who being in the form of God, thought it not robbery to be equal with God; but made Himself of no reputation, and took upon Him the form of a servant.

℟. My lovers and My neighbours did stand looking upon My trouble. ℣. And My kinsmen stood afar off. ℟. Looking upon My trouble. My lovers and My neighbours did stand looking upon My trouble.

℣. Save Me from the lion's mouth.

℟. Thou hast heard Me also from among the horns of the unicorns.

Collects as at the First Vespers.

AT SEXT.

Antiphon. And as He went: they spread their clothes in the way, saying, Blessed be the King that cometh in the Name of the Lord; peace in heaven, and glory in the highest.

The Chapter, Phil. ii. 8.

He humbled Himself, and became obedient unto death, even the death of the Cross.

℟. Give heed to Me, O Lord, and hearken to the voice of them that contend with Me. Shall evil be recompensed for good? for they have digged a pit for My Soul. ℣. Remember that I stood before Thee to speak for them. ℟. Shall evil be recompensed for good? for they have digged a pit for My Soul. Give heed to Me, O Lord, and hearken to the voice of them that contend with Me. Shall evil be recompensed for good? for they have digged a pit for My Soul.

℣. O shut not up My Soul with the sinners.

℟. Nor My Life with the bloodthirsty.

Collects as at the First Vespers.

AT NONE.

Antiphon. Much people : took branches of palm trees, and cried, Hosanna; Blessed is the King of Israel, that cometh in the Name of the Lord.

The Chapter, Phil. ii. 9, 10.

Wherefore God also hath highly exalted Him, and given Him a Name which is above every name; that at the Name of Jesus every knee should bow, of things in heaven, and things in earth, and things under the earth.

℟. Save Me, O God : for the waters are come in, even unto My Soul. And hide not Thy Face from Thy Servant, for I am in trouble. O haste Thee, and hear Me. ℣. Draw nigh unto My Soul, and save It : O deliver Me, because of Mine enemies. ℟. For I am in trouble. O haste Thee, and hear Me. Save Me, O God, for the waters are come in, even unto My Soul. And hide not Thy Face from Thy Servant, for I am in trouble. O haste Thee, and hear Me.

℣. Deliver Me, O Lord, from the evil man.

℟. And preserve Me from the wicked man.

Collects as at the First Vespers.

AT THE SECOND VESPERS.

Antiphons and Psalms as in the Psalter.

The Chapter as at Lauds.

R. When He was come near, He beheld the city and wept over it. ℣. O Israel, return unto the Lord thy God. ℞. When He was come near, He beheld the city and wept over it.

Hymn, Vexilla Regis prodeunt, ℣. and ℞., *p.* 76.

Antiphon to Magnificat.

A multitude with branches of palm go forth to meet their Lord, and worship the Son of God. All people adore Him, and in His praise is thundered through the sky, Hosanna in the highest.

Collects as at the First Vespers.

Monday before Easter.

AT LAUDS.

Antiphons. (1.) I hid not My Face : from shame and spitting.

Psalms as on Mondays.

(2.) Smite the Shepherd : and the sheep shall be scattered.
(3.) So they weighed for My price : thirty pieces of silver; a goodly price that I was prised at of them.
(4.) Waters flowed over Mine Head : then I said, I am cut off, I called upon Thy Name, O Lord, out of the low dungeon.
(5.) Behold, O Lord : the lips of those that rise up against Me, and their devices against Me all the day.

The Chapter, Jer. xi. 18, 19.

The Lord hath given Me knowledge of it and I know it : then Thou showedst Me their doings. But I was like a Lamb or an ox that is brought to the slaughter.

℞. Thanks be to God.

Hymn, Pange lingua, ℣. and ℞., *p.* 77.

Antiphon to Benedictus.

Thou couldest have no power : at all against Me, except it were given thee from above.

The Collects as on Sunday.

AT PRIME.

Antiphon. The ungodly are minded : to do Me some mischief, and My heart is disquieted within Me.

AT TERCE.

Antiphon. O Lord, Thou hast pleaded : the causes of My Soul; Thou hast redeemed My Life.

The Chapter, Isa. l. 6, 7.

I gave My Back to the smiters; and My Cheeks to them that plucked off the hair : I hid not My Face from shame and spitting. For the Lord God will help Me; therefore shall I not be confounded.

R. My lovers and My neighbours did stand looking upon My trouble. ℣. And My kinsmen stood afar off. ℞. Looking upon My trouble. My lovers and My neighbours did stand looking upon My trouble.

℣. Save Me from the lion's mouth.

℟. Thou hast heard Me also from among the horns of the unicorns.

The Collects as on Sunday.

AT SEXT.

Antiphon. O My people, what have I done unto thee: and wherein have I wearied thee? testify against Me.

The Chapter, Isa. l. 7.

For the Lord God will help Me; therefore shall I not be confounded: therefore have I set My Face like a flint, and I know that I shall not be ashamed.

R. Give heed to Me, O Lord, and hearken to the voice of them that contend with Me. Shall evil be recompensed for good? for they have digged a pit for My Soul. ℣. Remember that I stood before Thee to speak good for them. ℟. Shall evil be recompensed for good? for they have digged a pit for My Soul. Give heed to Me, O Lord, and hearken to the voice of them that contend with Me. Shall evil be recompensed for good? for they have digged a pit for My Soul.

℣. O shut not up My Soul with the sinners.

℟. Nor My Life with the bloodthirsty.

The Collects as on Sunday.

AT NONE.

Antiphon. Shall evil be recompensed for good: for they have digged a pit for My Soul.

The Chapter, Jer. xvii. 18.

Let them be confounded that persecute Me, but let not Me be confounded; let them be dismayed, but let not Me be dismayed: bring upon them the day of evil, and destroy them with double destruction.

R. Save Me, O God: for the waters are come in, even unto My Soul. And hide not Thy Face from Thy Servant, for I am in trouble. O haste Thee, and hear Me. ℣. Draw nigh unto My Soul, and save It: O deliver Me because of Mine enemies. ℟. For I am in trouble. O haste Thee, and hear Me. Save Me, O God, for the waters are come in, even unto My Soul. And hide not Thy Face from Thy Servant, for I am in trouble. O haste Thee, and hear Me.

℣. Deliver Me, O Lord, from the evil man.

℟. And preserve Me from the wicked man.

The Collect as on Sunday.

Prime, Terce, Sext, and None are thus said till Wednesday inclusive.

AT VESPERS.

Antiphons and Psalms as in the Psalter.

The Chapter, Lam. iii. 58.

O Lord, Thou hast pleaded the causes of My Soul: Thou hast redeemed My Life.

℟. Sinners have said, Let us lay wait for blood, let us lurk privily for the Innocent without cause, let us swallow them up alive as the grave. We shall fill our houses with spoil. ℣. Such things did they imagine, and were deceived: for their own wickedness hath blinded them. ℟. We shall fill our houses with spoil. Sinners have said, Let us lay wait for blood, let us lurk privily for the Innocent without cause, let us swallow them up alive as the grave. We shall fill our houses with spoil.

This ℟. is said till Wednesday inclusive.

Hymn. Vexilla Regis prodeunt, ℣. and ℟., *p.* 76.

Antiphon to Magnificat.

I have power: to lay down My life, and I have power to take it again.

The Collects as on Sunday.

Tuesday before Easter.

AT LAUDS.

Antiphons. (1.) Hide not Thy Face from Me: for I am in trouble. O haste Thee, and hear Me.

Psalms as on Tuesday.

(2.) Defend My cause: against the ungodly people. O deliver Me from the deceitful and wicked man.

(3.) When I was in trouble: I called upon the Lord, and He heard Me out of the belly of hell.

(4.) O Lord, I am oppressed: undertake for Me.

(5.) Let us oppress the poor Righteous Man: because He is clean contrary to our doings.

The Chapter, &c., as on Monday, p. 85.

Hymn, ℣. *and* ℟., *p.* 77.

Antiphon to Benedictus.

No man taketh from Me My life: but I lay it down of Myself.

The Collects as on Sunday.

AT VESPERS.

Antiphons and Psalms as in the Psalter.

Chapter, &c., as on Monday.

Antiphon to Magnificat.

I sat daily with you: teaching in the temple, and ye laid no hold on Me.

The Collects as on Sunday.

Wednesday before Easter.

AT LAUDS.

Antiphons. (1.) Deliver me from bloodguiltiness: O God, Thou that art the God of my health; and my tongue shall sing of Thy Righteousness.

Psalms of Wednesday.

(2.) I heard the defaming of many: fear on every side; but the Lord is with Me as a mighty terrible One.

(3.) These also that seek the hurt of My Soul: they shall go under the earth.

(4.) All Mine enemies have heard of My trouble: they are glad that Thou hast done it.

(5.) Bind, O Lord, the kings of the heathen in chains : and their nobles with links of iron.

The Chapter, &c., as on Monday, p. 85.

Hymn, V̇. and Ṙ., p. 77.

Antiphon to Benedictus.

Peter, what, could ye not watch with Me : one hour?

The Collects as on Sunday.

AT VESPERS.

Antiphons and Psalms as in the Psalter.

The Chapter, Isa. liii. 6, 7.

All we like sheep have gone astray : we have turned every one to his own way ; and the Lord hath laid on Him the iniquity of us all. He was oppressed, and He was afflicted, yet He opened not His Mouth.

R. *as on Monday, p. 87.*

Hymn, V̇. and Ṙ., p. 76.

Antiphon to Magnificat.

I was daily with you : in the temple teaching, and ye took Me not.

The Collect.

ALMIGHTY God, we beseech Thee graciously to behold this Thy family, for which our Lord Jesus Christ was contented to be Betrayed, and given up into the hands of wicked men, and to suffer death upon the Cross ; Who now liveth and reigneth with Thee and the Holy Ghost, ever one God, world without end. *Amen.*

Maundy Thursday.

AT LAUDS.

The customary Invocation of the Blessed Trinity, &c., shall be said in silence, and the reader shall immediately begin the Antiphon ; and this shall be so done at all the Hours, till the Lauds of Easter Day.

Antiphons. (1.) Thou wilt be justified in Thy saying : and clear when Thou art judged.

The Psalms for Thursday, all without Glory be to the Father, *which is not said again until the First Vespers of Easter Day.*

(2.) He is brought as a Lamb to the slaughter : He openeth not His Mouth.

(3.) Mine Heart within Me is broken : all My Bones shake.

(4.) He shall not cry nor lift up : nor cause His Voice to be heard in the street.

(5.) Surely He hath borne our griefs : and carried our sorrows.

Then immediately is begun the Antiphon to Benedictus.

Now he that betrayed Him : gave them a sign, saying, Whomsoever I shall kiss, that Same is He : hold Him fast.

Benedictus.

After the Antiphon is ended, is said, all kneeling,

Lord, have mercy upon us.
Christ, have mercy upon us.
Lord, have mercy upon us.

V̇. Christ became obedient for us unto death.

℟. Even the death of the Cross. Our Father.

Miserere mei Deus. Ps. li.

And then, without The Lord be with you, &c., *is immediately said*

The Collect.

ALMIGHTY God, we beseech Thee graciously to behold this Thy family, for which our Lord Jesus Christ was contented to be Betrayed, and given up into the hands of wicked men, and to suffer death upon the Cross; Who now liveth and reigneth with Thee and the Holy Ghost, ever one God, world without end. Amen.

Thus end the Lauds.

The Psalm Ad Te levavi *and the Prayers for the Peace of the Church now cease till the day after Trinity Sunday.*

The Memorials usually said at Lauds and Vespers are omitted until after Low Sunday.

AT PRIME.

Immediately after the customary Invocation of the Blessed Trinity and the Lord's Prayer in silence,

Antiphon. Christ became obedient : for us unto death, even the death of the Cross.

Deus, in nomine Tuo. Ps. liv.
Beati immaculati, and *Retribue servo Tuo,* Ps. cxix., *as in the Psalter.*

Then immediately follows,

Lord, have mercy upon us, *and the rest as at Lauds, and after the Collect,*

℣. The Lord be with you.
℟. And with thy spirit.
℣. Bless we the Lord.
℟. Thanks be to God.

Thus endeth Prime, and so shall be said Terce, Sext, None, on this day, except, of course, with their own Psalms.

AT VESPERS.

After the customary Invocation of the Blessed Trinity and the Lord's Prayer in silence shall be begun immediately the

Antiphon (1.) I will receive the Cup of Salvation.

Credidi. Ps. cxvi. 10.

10 I believed, and therefore will I speak ; but I was sore troubled : I said in my haste, All men are liars.

11 What reward shall I give unto the Lord : for all the benefits that He hath done unto me?

12 I will receive the cup of salvation : and call upon the Name of the Lord.

13 I will pay my vows now in the presence of all His people : right dear in the sight of the Lord is the death of His saints.

14 Behold, O Lord, how that I am Thy servant : I am Thy servant, and the son of Thine handmaid ; Thou hast broken my bonds in sunder.

15 I will offer to Thee the sacrifice of thanksgiving : and will call upon the Name of the Lord.

16 I will pay my vows unto the Lord, in the sight of all His people : in the courts of the Lord's house, even in the midst of thee, O Jerusalem. Praise the Lord.

Antiphon (1.) I will receive the Cup of Salvation : and call upon the Name of the Lord.

(2.) I labour for peace.

Ad Dominum. Ps. cxx.

1 When I was in trouble I called upon the Lord : and He heard me.
2 Deliver my soul, O Lord, from lying lips : and from a deceitful tongue.
3 What reward shall be given or done unto thee, thou false tongue : even mighty and sharp arrows, with hot burning coals.
4 Wo is me, that I am constrained to dwell with Mesech : and to have my habitation among the tents of Kedar.
5 My soul hath long dwelt among them : that are enemies unto peace.
6 I labour for peace, but when I speak unto them thereof : they make them ready to battle.

(2.) I labour for peace : but when I speak unto them thereof they make them ready to battle.

(3.) Keep Me, O Lord.

Eripe me, Domine. Ps. cxl.

1 Deliver me, O Lord, from the evil man : and preserve me from the wicked man.
2 Who imagine mischief in their hearts : and stir up strife all the day long.
3 They have sharpened their tongues like a serpent : adder's poison is under their lips.
4 Keep me, O Lord, from the hands of the ungodly : preserve me from the wicked men, who are purposed to overthrow my goings.
5 The proud have laid a snare for me, and spread a net abroad with cords : yea, and set traps in my way.
6 I said unto the Lord, Thou art my God : hear the voice of my prayers, O Lord.
7 O Lord God, Thou strength of my health : Thou hast covered my head in the day of battle.
8 Let not the ungodly have his desire, O Lord : let not his mischievous imagination prosper, lest they be too proud.
9 Let the mischief of their own lips fall upon the head of them : that compass me about.
10 Let hot burning coals fall upon them : let them be cast into the fire, and into the pit, that they never rise up again.
11 A man full of words shall not prosper upon the earth : evil shall hunt the wicked person to overthrow him.
12 Sure I am that the Lord will avenge the poor : and maintain the cause of the helpless.
13 The righteous also shall give thanks unto Thy Name : and the just shall continue in Thy sight.

(3.) Keep Me, O Lord, from the hands of the ungodly.

(4.) Keep Me from the snare.

Domine, clamavi. Ps. cxli.

1 Lord, I call upon Thee, haste Thee unto me : and consider my voice when I cry unto Thee.
2 Let my prayer be set forth in Thy sight as the incense : and let the lifting up of my hands be an evening sacrifice.

3 Set a watch, O Lord, before my mouth : and keep the door of my lips.

4 O let not mine heart be inclined to any evil thing : let me not be occupied in ungodly works with the men that work wickedness, lest I eat of such things as please them.

5 Let the righteous rather smite me friendly : and reprove me.

6 But let not their precious balms break my head : yea, I will pray yet against their wickedness.

7 Let their judges be overthrown in stony places : that they may hear my words, for they are sweet.

8 Our bones lie scattered before the pit : like as when one breaketh and heweth wood upon the earth.

9 But mine eyes look unto Thee, O Lord God : in Thee is my trust, O cast not out my soul.

10 Keep me from the snare that they have laid for me : and from the traps of the wicked doers.

11 Let the ungodly fall into their own nets together : and let me ever escape them.

(4.) Keep Me from the snare that they have laid for Me, and from the traps of the wicked doers.

(5.) I looked also upon My Right Hand.

Voce mea ad Dominum. Ps. cxlii.

1 I cried unto the Lord with my voice : yea, even unto the Lord did I make my supplication.

2 I poured out my complaints before Him : and showed Him of my trouble.

3 When my spirit was in heaviness Thou knewest my path : in the way wherein I walked have they privily laid a snare for me.

4 I looked also upon my right hand : and saw there was no man that would know me.

5 I had no place to flee unto : and no man cared for my soul.

6 I cried unto Thee, O Lord, and said : Thou art my hope, and my portion in the land of the living.

7 Consider my complaint : for I am brought very low.

8 O deliver me from my persecutors : for they are too strong for me.

9 Bring my soul out of prison, that I may give thanks unto Thy Name : which thing if Thou wilt grant me, then shall the righteous resort unto my company.

(5.) I looked also upon My Right Hand : and saw there was no man that would know Me.

And then immediately follows the Antiphon to Magnificat.

And as they were eating : Jesus took Bread, and blessed It, and brake It, and gave It to the disciples.

Magnificat.

And the Vespers shall forthwith end, all kneeling, with Lord, have mercy upon us, &c., *and the Collect as at Prime.*

GOOD FRIDAY.

Good Friday.

Me: and My heart within Me is desolate.

(3.) But the other malefactor answering rebuked him: saying, We receive the due reward of our deeds, but this Man hath done nothing amiss. Lord, remember me when Thou comest into Thy Kingdom.

(4.) Is it nothing to you, all ye that pass by: behold and see if there be any sorrow like unto My sorrow, which is done unto Me.

(5.) What are these Wounds in Thy Hands? Those with which I was wounded in the house of My friends.

AT LAUDS.

Antiphons. (1.) God spared not His Own Son: but delivered Him up for us all.

Psalms of Friday.

(2.) My spirit is vexed within

Antiphon to Benedictus.

And they set up over His Head, His accusation: written, THIS IS JESUS THE KING OF THE JEWS.

Benedictus.

EASTER EVEN.

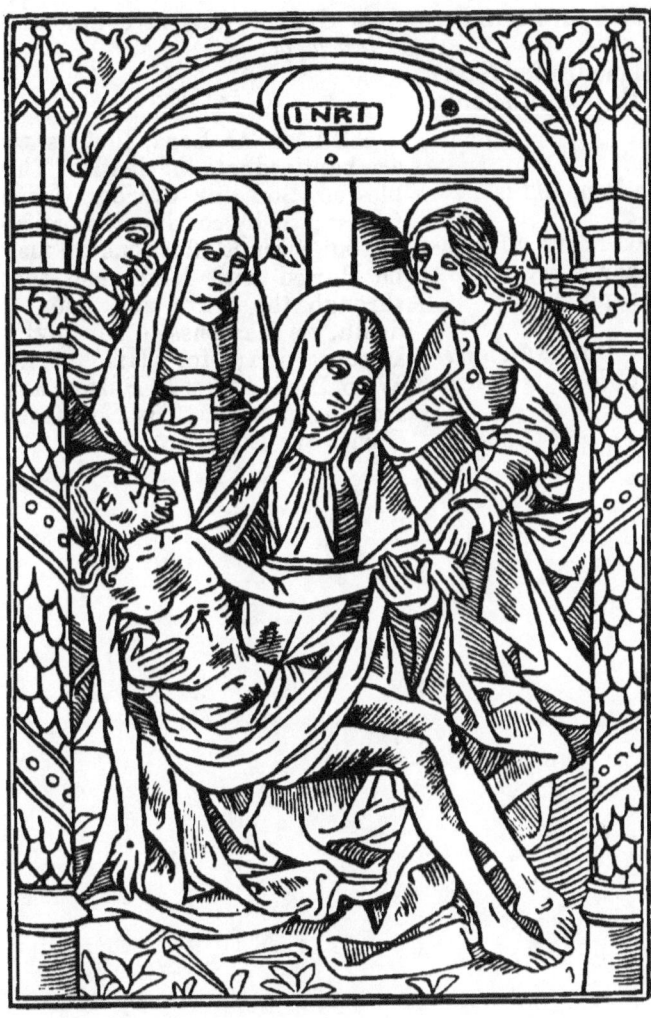

Vespers as on Maundy Thursday till the

Antiphon to Magnificat.

Now there stood by the Cross of Jesus: His Mother.

After the Antiphon is ended is said, all kneeling, Lord, have mercy upon us, *and the rest as at Lauds, p. 88, the Collect ending at the word* Cross.

𝕰aster 𝕰ven.

AT LAUDS.

Antiphons.
(1.) O death, I will be thy plagues : O grave, I will be thy destruction.

Psalms as on Saturday.

(2.) Behold, and see : if there be any sorrow like unto My sorrow.

(3.) Thou hast laid Me in the lowest pit : in the place of darkness, and in the deep.

(4.) I will break in pieces the

And the Lauds shall continue and end as on Maundy Thursday, except that the Collect shall end at the word Cross.

Prime, Terce, Sext, and None, as on Maundy Thursday, except that at the commencement of the ℣. Christ became obedient, *a genuflection is made.*

The Collect shall end as at Lauds.

gates of brass : and cut in sunder the bars of iron.

(5.) They shall mourn for Him : as one mourneth for his only son.

Antiphon to Benedictus.

And there was Mary Magdalene : and the other Mary, sitting over against the sepulchre.

And the rest as on Maundy Thursday, except the Collect as below.

Prime, Terce, Sext, and None, as on Good Friday, except the Collect as below.

The Collect.

GRANT, O Lord, that as we are baptized into the death of Thy blessed Son our Saviour Jesus Christ; so by continual mortifying our corrupt affections we may be Buried with Him; and that through the grave and gate of death, we may pass to our joyful Resurrection; for His merits, Who Died, and was Buried, and Rose again for us, Thy Son Jesus Christ our Lord. *Amen.*

EASTER DAY.

AT THE FIRST VESPERS.

These Vespers shall begin at once with the

Antiphon. Alleluia. Alleluia. Alleluia. Alleluia.

Laudate Dominum omnes gentes. Ps. cxvii.

1 O praise the Lord, all ye heathen : praise Him, all ye nations.

2 For His merciful kindness is ever more and more towards us : and the truth of the Lord endureth for ever. Praise the Lord.

Glory be to the Father, &c.

Antiphon. Alleluia. Alleluia. Alleluia. Alleluia.

Antiphon. In the end of the Sabbath, as it began to dawn toward the first day of the week, came Mary Magdalene and the other Mary to see the sepulchre. Alleluia.

Magnificat.

After the repetition of the Antiphon,

℣. The Lord be with you.

℟. And with thy spirit.

Let us pray.

The Collect.

ALMIGHTY God, Who through Thine Only-begotten Son Jesus Christ hast overcome death, and opened unto us the gate of everlasting Life; We humbly beseech Thee, that, as by Thy special grace preventing us Thou dost put into our minds good desires, so by Thy continual help we may bring the same to good effect; through Jesus Christ our Lord, Who liveth and reigneth with Thee and the Holy Ghost, ever one God, world without end. Amen.

℣. The Lord be with you.

℟. And with thy spirit.

℣. Bless we the Lord.

℟. Thanks be to God. [*At Lauds add* Alleluia.]

And thus shall end all the Hours until Low Sunday.

AT LAUDS.

℣. In Thy Resurrection, O Christ.

℟. Let heaven and earth rejoice. Alleluia.

℣. O God, make speed to save us.

℟. O Lord, make haste to help us.

℣. Glory be to the Father, and to the Son: and to the Holy Ghost.

℟. As it was in the beginning, is now, and ever shall be: world without end. Amen. Alleluia.

Antiphons. (1.) The Angel of the Lord: descended from heaven, and came and rolled back the stone from the door, and sat upon it. Alleluia, Alleluia.

Psalms for Sundays and Feast-days.

(2.) And, behold, there was a great earthquake: for the Angel of the Lord descended from heaven. Alleluia.

(3.) His countenance was like lightning: and his raiment white as snow. Alleluia, Alleluia.

(4.) And for fear of him: the keepers did shake, and became as dead men. Alleluia.

(5.) And the Angel answered and said unto the women, Fear not ye: for I know that ye seek Jesus. Alleluia.

Then shall be said no Chapter, but immediately this,

℣. The Lord is Risen from the Tomb.

℟. Who died to save us from our doom. Alleluia.

No Hymn is said at any Hour till the First Vespers of Low Sunday.

Antiphon to Benedictus.

And very early in the morning the first day of the week, they came unto the Sepulchre at the Rising of the Sun. Alleluia.

Collect as at the First Vespers.

"Bless we the Lord," *and* "Thanks be to God," *are said with* Alleluia, *from now to Trinity Sunday.*

Lauds are thus said till Low Sunday, except that the Antiphon to Benedictus *is changed as below.*

EASTER DAY.

AT PRIME.

℣. O God, make speed, &c.

The Hymn is not said.

Antiphon (1.) The Angel of the Lord : descended from heaven, and came and rolled back the stone from the door, and sat upon it. Alleluia, Alleluia.

Deus, in nomine Tuo. Ps. liv.
Confitemini Domino. Ps. cxviii.
Beati immaculati, and *Retribue servo Tuo.* Ps. cxix.

After the Antiphon is added,

This is the Day which the Lord hath made; we will rejoice and be glad in it.

The Chapter is not said.

℣. The Lord is Risen.

℟. As He said. Alleluia.

Collect, &c., as at Lauds.

Prime is thus said till Low Sunday.

AT TERCE.

℣. O God, make speed, &c.

The Hymn is not said.

Antiphon (2.) And, behold, there was a great earthquake : for the Angel of the Lord descended from heaven. Alleluia.

Legem pone, &c. Ps. cxix.

After the Antiphon is added,

This is the Day which the Lord hath made; we will rejoice and be glad in it.

The Chapter is not said.

℣. The Lord is Risen indeed.

℟. And hath appeared unto Simon. Alleluia.

Collect, &c., as at Lauds.

Terce is thus said till Low Sunday.

AT SEXT.

℣. O God, make speed, &c.

The Hymn is not said.

Antiphon (3.) His countenance was like lightning : and his raiment white as snow. Alleluia.

Defecit anima mea, &c. Ps. cxix.

After the Antiphon is added,

This is the Day which the Lord hath made; we will rejoice and be glad in it.

The Chapter is not said.

℣. The Lord is Risen from the Tomb.

℟. Who died to save us from our doom. Alleluia.

Collect, &c., as at Lauds.

Sext is thus said till Low Sunday.

AT NONE.

℣. O God, make speed, &c.

The Hymn is not said.

Antiphon (4.) And for fear of him : the keepers did shake, and became as dead men. Alleluia.

Mirabilia, &c. Ps. cxix.

After the Antiphon is added,

This is the Day which the Lord hath made; we will rejoice and be glad in it.

The Chapter is not said.

℣. In Thy Resurrection, O Christ.

H

℟. Let heaven and earth rejoice. Alleluia.

Collect, &c., as at Lauds.

None is thus said till Low Sunday.

AT THE SECOND VESPERS.

The Second Vespers shall begin thus:

Lord, have mercy upon us.
Christ, have mercy upon us.
Lord, have mercy upon us.

Antiphon. Alleluia. Alleluia. Alleluia. Alleluia.

Dixit Dominus, Ps. cx., *and the other Sunday Psalms.*

After the Antiphon is added,

This is the Day which the Lord hath made; we will rejoice and be glad in it.

℣. O give thanks unto the Lord, for He is gracious.

℟. Because His mercy endureth for ever. Alleluia.

℣. Christ our Passover is sacrificed for us, therefore let us keep the Feast.

℟. Not with the old leaven, nor with the leaven of malice and wickedness; but with the unleavened Bread of sincerity and truth. Alleluia.

℣. The Lord is Risen.

℟. As He said. Alleluia.

Antiphon to Magnificat.

And when they looked they saw that the stone was rolled away; for it was great. Alleluia.

Collect, &c., as at Lauds.

Vespers are thus said, with the Sunday Psalms, till Low Sunday, except that the Antiphon to Magnificat *is changed.*

Easter Monday.

Antiphon to Benedictus.

What manner of communications are these that ye have one to another, as ye walk, and are sad? And the one of them, whose name was Cleopas, answering, said unto Him, Art Thou only a stranger in Jerusalem, and hast not known the things that are come to pass there in these days? And He said unto them, What things? And they said unto Him, Concerning Jesus of Nazareth, Who was a Prophet mighty in deed and word, before God and all the people. Alleluia.

The week-day Prayers are not said till the day after Trinity Sunday.

Antiphon to Magnificat.

Did not our heart burn within us, while He talked with us by the way? Alleluia.

Easter Tuesday.

Antiphon to Benedictus.

Jesus Himself stood in the midst of them, and saith unto them, Peace be unto you. Alleluia.

Antiphon to Magnificat.

Behold My Hands and My Feet, that it is I Myself. Alleluia.

WEDNESDAY IN EASTER WEEK.

Antiphon to Benedictus.

Cast the net: on the right side of the ship, and ye shall find. Alleluia.

Antiphon to Magnificat.

This is now the third time: that Jesus showed Himself to His disciples, after that He was Risen from the dead. Alleluia.

THURSDAY IN EASTER WEEK.

Antiphon to Benedictus.

Mary stood without : at the Sepulchre weeping ; and seeth two Angels in white sitting, the one at the Head, the other at the Feet, where the Body of Jesus had lain. Alleluia.

Antiphon to Magnificat.

They have taken away my Lord : and I know not where they have laid Him. If thou hast borne Him hence, tell me where thou hast laid Him, and I will take Him away. Alleluia.

FRIDAY IN EASTER WEEK.

Antiphon to Benedictus.

Then the eleven disciples went away : into Galilee, and when they saw Him, they worshipped Him. Alleluia.

Antiphon to Magnificat.

All power is given unto Me : in heaven and earth. Alleluia.

SATURDAY IN EASTER WEEK.

Antiphon to Benedictus.

So they ran both together : and the other disciple did outrun Peter, and came first to the Sepulchre. Alleluia.

The First Sunday after Easter, or Low Sunday.

AT THE FIRST VESPERS.

℣. O God, make speed, &c.

Antiphon. Alleluia. Alleluia. Alleluia. Alleluia.

Psalms for Saturday.

The Chapter, Rom. vi. 9, 10.

Christ being raised from the dead dieth no more ; death hath no more dominion over Him. For in that He died, He died unto sin once ; but in that He liveth, He liveth unto God.

℟. Thanks be to God.

Hymn. Chorus novæ Hierusalem.

Ye Choirs of New Jerusalem !
To sweet new strains attune your theme ;
The while we keep, from care released,
With sober joy our Paschal Feast.

When Christ, unconquered Lion, first
The Dragon's chains by rising burst :
And while with living voice He cries,
The dead of other ages rise.

Engorged in former years, their prey
Must Death and Hell restore to-day :
And many a captive soul, set free,
With Jesus leaves captivity.

Right gloriously He triumphs now,
Worthy to Whom should all things bow :
And joining heaven and earth again
Links in one commonweal the twain.

And we, as these His deeds we sing,
His suppliant soldiers, pray our King,
That in His Palace, bright and vast,
We may keep watch and ward at last.

Long as unending ages run,
To God the Father laud be done,
To God the Son our equal praise,
And God the Holy Ghost, we raise.
                            Amen.

℣. Abide with us.

℟. For it is toward evening, and the day is far spent. Alleluia.

Antiphon to Magnificat.

Now when Jesus was risen : early the first day of the week, He appeared first unto Mary Magdalene, out of whom He had cast seven devils. Alleluia.

The Collect.

ALMIGHTY Father, Who hast given Thine only Son to die for our sins, and to Rise again for our justification; Grant us so to put away the leaven of malice and wickedness, that we may alway serve Thee in pureness of living and truth; through the merits of the Same Thy Son Jesus Christ our Lord. *Amen.*

AT LAUDS.

The Antiphons and Psalms as on Easter Day, p. 96.

The Chapter, 1 St. John v. 4.

Whatsoever is born of God overcometh the world; and this is the victory that overcometh the world, even our faith.

R⁊. Thanks be to God.

Hymn. Sermone blando Angelus.

With gentle voice the Angel gave
The women tidings at the Grave;
"Forthwith your Master shall ye see:
He goes before to Galilee."

And while with fear and joy they pressed
To tell these tidings to the rest,
Their Lord, their living Lord they meet,
And see His Form, and kiss His Feet.

The Eleven, when they hear, with speed
To Galilee forthwith proceed;
That there they may behold once more
The Lord's dear Face, as oft afore.

In this our bright and Paschal day
The sun shines out with purer ray:
When Christ, to earthly sight made plain,
The glad Apostles see again.

The Wounds, the riven Wounds, He shows,
In that His Flesh with light that glows,
With loud accord, both far and nigh,
The Lord's Arising testify.

O Christ, O King, Who lovest to bless,
Do Thou our hearts and souls possess;
To Thee our praise that we may pay,
To Whom our laud is due, for aye.

We pray Thee, King with glory decked,
In this our Paschal joy, protect
From all that Death would fain effect,
Thy ransomed flock, Thine own elect.

To Thee Who, dead, again dost live,
All glory, Lord, Thy people give;
All glory, as is ever meet,
To Father and to Paraclete. Amen.

So end the Hymns at all the Hours, till the Ascension, except the Saturday Vespers.

℣. The Lord is Risen from the Tomb.

R⁊. Who died to save us from our doom. Alleluia.

Antiphon to Benedictus.

Then the same day at evening, being the first day of the week, when the doors were shut where the disciples were assembled for fear of the Jews, came Jesus and stood in the midst, and saith unto them, Peace be unto you. Alleluia.

Collect as at the First Vespers.

Memorial of the Resurrection.

Antiphon. And very early in the morning, the first day of the week, they came unto the Sepulchre at the Rising of the Sun. Alleluia.

℣. The Lord is Risen indeed.

R⁊. And hath appeared to Simon. Alleluia.

The Collect.

ALMIGHTY God, Who through Thy Only-begotten Son Jesus Christ hast overcome death, and opened unto us the gate of everlasting Life; We humbly beseech Thee, that, as by Thy special grace preventing us Thou dost put into our minds good desires, so by Thy continual help we may bring the same to good effect: through Jesus Christ our Lord, Who liveth and reigneth with Thee and the Holy Ghost, ever one God, world without end. Amen.

This Memorial is said at Lauds, on Sundays, till the Ascension.

AT PRIME.

Hymn, Jam lucis, *with the Doxology of Easter*, To Thee, Who, dead, again dost live, &c., *p.* 100.

Antiphon. The Angel of the Lord: descended from heaven, and came and rolled back the stone from the door, and sat upon it. Alleluia.

Deus in nomine Tuo. Ps. liv.
Beati immaculati, and *Retribue servo Tuo.* Ps. cxix.

Ps. *Quicunque vult.*

The Chapter, 1 Tim. i. 17.

Now unto the King Eternal, Immortal, Invisible, the only Wise God, be honour and glory for ever and ever. Amen.

R. Jesus Christ, Son of the living God, have mercy upon us. Alleluia, Alleluia. ℣. Thou Who hast risen from the dead. Alleluia. ℟. Have mercy upon us. Alleluia, Alleluia. ℣. Glory be to the Father, and to the Son: and to the Holy Ghost. ℟. Jesus Christ, Son of the living God, have mercy upon us. Alleluia, Alleluia.

This R. *is so said, daily, till the Ascension.*

℣. O Lord, arise, help us.

℟. And deliver us for Thy Name's sake.

And the rest as usual.

AT TERCE.

Hymn, Nunc sancte nobis Spiritus, *with the Doxology of Easter, p.* 100.

Antiphon. And behold, there was a great earthquake: for the Angel of the Lord descended from heaven. Alleluia.

Psalms as usual.

The Chapter, 1 St. John v. 4.

Whatsoever is born of God overcometh the world: and this is the victory that overcometh the world, even our faith.

R. The Lord is Risen. Alleluia, Alleluia. ℣. As He said. ℟. Alleluia, Alleluia. ℣. Glory be to the Father, and to the Son: and to the Holy Ghost. ℟. The Lord is Risen. Alleluia, Alleluia.

℣. The Lord is Risen indeed.

℟. And hath appeared to Simon. Alleluia.

Collect as at the First Vespers.

AT SEXT.

Hymn, Rector potens verax Deus, *with the Doxology of Easter, p.* 100.

Antiphon. His countenance was like lightning: and his raiment white as snow. Alleluia.

Psalms as usual.

The Chapter, 1 St. John v. 5.

Who is he that overcometh the world, but he that believeth that Jesus is the Son of God? This is He that came by water and blood, even Jesus Christ.

R. The Lord is Risen indeed. Alleluia, Alleluia. ℣. And hath appeared to Simon. ℟. Alleluia, Alleluia. ℣. Glory be to the Father, and to the Son: and to the Holy Ghost. ℟. The Lord is Risen indeed. Alleluia, Alleluia.

℣. The Lord is Risen from the Tomb.

℟. Who died to save us from our doom. Alleluia.

Collect as at the First Vespers.

AT NONE.

Hymn, Rerum Deus tenax vigor, *with the Doxology of Easter, p.* 100.

Antiphon. And for fear of him: the keepers did shake, and became as dead men. Alleluia.

Psalms as usual.

The Chapter, 1 St. John v. 7.

And there are three that bear witness in earth, the spirit, and the water, and the blood: and these three agree in one.

R. The Lord is Risen from the Tomb. Alleluia, Alleluia. ℣. Who died to save us from our doom. ℟. Alleluia, Alleluia. ℣. Glory be to the Father, and to the Son: and to the Holy Ghost. ℟. The Lord is Risen from the Tomb. Alleluia, Alleluia.

℣. In Thy Resurrection, O Christ.

℟. Let heaven and earth rejoice. Alleluia.

Collect as at the First Vespers.

Prime, Terce, Sext, and None, are thus said till the Ascension, except the Chapter and Collect.

AT THE SECOND VESPERS.

Antiphon. Alleluia. Alleluia. Alleluia. Alleluia.

The Chapter, 1 St. John v. 4.

Whatsoever is born of God overcometh the world: and this is the victory that overcometh the world, even our faith.

℟. Thanks be to God.

Hymn. Ad Cœnam Agni providi.

The Lamb's high banquet we await,
In snow-white robes of royal state:
And now, the Red Sea's channel past,
To Christ our Prince we sing at last.

Upon the Altar of the Cross,
His Body hath redeemed our loss:
And tasting of His roseate Blood,
Our life is hid with Him in God.

That Paschal Eve God's arm was bared:
The devastating Angel spared:
By strength of hand our hosts went free
From Pharaoh's ruthless tyranny.

Now Christ, our Paschal Lamb, is slain,
The Lamb of God that knows no stain,
The true Oblation offered here,
Our own unleavened Bread sincere.

O Thou from Whom hell's monarch flies,
O great, O very Sacrifice,
Thy captive people are set free,
And endless life restored in Thee.

For Christ, arising from the dead,
From conquered hell victorious sped:
And thrust the tyrant down to chains,
And Paradise for man regains.

To Thee Who, dead, again dost live,
All glory, Lord, Thy people give;
All glory, as is ever meet,
To Father and to Paraclete. Amen.

℣. Abide with us.

℟. For it is toward evening, and the day is far spent. Alleluia.

Antiphon to Magnificat.

And after eight days came Jesus, the doors being shut, and

stood in the midst, and said, Peace be unto you. Alleluia.

Collect as at the First Vespers.

Memorial of the Resurrection.

Antiphon. And when they looked they saw that the stone was rolled away, for it was very great. Alleluia.

℣. The Lord is Risen.

℟. As He said. Alleluia.

Collect for Easter Day.

This Memorial is said at Vespers on Sundays till the Ascension.

Throughout the week, and till the Ascension.

Lauds are said as on Low Sunday, p. 100, except that the Psalms, (which shall be those of Sunday) are said under this one Antiphon, Alleluia, Alleluia, Alleluia, Alleluia : *the Chapter and Collect changing with the week.*

One of the Antiphons given below is said to Benedictus, *during this week.*

Prime, Terce, Sext, and None, are said as on Low Sunday, p. 101, *the Chapters and Collect changing with the week.*

Vespers are said as at the Second Vespers of Low Sunday, p. 102, *except that the Psalms are those for each day of the week, and are said under the one Antiphon,* Alleluia, Alleluia, Alleluia, Alleluia : *the Chapter and Collect changing with the week.*

One of the Antiphons given below is said to Magnificat *during this week.*

Antiphons to Benedictus *and* Magnificat *for the week.*

a. Thomas, because thou hast seen : Me, thou hast believed ; blessed are they that have not seen, and yet have believed. Alleluia.

b. And many other signs truly did Jesus : in the presence of His disciples. Alleluia. Which are not written in this book. Alleluia.

c. But these are written : that ye might believe that Jesus is the Christ, the Son of God : and that believing ye might have life through His Name. Alleluia.

Memorial of the Resurrection, to be said daily at Lauds till the Ascension, except on Sundays.

Antiphon. The Lord is Risen from the Tomb, Who died to save us from our doom. Alleluia.

℣. The Lord is Risen.

℟. As He said. Alleluia.

Collect for Easter Day.

Memorial of the Resurrection, to be said daily at Vespers till the Ascension, except on Sundays.

Antiphon. Go quickly, and tell His disciples that He is Risen from the dead. Alleluia.

℣. The Lord is Risen indeed.

℟. And hath appeared to Simon. Alleluia.

Collect for Easter Day.

The Second Sunday after Easter.

AT THE FIRST VESPERS.

Everything as at the First Vespers of Low Sunday, p. 99, till the

Antiphon to Magnificat.

Thou art worthy, O Lord : to receive glory, and honour, and power, for Thou hast created all things, and for Thy pleasure they are, and were created. Salvation to our God, Which sitteth upon the throne, and unto the Lamb. Alleluia.

The Collect.

ALMIGHTY God, Who hast given Thine only Son to be unto us both a Sacrifice for sin, and also an Ensample of godly life; Give us grace that we may always most thankfully receive that His inestimable Benefit, and also daily endeavour ourselves to follow the blessed steps of His most holy Life; through the Same Jesus Christ our Lord. *Amen.*

AT LAUDS.

Antiphons and Psalms as during the preceding week, and so till the Ascension.

The Chapter, 1 St. Pet. ii. 21, 22.

Christ also suffered for us, leaving us an Example, that ye should follow His steps : Who did no sin, neither was guile found in His Mouth.

℟. Thanks be to God.

Hymn, Sermone blando Angelus, ℣. *and* ℟. *as on Low Sunday, p.* 100.

Antiphon to Benedictus.

I am the Good Shepherd; the Good Shepherd giveth His Life for His sheep. Alleluia, Alleluia.

Collect as at the First Vespers.

AT PRIME.

Everything as on Low Sunday.

AT TERCE.

Everything as on Low Sunday, except

The Chapter, 1 St. Pet. ii. 21, 22.

Christ also suffered for us, leaving us an Example, that ye should follow His steps : Who did no sin, neither was guile found in His Mouth.

Collect as at the First Vespers.

AT SEXT.

Everything as on Low Sunday, except

The Chapter, 1 St. Pet. ii. 23, 24.

Who when He was reviled, reviled not again; when He suffered, He threatened not; but committed Himself to Him that judgeth righteously : Who His own Self bare our sins in His own Body on the tree, by Whose Stripes ye were healed.

Collect as at the First Vespers.

AT NONE.

Everything as on Low Sunday, except

The Chapter, 1 St. Pet. ii. 25.

For ye were as sheep going

astray; but are now returned unto the Shepherd and Bishop of your souls.

Collect as at the First Vespers.

AT THE SECOND VESPERS.

Everything as on Low Sunday, except

The Chapter, 1 St. Pet. ii. 21, 22.

Christ also suffered for us, leaving us an Example, that ye should follow His steps: Who did no sin, neither was guile found in His Mouth.

Antiphon to Magnificat.

I am the Good Shepherd, and know My sheep, and am known of Mine; and I lay down My Life for the sheep. Alleluia, Alleluia.

Collect as at the First Vespers.

Antiphons to Benedictus *and* Magnificat *for the week.*

a. Jesus said, I am the Good Shepherd: the Good Shepherd giveth His Life for the sheep. Alleluia.

b. As the Father knoweth Me, even so know I the Father: and I lay down My Life for the sheep. Alleluia.

c. But he that is an hireling: and not the Shepherd, whose own the sheep are not, seeth the wolf coming, and leaveth the sheep and fleeth, and the wolf catcheth them, and scattereth the sheep. Alleluia.

d. And other sheep I have: which are not of this fold; them also I must bring, and they shall hear My Voice; and there shall be One Fold under One Shepherd. Alleluia.

The Third Sunday after Easter.

AT THE FIRST VESPERS.

Everything as at the First Vespers of Low Sunday, p. 99, *till the*

Antiphon to Magnificat.

I am Alpha and Omega: the Beginning and the End, the First and the Last. I am the Root and Offspring of David, and the bright and morning Star. Alleluia.

The Collect.

ALMIGHTY God, Who showest to them that be in error the Light of Thy truth, to the intent that they may return into the way of righteousness; Grant unto all them that are admitted into the fellowship of Christ's Religion, that they may eschew those things that are contrary to their profession, and follow all such things as are agreeable to the same; through our Lord Jesus Christ. *Amen.*

AT LAUDS.

Everything as on Low Sunday, except

The Chapter, 1 St. Pet. ii. 11.

Dearly beloved, I beseech you as strangers and pilgrims, abstain from fleshly lusts, which war against the soul.

℟. Thanks be to God.

Antiphon to Benedictus.

Jesus said to His disciples, A little while and ye shall not see Me; and again a little while and ye shall see Me; because I go to the Father. Alleluia, Alleluia.

Collect as at the First Vespers.

AT PRIME.

Everything as on Low Sunday.

AT TERCE.

Everything as on Low Sunday, except

The Chapter, 1 St. Pet. ii. 11.

Dearly beloved, I beseech you as strangers and pilgrims, abstain from fleshly lusts, which war against the soul.

Collect as at the First Vespers.

AT SEXT.

The Chapter, 1 St. Pet. ii. 13, 14.

Submit yourselves to every ordinance of man for the Lord's sake : whether it be to the King, as supreme ; or unto governors, as unto them that are sent by Him, for the punishment of evil doers, and for the praise of them that do well.

AT NONE.

The Chapter, 1 St. Pet. ii. 15.

For so is the Will of God, that with well-doing ye may put to silence the ignorance of foolish men.

AT THE SECOND VESPERS.

The Chapter, 1 St. Pet. ii. 11.

Dearly beloved, I beseech you as strangers and pilgrims, abstain from fleshly lusts, which war against the soul.

Antiphon to Magnificat.

What is this that He saith, A little while ? we cannot tell what He saith. Alleluia.

Collect as at the First Vespers.

Antiphons to Benedictus *and* Magnificat *for the week.*

a. Verily, verily, I say unto you : that ye shall weep and lament, but the world shall rejoice ; and ye shall be sorrowful, but your sorrow shall be turned into joy. Alleluia.

b. Ye now therefore have sorrow : but your sorrow shall be turned into joy. Alleluia.

c. I will see you again : and your heart shall rejoice, and your joy no man taketh from you. Alleluia.

The Fourth Sunday after Easter.

AT THE FIRST VESPERS.

Everything as at the First Vespers of Low Sunday, p. 99, *till the*

Antiphon to Magnificat.

Great and marvellous are Thy works, Lord God Almighty : just and true are Thy ways, Thou King of Saints. Who shall not fear Thee, O Lord, and glorify Thy Name ? for Thou only art Holy ; for all nations shall come and worship before Thee ; for Thy judgments are made manifest. Alleluia.

The Collect.

O ALMIGHTY God, Who alone canst order the unruly wills and affections of sinful men ; Grant unto Thy people, that they may love the thing which Thou commandest, and desire that which Thou dost promise ; that so, among the sundry and manifold changes of the world, our hearts may surely there be fixed, where true Joys are to be found; through Jesus Christ our Lord. *Amen.*

AT LAUDS.

The Chapter, St. James i. 17.

Every good gift and every perfect gift is from above, and cometh down from the Father of lights, with Whom is no variableness, neither shadow of turning.

℟. Thanks be to God.

Antiphon to Benedictus.

Jesus said unto His disciples, Now I go My way to Him that sent Me, and none of you asketh Me, Whither goest Thou? But, because I have said these things unto you, sorrow hath filled your heart. Alleluia.

Collect as at the First Vespers.

AT PRIME.

Everything as on Low Sunday.

AT TERCE.

The Chapter, St. James i. 17.

Every good gift and every perfect gift is from above, and cometh down from the Father of lights, with Whom is no variableness, neither shadow of turning.

AT SEXT.

The Chapter, St. James i. 19.

Wherefore, my beloved brethren, let every man be swift to hear, slow to speak, slow to wrath.

AT NONE.

The Chapter, St. James i. 21.

Wherefore lay apart all filthiness and superfluity of naughtiness, and receive with meekness the engrafted Word, which is able to save your souls.

AT THE SECOND VESPERS.

The Chapter, St. James i. 17.

Every good gift and every perfect gift is from above, and cometh down from the Father of lights, with Whom is no variableness, neither shadow of turning.

Antiphon to Magnificat.

Nevertheless, I tell you the truth; it is expedient for you that I go away; for if I go not away, the Comforter will not come unto you. Alleluia.

Collect as at the First Vespers.

Antiphons to Benedictus *and* Magnificat *for the week.*

a. When the Comforter is come: He will reprove the world of sin, and of righteousness, and of judgment. Alleluia.

b. I have yet many things to say unto you: but ye cannot bear them now. Howbeit, when He, the Spirit of truth, is come, He will guide you into all truth. Alleluia.

c. When He, the Spirit of truth, is come: He will guide you into all truth: and He will show you things to come. Alleluia.

d. He shall glorify Me: for He shall receive of Mine, and shall show it unto you. Alleluia.

The Fifth Sunday after Easter.

AT THE FIRST VESPERS.

Everything as at the First Vespers of Low Sunday, p. 99, till the

Antiphon to Magnificat.

Hear, O Israel : the Lord our God is One Lord : and thou shalt love the Lord thy God with all thine heart, and with all thy soul, and with all thy might. Alleluia.

The Collect.

O LORD, from Whom all Good Things do come ; Grant to us Thy humble servants, that by Thy holy inspiration we may think those things that be good, and by Thy merciful guiding may perform the same ; through our Lord Jesus Christ. *Amen.*

AT LAUDS.

The Chapter, St. James i. 22, 23.

Be ye doers of the Word, and not hearers only, deceiving your own selves. For if any be a hearer of the Word, and not a doer, he is like unto a man beholding his natural face in a glass.

℟. Thanks be to God.

Antiphon to Benedictus.

Hitherto have ye asked nothing in My Name ; ask, and ye shall receive. Alleluia.

Collect as at the First Vespers.

AT PRIME.

Everything as on Low Sunday.

AT TERCE.

The Chapter, St. James i. 22, 23.

Be ye doers of the Word, and not hearers only, deceiving your own selves. For if any be a hearer of the Word, and not a doer, he is like unto a man beholding his natural face in a glass.

AT SEXT.

The Chapter, St. James i. 25.

But whoso looketh into the perfect law of liberty, and continueth therein, he being not a forgetful hearer, but a doer of the work, this man shall be blessed in his deed.

AT NONE.

The Chapter, St. James i. 25.

Pure Religion and undefiled before God and the Father is this, To visit the fatherless and widows in their affliction, and to keep himself unspotted from the world.

AT THE SECOND VESPERS.

The Chapter, St. James i. 22, 23.

Be ye doers of the Word, and not hearers only, deceiving your own selves. For if any be a hearer of the Word, and not a doer, he is like unto a man beholding his natural face in a glass.

Antiphon to Magnificat.

Ask, and ye shall receive, that your joy may be full ; for the Father Himself loveth you, because ye have loved Me, and have believed. Alleluia.

Collect as at the First Vespers.

The Rogation Days.

MONDAY.

Antiphon to Benedictus.

Ask, and it shall be given you : seek, and ye shall find ; knock, and it shall be opened unto you. Alleluia.

Antiphon to Magnificat.

I go to prepare : a place for you. Alleluia.

TUESDAY.

Antiphon to Benedictus.

If ye shall ask anything : in My Name, I will do it. Alleluia.

Antiphon to Magnificat.

Lo, now speakest Thou plainly : and speakest no proverb. Now are we sure that Thou knowest all things, and needest not that any man should ask Thee. Alleluia.

WEDNESDAY.

Antiphon to Benedictus.

Now, O Father, glorify Thou Me : with Thine own Self, with the Glory which I had with Thee before the world was. Alleluia.

The Ascension of Our Lord Jesus Christ.

AT THE FIRST VESPERS.

Antiphon. I will not leave you comfortless; Alleluia; I will come to you. Alleluia. Let not your heart be troubled, neither let it be afraid. Alleluia, Alleluia.

Nisi Dominus, Ps. cxxvii., *and the rest of the Psalms of Wednesday.*

The Chapter, Acts i. 1.

The former treatise have I made, O Theophilus, of all that Jesus began both to do and teach, until the day in which He was Taken Up, after that He through the Holy Ghost had given commandments unto the Apostles whom He had chosen.

R. Let not your heart be troubled: ye believe in God, believe also in Me. Alleluia. ℣. I go to prepare a place for you. R. Ye believe in God, believe also in Me. Alleluia. ℣. Glory be to the Father, and to the Son: and to the Holy Ghost. R. Let not your heart be troubled: ye

THE ASCENSION OF OUR LORD JESUS CHRIST. 111

believe in God, believe also in Me. Alleluia.

Hymn. Æterne Rex Altissime.

This Hymn is said at Vespers daily, till Whitsun Eve.

Eternal Monarch, King most high,
Whose Blood hath brought Redemption nigh,
By Whom the death of Death was wrought,
And conquering Grace's battle fought;

Ascending to the Throne of might,
And seated at the Father's right,
All power in Heaven is Jesu's own,
That here His Manhood had not known.

That so, in Nature's triple frame,
Each heavenly and each earthly name,
And things in hell's abyss abhorred,
May bend the knee and own Him Lord.

Yea, Angels tremble when they see
How changed is our humanity,
That Flesh hath purged what flesh had stained,
And God, the Flesh of God, hath reigned.

Be Thou our Joy and Thou our Guard,
Who art to be our great Reward:
Our glory and our boast in Thee
For ever and for ever be!

All glory, Lord, to Thee we pay,
Ascending o'er the stars to-day;
All glory, as is ever meet,
To Father and to Paraclete. Amen.

℣. Thou art Gone Up on high, O Christ.

℞. Thou hast led captivity captive. Alleluia.

Antiphon to Magnificat.

Father, I have manifested Thy Name unto the men which Thou gavest Me out of the world. I pray for them, I pray not for the world. And now I come to Thee. Alleluia.

The Collect.

GRANT, we beseech Thee, Almighty God, that like as we do believe Thy Only-begotten Son our Lord Jesus Christ to have Ascended into the heavens; so we may also in heart and mind thither ascend, and with Him continually dwell, Who liveth and reigneth with Thee and the Holy Ghost, One God, world without end. *Amen.*

The Memorials usually said at Lauds and Vespers are omitted until after Trinity Sunday.

AT LAUDS.

℣. I Ascend to My Father, and your Father.

℞. And to My God, and your God. Alleluia.

℣. O God, make speed, &c.

Antiphons. (1.) Ye men of Galilee: why stand ye gazing up into heaven? This Same Jesus, Which is Taken Up from you into heaven, shall so come in like manner. Alleluia.

Psalms as on Sundays and Feast-days.

(2.) And while they looked: steadfastly toward heaven, as He Went Up, they said, Alleluia.

(3.) While He blessed them: He was parted from them, and Carried Up into heaven. Alleluia.

(4.) For Thou, Lord, art higher: than all that are in the earth; Thou art Exalted. Alleluia.

(5.) While they beheld: He was Taken Up; and a cloud received Him out of their sight. Alleluia.

The Chapter, Acts i. 1.

The former treatise have I made, O Theophilus, of all that

Jesus began both to do and teach, until the day in which He was Taken Up, after that He through the Holy Ghost had given commandments unto the Apostles whom He had chosen.

℟. Thanks be to God.

Hymn. Hymnum canamus gloriæ.

This Hymn is said at Lauds daily, till Whitsun Day.

Sing we triumphant hymns of praise,
New hymns to heaven exulting raise;
Christ by a road before untrod,
Ascendeth to the Throne of God.

The holy Apostolic band
Upon the Mount of Olives stand,
And with the Virgin Mother see
Jesu's resplendent Majesty.

To whom the Angels, drawing nigh,
"Why stand and gaze upon the sky?
This is the Saviour," thus they say,
"This is His noble triumph-day.

"Again shall ye behold Him—so
As ye to-day have seen Him go,
In glorious pomp Ascending high,
Up to the portals of the sky."

O grant us thitherward to tend,
And with unwearied hearts ascend
Toward Thy Kingdom's Throne, where Thou,
In very flesh, art seated now.

Be Thou our Joy and Thou our Guard,
Who art to be our great Reward:
Our glory and our boast in Thee
For ever and for ever be!

All glory, Lord, to Thee we pay,
Ascending o'er the stars to-day;
All glory, as is ever meet,
To Father and to Paraclete. Amen.

℣. God is Gone Up with a merry noise.

℟. And the Lord with the sound of the trumpet. Alleluia.

Antiphon to Benedictus.

I Ascend unto My Father, and your Father; and to My God, and your God. Alleluia.

The Collect.

GRANT, we beseech Thee, Almighty God, that like as we do believe Thy Only-begotten Son our Lord Jesus Christ to have Ascended into the heavens; so we may also in heart and mind thither ascend, and with Him continually dwell, Who liveth and reigneth with Thee and the Holy Ghost, One God, world without end. *Amen.*

AT PRIME.

Antiphon (1.) Ye men of Galilee: why stand ye gazing up into heaven? This Same Jesus, which is Taken Up, shall so come in like manner. Alleluia.

Deus in nomine. Ps. liv.

Beati immaculati, and *Retribue servo Tuo.* Ps. cxix.

Ps. *Quicunque vult.*

The Chapter, 1 Tim. i. 17.

Now unto the King Eternal, Immortal, Invisible, the only Wise God, be honour and glory for ever and ever. Amen.

R. Jesus Christ, Son of the living God, have mercy upon us. Alleluia, Alleluia. ℣. Thou that sittest at the Right Hand of God the Father. Alleluia, Alleluia. ℟. Have mercy upon us. Alleluia, Alleluia. ℣. Glory be to the Father, and to the Son: and to the Holy Ghost. ℟. Jesus Christ, Son of the living God, have mercy upon us. Alleluia, Alleluia.

℣. O Lord, arise, help us.

℟. And deliver us for Thy Name's sake.

AT TERCE.

Antiphon (2.) And while they looked : steadfastly toward heaven as He Went Up, they said, Alleluia.

The Chapter, Acts i. 1, 2.

The former treatise have I made, O Theophilus, of all that Jesus began both to do and teach, until the day in which He was Taken Up, after that He through the Holy Ghost had given commandments unto the Apostles whom He had chosen.

R. Thou hast set Thy Glory, O Lord. Alleluia, Alleluia. ℣. Above the heavens. ℟. Alleluia, Alleluia. ℣. Glory be to the Father, and to the Son : and to the Holy Ghost. ℟. Thou hast set Thy Glory, O Lord. Alleluia, Alleluia.

℣. God is Gone Up with a merry noise.

℟. And the Lord with the sound of the trumpet. Alleluia.

Collect as at Lauds.

AT SEXT.

Antiphon (3.) While He blessed them : He was parted from them, and Carried Up into heaven. Alleluia.

The Chapter, Acts i. 4.

He being assembled together with them, commanded them that they should not depart from Jerusalem, but wait for the promise of the Father, which, saith He, ye have heard of Me.

R. God is Gone Up with a merry noise. Alleluia, Alleluia. ℣. And the Lord with the sound of the trumpet. ℟. Alleluia, Alleluia. ℣. Glory be to the Father, and to the Son : and to the Holy Ghost. ℟. God is Gone Up with a merry noise. Alleluia, Alleluia.

℣. Thou art Gone Up on high, O Christ.

℟. Thou hast led captivity captive. Alleluia.

Collect as at Lauds.

AT NONE.

Antiphon (5.) While they beheld : He was Taken Up; and a Cloud received Him out of their sight. Alleluia.

The Chapter, Acts i. 5.

For John truly baptized with water, but ye shall be baptized with the Holy Ghost not many days hence.

R. Thou hast Gone Up on high, O Christ. Alleluia, Alleluia. ℣. Thou hast led captivity captive. ℟. Alleluia. ℣. Glory be to the Father, and to the Son : and to the Holy Ghost. ℟. Thou hast Gone Up on high, O Christ. Alleluia, Alleluia.

℣. I Ascend to My Father, and your Father.

℟. To My God, and your God. Alleluia.

Prime, Terce, Sext and None, shall be thus said daily, till the Octave, except that on and after Sunday the Chapters and Collects are changed.

Collect as at Lauds.

AT THE SECOND VESPERS.

Antiphon. Ye men of Galilee; why stand ye gazing up into heaven? This Same Jesus, Which is Taken Up, shall so come in like manner. Alleluia, Alleluia.

Dixit Dominus, Ps. cx., and the other Sunday Psalms.

This Antiphon, and these Psalms are said at Vespers daily throughout the Octave.

The Chapter, Acts i. 1, 2.

The former treatise have I made, O Theophilus, of all that Jesus began both to do and teach, until the day in which He was Taken Up, after that He through the Holy Ghost, had given commandments unto the Apostles, whom He had chosen.

R. Go ye into all the world and preach. Alleluia. He that believeth and is baptized shall be saved. Alleluia, Alleluia, Alleluia. ℣. But the Comforter, Which is the Holy Ghost, Whom the Father will send in My Name, He shall teach you all things, and bring all things to your remembrance, whatsoever I have said unto you. ℟. He that believeth and is baptized shall be saved. Alleluia, Alleluia, Alleluia. ℣. Glory be to the Father, and to the Son : and to the Holy Ghost. ℟. Go ye into all the world and preach. Alleluia. He that believeth and is baptized shall be saved. Alleluia, Alleluia, Alleluia.

Hymn, Æterne Rex Altissime, ℣. *and* ℟., *as at the First Vespers, p.* 111.

Antiphon to Magnificat.

Seek those things which are above, where Christ sitteth on the Right Hand of God. Alleluia.

Collect as at Lauds.

FRIDAY. AT LAUDS.

Antiphon. Ye men of Galilee : why stand ye gazing up into heaven? This Same Jesus, Which is Taken Up into heaven, shall so come in like manner. Alleluia.

Psalms of the Sunday.

The Chapter, Hymn, ℣. *and* ℟., *as on Ascension Day, p.* 111; *and thus shall Lauds be said daily till the Octave, except that on and after Sunday the Chapter and Collect are changed; also the Antiphon to* Benedictus *is changed daily.*

Antiphon to Benedictus.

Go ye into all the world : and preach the Gospel to every creature. Alleluia. He that believeth and is baptized shall be saved. Alleluia. But he that believeth not shall be damned. Alleluia.

Collect as on Ascension Day, which is said at all the Hours till the First Vespers of Sunday.

AT VESPERS.

Everything as on Ascension Day till the

Antiphon to Magnificat.

I will pray the Father : and He shall give you another Comforter. Alleluia.

And thus shall Vespers be said till Whitsun Day, except the Antiphon to Magnificat, *but after Sunday are said the Chapter and Collect of the week.*

SATURDAY.

Antiphon to Benedictus.

If I go not away, the Comforter will not come : unto you ; but if I depart, I will send Him unto you. Alleluia.

Sunday after Ascension Day.

AT THE FIRST VESPERS.

Antiphon to Magnificat.

After the Lord had spoken unto them : He was received up into heaven, and sat at the Right Hand of God.   Alleluia.

The Collect.

O GOD the King of glory, Who hast exalted Thine only Son Jesus Christ with great triumph unto Thy Kingdom in heaven ; We beseech Thee, leave us not comfortless ; but send to us Thine Holy Ghost to comfort us, and exalt us unto the same place whither our Saviour Christ is gone before, Who liveth and reigneth with Thee and the Holy Ghost, One God, world without end. *Amen.*

AT LAUDS.

The Chapter, 1 St. Pet. iv. 7, 8.

The end of all things is at hand ; be ye therefore sober, and watch unto prayer. And above all things have fervent charity among yourselves : for charity shall cover the multitude of sins.

R̷. Thanks be to God.

Antiphon to Benedictus.

When the Comforter is come, Whom I will send unto you from the Father, even the Spirit of Truth, Which proceedeth from the Father, He shall testify of Me. Alleluia.

Collect as at the First Vespers.

AT TERCE.

The Chapter, 1 St. Pet. iv. 7, 8.

The end of all things is at hand ; be ye therefore sober, and watch unto prayer. And above all things have fervent charity among yourselves : for charity shall cover the multitude of sins.

R̷. *as on Ascension Day, p.* 113.

Collect as at the First Vespers.

AT SEXT.

The Chapter, 1 St. Pet. iv. 9, 10.

Use hospitality one to another without grudging. As every man hath received the gift, even so minister the same one to another, as good stewards of the manifold grace of God.

R̷. *as on Ascension Day, p.* 113.

Collect as at the First Vespers.

AT NONE.

The Chapter, 1 St. Pet. iv. 11.

If any man speak, let him speak as the oracles of God : if any man minister, let him do it as of the ability which God giveth ; that God in all things may be glorified through Jesus Christ.

R̷. *as on Ascension Day, p.* 113.

Collect as at the First Vespers.

AT THE SECOND VESPERS.

The Chapter, 1 St. Pet. iv. 7, 8.

The end of all things is at hand; be ye therefore sober, and watch unto prayer. And above all things have fervent charity among yourselves: for charity shall cover the multitude of sins.

Antiphon to Magnificat.

These things have I told you that, when the time shall come, ye may remember that I told you of them. Alleluia.

Collect as at the First Vespers.

MONDAY.

Antiphon to Benedictus.

And they went forth : and preached everywhere, the Lord working with them, and confirming the Word with signs following. Alleluia, Alleluia.

Antiphon to Magnificat.

Go ye into all the world : and preach. Alleluia. He that believeth and is baptized shall be saved. Alleluia.

TUESDAY.

Antiphon to Benedictus.

I will pray the Father : and He shall give you another Comforter. Alleluia.

Antiphon to Magnificat.

If I go not away : the Comforter will not come unto you; but if I depart, I will send Him unto you. Alleluia.

WEDNESDAY.

Antiphon to Benedictus.

And they went forth : and preached everywhere, the Lord working with them, and confirming the Word with signs following. Alleluia, Alleluia.

Thursday after Ascension Day.

AT THE FIRST VESPERS.

Everything as at the First Vespers of Ascension Day, p. 110, except

The Collect.

O GOD the King of Glory, Who hast exalted Thine only Son Jesus Christ with great triumph unto Thy kingdom in heaven; We beseech Thee, leave us not comfortless; but send to us Thine Holy Ghost to comfort us, and exalt us unto the same place whither our Saviour Christ has gone before, Who liveth and reigneth with Thee and the Holy Ghost, One God, world without end. *Amen.*

AT LAUDS, *and all the Hours.*

Everything as on Ascension Day, except the Collect, which shall be that of the Sunday.

FRIDAY. AT LAUDS.

Antiphon to Psalms.

Alleluia. Alleluia. Alleluia. Alleluia.

The Psalms, and everything of the Sunday after Ascension Day. Prime, Terce, Sext, and None as on the Sunday.

AT VESPERS.

Antiphon to Psalms.

Alleluia. Alleluia. Alleluia. Alleluia.

The Psalms of Friday, but everything else of the Sunday after Ascension Day.

SATURDAY. AT LAUDS.

Antiphon to Psalms.

Alleluia. Alleluia. Alleluia. Alleluia.

The Psalms, and everything of the Sunday after Ascension Day, till the

Antiphon to Benedictus.

If ye love Me : keep My commandments. Alleluia, Alleluia, Alleluia.

Prime, Terce, Sext, and None as on the Sunday.

WHITSUN DAY.

AT THE FIRST VESPERS.
Antiphon to Psalms.

Come, Holy Ghost, and fill the hearts of Thy faithful people, inflaming them with Thy love: Thou Who, through divers tongues, gatherest together Thine elect in the Unity of the Faith. Alleluia, Alleluia, Alleluia.

Psalms of Saturday.

The Chapter, Acts ii. 1.

When the Day of Pentecost was fully come, they were all with one accord in one place.

℞. The Apostles did speak in other tongues. Alleluia. The wonderful works of God. Alleluia. ℣. They were all filled with the Holy Ghost, and began to speak. ℞. The wonderful works of God. Alleluia. ℣. Glory be to the Father, and to the Son: and to the Holy Ghost. ℞. The Apostles did speak in other tongues. Alleluia. The wonderful works of God. Alleluia.

Hymn. Jam Christus astra ascenderat.

Now Christ ascending whence He came,
Had mounted o'er the starry frame ;
The Holy Ghost on man to pour,
As God the Father's promise bore.

The solemn time was drawing nigh,
Replete with heavenly mystery,
On seven days' sevenfold circles borne,
That first and blessed Whitsun morn.

When the third hour shone all around,
There came a rushing mighty Sound,
And told the Apostles, while in prayer,
That, as 'twas promised, God was there.

Forth from the Father's Light it came,
That beautiful and kindly Flame :
To fill, with fervour of His word,
The spirits faithful to their Lord.

Thou once in every holy breast
Didst bid indwelling grace to rest :
This day our sins, we pray, release,
And in our time, O Lord, give peace.

To God the Father, God the Son,
And God the Spirit praise be done :
And Christ the Lord upon us pour
The Spirit's gift for evermore. Amen.

So ends the Hymn at Prime, Sext, and None, till Trinity Sunday.

℣. The Spirit of the Lord filleth the world.

℟. That which containeth all things hath knowledge of the Voice. Alleluia.

Antiphon to Magnificat.

If a man love Me he will keep My words, and My Father will love him, and We will come unto him, and make Our abode with him. Alleluia.

The Collect.

GOD, Who as at this time didst teach the hearts of Thy faithful people, by the sending to them the light of Thy Holy Spirit ; Grant us by the same Spirit to have a right judgment in all things, and evermore to rejoice in His holy Comfort : through the merits of Christ Jesus our Saviour, Who liveth and reigneth with Thee in the unity of the same Spirit, one God, world without end. *Amen.*

AT LAUDS.

℣. When Thou lettest Thy Breath go forth they shall be made.

℟. And Thou shalt renew the face of the earth. Alleluia.

℣. O God, make speed, &c.

Antiphons. (1.) When the Day of Pentecost was fully come : they were all with one accord in one place. Alleluia.
(2.) The Spirit of the Lord : filleth the world. Alleluia.
(3.) They were all filled with the Holy Ghost : and began to speak. Alleluia.
(4.) All that move upon the face of the waters : bless ye the Lord. Alleluia.
(5.) The Apostles did speak : in other tongues the wonderful works of God. Alleluia, Alleluia, Alleluia.

The Chapter, Acts ii. 1.

When the Day of Pentecost was fully come, they were all with one accord in one place.

℟. Thanks be to God.

Hymn. Veni Creator Spiritus.

This Hymn is said at Lauds daily, till Trinity Sunday.

Come, Holy Ghost, our souls inspire,
And lighten with celestial fire :
Thou the anointing Spirit art,
Who dost Thy sevenfold gifts impart.

WHITSUN DAY.

Thy blessed Unction from above,
Is comfort, life, and fire of love:
Enable with perpetual light
The dulness of our blinded sight.

Anoint and cheer our soiléd face,
With the abundance of Thy grace;
Keep far our foes, give peace at home:
Where Thou art Guide, no ill can come.

Teach us to know the Father, Son,
And Thee, of Both, to be but One;
That through the ages all along,
This may be our endless song:
  Praise to Thy eternal merit,
  Father, Son, and Holy Spirit. Amen.

℣. The Apostles did speak with other tongues.

℟. The wonderful works of God. Alleluia.

Antiphon to Benedictus.

Receive ye the Holy Ghost; whosesoever sins ye remit, they are remitted unto them. Alleluia.

The Collect.

GOD, Who as at this time didst teach the hearts of Thy faithful people, by the sending to them the light of Thy Holy Spirit; Grant us by the same Spirit to have a right judgment in all things, and evermore to rejoice in His holy Comfort; through the merits of Christ Jesus our Saviour, Who liveth and reigneth with Thee in the unity of the same Spirit, one God, world without end. *Amen.*

AT PRIME.

Antiphon (1.) When the Day of Pentecost was fully come: they were all with one accord in one place. Alleluia.

And the rest as on Ascension Day.

Prime is thus said through the week.

AT TERCE.

Instead of the Hymn Nunc Sancte nobis Spiritus, *is said* Veni Creator, *as at Lauds, p.* 119.

Antiphon (2.) The Spirit of the Lord: filleth the world. Alleluia.

The Chapter, Acts ii. 1.

When the Day of Pentecost was fully come, they were all with one accord in one place.

R. They were all filled with the Holy Ghost. Alleluia, Alleluia. ℣. And began to speak with other tongues. ℟. Alleluia, Alleluia. ℣. Glory be to the Father, and to the Son: and to the Holy Ghost. ℟. They were all filled with the Holy Ghost. Alleluia, Alleluia.

℣. The Apostles did speak with other tongues.

℟. The wonderful works of God. Alleluia.

Collect as at Lauds.

AT SEXT.

Antiphon (3.) They were all filled with the Holy Ghost: and began to speak. Alleluia.

The Chapter, Acts ii. 2.

And suddenly there came a Sound from heaven, as of a rushing mighty Wind, and It filled all the house where they were sitting.

R. The Apostles did speak with other tongues. Alleluia, Alleluia. ℣. The wonderful works of God. ℟. Alleluia, Alleluia. ℣. Glory be to the Father, and to the Son:

and to the Holy Ghost. ℞. The Apostles did speak with other tongues. Alleluia, Alleluia.

℣. The Spirit of the Lord filleth the world.

℞. And that which containeth all things hath knowledge of the Voice. Alleluia.

Collect as at Lauds.

AT NONE.

Antiphon (5.) The Apostles did speak : in other tongues the wonderful works of God. Alleluia.

The Chapter, Acts ii. 3.

And there appeared unto them cloven tongues like as of Fire, and It sat upon each of them.

℞. The Spirit of the Lord filleth the world. Alleluia, Alleluia. ℣. And that which containeth all things hath knowledge of the Voice. ℞. Alleluia, Alleluia. ℣. Glory be to the Father, and to the Son : and to the Holy Ghost. ℞. The Spirit of the Lord filleth the world. Alleluia, Alleluia.

℣. When Thou lettest Thy Breath go forth they shall be made.

℞. And Thou shalt renew the face of the earth. Alleluia.

Collect as at Lauds.

AT THE SECOND VESPERS.

Antiphon. When the Day of Pentecost was fully come, they were all with one accord in one place. Alleluia.

The Sunday Psalms.

The Chapter, Acts ii. 6.

The multitude came together, and were confounded, because that every man heard them speak in his own language.

℞. All thy children shall be taught of the Lord. Alleluia, Alleluia. ℣. For I have poured out My Spirit. ℞. Alleluia, Alleluia. ℣. Glory be to the Father, and to the Son : and to the Holy Ghost. ℞. All thy children shall be taught of the Lord. Alleluia, Alleluia.

Hymn. Beata nobis gaudia.

This Hymn is said daily till the First Vespers of Trinity Sunday.

Blest joys for mighty wonders wrought
The year's revolving orb has brought,
What time the Holy Ghost in flame
Upon the Lord's disciples came.

The quivering fire their heads bedew'd,
In cloven tongues' similitude,
That eloquent their words might be,
And fervid all their charity.

In varying tongues the Lord they praised,
The gathering people stood amazed;
And whom the Comforter Divine
Inspired, they mocked as full of wine.

These things were done in type to-day,
When Eastertide had worn away,
The number told which once set free
The captive at the Jubilee.

Thy servants, falling on their face,
Beseech Thy mercy, God of grace,
To send us, from Thy heavenly Seat,
The blessings of the Paraclete.

To God the Father, God the Son,
And God the Spirit, praise be done :
And Christ the Lord upon us pour
The Spirit's gift for evermore. Amen.

℣. The Spirit of the Lord filleth the world.

℞. And that which containeth all things hath knowledge of the Voice. Alleluia.

Antiphon to Magnificat.

To-day is the feast of Pentecost fully come. To-day is the Holy Ghost shed abroad in fiery tongues with promised Gifts on the disciples, sent into all the world to preach. He that believeth and is baptized shall be saved. Alleluia.

Collect as at Lauds.

Vespers are thus said through the week, except that the Antiphon to Magnificat *is changed.*

Whitsun Monday.

AT LAUDS.

Antiphon. When the Day of Pentecost was fully come, they were all with one accord in one place. Alleluia.

Psalms as on Sundays and Feastdays.

The Chapter, Acts ii. 2.

And suddenly there came a Sound from heaven as of a rushing mighty Wind, and It filled all the house where they were sitting.

℟. Thanks be to God.

Hymn, Veni Creator Spiritus, ℣. *and* ℟., *as on Whitsun Day, p.* 119.

Antiphon to Benedictus.

God so loved the world that He gave His Only-begotten Son, that whosoever believeth in Him should not perish, but have everlasting life. Alleluia.

The Collect as on Whitsun Day.

Lauds are thus said through the week, except that the Antiphon to Benedictus *is changed.*

Terce, Sext, and None through the week, as on Whitsun Day, except the Chapters which are given here.

AT TERCE.

The Chapter, Acts ii. 2.

And suddenly there came a Sound from heaven as of a rushing mighty Wind, and It filled all the house where they were sitting.

AT SEXT.

The Chapter, Acts ii. 3.

And there appeared unto them cloven tongues, like as of Fire, and It sat upon each of them.

AT NONE.

The Chapter, Acts ii. 4.

And they were all filled with the Holy Ghost, and began to speak with other tongues, as the Spirit gave them utterance.

AT VESPERS.

Antiphon to Magnificat.

For God sent not His Son into the world to condemn the world, but that the world through Him might be saved. Alleluia.

Whitsun Tuesday.

Antiphon to Benedictus.

Verily, verily, I say unto you, He that entereth not by the Door into the Sheep-fold, but climbeth up some other way, the same is a thief and a robber. But he that entereth in by the Door is the shepherd of the sheep. Alleluia.

Antiphon to Magnificat.

I am the Door; by Me if any man enter in, he shall be saved, and shall go in and out, and find pasture. Alleluia.

WEDNESDAY.

Antiphon to Benedictus.

Verily, verily, I say unto you: He that believeth on Me hath everlasting life. Alleluia, Alleluia.

Antiphon to Magnificat.

I am the living Bread: Which came down from heaven; if any man eat of this Bread he shall live for ever; and the Bread that I will give is My Flesh, Which I will give for the life of the world. Alleluia, Alleluia.

THURSDAY.

Antiphon to Benedictus.

Jesus called His twelve disciples together: and gave them power and authority over all devils, and to cure diseases. And He sent them to preach the Kingdom of God, and to heal the Sick. Alleluia, Alleluia.

Antiphon to Magnificat.

The Twelve departed: and went through the towns preaching the Gospel, and healing everywhere. Alleluia, Alleluia.

FRIDAY.

Antiphon to Benedictus.

And it came to pass: on a certain day, as He was teaching, that there were Pharisees and doctors of the law sitting by, which were come out of every town of Galilee, and Judea, and Jerusalem; and the power of the Lord was present to heal them. Alleluia, Alleluia.

Antiphon to Magnificat.

And the sick of the palsy: took up that whereon he lay, glorifying God. And they were all amazed, and glorified God. Alleluia.

SATURDAY.

Antiphon to Benedictus.

Now when the sun was setting: all they that had any sick with divers diseases brought them unto Jesus; and He laid His Hands on every one of them, and healed them. Alleluia.

Trinity Sunday.

AT THE FIRST VESPERS.

Antiphon (1.) Glory be to Thee, Co-equal Trinity.

Laudate, pueri. Ps. cxiii.

1 Praise the Lord, ye servants : O praise the Name of the Lord.
2 Blessed be the Name of the Lord : from this time forth for evermore.
3 The Lord's Name is praised : from the rising up of the sun unto the going down of the same.
4 The Lord is high above all heathen : and His glory above the heavens.
5 Who is like unto the Lord our God, that hath His dwelling so high : and yet humbleth Himself to behold the things that are in heaven and earth?
6 He taketh up the simple out of the dust : and lifteth the poor out of the mire;
7 That He may set him with the princes : even with the princes of His people.
8 He maketh the barren woman to keep house : and to be a joyful mother of children.
Glory be to the Father, &c.

Antiphon (1.) Glory be to Thee, Co-equal Trinity : One God before all worlds began, and now and ever, and to ages of ages.

(2.) Praise and glory be to God.

Laudate Dominum. Ps. cxvii.

1 O praise the Lord, all ye heathen : praise Him, all ye nations.
2 For His merciful kindness is ever more and more towards us : and the truth of the Lord endureth for ever. Praise the Lord.
Glory be to the Father, &c.

(2.) Praise and glory be to God : the Father, the Son, and the Holy Ghost, now and ever, and to ages of ages.

(3.) Holy, Holy, Holy.

Lauda, anima mea. Ps. cxlvi.

1 Praise the Lord, O my soul ; while I live will I praise the Lord : yea, as long as I have any being I will sing praises unto my God.
2 O put not your trust in princes, nor in any child of man : for there is no help in them.
3 For when the breath of man goeth forth he shall turn again to his earth : and then all his thoughts perish.
4 Blessed is he that hath the God of Jacob for his help : and whose hope is in the Lord his God :
5 Who made heaven and earth, the sea, and all that therein is : Who keepeth His promise for ever ;
6 Who helpeth them to right that suffer wrong : Who feedeth the hungry.
7 The Lord looseth men out of prison : the Lord giveth sight to the blind.
8 The Lord helpeth them that are fallen : the Lord careth for the righteous.
9 The Lord careth for the strangers ; He defendeth the fatherless and widow : as for the way of

the ungodly, He turneth it upside down.

10 The Lord thy God, O Sion, shall be King for evermore : and throughout all generations.

Glory be to the Father, &c.

(3.) Holy, Holy, Holy : is the Lord of hosts : the whole earth is full of His glory; the Lord God of our fathers, the God of Abraham, the God of Isaac, and the God of Jacob.

(4.) Hear ye this.

Laudate Dominum. Ps. cxlvii. 1—11.

1 O praise the Lord, for it is a good thing to sing praises unto our God : yea, a joyful and pleasant thing it is to be thankful.

2 The Lord doth build up Jerusalem : and gather together the outcasts of Israel.

3 He healeth those that are broken in heart : and giveth medicine to heal their sickness.

4 He telleth the number of the stars : and calleth them all by their names.

5 Great is our Lord, and great is His power : yea, and His wisdom is infinite.

6 The Lord setteth up the meek: and bringeth the ungodly down to the ground.

7 O sing unto the Lord with thanksgiving : sing praises upon the harp unto our God;

8 Who covereth the heaven with clouds, and prepareth rain for the earth : and maketh the grass to grow upon the mountains: and herb for the use of men;

9 Who giveth fodder unto the cattle : and feedeth the young ravens that call upon Him.

10 He hath no pleasure in the strength of an horse : neither delighteth He in any man's legs.

11 But the Lord's delight is in them that fear Him : and put their trust in His mercy.

Glory be to the Father, &c.

(4.) Hear ye this : I have not spoken in secret from the beginning; from the time that it was, there am I; and now the Lord God, and His Spirit, hath sent Me.

(5.) Praise God, from Whom all blessings flow.

Lauda Hierusalem. Ps. cxlvii. 12.

12 Praise the Lord, O Jerusalem : praise thy God, O Sion.

13 For He hath made fast the bars of thy gates : and hath blessed thy children within thee.

14 He maketh peace in thy borders : and filleth thee with the flour of wheat.

15 He sendeth forth His commandment upon earth : and His word runneth very swiftly.

16 He giveth snow like wool : and scattereth the hoar-frost like ashes.

17 He casteth forth His ice like morsels : who is able to abide His frost?

18 He sendeth out His word, and melteth them : He bloweth with His wind, and the waters flow.

19 He showeth His word unto Jacob : His statutes and ordinances unto Israel.

20 He hath not dealt so with any nation : neither have the heathen knowledge of His laws.

Glory be to the Father, &c.

(5.) Praise God, from Whom all blessings flow,

Praise Him, all people here below,
Praise Him above, ye heavenly host,
Praise Father, Son, and Holy Ghost.

The Chapter, 2 Cor. xiii. 14.

The Grace of our Lord Jesus Christ, and the Love of God, and the Fellowship of the Holy Ghost, be with you all evermore.

R. And the Lord appeared unto Abraham in the plains of Mamre; and he sat at the tent door in the heat of the day; and he lift up his eyes and looked, and lo, Three Men stood by him. ℣. Holy, Holy, Holy, Lord God Almighty, Which was, and is, and is to come. ℟. And lo, Three Men stood by him. ℣. Glory be to the Father, and to the Son: and to the Holy Ghost. ℟. And the Lord appeared unto Abraham in the plains of Mamre; and he sat at the tent door in the heat of the day; and he lift up his eyes, and looked, and lo, Three Men stood by him.

Hymn. Adesto Sancta Trinitas.

Be present, Holy Trinity;
Like splendour, and one Deity:
Of things above, and things below,
Beginning that no end shall know.

That all the armies of the sky
Adore, and laud, and magnify;
While Nature, in her triple frame,
For ever sanctifies Thy Name.

And we, too, thanks and homage pay,
Thine own adoring flock to-day;
O join to that celestial Song
The praises of our suppliant throng!

Light, sole and one, we Thee confess,
With triple praise we rightly bless;
Alpha and Omega we own,
With every spirit round Thy throne.

To Thee, O Unbegotten One,
And Thee, O Sole-begotten Son,
And Thee, O Holy Ghost, we raise
Our equal and eternal praise. Amen.

℣. Let us bless the Father, and the Son, and the Holy Ghost.

℟. Praise Him and magnify Him for ever.

Antiphon to Magnificat.

We thank Thee, O God, O One and very Trinity, One and mighty Godhead, One in Unity now and ever, and to ages of ages.

The Collect.

ALMIGHTY and Everlasting God, Who hast given unto us Thy servants grace by the confession of a true faith to acknowledge the glory of the Eternal Trinity, and in the Power of the Divine Majesty to worship the Unity; We beseech Thee, that Thou wouldest keep us steadfast in this faith, and evermore defend us from all adversities, Who livest and reignest, One God, world without end. Amen.

AT LAUDS.

℣. Blessed art Thou, O Lord God of our Fathers.

℟. And to be praised and exalted above all for ever.

℣. O God, make speed, &c.

Antiphon (1.) O Holy, Blessed, and Glorious Trinity: Three Persons and One God, have mercy upon us now and ever, and to ages of ages.

And this Antiphon is said to each of the five Psalms of the Sunday Lauds.

TRINITY SUNDAY.

The Chapter, Rom. xi. 33, 36.

O the depth of the riches both of the wisdom and knowledge of God! For of Him, and through Him, and to Him, are all things: to Whom be glory for ever. Amen.

℞. Thanks be to God.

Hymn.   Ave colenda Trinitas.

All hail! Adored Trinity!
All hail! Adored Unity!
The Father God, and God the Son,
And God the Spirit, Three in One!

Behold, to Thee this blessed Day
Our grateful thanks we duly pay
For Thy rich gifts of priceless worth,
The saving health of all on earth.

Thee Three in One we thus adore,
Thee One in Three for evermore;
In Thy sweet mercy shall we find
A shelter sure for all mankind.

O Trinity! O Unity!
Be with us as we worship Thee;
And to the Angels' songs in light
Our prayers and praises now unite!
Amen.

℣. Blessed be the Name of the Lord.

℞. From this time forth for evermore.

Antiphon to Benedictus.

Blessed be the Holy and Undivided Trinity, the Creator and Preserver of all things, now and ever, and to ages of ages.

Collect as at the First Vespers.

AT PRIME.

The Antiphon, O Holy, Blessed, and Glorious Trinity: Three Persons, and One God, have mercy upon us now and ever, and to ages of ages, *is said at Prime, Terce, Sext, and None.*

AT TERCE.

The Chapter, Rev. iv. 8.

And they rest not day and night, saying, Holy, Holy, Holy, Lord God Almighty, Which was, and is, and is to come.

℞. Let us bless the Father, and the Son, and the Holy Ghost. Alleluia, Alleluia. ℣. Praise Him and magnify Him for ever. ℞. Alleluia, Alleluia. ℣. Glory be to the Father, and to the Son: and to the Holy Ghost. ℞. Let us bless the Father, and the Son, and the Holy Ghost. Alleluia, Alleluia.

℣. Blessed art Thou in the firmament of heaven.

℞. And above all to be praised and glorified for ever.

Collect as at the First Vespers.

AT SEXT.

The Chapter, 1 St. John v. 7.

There are Three that bear record in heaven, the Father, the Word, and the Holy Ghost: and these Three are One.

℞. Blessed art Thou in the firmament of heaven. Alleluia, Alleluia. ℣. And above all to be praised and glorified for ever. ℞. Alleluia, Alleluia. ℣. Glory be to the Father, and to the Son: and to the Holy Ghost. ℞. Blessed art Thou in the firmament of heaven. Alleluia, Alleluia.

℣. By the Word of the Lord were the heavens made.

℞. And all the hosts of them by the Breath of His mouth.

Collect as at the First Vespers.

AT NONE.

The Chapter, Eph. iv. 5, 6.

There is One Lord, one faith, one Baptism, One God and Father of all, Who is above all, and through all, and in you all.

R. By the Word of the Lord were the heavens made. Alleluia, Alleluia. ℣. And all the hosts of them by the Breath of His Mouth. ℟. Alleluia, Alleluia. ℣. Glory be to the Father, and to the Son: and to the Holy Ghost. ℟. By the Word of the Lord were the heavens made. Alleluia, Alleluia.

℣. Blessed be the Name of the Lord.

℟. From this time forth for evermore.

Collect as at the First Vespers.

AT THE SECOND VESPERS.

The Antiphons shall be said as at Lauds, but with the Psalms of the Sunday Vespers.

The Chapter, Rom. xi. 33, 36.

O the depth of the riches both of the wisdom and knowledge of God! For of Him, and through Him, and to Him are all things: to Whom be glory for ever. Amen.

R. Let us bless the Father, and the Son, and the Holy Ghost. Alleluia, Alleluia. ℣. Praise Him and magnify Him for ever. ℟. Alleluia, Alleluia. ℣. Glory be to the Father, and to the Son: and to the Holy Ghost. ℟. Let us bless the Father, and the Son, and the Holy Ghost. Alleluia, Alleluia.

The Hymn, Adesto Sancta Trinitas, ℣. *and* ℟., *as at the First Vespers, p.* 126.

Antiphon to Magnificat.

Thee, the Father Unbegotten; Thee, the Only-begotten Son; Thee, the Holy Ghost the Comforter, One Holy and Undivided Trinity, with heart and mouth we confess. We praise Thee, we bless Thee, we glorify Thee; to Thee be glory now and ever, and to ages of ages.

Collect as at the First Vespers.

The First Sunday after Trinity.

AT THE FIRST VESPERS.

Everything as in the Psalter, till the

Antiphon to Magnificat.

It came to pass when the people heard the sound of the trumpet: and the people shouted with a great shout, that the wall fell down flat.

The Collect.

O GOD, the Strength of all them that put their trust in Thee, mercifully accept our prayers; and because through the weakness of our mortal nature we can do no good thing without Thee, grant us the help of Thy grace, that in keeping of Thy commandments we may please Thee, both in will and deed; through Jesus Christ our Lord. Amen.

AT LAUDS.

Antiphon to Benedictus.

Father Abraham, have mercy

on me, and send Lazarus, that he may dip the tip of his finger in water, and cool my tongue.

The Collect at Lauds and the Second Vespers is always the same as that said at the First Vespers.

AT THE SECOND VESPERS.

Antiphon to Magnificat.

Son, remember that thou in thy lifetime receivedst thy good things, and likewise Lazarus evil things.

The Collect as above.

The Second Sunday after Trinity.

AT THE FIRST VESPERS.

Antiphon to Magnificat.

They that are delivered from the noise of archers : in the places of drawing water, there shall they rehearse the righteous acts of the Lord.

The Collect.

O LORD, Who never failest to help and govern them whom Thou dost bring up in Thy steadfast fear and love ; Keep us, we beseech Thee, under the protection of Thy good Providence, and make us to have a perpetual fear and love of Thy Holy Name ; through Jesus Christ our Lord. *Amen.*

Antiphon to Benedictus.

A Certain Man made a great supper, and bade many ; and sent His servant at supper-time to say to them that were bidden, Come ; for all things are now ready.

AT THE SECOND VESPERS.

Antiphon to Magnificat.

Go out quickly into the streets and lanes of the city, and bring in hither the poor, the maimed, the halt and the blind, that My House may be filled.

The Third Sunday after Trinity.

AT THE FIRST VESPERS.

Antiphon to Magnificat.

Speak, Lord : for Thy servant heareth.

The Collect.

O LORD, we beseech Thee mercifully to hear us ; and grant that we, to whom Thou hast given an hearty desire to pray, may by Thy mighty aid be defended and comforted in all dangers and adversities ; through Jesus Christ our Lord. *Amen.*

Antiphon to Benedictus.

What man of you having an hundred sheep, if he lose one of them, doth not leave the ninety and nine in the wilderness, and go after that which is lost until he find it ?

AT THE SECOND VESPERS.

Antiphon to Magnificat.

What woman having ten pieces of silver, if she lose one piece, doth not light a candle, and sweep the house, and seek diligently until she find it ?

The Fourth Sunday after Trinity.

AT THE FIRST VESPERS.

Antiphon to Magnificat.

Only fear the Lord : and serve

Him in truth, with all your heart; for consider how great things He hath done for you.

The Collect.

O GOD, the Protector of all that trust in Thee, without Whom nothing is strong, nothing is holy; Increase and multiply upon us Thy mercy; that, Thou being our Ruler and Guide, we may so pass through things temporal, that we finally lose not the Things Eternal: Grant this, O Heavenly Father, for Jesus Christ's sake our Lord. Amen.

Antiphon to Benedictus.

Be ye therefore merciful, as your Father also is merciful, saith the Lord.

AT THE SECOND VESPERS.

Antiphon to Magnificat.

Judge not, and ye shall not be judged; for with the same measure that ye mete withal, it shall be measured to you again.

The Fifth Sunday after Trinity.

AT THE FIRST VESPERS.

Antiphon to Magnificat.

Behold, to obey is better: than sacrifice, and to hearken than the fat of rams.

The Collect.

GRANT, O Lord, we beseech Thee, that the course of this world may be so peaceably ordered by Thy governance, that Thy Church may joyfully serve Thee in all godly quietness; through Jesus Christ our Lord. Amen.

Antiphon to Benedictus.

And Jesus entered into one of the ships, and sat down, and taught the people out of the ship.

AT THE SECOND VESPERS.

Antiphon to Magnificat.

Master, we have toiled all the night, and have taken nothing; nevertheless, at Thy word I will let down the net.

The Sixth Sunday after Trinity.

AT THE FIRST VESPERS.

Antiphon to Magnificat.

The Lord also hath put away thy sin: thou shalt not die.

The Collect.

O GOD, Who hast prepared for them that love Thee such Good Things as pass man's understanding; Pour into our hearts such love towards Thee, that we, loving Thee above all things, may obtain Thy Promises, which exceed all that we can desire; through Jesus Christ our Lord. Amen.

Antiphon to Benedictus.

Ye have heard that it was said by them of old time, Thou shalt not kill: and, whosoever shall kill, shall be in danger of the judgment.

AT THE SECOND VESPERS.

Antiphon to Magnificat.

If thou bring thy gift to the Altar, and there rememberest that thy brother hath aught against thee; leave there thy gift before the Altar, and go thy way; first be reconciled to thy brother, and then come and offer thy gift.

The Seventh Sunday after Trinity.

AT THE FIRST VESPERS.

Antiphon to Magnificat.

Let me fall now into the hand of the Lord: for very great are His mercies.

The Collect.

LORD of all power and might, Who art the Author and Giver of all good things; Graft in our hearts the love of Thy Name, increase in us true religion, nourish us with all goodness, and of Thy great mercy keep us in the same; through Jesus Christ our Lord. *Amen.*

Antiphon to Benedictus.

I have compassion on the multitude, because they have now been with Me three days, and have nothing to eat; and if I send them away fasting to their own houses, they will faint by the way.

AT THE SECOND VESPERS.

Antiphon to Magnificat.

And Jesus took the seven loaves, and gave thanks, and brake, and gave to His disciples to set before them; and they did set them before the people.

The Eighth Sunday after Trinity.

AT THE FIRST VESPERS.

Antiphon to Magnificat.

Because this was in thine heart, and thou hast not asked riches, wealth, or honour: nor the life of thine enemies, neither yet hast asked long life; but hast asked wisdom and knowledge for thyself, that thou mayest judge My people, over whom I have made thee king: wisdom and knowledge is granted unto thee.

The Collect.

O GOD, Whose never-failing Providence ordereth all things both in heaven and earth; We humbly beseech Thee to put away from us all hurtful things, and to give us those things which be profitable to us; through Jesus Christ our Lord. *Amen.*

Antiphon to Benedictus.

Beware of false prophets, which come to you in sheep's clothing, but inwardly they are ravening wolves. Ye shall know them by their fruits.

AT THE SECOND VESPERS.

Antiphon to Magnificat.

Not every one that saith unto Me, Lord, Lord, shall enter into the kingdom of Heaven; but he that doeth the will of My Father, Which is in heaven.

The Ninth Sunday after Trinity.

AT THE FIRST VESPERS.

Antiphon to Magnificat.

Happy are these Thy servants: which stand continually before Thee, and that hear Thy wisdom.

The Collect.

GRANT to us, Lord, we beseech Thee, the spirit to think

and do always such things as be rightful; that we who cannot do anything that is good without Thee, may by Thee be enabled to live according to Thy Will; through Jesus Christ our Lord. *Amen.*

Antiphon to Benedictus.

And the Rich Man called him, and said unto him, How is it that I hear this of thee? Give an account of thy stewardship.

AT THE SECOND VESPERS.

Antiphon to Magnificat.

What shall I do? for my Lord taketh away from me the stewardship; I cannot dig, to beg I am ashamed. I am resolved what to do, that, when I am put out of the stewardship, they may receive me into their houses.

The Tenth Sunday after Trinity.

AT THE FIRST VESPERS.

Antiphon to Magnificat.

It is the man of God who was disobedient: unto the word of the Lord.

The Collect.

LET Thy merciful ears, O Lord, be open to the prayers of Thy humble servants; and that they may obtain their petitions make them to ask such things as shall please Thee; through Jesus Christ our Lord. *Amen.*

Antiphon to Benedictus.

And when He was come near He beheld the city, and wept over it, saying, If thou hadst known, even thou, at least in this thy day, the things which belong unto thy peace! but now they are hid from thine eyes. For the days shall come upon thee, that thine enemies shall cast a trench about thee, and compass thee round, and keep thee in on every side, and shall lay thee even with the ground, and thy children within thee; and they shall not leave in thee one stone upon another; because thou knewest not the time of thy visitation.

AT THE SECOND VESPERS.

Antiphon to Magnificat.

It is written, My house is the house of prayer; but ye have made it a den of thieves. And He taught daily in the temple.

The Eleventh Sunday after Trinity.

AT THE FIRST VESPERS.

Antiphon to Magnificat.

And after the earthquake a fire; but the Lord was not in the fire: and after the fire a still small Voice.

The Collect.

O GOD, Who declarest Thy Almighty power most chiefly in showing mercy and pity; Mercifully grant unto us such a measure of Thy Grace, that we, running the way of Thy commandments, may obtain Thy gracious promises, and be made partakers of Thy Heavenly Treasure; through Jesus Christ our Lord. *Amen.*

Antiphon to Benedictus.

Two men went up into the temple to pray; the one a Pharisee, and the other a publican; I tell you this man went down to his house justified.

AT THE SECOND VESPERS.

Antiphon to Magnificat.

The publican, standing afar off, would not so much as lift up his eyes unto heaven, but smote upon his breast, saying, God be merciful unto me a sinner.

The Twelfth Sunday after Trinity.

AT THE FIRST VESPERS.

Antiphon to Magnificat.

I saw the Lord, sitting on His throne: and all the host of heaven standing by Him on His Right Hand and on His Left.

The Collect.

ALMIGHTY and Everlasting God, Who art always more ready to hear than we to pray, and art wont to give more than either we desire or deserve; Pour down upon us the abundance of Thy mercy; forgiving us those things whereof our conscience is afraid, and giving us those Good Things which we are not worthy to ask, but through the merits and mediation of Jesus Christ Thy Son our Lord. *Amen.*

Antiphon to Benedictus.

Jesus departing from the coasts of Tyre and Sidon, came unto the sea of Galilee, through the midst of the coasts of Decapolis.

AT THE SECOND VESPERS.

Antiphon to Magnificat.

He hath done all things well; He maketh both the deaf to hear, and the dumb to speak.

The Thirteenth Sunday after Trinity.

AT THE FIRST VESPERS.

Antiphon to Magnificat.

Is it a time to receive money: and to receive garments, and oliveyards, and vineyards, and sheep and oxen, and menservants and maidservants?

The Collect.

ALMIGHTY and merciful God, of Whose only gift it cometh that Thy faithful people do unto Thee true and laudable service; Grant, we beseech Thee, that we may so faithfully serve Thee in this life, that we fail not finally to attain Thy Heavenly Promises; through the merits of Jesus Christ our Lord. *Amen.*

Antiphon to Benedictus.

A certain man went down from Jerusalem to Jericho, and fell among thieves, which stripped him of his raiment, and wounded him, and departed, leaving him half dead.

AT THE SECOND VESPERS.

Antiphon to Magnificat.

Which now of these three, thinkest thou, was neighbour unto him that fell among the thieves? And he said, He that showed mercy on him. Then said Jesus unto him, Go, and do thou likewise.

The Fourteenth Sunday after Trinity.

AT THE FIRST VESPERS.

Antiphon to Magnificat.

There shall fall unto the earth nothing : of the word of the Lord.

The Collect.

ALMIGHTY and Everlasting God, give unto us the increase of faith, hope, and charity ; and, that we may obtain that which Thou dost promise, make us to love that which Thou dost command ; through Jesus Christ our Lord. Amen.

Antiphon to Benedictus.

And as He entered into a certain village, there met Him ten men that were lepers, which stood afar off. And they lifted up their voices and said, Jesus, Master, have mercy on us.

AT THE SECOND VESPERS.

Antiphon to Magnificat.

Were there not ten cleansed? but where are the nine? There are not found that returned to give glory to God, save this stranger. And He said unto him, Arise, go thy way, thy faith hath made thee whole.

The Fifteenth Sunday after Trinity.

AT THE FIRST VESPERS.

Antiphon to Magnificat.

Hast thou not heard long ago how I have done it : and of ancient times that I have formed it?

The Collect.

KEEP, we beseech Thee, O Lord, Thy Church with Thy perpetual mercy : and, because the frailty of man without Thee cannot but fall, keep us ever by Thy help from all things hurtful, and lead us to all things profitable to our salvation ; through Jesus Christ our Lord. Amen.

Antiphon to Benedictus.

Take no thought, saying, What shall we eat? or what shall we drink? or wherewithal we shall be clothed? for your heavenly Father knoweth that ye have need of all these things.

AT THE SECOND VESPERS.

Antiphon to Magnificat.

Seek ye first the kingdom of God, and His Righteousness, and all these things shall be added unto you.

The Sixteenth Sunday after Trinity.

AT THE FIRST VESPERS.

Antiphon to Magnificat.

The Lord God of their fathers sent to them : by His messengers rising up betimes and sending.

The Collect.

O LORD, we beseech Thee, let Thy continual Pity cleanse and defend Thy Church ; and, because it cannot continue in safety without Thy succour, preserve it evermore by Thy help and goodness ; through Jesus Christ our Lord. Amen.

Antiphon to Benedictus.

And it came to pass the day after, that Jesus went into a city called Nain ; and behold, there was a dead man carried out, the only son of his mother.

AT THE SECOND VESPERS.

Antiphon to Magnificat.

And there came a fear on all, and they glorified God, saying, That a Great Prophet is risen up among us, and that God hath visited His people.

The Seventeenth Sunday after Trinity.

AT THE FIRST VESPERS.

Antiphon to Magnificat.

Execute judgment and righteousness : and deliver the spoiled out of the hand of the oppressor; and do no wrong, do no violence to the stranger, the fatherless, and the widow, neither shed innocent blood.

The Collect.

LORD, we pray Thee that Thy Grace may always prevent and follow us, and make us continually to be given to all good works; through Jesus Christ our Lord. Amen.

Antiphon to Benedictus.

And Jesus spake unto the lawyers and Pharisees, saying, Is it lawful to heal on the sabbath-day? And they held their peace. And He took him, and healed him, and let him go.

AT THE SECOND VESPERS.

Antiphon to Magnificat.

When thou art bidden to a wedding, go and sit down in the lowest room; that, when he that bade thee cometh, he may say unto thee, Friend, go up higher; then shalt thou have worship in the presence of them that sit at meat with thee.

The Eighteenth Sunday after Trinity.

AT THE FIRST VESPERS.

Antiphon to Magnificat.

It may be that the house of Judah will hear all the evil which I purpose : to do unto them; that they may return every man from his evil way; that I may forgive their iniquity and their sin.

The Collect.

LORD, we beseech Thee, grant Thy people grace to withstand the temptations of the world, the flesh, and the devil, and with pure hearts and minds to follow Thee the only God; through Jesus Christ our Lord. Amen.

Antiphon to Benedictus.

Master, which is the great commandment in the Law? Jesus said unto him, Thou shalt love the Lord thy God with all thy heart, and with all thy soul, and with all thy mind.

AT THE SECOND VESPERS.

Antiphon to Magnificat.

What think ye of Christ? whose son is He? They say unto Him, The Son of David. He saith unto them, How then doth David in spirit call Him Lord, saying, The Lord said unto my Lord, Sit Thou on My right hand.

The Nineteenth Sunday after Trinity.

AT THE FIRST VESPERS.

Antiphon to Magnificat.

Every man of the house of Israel that setteth up his idols in his heart : and putteth the stumbling-block of his iniquity before his face, and cometh to the prophet; I the Lord will answer him that cometh according to the multitude of his idols.

The Collect.

O GOD, forasmuch as without Thee, we are not able to please Thee; Mercifully grant, that Thy Holy Spirit may in all things direct and rule our hearts; through Jesus Christ our Lord. *Amen.*

Antiphon to Benedictus.

Jesus said unto the sick of the palsy, Son, be of good cheer, thy sins be forgiven thee.

AT THE SECOND VESPERS.

Antiphon to Magnificat.

But when the multitude saw it, they marvelled, and glorified God, Who had given such power unto men.

The Twentieth Sunday after Trinity.

AT THE FIRST VESPERS.

Antiphon to Magnificat.

As a shepherd seeketh out his flock : in the day that he is among his sheep that are scattered, so will I seek out My sheep and will deliver them.

The Collect.

O ALMIGHTY and most merciful God, of Thy bountiful goodness keep us, we beseech Thee, from all things that may hurt us; that we, being ready both in body and soul, may cheerfully accomplish those things that Thou wouldest have done; through Jesus Christ our Lord. *Amen.*

Antiphon to Benedictus.

Tell them which are bidden, Behold, I have prepared My dinner; come unto the marriage.

AT THE SECOND VESPERS.

Antiphon to Magnificat.

The wedding is ready, but they who were bidden were not worthy. Go ye therefore into the highways, and as many as ye shall find bid to the marriage.

The Twenty-first Sunday after Trinity.

AT THE FIRST VESPERS.

Antiphon to Magnificat.

Then Nebuchadnezzar the king was astonied : and rose up in haste and spake and said unto his counsellors, Did we not cast three men bound into the midst of the fire? They answered and said unto the king, True, O king. He answered and said, Lo, I see four men loose, walking in the midst of the fire, and they have no hurt; and the form of the Fourth is like the Son of God.

The Collect.

GRANT, we beseech Thee, merciful Lord, to Thy faithful people pardon and peace, that they may be cleansed from all their sins, and serve Thee with a quiet mind; through Jesus Christ our Lord. *Amen.*

Antiphon to Benedictus.

There was a certain nobleman, whose son was sick at Capernaum. When he heard that Jesus was come out of Judæa into Galilee, he went unto Him, and besought

Him that He would come down and heal his son.

AT THE SECOND VESPERS.

Antiphon to Magnificat.

So the father knew that it was at the same hour, in the which Jesus said unto him, Thy son liveth; and himself believed and his whole house.

The Twenty-second Sunday after Trinity.

AT THE FIRST VESPERS.

Antiphon to Magnificat.

So Daniel was taken up out of the den : and no manner of hurt was found upon him, because he believed in his God.

The Collect.

LORD, we beseech Thee to keep Thy Household the Church in continual godliness; that through Thy protection it may be free from all adversities, and devoutly given to serve Thee in good works, to the glory of Thy Name; through Jesus Christ our Lord. *Amen.*

Antiphon to Benedictus.

And the lord commanded his servant to be sold, and his wife, and children, and all that he had, and payment to be made. The servant, therefore, fell down and worshipped him, saying, Lord, have patience with me, and I will pay thee all.

AT THE SECOND VESPERS.

Antiphon to Magnificat.

O thou wicked servant, I forgave thee all that debt, because thou desiredst me; shouldest not thou also have had compassion on thy fellow-servant, even as I had pity on thee?

The Twenty-third Sunday after Trinity.

AT THE FIRST VESPERS.

Antiphon to Magnificat.

The ways of the Lord are right : and the just shall walk in them.

The Collect.

O GOD, our Refuge and Strength, Who art the Author of all godliness; Be ready, we beseech Thee, to hear the devout prayers of Thy Church; and grant that those things which we ask faithfully we may obtain effectually; through Jesus Christ our Lord. *Amen.*

Antiphon to Benedictus.

Master, we know that Thou art true, and teachest the way of God in truth.

AT THE SECOND VESPERS.

Antiphon to Magnificat.

Render therefore unto Cæsar the things that are Cæsar's; and unto God, the things that are God's.

The Twenty-fourth Sunday after Trinity.

AT THE FIRST VESPERS.

Antiphon to Magnificat.

In that day : will I raise up the tabernacle of David that is fallen, and close up the breaches thereof.

The Collect.

O LORD, we beseech Thee, absolve Thy people from their offences; that through Thy bountiful goodness we may all be delivered from the bands of those sins, which by our frailty we have committed: Grant this, O Heavenly Father, for Jesus Christ's sake, our blessed Lord and Saviour. Amen.

Antiphon to Benedictus.

While Jesus spake these things unto John's disciples, behold, there came a certain ruler, and worshipped Him, saying, My daughter is even now dead; but come and lay Thy Hand upon her, and she shall live.

AT THE SECOND VESPERS.

Antiphon to Magnificat.

Daughter, be of good comfort, thy faith hath made thee whole. And the woman was made whole from that hour.

The Twenty-fifth Sunday after Trinity.

AT THE FIRST VESPERS.

Antiphon to Magnificat.

Let us hear the conclusion: of the whole matter; Fear God and keep His commandments; for this is the whole duty of man. For God shall bring every work into Judgment.

The Collect.

STIR up, we beseech Thee, O Lord, the wills of Thy faithful people; that they, plenteously bringing forth the fruit of good works, may of Thee be plenteously rewarded; through Jesus Christ our Lord. Amen.

Antiphon to Benedictus.

When Jesus then lift up His Eyes, and saw a great company come unto Him, He saith unto Philip, Whence shall we buy bread, that these may eat? And this He said to prove him; for He Himself knew what He would do.

AT THE SECOND VESPERS.

Antiphon to Magnificat.

Then those men, when they had seen the miracle that Jesus did, said, This is of a truth that Prophet that should come into the world.

¶ *If there be any more Sundays before Advent Sunday, the Service of some of those Sundays that were omitted after the Epiphany shall be taken in to supply so many as are here wanting. And if there be fewer, the overplus may be omitted: Provided that this last Collect, with the Antiphons to* Benedictus *and* Magnificat, *shall always be used upon the Sunday next before Advent.*

Antiphon to Magnificat *at the First Vespers of the Twenty-fifth Sunday after Trinity, when it is not the Sunday next before Advent.*

Hear ye, O mountains, the Lord's controversy: and ye strong foundations of the earth.

Antiphon to Magnificat *at the First Vespers of the Twenty-sixth Sunday after Trinity.*

The vision is yet for an appointed time: but at the end it shall speak and not lie; though it tarry, wait for it, because it will surely come, it will not tarry.

Here endeth the Service Proper for the Seasons.

THE PSALTER.

AT LAUDS, SUNDAY.

℣. The Lord is high above all people.

℟. And His glory above the heavens.

℣. O God, make speed to save us.

℟. O Lord, make haste to help us.

℣. Glory be to the Father, and to the Son : and to the Holy Ghost;

℟. As it was in the beginning, is now, and ever shall be : world without end. Amen.

Alleluia.

But from Septuagesima Sunday to Wednesday in Holy Week, inclusive, is said, instead of Alleluia,

Praise to Thee, O Lord, we sing, Of Glory the Eternal King.

Antiphon when not otherwise ordered. The Lord is King.

Dominus regnavit. Ps. xciii.

1 The Lord is King, and hath put on glorious apparel : the Lord hath put on His apparel, and girded Himself with strength.

2 He hath made the round world so sure : that it cannot be moved.

3 Ever since the world began hath Thy seat been prepared : Thou art from everlasting.

4 The floods are risen, O Lord, the floods have lift up their voice : the floods lift up their waves.

5 The waves of the sea are mighty, and rage horribly : but yet the Lord Who dwelleth on high is mightier.

6 Thy testimonies, O Lord, are very sure : holiness becometh Thine house for ever.

Glory be to the Father, &c.

Antiphon. The Lord is King, and hath put on glorious apparel; He hath girded Himself with strength, and His seat is from everlasting.

Antiphon. Be ye sure.

Jubilate Deo. Ps. c.

1 O be joyful in the Lord, all ye lands : serve the Lord with gladness, and come before His presence with a song.

2 Be ye sure that the Lord He is God : it is He that hath made us, and not we ourselves; we are His people, and the sheep of His pasture.

3 O go your way into His gates with thanksgiving, and into His courts with praise : be thankful unto Him and speak good of His Name.

4 For the Lord is gracious, His mercy is everlasting : and His Truth endureth from generation to generation.

Glory be to the Father, &c.

Antiphon. Be ye sure that the Lord He is God : in Him let us be joyful, and speak good of His Name.

Antiphon. As long as I live.

Deus, Deus meus. Ps. lxiii.

1 O God, Thou art my God : early will I seek Thee.

2 My soul thirsteth for Thee, my flesh also longeth after Thee : in a barren and dry land, where no water is.

3 Thus have I looked for Thee in holiness : that I might behold Thy power and glory.

4 For Thy loving-kindness is better than the life itself : my lips shall praise Thee.

5 As long as I live will I magnify Thee on this manner : and lift up my hands in Thy Name.

6 My soul shall be satisfied even as it were with marrow and fatness : when my mouth praiseth Thee with joyful lips.

7 Have I not remembered Thee in my bed : and thought upon Thee when I was waking?

8 Because Thou hast been my helper : therefore under the shadow of Thy wings will I rejoice.

9 My soul hangeth upon Thee : Thy right hand hath upholden me.

10 These also that seek the hurt of my soul : they shall go under the earth.

11 Let them fall upon the edge of the sword : that they may be a portion for foxes.

12 But the King shall rejoice in God; all they also that swear by Him shall be commended : for the mouth of them that speak lies shall be stopped.

Here is not said Gloria Patri.

Deus misereatur. Ps. lxvii.

1 God be merciful unto us, and bless us : and show us the light of His countenance, and be merciful unto us.

2 That Thy way may be known upon earth : Thy saving health among all nations.

3 Let the people praise Thee, O God : yea, let all the people praise Thee.

4 O let the nations rejoice and be glad : for Thou shalt judge the folk righteously, and govern the nations upon earth.

5 Let the people praise Thee, O God : let all the people praise Thee.

6 Then shall the earth bring forth her increase : and God, even our own God, shall give us His blessing.

7 God shall bless us : and all the ends of the world shall fear Him.

Glory be to the Father, &c.

Antiphon. As long as I live will I magnify Thee, that I may behold Thy power and glory.

Antiphon. Let every creature.

Benedicite, omnia opera.

O all ye Works of the Lord, bless ye the Lord : praise Him, and magnify Him for ever.

O ye Angels of the Lord, bless ye the Lord : praise Him, and magnify Him for ever.

O ye Heavens, bless ye the Lord : praise Him, and magnify Him for ever.

O ye Waters that be above the Firmament, bless ye the Lord : praise Him, and magnify Him for ever.

O all ye Powers of the Lord, bless ye the Lord : praise Him, and magnify Him for ever.

O ye Sun, and Moon, bless ye the Lord : praise Him, and magnify Him for ever.

O ye Stars of Heaven, bless ye

AT LAUDS.

the Lord : praise Him, and magnify Him for ever.

O ye Showers and Dew, bless ye the Lord : praise Him, and magnify Him for ever.

O ye Winds of God, bless ye the Lord : praise Him, and magnify Him for ever.

O ye Fire and Heat, bless ye the Lord : praise Him, and magnify Him for ever.

O ye Winter and Summer, bless ye the Lord : praise Him, and magnify Him for ever.

O ye Dews and Frosts, bless ye the Lord : praise Him, and magnify Him for ever.

O ye Frost and Cold, bless ye the Lord : praise Him, and magnify Him for ever.

O ye Ice and Snow, bless ye the Lord : praise Him, and magnify Him for ever.

O ye Nights and Days, bless ye the Lord : praise Him, and magnify Him for ever.

O ye Light and Darkness, bless ye the Lord : praise Him, and magnify Him for ever.

O ye Lightnings, and Clouds, bless ye the Lord : praise Him, and magnify Him for ever.

O let the Earth bless the Lord : yea, let it praise Him, and magnify Him for ever.

O ye Mountains and Hills, bless ye the Lord : praise Him, and magnify Him for ever.

O all ye Green Things upon the Earth, bless ye the Lord : praise Him, and magnify Him for ever.

O ye Wells, bless ye the Lord : praise Him, and magnify Him for ever.

O ye Seas, and Floods, bless ye the Lord : praise Him, and magnify Him for ever.

O ye Whales, and all that move in the Waters, bless ye the Lord : praise Him, and magnify Him for ever.

O all ye Fowls of the Air, bless ye the Lord : praise Him, and magnify Him for ever.

O all ye Beasts and Cattle, bless ye the Lord : praise Him, and magnify Him for ever.

O ye Children of men, bless ye the Lord : praise Him, and magnify Him for ever.

O let Israel bless the Lord : praise Him, and magnify Him for ever.

O ye Priests of the Lord, bless ye the Lord : praise Him, and magnify Him for ever.

O ye Servants of the Lord, bless ye the Lord : praise Him, and magnify Him for ever.

O ye Spirits and Souls of the Righteous, bless ye the Lord : praise Him, and magnify Him for ever.

O ye holy and humble Men of heart, bless ye the Lord : praise Him, and magnify Him for ever.

O Ananias, Azarias, and Misael, bless ye the Lord : praise Him, and magnify Him for ever.

Glory be to the Father, &c.

Antiphon. Let every creature which is in heaven and on the earth bless the Lord; praise Him, and magnify Him for ever.

Antiphon. Let every thing that hath breath.

Laudate Dominum. Ps. cxlviii.

1 O praise the Lord of heaven : praise Him in the height.

2 Praise Him, all ye Angels of His : praise Him, all His host.

3 Praise Him, sun and moon : praise Him, all ye stars and light.

4 Praise Him, all ye heavens : and ye waters that are above the heavens.

5 Let them praise the Name of the Lord : for He spake the word, and they were made ; He commanded, and they were created.

6 He hath made them fast for ever and ever : He hath given them a law which shall not be broken.

7 Praise the Lord upon earth : ye dragons and all deeps ;

8 Fire and hail, snow and vapours : wind and storm, fulfilling His word ;

9 Mountains and all hills : fruitful trees and all cedars ;

10 Beasts and all cattle : worms and feathered fowls ;

11 Kings of the earth and all people : princes and all judges of the world ;

12 Young men and maidens, old men and children, praise the Name of the Lord : for His Name only is excellent, and His praise above heaven and earth.

13 He shall exalt the horn of His people ; all His saints shall praise Him : even the children of Israel, even the people that serveth Him.

Here is not said Gloria Patri.

Cantate Domino. Ps. cxlix.

1 O sing unto the Lord a new song : let the congregation of saints praise Him.

2 Let Israel rejoice in Him that made him : and let the children of Sion be joyful in their King.

3 Let them praise His Name in the dance : let them sing praises unto Him with tabret and harp.

4 For the Lord hath pleasure in His people : and helpeth the meek-hearted.

5 Let the saints be joyful with glory : let them rejoice in their beds.

6 Let the praises of God be in their mouth : and a two-edged sword in their hands ;

7 To be avenged of the heathen : and to rebuke the people ;

8 To bind their kings in chains : and their nobles with links of iron.

9 That they may be avenged of them, as it is written : Such honour have all His Saints.

Here is not said Gloria Patri.

Laudate Dominum. Ps. cl.

1 O praise God in His holiness : praise Him in the firmament of His power.

2 Praise Him in His noble acts : praise Him according to His excellent greatness.

3 Praise Him in the sound of the trumpet : praise Him upon the lute and harp.

4 Praise Him in the cymbals and dances : praise Him upon the strings and pipe.

5 Praise Him upon the well-tuned cymbals : praise Him upon the loud cymbals.

6 Let every thing that hath breath : praise the Lord.

Glory be to the Father, &c.

Antiphon. Let every thing that hath breath praise the Lord ; for He spake the word, and they were made ; He commanded, and they were created.

The Chapter, Rev. vii. 12, (*for all Sundays from Epiphany to Septuagesima, and from Trinity to Advent.*)

Blessing, and glory, and wisdom, and thanksgiving, and honour, and power, and might, be unto our God for ever and ever. Amen.

℞. Thanks be to God.

Hymn, (on Sundays from Epiphany to Lent.) Æterne rerum Conditor.

Creator Blest, Eternal King,
Who day and night about dost bring,
Who weary mortals to relieve,
Dost in their times the seasons give.

Now the shrill cock proclaims it day,
And calls the sun's awakening ray,
The wandering pilgrim's guiding Light,
That marks the watches night by night.

Roused at the note, the morning star
Heaven's dusky veil uplifts afar;
Night's wicked bands no longer roam,
But from their dark ways hie them home.

The encouraged sailor's fears are o'er,
The foaming waters rage no more:
Repentance once the crowing cock
Brought to the Church's promised Rock.

O let us then like men arise;
The cock rebukes our slumbering eyes;
Bestirs who still in sleep would lie,
And shames who would their Lord deny;

Revives once more hope's fading fires,
Through the sick frame new health inspires,
Sheathes the wild robber's weapon dark,
Lights in the fall'n, faith's dying spark.

Look on us, Jesu, when we fall,
And with that look our souls recall:
If Thou but look, our stains are gone,
And with due tears our pardon won.

Shed through our souls Thy piercing ray,
Our souls' dull slumber drive away;—
Thy Name be first on every tongue,
To Thee our earliest praises sung.

All praise to God the Father be,
All praise, Eternal Son, to Thee;
All praise for ever, as is meet,
To God the Holy Paraclete. Amen.

℣. (*From Epiphany to Septuagesima.*) The Lord is King.

℞. He hath put on glorious apparel. Alleluia!

℣. (*From Septuagesima till Lent.*) Lord, Thou hast been our Refuge.

℞. From one generation to another.

On Sundays and week-days after Trinity is said the

Hymn. Ecce jam noctis.

Lo! now the melting shades of night are ending,
Flickers the golden gleam of dawning day,
Let us before the Lord of all, low bending,
 Suppliants pray;

That He would of the stain of guilt relieve us,
Grant our soul's health, of His most blessed love,
And of His pitying grace and mercy give us
 Heaven above.

Be this by Thy thrice Holy Godhead granted,
Father, and Son, and Spirit ever blest,
Whose glory by the firmament is chanted,
 By all confess'd. Amen.

℣. The Lord is King.

℞. He hath put on glorious apparel. Alleluia.

Antiphon (*as in the Proper Services.*)

Benedictus. St. Luke i. 68.

Blessed be the Lord God of Israel: for He hath visited and redeemed His people;

And hath raised up a mighty Salvation for us: in the house of His servant David;

As He spake by the mouth of His holy Prophets: which have been since the world began;

That we should be Saved from our enemies: and from the hands of all that hate us;

To perform the Mercy promised to our forefathers : and to remember His holy covenant ;

To perform the oath which He sware to our forefather Abraham : that He would give us ;

That we being delivered out of the hand of our enemies : might serve Him without fear ;

In holiness and righteousness before Him : all the days of our life.

And thou, Child, shalt be called the Prophet of the Highest : for thou shalt go before the face of the Lord to prepare His ways ;

To give knowledge of Salvation unto His people : for the remission of their sins.

Through the tender mercy of our God : whereby the Day-Spring from on high hath visited us ;

To give light to them that sit in darkness, and in the shadow of death : and to guide our feet into the way of Peace.

Glory be to the Father, &c.

Antiphon (as in the Proper Services.)

℣. The Lord be with you.

℟. And with thy spirit.

Let us pray.

The Collect (as in the Proper Service.)

℣. The Lord be with you.

℟. And with thy spirit.

℣. Bless we the Lord.

℟. Thanks be to God.

MEMORIALS AT LAUDS.

Of the Incarnation of our Lord in Advent.

Antiphon (except on Advent Sunday.) The Holy Ghost shall come upon thee, Mary ; That Holy Thing which shall be born of thee shall be called the Son of God. (*On Sundays and Holy Days is added* Alleluia.)

℣. There shall come forth a Rod out of the stem of Jesse.

℟. A branch shall grow out of his roots.

Let us pray.

WE beseech Thee, O Lord, pour Thy grace into our hearts ; that as we have known the Incarnation of Thy Son Jesus Christ by the message of an Angel, so by His Cross and Passion we may be brought to the glory of His Resurrection : through the same Jesus Christ our Lord. *Amen.*

At other times (except during the Octave of Christmas and upon the second, third, fourth, and fifth days of January, and also from Maundy Thursday to Low Sunday inclusive.)

Antiphon. Lo ! Mary hath brought forth the Saviour, of Whom, when John saw Him, he said, Behold the Lamb of God Which taketh away the sins of the world. (*On Sundays and Holy Days is added*, Alleluia.)

℣. Thou art fairer than the children of men.

℟. Full of grace are Thy lips.

Let us pray.

WE beseech Thee, O Lord, pour Thy grace into our hearts ; that as we have known the Incarnation of Thy Son Jesus Christ by the message of an Angel, so by His Cross and Passion we may be brought to the glory of His Resurrection :

through the same Jesus Christ our Lord. *Amen.*

Of All Saints in Advent.

Antiphon. Behold the Lord my God shall come, and All His Saints with Him, and there shall be in that day a great Light. (*On Sundays and Holy Days is added,* Alleluia.)

℣. O God, wonderful art Thou in Thy Saints.

℟. And glorious in Thy Majesty.

When this ℣. and ℟. are said at Lauds in a Black Letter Day Memorial, then in this Memorial is said instead,

℣. The Souls of the Righteous are in the Hand of God.

℟. And there shall no torment touch them.

Let us pray.

O LORD, we beseech Thee, visit and cleanse our consciences, that Thy Son our Lord Jesus Christ when He cometh with All His Saints, may find in us a dwelling-place prepared for Him, Who liveth and reigneth with Thee and the Holy Ghost, ever one God, world without end. *Amen.*

At other times.

Antiphon. The Saints shall be joyful with glory; they shall rejoice in their beds. (*On Sundays and Holy Days is added,* Alleluia.)

℣. O God, wonderful art Thou in Thy Saints.

℟. And glorious in Thy Majesty.

When this ℣. and ℟. are said at Lauds in a Black Letter Day Memorial, then in this Memorial is said instead,

℣. The Souls of the Righteous are in the Hand of God.

℟. And there shall no torment touch them.

Let us pray.

O ALMIGHTY God, Who hast knit together Thine elect in one Communion and fellowship, in the mystical Body of Thy Son Christ our Lord; Grant us grace so to follow Thy blessed Saints in all virtuous and godly living, that we may come to those unspeakable Joys, which Thou hast prepared for them that unfeignedly love Thee; through Jesus Christ our Lord. *Amen.*

Memorial of penitent sinners, to be said at Lauds from Ash-Wednesday till Wednesday in Holy Week inclusive.

Antiphon. Turn ye even unto Me, saith the Lord, with all your heart, and with fasting, and with weeping, and with mourning.

℣. We have sinned with our fathers.

℟. We have done amiss, and dealt wickedly.

Let us pray.

O LORD, we beseech Thee, mercifully hear our prayers, and spare all those who confess their sins unto Thee; that they, whose consciences by sin are accused, by Thy merciful pardon may be absolved; through Christ our Lord. *Amen.*

Memorial of the Resurrection, to be said at Lauds on Sundays, from Low Sunday till the Ascension.

Antiphon. And very early in the morning, the first day of the week, they came unto the Sepulchre at the Rising of the Sun. Alleluia.

℣. The Lord is Risen indeed.

℟. And hath appeared to Simon. Alleluia.

Let us pray.

ALMIGHTY God, Who through Thy Only-begotten Son Jesus Christ hast overcome death, and opened unto us the gate of everlasting Life; We humbly beseech Thee, that, as by Thy special grace preventing us Thou dost put into our minds good desires, so by Thy continual help we may bring the same to good effect; through Jesus Christ our Lord, Who liveth and reigneth with Thee and the Holy Ghost, ever one God, world without end. Amen.

Memorial of the Resurrection, to be said daily at Lauds on week-days from Low Sunday till the Ascension.

Antiphon. The Lord is Risen from the Tomb, Who died to save us from our doom. Alleluia.

℣. The Lord is Risen.

℟. As He said. Alleluia.

With the Collect of Easter Day.

Memorial of the Passion, to be said at Lauds daily from Trinity Monday to Advent.

Antiphon. It behoveth us to glory in the Cross of our Lord Jesus Christ. (*On Sundays and Holy Days is added,* Alleluia.)

℣. All the world shall worship Thee, O God.

℟. Sing of Thee and praise Thy power.

Let us pray.

KEEP, we beseech Thee, O Saviour of the world, in continual peace, those whom Thou hast been pleased to redeem by Thy Cross and Passion, Who livest and reignest with the Father and the Holy Ghost, ever one God, world without end. *Amen.*

For the Peace of the Church.

Ad Te levavi oculos meos. Ps. cxxiii.

1 Unto Thee lift I up mine eyes : O Thou that dwellest in the heavens.

2 Behold, even as the eyes of servants look unto the hand of their masters, and as the eyes of a maiden unto the hand of her mistress : even so our eyes wait upon the Lord our God, until He have mercy upon us.

3 Have mercy upon us, O Lord, have mercy upon us : for we are utterly despised.

4 Our soul is filled with the scornful reproof of the wealthy : and with the despitefulness of the proud.

Glory be to the Father, &c.

Lord, have mercy upon us.
Christ, have mercy upon us.
Lord, have mercy upon us.

Our Father, &c.

℣. O Lord, arise, help us.

℟. And deliver us for Thy Name's sake.

℣. Turn us again, Thou God of Hosts.

℟. Show the light of Thy Countenance, and we shall be whole.

℣. Lord, hear our prayer.

℟. And let our cry come unto Thee.

℣. The Lord be with you.

℟. And with thy spirit.

Let us pray.

O LORD, we beseech Thee, mercifully to hear the prayers of Thy Church, that we, being delivered from all adversities, and serving Thee with a quiet mind, may enjoy Thy peace all the days of our life; through Jesus Christ our Lord, Who liveth and reigneth with Thee and the Holy Ghost, one God, world without end. *Amen.*

℣. The Lord be with you.

℟. And with thy spirit.

℣. Bless we the Lord.

℟. Thanks be to God.

MONDAY. AT LAUDS.

℣. Let Thy merciful kindness, O Lord, be upon us.

℟. As we do put our trust in Thee.

This ℣. and ℟. are said on all week-days from Epiphany to Lent, and from Trinity to Advent.

℣. O God, make speed to save us.

℟. O Lord, make haste to help us.

℣. Glory be to the Father, and to the Son : and to the Holy Ghost;

℟. As it was in the beginning, is now, and ever shall be : world without end. Amen.

Alleluia.

But from Septuagesima Sunday to Wednesday in Holy Week, inclusive, is said instead of Alleluia,

Praise to Thee, O Lord, we sing, Of Glory the Eternal King.

Antiphon. Have mercy.

Miserere mei, Deus. Ps. li.

1 Have mercy upon me, O God, after Thy great goodness : according to the multitude of Thy mercies, do away mine offences.

2 Wash me throughly from my wickedness : and cleanse me from my sin.

3 For I acknowledge my faults : and my sin is ever before me.

4 Against Thee only have I sinned, and done this evil in Thy sight : that Thou mightest be justified in Thy saying, and clear when Thou art judged.

5 Behold, I was shapen in wickedness : and in sin hath my mother conceived me.

6 But lo, Thou requirest truth in the inward parts : and shalt make me to understand wisdom secretly.

7 Thou shalt purge me with hyssop, and I shall be clean : Thou shalt wash me, and I shall be whiter than snow.

8 Thou shalt make me hear of

joy and gladness : that the bones which Thou hast broken may rejoice.

9 Turn Thy Face from my sins : and put out all my misdeeds.

10 Make me a clean heart, O God : and renew a right spirit within me.

11 Cast me not away from Thy presence : and take not Thy Holy Spirit from me.

12 O give me the comfort of Thy help again : and stablish me with Thy free Spirit.

13 Then shall I teach Thy ways unto the wicked : and sinners shall be converted unto Thee.

14 Deliver me from blood-guiltiness, O God, Thou that art the God of my health : and my tongue shall sing of Thy righteousness.

15 Thou shalt open my lips, O Lord : and my mouth shall show Thy praise.

16 For Thou desirest no sacrifice, else would I give it Thee : but Thou delightest not in burnt-offerings.

17 The sacrifice of God is a troubled spirit : a broken and contrite heart, O God, shalt Thou not despise.

18 O be favourable and gracious unto Sion : build Thou the walls of Jerusalem.

19 Then shalt Thou be pleased with the sacrifice of righteousness, with the burnt-offerings and oblations : then shall they offer young bullocks upon Thine Altar.

Glory be to the Father, &c.

Antiphon. Have mercy upon me, O God.

Antiphon. Consider.

Verba mea auribus. Ps. v.

1 Ponder my words, O Lord : consider my meditation.

2 O hearken Thou unto the voice of my calling, my King and my God : for unto Thee will I make my prayer.

3 My voice shalt Thou hear betimes, O Lord : early in the morning will I direct my prayer unto Thee, and will look up.

4 For Thou art the God that hast no pleasure in wickedness : neither shall any evil dwell with Thee.

5 Such as be foolish shall not stand in Thy Sight : for Thou hatest all them that work vanity.

6 Thou shalt destroy them that speak leasing : the Lord will abhor both the blood-thirsty and deceitful man.

7 But as for me, I will come into Thine House, even upon the multitude of Thy mercy : and in Thy fear will I worship toward Thy holy temple.

8 Lead me, O Lord, in Thy righteousness, because of mine enemies : make Thy way plain before my face.

9 For there is no faithfulness in his mouth : their inward parts are very wickedness.

10 Their throat is an open sepulchre : they flatter with their tongue.

11 Destroy Thou them, O God ; let them perish through their own imaginations : cast them out in the multitude of their ungodliness ; for they have rebelled against Thee.

12 And let all them that put their trust in Thee rejoice : they shall ever be giving of thanks, because Thou defendest them ; they that love Thy Name shall be joyful in Thee.

13 For Thou, Lord, wilt give Thy blessing unto the righteous :

and with Thy favourable kindness wilt Thou defend him as with a shield.

Glory be to the Father, &c.

Antiphon. Consider my meditation.

Antiphon. O God.

Deus, Deus meus. Ps. lxiii.
Deus misereatur. Ps. lxvii.
As in the Sunday Lauds, p. 140.

Antiphon. O God, Thou art my God : early will I seek Thee.

Antiphon. Thine anger is turned away.

The Song of Isaiah, chap. xii., Confitebor Tibi.

1 O Lord, I will praise Thee, though Thou wast angry with me : Thine anger is turned away, and Thou comfortedst me.

2 Behold, God is my Salvation : I will trust, and not be afraid :

For the Lord JEHOVAH is my Strength and my Song : He also is become my Salvation.

3 Therefore with joy shall ye draw water out of the wells of salvation : and in that day shall ye say, Praise the Lord, call upon His Name.

4 Declare His doings among the people : make mention that His Name is exalted.

5 Sing unto the Lord, for He hath done excellent things : this is known in all the earth.

6 Cry out and shout, thou inhabitant of Zion : for great is the Holy One of Israel in the midst of thee.

Glory be to the Father, &c.

Antiphon. Thine anger is turned away : and Thou comfortedst me.

Antiphon. O praise.

Laudate Dominum. Ps. cxlviii.
Cantate Domino. Ps. cxlix.
Laudate Dominum. Ps. cl.
As in the Sunday Lauds, p. 141.

Antiphon. O praise the Lord of heaven.

The Chapter, 1 Cor. xvi. 13, 14.

Watch ye, stand fast in the faith, quit you like men, be strong. Let all your things be done with charity.

℟. Thanks be to God.

In week-day Services this Chapter is said (1.) *daily from Epiphany to Ash-Wednesday, and* (2.) *daily from Trinity to Advent.*

Hymn, (for Mondays from Epiphany to Lent.) Splendor Paternæ Gloriæ.

Thou Brightness of the Father's ray,
True Light of light, and Day of day ;
Light's fountain and eternal spring :
Thou Morn the morn illumining !

Glide in, Thou very Sun divine ;
With everlasting brightness shine :
And shed abroad on every sense
The Spirit's light and influence.

Thee, Father, let us seek aright :
The Father of perpetual light :
The Father of Almighty grace :
Each wile of sin away to chase.

Our acts with courage do Thou fill :
Blunt Thou the Tempter's tooth of ill.
Misfortune into good convert,
Or give us grace to bear unhurt.

Our spirits, whatsoe'er betide,
In chaste and loyal bodies guide ;
Let Faith, with fervour unalloyed,
The bane of falsehood still avoid.

And Christ our daily food be nigh ;
And Faith our daily cup supply :
So may we quaff, to calm and bless,
The Spirit's rapturous holiness.

Now let the day in joy pass on :
Our modesty like early dawn,
Our faith like noontide splendour glow ;
Our souls the twilight never know.

All laud to God the Father be :
All laud, Eternal Son, to Thee :
All laud, as is for ever meet,
To God the Holy Paraclete. Amen.

℣. Have I not thought upon Thee when I was waking?

℟. Because Thou hast been my Helper.

On Monday, from Trinity to Advent, is said the Hymn, Ecce jam noctis, *as in the Sunday Lauds, p. 143, with the*

℣. Have I not thought upon Thee when I was waking?

℟. Because Thou hast been my Helper.

Antiphon. Blessed be.

Benedictus, St. Luke i. 68, *as in the Sunday Lauds, p.* 143.

Antiphon. Blessed be : the Lord God of Israel.

[*From Easter to Trinity the weekday Prayers are not said at Lauds, and the Lauds end as on Sunday.*]

Here follow the week-day Prayers, thus, (all kneeling.)

Lord, have mercy upon us.
Christ, have mercy upon us.
Lord, have mercy upon us.
Our Father, &c.

℣. I said, Lord, be merciful unto me.

℟. Heal my soul, for I have sinned against Thee.

℣. Turn Thee again, O Lord, at the last.

℟. And be gracious unto Thy servants.

℣. Let Thy merciful kindness, O Lord, be upon us.

℟. As we do put our trust in Thee.

℣. Let Thy Priests be clothed with righteousness.

℟. And Thy Saints sing with joyfulness.

℣. O Lord, save the Queen.

℟. And mercifully hear us when we call upon Thee.

℣. O God, save Thy servants and handmaidens.

℟. Which put their trust in Thee.

℣. O Lord, save Thy people.

℟. And bless Thine inheritance.

℣. Peace be within Thy walls.

℟. And plenteousness within Thy palaces.

℣. Let us pray for the dead in Christ.

℟. Grant them, O Lord, eternal rest, and let everlasting light shine upon them.

℣. Hearken unto my voice, O Lord, when I cry unto Thee.

℟. Have mercy upon me, and hear me.

Miserere mei Deus. Ps. li., *p.* 147.

[*This Psalm may be omitted except on week-days in Lent, when it shall always be said and followed by*

Domine, ne in furore. Ps. vi.

Against Anger.

1 O Lord, rebuke me not in Thine indignation : neither chasten me in Thy displeasure.

2 Have mercy upon me, O Lord, for I am weak : O Lord, heal me, for my bones are vexed.

3 My soul also is sore troubled : but, Lord, how long wilt Thou punish me?

4 Turn Thee, O Lord, and deliver my soul : O save me for Thy mercy's sake.

5 For in death no man remem-

bereth Thee: and who will give Thee thanks in the pit?

6 I am weary of my groaning; every night wash I my bed: and water my couch with my tears.

7 My beauty is gone for very trouble: and worn away because of all mine enemies.

8 Away from me, all ye that work vanity: for the Lord hath heard the voice of my weeping.

9 The Lord hath heard my petition: the Lord will receive my prayer.

10 All mine enemies shall be confounded, and sore vexed: they shall be turned back, and put to shame suddenly.

Glory be to the Father, &c.]

Then let the reader, [if a Priest, rise from his knees, go to the steps of the Sanctuary, and] say,

O Lord, arise, help us.

℟. And deliver us for Thy Name's sake.

℣. Turn Thee again, O Lord God of Hosts.

℟. Show the light of Thy Countenance, and we shall be whole.

℣. Lord, hear our prayer.

℟. And let our cry come unto Thee.

℣. The Lord be with you.

℟. And with thy spirit.

Let us pray.

The Collect as in the Proper Services.

Then follow the Memorials, &c., as at the Sunday Lauds, pp. 144—146.

TUESDAY. AT LAUDS.

℣. Let Thy merciful kindness, O Lord, be upon us.

℟. As we do put our trust in Thee.

℣. O God, make speed to save us.

℟. O Lord, make haste to help us.

℣. Glory be to the Father, and to the Son: and to the Holy Ghost;

℟. As it was in the beginning, is now, and ever shall be: world without end. Amen.

Alleluia.

But from Septuagesima Sunday to Wednesday in Holy Week, inclusive, is said instead of Alleluia,

Praise to Thee, O Lord, we sing, Of Glory the Eternal King.

Antiphon. According to the multitude.

Miserere mei Deus. Ps. li., *as in Monday Lauds, p.* 147.

Antiphon. According to the multitude: of Thy mercies have mercy on me, O God.

Antiphon. The Help of my countenance.

Judica me, Deus. Ps. xliii.

1 Give sentence with me, O God, and defend my cause against the ungodly people: O deliver me from the deceitful and wicked man.

2 For Thou art the God of my strength; why hast Thou put me from Thee: and why go I so

heavily, while the enemy oppresseth me?

3 O send out Thy light and Thy truth, that they may lead me : and bring me unto Thy holy hill, and to Thy dwelling.

4 And that I may go unto the Altar of God, even unto the God of my joy and gladness : and upon the harp will I give thanks unto Thee, O God my God.

5 Why art thou so heavy, O my soul : and why art thou so disquieted within me?

6 O put thy trust in God : for I will yet give Him thanks, which is the Help of my countenance, and my God.

Glory be to the Father, &c.

Antiphon. The Help of my countenance : and my God.

Antiphon. Early.

Deus, Deus meus. Ps. lxiii.
Deus misereatur. Ps. lxvii.

As in the Sunday Lauds, p. 140.

Antiphon. Early : will I seek Thee.

Antiphon. All the days of my life.

The Song of Hezekiah. Ego dixi, Isaiah xxxviii. 10.

10 I said, in the cutting off of my days : I shall go to the gates of the grave.

I am deprived of the residue of my years : I said, I shall not see the Lord, even the Lord, in the land of the living.

11 I shall behold man no more : with the inhabitants of the world.

12 Mine age is departed : and is removed from me as a shepherd's tent.

I have cut off like a weaver my life : He will cut me off with pining sickness.

From day even to night : wilt Thou make an end of me.

13 I reckoned till morning that, as a lion, so will He break all my bones : from day even to night wilt Thou make an end of me.

14 Like a crane or a swallow, so did I chatter : I did mourn as a dove.

Mine eyes fail with looking upward : O Lord, I am oppressed; undertake for me.

15 What shall I say? He hath both spoken unto me, and Himself hath done it : I shall go softly all my years in the bitterness of my soul.

16 O Lord, by these things men live, and in all these things is the life of my spirit ; so wilt Thou recover me, and make me to live.

17 Behold, for peace I had great bitterness ; but Thou hast in love to my soul delivered it from the pit of corruption : for Thou hast cast all my sins behind Thy back.

18 For the grave cannot praise Thee, death cannot celebrate Thee : they that go down into the pit cannot hope for Thy truth.

19 The living, the living, he shall praise Thee, as I do this day : the father to the children shall make known Thy truth.

20 The Lord was ready to save me : therefore we will sing my songs to the stringed instruments all the days of our life in the house of the Lord.

Glory be to the Father, &c.

Antiphon. All the days of my life : the Lord was ready to save me.

AT LAUDS.

Antiphon. Praise Him.

Laudate Dominum. Ps. cxlviii.
Cantate Domino. Ps. cxlix.
Laudate Dominum. Ps. cl.

As in the Sunday Lauds, p. 141.

Antiphon. Praise Him : in the firmament of His power.

The Chapter, 1 Cor. xvi. 13, 14.

Watch ye, stand fast in the faith, quit you like men, be strong. Let all your things be done with charity.

℞. Thanks be to God.

In week-day Services this Chapter is said (1.) *daily from Epiphany to Ash-Wednesday, and* (2.) *daily from Trinity to Advent.*

Hymn for Tuesdays from Epiphany to Lent.

Ales diei nuntius.

The winged herald of the day
Proclaims the morn's approaching ray:
And Christ the Lord our souls excites,
And so to endless life invites.

Take up thy bed, to each He cries,
Who sick, or wrapped in slumber lies;
And chaste, and just, and sober stand,
And watch: My coming is at hand.

With earnest cry, with tearful care,
Call we the Lord to hear our prayer,
While supplication, pure and deep,
Forbids each chastened heart to sleep.

Do Thou, O Christ, our slumbers wake;
Do Thou the chains of darkness break;
Purge Thou our former sins away,
And in our souls new light display.

All laud to God the Father be;
All laud, Eternal Son, to Thee;
All laud, as is for ever meet,
To God the Holy Paraclete. Amen.

℣. Have I not thought upon Thee when I was waking?

℞. Because Thou hast been my Helper.

On Tuesdays, from Trinity to Advent, is said the Hymn, Ecce jam noctis, *as in the Sunday Lauds, p.* 143, *with the*

℣. Have I not thought upon Thee when I was waking?

℞. Because Thou hast been my Helper.

Antiphon. And the Lord shall be to us.

Benedictus, St. Luke i. 68.

Antiphon. And the Lord shall be to us : a mighty Salvation in the house of His servant David.

Then follow the week-day Prayers as at p. 150.

The Proper Collect.

℣. The Lord be with you.

℞. And with thy spirit.

℣. Bless ye the Lord.

℞. Thanks be to God.

Then follow the Memorials, &c., as at the Sunday Lauds, pp. 144—146.

WEDNESDAY. AT LAUDS.

℣. Let Thy merciful kindness, O Lord, be upon us.

℞. As we do put our trust in Thee.

℣. O God, make speed to save us.

℞. O Lord, make haste to help us.

℣. Glory be to the Father, and

to the Son : and to the Holy Ghost;

℟. As it was in the beginning, is now, and ever shall be : world without end. Amen.

Alleluia.

But from Septuagesima to Wednesday in Holy Week, inclusive, is said instead of Alleluia,

Praise to Thee, O Lord, we sing, Of Glory the Eternal King.

Antiphon. Wash me throughly.

Miserere mei Deus, Ps. li., *as in Monday Lauds, p.* 147.

Antiphon. Wash me throughly : from my wickedness, O God.

Antiphon. Thou, O God.

Te decet hymnus. Ps. lxv.

1 Thou, O God, art praised in Sion : and unto Thee shall the vow be performed in Jerusalem.

2 Thou that hearest the prayer : unto Thee shall all flesh come.

3 My misdeeds prevail against me : O be Thou merciful unto our sins.

4 Blessed is the man, whom Thou choosest, and receivest unto Thee : he shall dwell in Thy court, and shall be satisfied with the pleasures of Thy House, even of Thy holy temple.

5 Thou shalt show us wonderful things in Thy righteousness, O God of our salvation : Thou that art the Hope of all the ends of the earth, and of them that remain in the broad sea.

6 Who in His strength setteth fast the mountains : and is girded about with power.

7 Who stilleth the raging of the sea : and the noise of his waves, and the madness of the people.

8 They also that dwell in the uttermost parts of the earth shall be afraid at Thy tokens : Thou that makest the outgoings of the morning and evening to praise Thee.

9 Thou visitest the earth, and blessest it : Thou makest it very plenteous.

10 The river of God is full of water : Thou preparest their corn, for so Thou providest for the earth.

11 Thou waterest her furrows, Thou sendest rain into the little valleys thereof : Thou makest it soft with the drops of rain, and blessest the increase of it.

12 Thou crownest the year with Thy goodness : and Thy clouds drop fatness.

13 They shall drop upon the dwellings of the wilderness : and the little hills shall rejoice on every side.

14 The folds shall be full of sheep : the valleys also shall stand so thick with corn, that they shall laugh and sing.

Glory be to the Father, &c.

Antiphon. Thou, O God : art praised in Sion.

Antiphon. My lips shall praise.

Deus, Deus meus. Ps. lxiii.
Deus misereatur. Ps. lxvii.

As in the Sunday Lauds, p. 140.

Antiphon. My lips shall praise : Thee as long as I live.

Antiphon. The Lord shall judge.

The Song of Hannah, Exultavit cor meum. 1 Sam. ii. 1.

1 My heart rejoiceth in the Lord : mine horn is exalted in the Lord.

My mouth is enlarged over mine enemies : because I rejoice in Thy Salvation.

2 There is none holy as the Lord ; for there is none beside Thee : neither is there any rock like our God.

3 Talk no more so exceeding proudly : let not arrogancy come out of your mouth.

For the Lord is a God of knowledge : and by Him actions are weighed.

4 The bows of the mighty men are broken : and they that stumbled are girded with strength.

5 They that were full have hired out themselves for bread : and they that were hungry ceased.

So that the barren hath born seven : and she that hath many children is waxed feeble.

6 The Lord killeth and maketh alive : He bringeth down to the grave, and bringeth up.

7 The Lord maketh poor and maketh rich, He bringeth low and lifteth up : He raiseth up the poor out of the dust, and lifteth up the beggar from the dunghill ;

8 To set them among princes : and to make them inherit the throne of glory.

For the pillars of the Earth are the Lord's : and He hath set the World upon them.

9 He will keep the feet of His Saints, and the wicked shall be silent in darkness : for by strength shall no man prevail.

10 The adversaries of the Lord shall be broken in pieces : out of heaven shall He thunder upon them.

The Lord shall judge the ends of the earth ; and He shall give strength unto His King : and exalt the horn of His Anointed.

Glory be to the Father, &c.

Antiphon. The Lord shall judge : the ends of the earth.

Antiphon. O praise God.

Laudate Dominum. Ps. cxlviii.
Cantate Domino. Ps. cxlix.
Laudate Dominum. Ps. cl.

As in the Sunday Lauds, p. 141.

Antiphon. O praise God : all ye heavens.

The Chapter, 1 Cor. xvi. 13, 14.

Watch ye, stand fast in the faith, quit you like men, be strong. Let all your things be done with charity.

℟. Thanks be to God.

In week-day Services this Chapter is said (1.) *daily from Epiphany to Ash-Wednesday, and* (2.) *daily from Trinity to Advent.*

Hymn for Wednesdays from Epiphany to Lent.

Nox et tenebræ et nubila.

Hence, night and clouds that night-
  time brings,
Confused and dark and troubled things :
The dawn is here ; the sky grows white ;
Christ is at hand : depart from sight !

Earth's dusky veil is torn away,
Pierced by the sparkling beams of day :
The world resumes its hues apace
Soon as the Day-star shows its face.

But Thee, O Christ, alone we seek,
With conscience pure and temper meek,
With tears and chants we humbly pray :
That Thou wouldst guide us through the
  day.

For many a shade obscures each sense,
Which needs Thy beams to purge it
 thence:
Light of the Morning Star, illume,
Serenely shining, all our gloom.

All laud to God the Father be;
All laud, Eternal Son, to Thee;
All laud, as is for ever meet,
To God the Holy Paraclete.   Amen.

℣. Have I not thought upon Thee when I was waking?

℟. Because Thou hast been my Helper.

On Wednesdays, from Trinity to Advent, is said the Hymn, Ecce jam noctis, *as in the Sunday Lauds, p.* 143, *with the*

℣. Have I not thought upon Thee when I was waking?

℟. Because Thou hast been my Helper.

Antiphon. That we should be saved.

Benedictus, St. Luke i. 68.

Antiphon. That we should be saved : from our enemies; and from the hands of all that hate us, Good Lord, deliver us.

Then follow the week-day Prayers, as at p. 150.

The Proper Collect.

℣. The Lord be with you.

℟. And with thy spirit.

℣. Bless we the Lord.

℟. Thanks be to God.

Then follow the Memorials, &c., as at the Sunday Lauds, pp. 144—146.

THURSDAY, AT LAUDS.

℣. Let Thy merciful kindness, O Lord, be upon us.

℟. As we do put our trust in Thee.

℣. O God, make speed to save us.

℟. O Lord, make haste to help us.

℣. Glory be to the Father, and to the Son : and to the Holy Ghost.

℟. As it was in the beginning, is now, and ever shall be : world without end.   Amen.

Alleluia.

But from Septuagesima to Wednesday in Holy Week, inclusive, is said instead of Alleluia,

Praise to Thee, O Lord, we sing,
Of Glory the Eternal King.

Antiphon. Against Thee only.

Miserere mei Deus, Ps. li., *as in the Monday Lauds, p.* 147.

Antiphon. Against Thee only : have I sinned. Have mercy upon me, O God.

Antiphon. Lord, Thou hast been.

Domine refugium.   Ps. xc.

1 Lord, Thou hast been our Refuge : from one generation to another.

2 Before the mountains were brought forth, or ever the earth and the world were made : Thou art God from everlasting, and world without end.

3 Thou turnest man to destruction : again Thou sayest, Come again, ye children of men.

4 For a thousand years in Thy sight are but as yesterday : seeing that is past as a watch in the night.

5 As soon as Thou scatterest them they are even as a sleep : and fade away suddenly like the grass.

6 In the morning it is green, and groweth up : but in the evening it is cut down, dried up, and withered.

7 For we consume away in Thy displeasure : and are afraid at Thy wrathful indignation.

8 Thou hast set our misdeeds before Thee : and our secret sins in the light of Thy Countenance.

9 For when Thou art angry all our days are gone : we bring our years to an end, as it were a tale that is told.

10 The days of our age are threescore years and ten; and though men be so strong that they come to fourscore years : yet is their strength then but labour and sorrow; so soon passeth it away, and we are gone.

11 But who regardeth the power of Thy wrath : for even thereafter as a man feareth, so is Thy displeasure.

12 So teach us to number our days : that we may apply our hearts unto wisdom.

13 Turn Thee again, O Lord, at the last : and be gracious unto Thy servants.

14 O satisfy us with Thy Mercy, and that soon : so shall we rejoice and be glad all the days of our life.

15 Comfort us again now after the time that Thou hast plagued us : and for the years wherein we have suffered adversity.

16 Show Thy servants Thy work : and their children Thy Glory.

17 And the glorious Majesty of the Lord our God be upon us : prosper Thou the work of our hands upon us, O prosper Thou our handywork.

Glory be to the Father, &c.

Antiphon. O Lord, Thou hast been : our Refuge.

Antiphon. Have I not thought?

Deus, Deus meus. Ps. lxiii.
Deus misereatur. Ps. lxvii.

As in the Sunday Lauds, p. 140.

Antiphon. Have I not thought : upon Thee when I was waking?

Antiphon. The Lord shall reign.

The Song of Moses, Cantemus Domino. Exodus xv. 1.

1 I will sing unto the Lord, for He hath triumphed gloriously : the horse and his rider hath He thrown into the sea.

2 The Lord is my Strength and my Song : and is become my Salvation.

He is my God, and I will prepare Him an habitation : my father's God, and I will exalt Him.

3 The Lord is a Man of War : the Lord is His Name.

4 Pharaoh's chariots and his host hath He cast into the sea : his chosen captains are drowned in the Red Sea.

5 The depths have covered them : they sank into the bottom as a stone.

6 Thy Right Hand, O Lord, is become glorious in power : Thy Right Hand, O Lord, hath dashed in pieces the enemy.

7 And in the greatness of Thine Excellency Thou hast overthrown

them that rose up against Thee: Thou sentest forth Thy wrath, which consumed them as stubble.

8 And with the blast of Thy nostrils the waters were gathered together, the flood stood upright as an heap : and the depths were congealed in the heart of the sea.

9 The enemy said, I will pursue, I will overtake, I will divide the spoil : my lust shall be satisfied upon them; I will draw my sword, my hand shall destroy them.

10 Thou didst blow with Thy Wind, the sea covered them : they sank as lead in the mighty waters.

11 Who is like unto Thee, O Lord, among the gods : who is like Thee, glorious in holiness, fearful in praises, doing wonders?

12 Thou stretchedst out Thy Right Hand : the earth swallowed them.

13 Thou in Thy mercy hast led forth the people which Thou hast Redeemed : Thou hast guided them in Thy strength, unto Thy holy habitation.

14 The people shall hear, and be afraid : sorrow shall take hold of the inhabitants of Palestina.

15 Then the dukes of Edom shall be amazed; the mighty men of Moab, trembling shall take hold upon them : all the inhabitants of Canaan shall melt away.

16 Fear and dread shall fall upon them; by the greatness of Thine Arm they shall be as still as a stone : till Thy people pass over, O Lord, till Thy people pass over, which Thou hast purchased.

17 Thou shalt bring them in, and plant them in the Mountain of Thine inheritance : in the Place, O Lord, which Thou hast made for Thee to dwell in, in the Sanctuary, O Lord, which Thy hands have established.

18 The Lord shall reign : for ever and ever.

19 For the horse of Pharaoh went in with his chariots and with his horsemen into the sea, and the Lord brought again the waters of the sea upon them : but the children of Israel went on dry land in the midst of the sea.

Glory be to the Father, &c.

Antiphon. The Lord shall reign: for ever and ever.

Antiphon. O praise.

Laudate Dominum. Ps. cxlviii.
Cantate Domino. Ps. cxlix.
Laudate Dominum. Ps. cl.

As in the Sunday Lauds, p. 141.

Antiphon. O praise : the Lord of heaven.

The Chapter, 1 Cor. xvi. 13, 14.

Watch ye, stand fast in the faith, quit you like men, be strong. Let all your things be done with charity.

R̲. Thanks be to God.

In week-day Services this Chapter is said (1.) *daily from Epiphany to Ash-Wednesday, and* (2.) *daily from Trinity to Advent.*

Hymn for Thursdays from Epiphany to Lent.

Lux ecce surgit aurea.

Behold the golden dawn arise;
The paling night forsakes the skies :
Those shades that hid the world from view,
And us to dangerous error drew.

May this new day be calmly pass'd,
May we keep pure while it shall last ;
Nor let our lips from truth depart,
Nor dark designs engage the heart.

So may the day speed on ; the tongue
No falsehood know, the hands no wrong ;
Our eyes from wanton gaze refrain ;
No guilt our guarded bodies stain.

For God, All-seeing, from on high
Surveys us with a watchful Eye ;
Each day our every act He knows,
From early dawn to evening's close.

All laud to God the Father be ;
All laud, Eternal Son, to Thee ;
All laud, as is for ever meet,
To God the Holy Paraclete.   Amen.

℣. Have I not thought upon Thee when I was waking?

℞. Because Thou hast been my Helper.

On Thursdays from Trinity to Advent is said the Hymn, Ecce jam noctis, *as in the Sunday Lauds, p. 143, with the*

℣. Have I not thought upon Thee when I was waking?

℞. Because Thou hast been my Helper.

Antiphon. Let us serve the Lord.

Benedictus, St. Luke i. 68.

Antiphon. Let us serve the Lord : in holiness and righteousness before Him ; and He shall deliver us out of the hand of our enemies.

Then follow the week-day Prayers, as at p. 150.

The Proper Collect.

℣. The Lord be with you.

℞. And with thy spirit.

℣. Bless we the Lord.

℞. Thanks be to God.

Then follow the Memorials, &c., p. 144—146.

FRIDAY, AT LAUDS.

℣. Let Thy merciful kindness, O Lord, be upon us.

℞. As we do put our trust in Thee.

℣. O God, make speed to save us.

℞. O Lord, make haste to help us.

℣. Glory be to the Father, and to the Son : and to the Holy Ghost ;

℞. As it was in the beginning, is now, and ever shall be : world without end.   Amen.

Alleluia.

But from Septuagesima to Wednesday in Holy Week, inclusive, is said instead of Alleluia,

Praise to Thee, O Lord, we sing,
Of Glory the Eternal King.

Antiphon. O stablish me.

Miserere mei Deus, Ps. li., *p.* 147.

Antiphon. O stablish me : with Thy free Spirit.

Antiphon. Hearken unto me.

Domine, exaudi. Psalm cxliii.

1 Hear my prayer, O Lord, and consider my desire : hearken unto me for Thy truth and righteousness' sake.

2 And enter not into judgment with Thy servant : for in Thy sight shall no man living be justified.

3 For the enemy hath persecuted my soul ; he hath smitten my life down to the ground : he hath laid me in the darkness, as the men that have been long dead.

4 Therefore is my spirit vexed within me : and my heart within me is desolate.

5 Yet do I remember the time past; I muse upon all Thy works : yea, I exercise myself in the works of Thy hands.

6 I stretch forth my hands unto Thee : my soul gaspeth unto Thee as a thirsty land.

7 Hear me, O Lord, and that soon, for my spirit waxeth faint : hide not Thy face from me, lest I be like unto them that go down into the pit.

8 O let me hear Thy lovingkindness betimes in the morning, for in Thee is my trust : show Thou me the way that I should walk in, for I lift up my soul unto Thee.

9 Deliver me, O Lord, from mine enemies : for I flee unto Thee to hide me.

10 Teach me to do the thing that pleaseth Thee, for Thou art my God : let Thy loving Spirit lead me forth into the land of righteousness.

11 Quicken me, O Lord, for Thy Name's sake : and for Thy righteousness' sake bring my soul out of trouble.

12 And of Thy goodness slay mine enemies : and destroy all them that vex my soul; for I am Thy servant.

Glory be to the Father, &c.

Antiphon. Hearken unto me : for Thy truth and righteousness' sake.

Antiphon. God show us.

Deus, Deus meus. Ps. lxiii.
Deus misereatur. Ps. lxvii.

As in the Sunday Lauds, p. 140.

Antiphon. God show us : the light of His countenance.

Antiphon. O Lord, I have heard.

The Song of Habakkuk, Domine audivi. Habakkuk iii.

2 O Lord, I have heard Thy speech, and was afraid : O Lord, revive Thy work in the midst of the years, in the midst of the years make known; in wrath remember mercy.

3 God came from Teman, and the Holy One from Mount Paran : His glory covered the heavens, and the earth was full of His praise.

4 And His brightness was as the light; He had horns coming out of His hand : and there was the hiding of His power.

5 Before Him went the pestilence : and burning coals went forth at His Feet.

6 He stood and measured the earth, He beheld and drove asunder the nations : and the everlasting mountains were scattered, the perpetual hills did bow; His ways are everlasting.

7 I saw the tents of Cushan in affliction : and the curtains of the land of Midian did tremble.

8 Was the Lord displeased against the rivers? was Thine anger against the rivers : was Thy wrath against the sea, that Thou didst ride upon Thine horses and Thy chariots of salvation?

9 Thy bow was made quite naked : according to the oaths of the tribes, even Thy word.

Thou didst cleave the earth with rivers : the mountains saw Thee, and trembled.

10 The overflowing of the water passed by : the deep uttered his voice, and lifted up his hands on high.

11 The sun and moon stood still

in their habitation : at the light of Thine arrows they went, and at the shining of Thy glittering spear.

12 Thou didst march through the land in indignation : Thou didst thresh the heathen in anger.

13 Thou wentest forth for the Salvation of Thy people, even for Salvation with Thine Anointed : Thou woundedst the head out of the house of the wicked, by discovering the foundation unto the neck.

14 Thou didst strike through with his staves the head of his villages ; they came out as a whirlwind to scatter me : their rejoicing was as to devour the poor secretly.

15 Thou didst walk through the sea with Thine horses : through the heap of great waters.

16 When I heard, my belly trembled ; my lips quivered at the voice ; rottenness entered into my bones ; and I trembled in myself : that I might rest in the day of trouble.

When He cometh up unto the people : He will invade them with His troops.

17 Although the fig-tree shall not blossom, neither shall fruit be in the vines : the labour of the olive shall fail, and the fields shall yield no meat ;

The flock shall be cut off from the fold : and there shall be no herd in the stalls ;

18 Yet I will rejoice in the Lord : I will joy in the God of my salvation.

19 The Lord God is my Strength, and He will make my feet like hinds' feet : and He will make me to walk upon mine high places.

Glory be to the Father, &c.

Antiphon. O Lord, I have heard : Thy speech and was afraid.

Antiphon. Praise Him in the cymbals.

Laudate Dominum. Ps. cxlviii.
Cantate Domino. Ps. cxlix.
Laudate Dominum. Ps. cl.

As in the Sunday Lauds, p. 141.

Antiphon. Praise Him in the cymbals : and dances ; praise Him upon the strings and pipe.

The Chapter, 1 Cor. xvi. 13, 14.

Watch ye, stand fast in the faith, quit you like men, be strong. Let all your things be done with charity.

℟. Thanks be to God.

In week-day Services this Chapter is said (1.) *daily from Epiphany to Ash-Wednesday, and* (2.) *daily from Trinity to Advent.*

Hymn for Fridays from Epiphany to Lent.

Æterna cœli Gloria.

Eternal Glory of the sky,
Blest Hope of frail humanity,
The Father's Sole-begotten One,
Yet born a spotless Virgin's Son :

Uplift us with Thine arm of might,
And let our hearts rise pure and bright ;
And ardent in God's praises, pay
The thanks we owe Him every day.

The Day-star's rays are glittering clear,
And tell that Day itself is near ;
The shadows of the night depart :
Thou, Holy Light, illume the heart !

Within our senses ever dwell,
And worldly darkness thence expel :
Long as the days of life endure
Preserve our souls devout and pure :

The Faith that first must be possess'd
Root deep within our inmost breast :
And joyous Hope in second place ;
Then Charity, Thy greatest grace.

All laud to God the Father be;
All laud, Eternal Son, to Thee;
All laud, as is for ever meet,
To God the Holy Paraclete. Amen.

℣. Have I not thought upon Thee when I was waking?

℟. Because Thou hast been my Helper.

On Fridays, from Trinity to Advent, is said the Hymn, Ecce jam noctis, *as in the Sunday Lauds, p.* 143, *with the*

℣. Have I not thought upon Thee when I was waking?

℟. Because Thou hast been my Helper.

Antiphon. Through the tender mercies.

Benedictus, St. Luke i. 68.

Antiphon. Through the tender mercies : of our God, whereby the Day-Spring from on high hath visited us.

Then follow the week-day Prayers, as at p. 150.

The Proper Collect.

℣. The Lord be with you.

℟. And with thy spirit.

℣. Bless we the Lord.

℟. Thanks be to God.

Then follow the Memorials, &c., as at the Sunday Lauds, pp. 144—147.

SATURDAY, AT LAUDS.

℣. Let Thy merciful kindness, O Lord, be upon us.

℟. As we do put our trust in Thee.

℣. O God, make speed to save us.

℟. O Lord, make haste to help us.

℣. Glory be to the Father, and to the Son : and to the Holy Ghost;

℟. As it was in the beginning, is now, and ever shall be : world without end. Amen.
Alleluia.

But from Septuagesima to Wednesday in Holy Week, inclusive, is said instead of Alleluia,

Praise to Thee, O Lord, we sing,
Of Glory the Eternal King.

Antiphon. O be favourable.

Miserere mei Deus, Ps. li., *as in the Monday Lauds, p.* 147.

Antiphon. O be favourable : and gracious unto Sion.

Antiphon. It is a good thing.

Bonum est confiteri. Ps. xcii.

1 It is a good thing to give thanks unto the Lord : and to sing praises unto Thy Name, O most Highest;

2 To tell of Thy loving-kindness early in the morning : and of Thy truth in the night season;

3 Upon an instrument of ten strings, and upon the lute : upon a loud instrument and upon the harp.

4 For Thou, Lord, hast made me glad through Thy works : and I will rejoice in giving praise for the operations of Thy Hands.

5 O Lord, how glorious are Thy works : Thy thoughts are very deep.

6 An unwise man doth not well consider this : and a fool doth not understand it.

7 When the ungodly are green as the grass, and when all the

workers of wickedness do flourish: then shall they be destroyed for ever; but Thou, Lord, art the most Highest for evermore.

8 For lo, Thine enemies, O Lord, lo, Thine enemies shall perish : and all the workers of wickedness shall be destroyed.

9 But mine horn shall be exalted like the horn of an unicorn : for I am anointed with fresh oil.

10 Mine eye also shall see his lust of mine enemies : and mine ear shall hear his desire of the wicked that rise up against me.

11 The righteous shall flourish like a palm-tree : and shall spread abroad like a cedar in Libanus.

12 Such as are planted in the house of the Lord : shall flourish in the courts of the House of our God.

13 They also shall bring forth more fruit in their age : and shall be fat and well-liking.

14 That they may show how true the Lord my Strength is : and that there is no unrighteousness in Him.

Glory be to the Father, &c.

Antiphon. It is a good thing : to give thanks unto the Lord.

Antiphon. All the ends of the world.

Deus, Deus meus. Ps. lxiii.
Deus misereatur. Ps. lxvii.

As in the Sunday Lauds, p. 140.

Antiphon. All the ends of the world : shall fear Him.

Antiphon. The Lord shall repent.

The Song of Moses, Audite cœli.
Deut. xxxii.

1 Give ear, O ye heavens, and I will speak : and hear, O earth, the words of my mouth.

2 My doctrine shall drop as the rain, my speech shall distil as the dew : as the small rain upon the tender herb, and as the showers upon the grass.

3 Because I will publish the Name of the Lord : ascribe ye greatness unto our God.

4 He is the Rock, His work is perfect. For all His ways are judgment : a God of truth and without iniquity, Just and Right is He.

5 They have corrupted themselves, their spot is not the spot of His children : they are a perverse and crooked generation.

6 Do ye thus requite the Lord, O foolish people and unwise : is not He thy Father that hath bought thee? hath He not made thee, and established thee?

7 Remember the days of old, consider the years of many generations : ask thy father, and he will show thee, thy elders, and they will tell thee.

8 When the Most High divided to the nations their inheritance, when He separated the sons of Adam : He set the bounds of the people, according to the number of the Children of Israel :

9 For the Lord's portion is His people : Jacob is the lot of His inheritance.

10 He found him in a desert land, and in the waste howling wilderness : He led him about, He instructed him, He kept him as the apple of His eye.

11 As an eagle stirreth up her nest, fluttereth over her young, spreadeth abroad her wings, taketh them, beareth them on her wings : so the Lord alone did lead him, and there was no strange god with him.

13 He made him ride on the

high places of the earth, that he might eat the increase of the fields : and He made him suck honey out of the Rock, and oil out of the flinty rock :

14 Butter of kine, and milk of sheep, with fat of lambs and rams of the breed of Basan, and goats with the fat of kidneys of Wheat: and thou didst drink the pure Blood of the grape.

15 But Jeshurun waxed fat, and kicked : thou art waxen fat, thou art grown thick, thou art covered with fatness.

Then he forsook God Which made him : and lightly esteemed the Rock of his salvation.

16 They provoked Him to jealousy with strange gods : with abominations provoked they Him to anger.

17 They sacrificed unto devils, not to God : to gods whom they knew not ; to new gods that came newly up, whom your fathers feared not.

18 Of the Rock that begat thee, thou art unmindful: and hast forgotten God that formed thee.

19 And when the Lord saw it He abhorred them : because of the provoking of His sons and of His daughters.

20 And He said, I will hide My Face from them, I will see what their end shall be : for they are a very froward generation, children in whom is no faith.

21 They have moved Me to jealousy with that which is not God : they have provoked Me to anger with their vanities :

And I will move them to jealousy with those which are not a people : I will provoke them to anger with a foolish nation.

22 For a fire is kindled in Mine anger, and shall burn unto the lowest hell : and shall consume the earth with her increase, and set on fire the foundations of the mountains.

23 I will heap mischiefs upon them : I will spend Mine arrows upon them.

24 They shall be burnt with hunger, and devoured with burning heat, and with bitter destruction : I will also send the teeth of beasts upon them, with the poison of serpents of the dust.

25 The sword without and terror within shall destroy both the young man and the virgin : the suckling also, with the man of grey hairs.

26 I said, I would scatter them into corners : I would make the remembrance of them to cease from among men :

27 Were it not that I feared the wrath of the enemy ; lest their adversaries should behave themselves strangely : and lest they should say, Our hand is high, and the Lord hath not done all this.

28 For they are a nation void of counsel : neither is there any understanding in them.

29 O that they were wise, that they understood this : that they would consider their latter end.

30 How should one chase a thousand, and two put ten thousand to flight : except their Rock had sold them, and the Lord had shut them up.

31 For their rock is not as our Rock : even our enemies themselves being judges.

32 For their vine is of the vine of Sodom, and of the fields of Gomorrah : their grapes are grapes of gall, their clusters are bitter, their wine is the poison of dragons, and the cruel venom of asps.

34 Is not this laid up in store with Me, and sealed up among My treasures: to Me belongeth vengeance and recompense.

35 Their foot shall slide in due time, for the day of their calamity is at hand: and the things that shall come upon them make haste.

36 For the Lord shall judge His people, and repent Himself for His servants: when He seeth that their power is gone, and there is none shut up, or left.

37 And He shall say, Where are their gods, their rock in whom they trusted: which did eat the fat of their sacrifices, and drank the wine of their drink offerings? Let them rise up and help you, and be your protection.

39 See now that I, even I, am He, and there is no god with Me: I kill, and I make alive; I wound, and I heal, neither is there any that can deliver out of My hand.

40 For I lift up My hand to heaven: and say, I live for ever.

41 If I whet My glittering sword, and Mine Hand take hold on judgment: I will render vengeance to Mine enemies, and will reward them that hate Me.

42 I will make Mine arrows drunk with blood, and My sword shall devour flesh: and that with the blood of the slain, and of the captives, from the beginning of revenges upon the enemy.

43 Rejoice, O ye nations, with His people: for He will avenge the blood of His servants, and will render vengeance to His adversaries, and will be merciful unto His land, and to His people.

Glory be to the Father, &c.

Antiphon. The Lord shall repent: Himself for His servants.

Antiphon. Praise Him.

Laudate Dominum. Ps. cxlviii.
Cantate Domino. Ps. cxlix.
Laudate Dominum. Ps. cl.

As in the Sunday Lauds, p. 141.

Antiphon. Praise Him: on the well-tuned cymbals.

The Chapter, 1 Cor. xvi. 13, 14.

Watch ye, stand fast in the faith, quit you like men, be strong. Let all your things be done with charity.

℟. Thanks be to God.

In week-day Services this Chapter is said at Lauds (1.) *daily from Epiphany to Ash-Wednesday, and* (2.) *daily from Trinity to Advent.*

Hymn for Saturdays from Epiphany to Lent.

Aurora jam spargit polum.

Dawn sprinkles all the East with light;
Day o'er the earth is gliding bright;
Morn's glittering rays their course begin;
Farewell to darkness and to sin.

Each phantom of the night depart,
Each thought of guilt forsake the heart;
Let every ill that darkness brought
Beneath its shade, now come to nought.

So that last morning, dread and great,
Which we with trembling hope await,
With blessed light for us shall glow,
Who chant the song we sang below,—

All laud to God the Father be;
All laud, Eternal Son, to Thee;
All laud, as is for ever meet,
To God the Holy Paraclete. Amen.

℣. Have I not thought upon Thee when I was waking?

℟. Because Thou hast been my Helper.

On Saturdays, from Trinity to Advent, is said the Hymn, Ecce jam noctis, *as in the Sunday Lauds, p.* 143, *with the*

℣. Have I not thought upon Thee when I was waking?

℟. Because Thou hast been my Helper.

Antiphon. Guide our feet.

Benedictus, St. Luke i. 68.

Antiphon. Guide our feet, O Lord, into the way of peace.

Then follow the week-day Prayers, as at p. 150.

The Proper Collect.
℣. The Lord be with you.
℟. And with thy spirit.
℣. Bless we the Lord.
℟. Thanks be to God.

Then follow the Memorials, &c., as at the Sunday Lauds, p. 144—147.

Here end the Lauds.

AT PRIME.

SUNDAY.

℣. O God, make speed to save us.

℟. O Lord, make haste to help us.

℣. Glory be to the Father, and to the Son : and to the Holy Ghost ;

℟. As it was in the beginning, is now, and ever shall be : world without end. Amen.

Alleluia.

But from Septuagesima Sunday to Wednesday in Holy Week, inclusive, is said instead of Alleluia,

Praise to Thee, O Lord, we sing,
Of Glory the Eternal King.

Hymn. Jam lucis orto sidere.

Now that the daylight fills the sky,
We lift our hearts to God on high,
That He, in all we do or say,
Would keep us free from harm to-day ;

Would guard our hearts and tongues from strife :
From anger's din would hide our life :
From all ill sights would turn our eyes ;
Would close our ears from vanities :

Would keep our inmost conscience pure :
Our souls from folly would secure :
Would bid us check the pride of sense
With due and holy abstinence.

So we, when this new day is gone,
And night in turn is drawing on,
With conscience by the world unstained
Shall praise His Name for victory gained.

All laud to God the Father be ;
All praise, Eternal Son, to Thee ;
All praise for ever, as is meet,
To God the Holy Paraclete. Amen.

Antiphon when no other is given in the Proper Service. Alleluia.

Deus, in nomine. Ps. liv.

1 Save me, O God, for Thy Name's sake : and avenge me in Thy strength.

2 Hear my prayer, O God : and hearken unto the words of my mouth.

3 For strangers are risen up against me : and tyrants, which have not God before their eyes, seek after my soul.

4 Behold, God is my Helper : the Lord is with them that uphold my soul.

5 He shall reward evil unto mine enemies : destroy Thou them in Thy truth.

6 An offering of a free heart will I give Thee, and praise Thy Name, O Lord : because It is so comfortable.

7 For He hath delivered me

out of all my trouble : and mine eye hath seen his desire upon mine enemies.

Glory be to the Father, &c.

Confitemini Domino. Ps. cxviii.

1 O give thanks unto the Lord, for He is gracious : because His mercy endureth for ever.

2 Let Israel now confess, that He is gracious : and that His mercy endureth for ever.

3 Let the house of Aaron now confess : that His mercy endureth for ever.

4 Yea, let them now that fear the Lord confess : that His mercy endureth for ever.

5 I called upon the Lord in trouble : and the Lord heard me at large.

6 The Lord is on my side : I will not fear what man doeth unto me.

7 The Lord taketh my part with them that help me : therefore shall I see my desire upon mine enemies.

8 It is better to trust in the Lord : than to put any confidence in man.

9 It is better to trust in the Lord : than to put any confidence in princes.

10 All nations compassed me round about : but in the Name of the Lord will I destroy them.

11 They kept me in on every side, they kept me in, I say, on every side : but in the Name of the Lord will I destroy them.

12 They came about me like bees, and are extinct even as the fire among the thorns : for in the Name of the Lord I will destroy them.

13 Thou hast thrust sore at me, that I might fall : but the Lord was my Help.

14 The Lord is my strength, and my song : and is become my Salvation.

15 The voice of joy and health is in the dwellings of the righteous : the Right Hand of the Lord bringeth mighty things to pass.

16 The Right Hand of the Lord hath the pre-eminence : the Right Hand of the Lord bringeth mighty things to pass.

17 I shall not die, but live : and declare the works of the Lord.

18 The Lord hath chastened and corrected me : but He hath not given me over unto death.

19 Open me the gates of righteousness : that I may go into them, and give thanks unto the Lord.

20 This is the Gate of the Lord : the righteous shall enter into it.

21 I will thank Thee, for Thou hast heard me : and art become my Salvation.

22 The same Stone which the builders refused : is become the Head-Stone in the corner.

23 This is the Lord's doing : and it is marvellous in our eyes.

24 This is the Day which the Lord hath made : we will rejoice and be glad in it.

25 Help me now, O Lord : O Lord, send us now prosperity.

26 Blessed be He that Cometh in the Name of the Lord : we have wished you good luck, ye that are of the house of the Lord.

27 God is the Lord Who hath showed us light : bind the Sacrifice with cords, yea, even unto the horns of the altar.

28 Thou art my God, and I will thank Thee : Thou art my God, and I will praise Thee.

29 O give thanks unto the Lord,

for He is gracious : and His mercy endureth for ever.

Glory be to the Father, &c.

Beati immaculati. Ps. cxix.

1 Blessed are those that are undefiled in the way : and walk in the law of the Lord.

2 Blessed are they that keep His testimonies : and seek Him with their whole heart.

3 For they who do no wickedness : walk in His ways.

4 Thou hast charged : that we shall diligently keep Thy commandments.

5 O that my ways were made so direct : that I might keep Thy statutes!

6 So shall I not be confounded : while I have respect unto all Thy commandments.

7 I will thank Thee with an unfeigned heart : when I shall have learned the judgments of Thy righteousness.

8 I will keep Thy ceremonies : O forsake me not utterly.

9 Wherewithal shall a young man cleanse his way : even by ruling himself after Thy Word.

10 With my whole heart have I sought Thee : O let me not go wrong out of Thy commandments.

11 Thy words have I hid within my heart : that I should not sin against Thee.

12 Blessed art Thou, O Lord : O teach me Thy statutes.

13 With my lips have I been telling : of all the judgments of Thy mouth.

14 I have had as great delight in the way of Thy testimonies : as in all manner of riches.

15 I will talk of Thy commandments : and have respect unto Thy ways.

16 My delight shall be in Thy statutes : and I will not forget Thy Word.

Glory be to the Father, &c.

Retribue servo Tuo.

17 O do well unto Thy servant : that I may live, and keep Thy Word.

18 Open Thou mine eyes : that I may see the wondrous things of Thy law.

19 I am a stranger upon earth : O hide not Thy commandments from me.

20 My soul breaketh out for the very fervent desire : that it hath alway unto Thy judgments.

21 Thou hast rebuked the proud : and cursed are they that do err from Thy commandments.

22 O turn from me shame and rebuke : for I have kept Thy testimonies.

23 Princes also did sit and speak against me : but Thy servant is occupied in Thy statutes.

24 For Thy testimonies are my delight : and my counsellors.

25 My soul cleaveth to the dust : O quicken Thou me according to Thy Word.

26 I have acknowledged my ways, and Thou heardest me : O teach me Thy statutes.

27 Make me to understand the way of Thy commandments : and so shall I talk of Thy wondrous works.

28 My soul melteth away for very heaviness : comfort Thou me according unto Thy Word.

29 Take from me the way of lying : and cause Thou me to make much of Thy law.

30 I have chosen the way of truth : and Thy judgments have I laid before me.

31 I have stuck unto Thy testimonies : O Lord, confound me not.

32 I will run the way of Thy commandments : when Thou hast set my heart at liberty.

Glory be to the Father, &c.

Antiphon. Alleluia.

[*From Septuagesima Sunday to Easter instead of Confitemini Domino*, Ps. cxviii., *is said*, *Dominus regnavit*, Ps. xciii.]

Antiphon. O Holy and Undivided Trinity.

Ps. *Quicunque vult.*

Whosoever will be saved : before all things it is necessary that he hold the Catholick Faith.

Which Faith except every one do keep whole and undefiled : without doubt he shall perish everlastingly.

And the Catholick Faith is this : That we worship one God in Trinity, and Trinity in Unity ;

Neither confounding the Persons : nor dividing the Substance.

For there is one Person of the Father, another of the Son : and another of the Holy Ghost.

But the Godhead of the Father, of the Son, and of the Holy Ghost, is all One : the Glory equal, the Majesty co-eternal.

Such as the Father is, such is the Son : and such is the Holy Ghost.

The Father uncreate, the Son uncreate : and the Holy Ghost uncreate.

The Father incomprehensible, the Son incomprehensible : and the Holy Ghost incomprehensible.

The Father eternal, the Son eternal : and the Holy Ghost eternal.

And yet They are not three eternals : but One Eternal.

As also there are not three incomprehensibles, nor three uncreated : but One Uncreated, and One Incomprehensible.

So likewise the Father is Almighty, the Son Almighty : and the Holy Ghost Almighty.

And yet They are not three almighties : but One Almighty.

So the Father is God, the Son is God : and the Holy Ghost is God.

And yet They are not three Gods : but One God.

So likewise the Father is Lord, the Son Lord : and the Holy Ghost Lord.

And yet not three Lords : but One Lord.

For like as we are compelled by the Christian Verity : to acknowledge every Person by Himself to be God and Lord ;

So are we forbidden by the Catholick Religion : to say, There be three Gods, or three Lords.

The Father is made of none : neither created, nor begotten.

The Son is of the Father alone : not made, nor created, but begotten.

The Holy Ghost is of the Father and of the Son : neither made, nor created, nor begotten, but Proceeding.

So there is one Father, not three Fathers ; one Son, not three Sons : one Holy Ghost, not three Holy Ghosts.

And in this Trinity none is afore, or after other : none is greater, or less than another ;

But the whole Three Persons are co-eternal together : and co-equal.

So that in all things, as is aforesaid : the Unity in Trinity, and the Trinity in Unity is to be worshipped.

He therefore that will be saved : must thus think of the Trinity.

Furthermore, it is necessary to everlasting Salvation : that he also believe rightly the Incarnation of our Lord Jesus Christ.

For the right Faith is, that we believe and confess : that our Lord Jesus Christ, the Son of God, is God and Man.

God, of the substance of the Father, begotten before the worlds : and Man of the substance of His Mother, born in the world ;

Perfect God, and perfect Man : of a reasonable soul and human flesh subsisting ;

Equal to the Father, as touching His Godhead : and Inferior to the Father, as touching His Manhood.

Who although He be God and Man : yet He is not two, but One Christ ;

One ; not by conversion of the Godhead into flesh : but by taking of the Manhood into God.

One altogether ; not by confusion of Substance : but by unity of Person.

For as the reasonable soul and flesh is one man : so God and Man is One Christ ;

Who suffered for our salvation : descended into hell, rose again the third day from the dead.

He ascended into heaven, He sitteth on the right hand of the Father, God Almighty : from whence He shall come to judge the quick and the dead.

At Whose coming all men shall rise again with their bodies : and shall give account for their own works.

And they that have done good shall go into life everlasting : and they that have done evil into everlasting fire.

This is the Catholick Faith : which except a man believe faithfully, he cannot be saved.

Glory be to the Father, &c.

Antiphon. O Holy and Undivided Trinity, with heart and mouth we confess, praise and bless Thee the Father Eternal, Thee the Only-begotten Son, Thee the Holy Ghost the Comforter : To Thee be glory for ever. (*In Eastertide is added*, Alleluia.)

The Chapter, 1 Tim. i. 17.

Now unto the King Eternal, Immortal, Invisible, the only wise God, be honour and glory for ever and ever. Amen.

R. Jesu Christ, Son of the living God, have mercy upon us. ℣. Thou that sittest at the Right Hand of the Father. ℞. Have mercy upon us. ℣. Glory be to the Father, and to the Son : and to the Holy Ghost. ℞. Jesu Christ, Son of the living God, have mercy upon us.

℣. O Lord, arise, help us.

℞. And deliver us, for Thy Name's sake.

(*This* ℣. Thou that sittest, *is altered on certain days, as is marked in the Proper Services.*)

℣. The Lord be with you.

℞. And with thy spirit.

Let us pray.

O LORD, our Heavenly Father, Almighty and Everlasting

God, Who hast safely brought us to the beginning of this day; Defend us in the same with Thy mighty Power; and grant that this day we fall into no sin, neither run into any kind of danger; but that all our doings may be ordered by Thy governance, to do always that is righteous in Thy sight; through Jesus Christ our Lord. *Amen.*

℣. The Lord be with you.

℟. And with thy spirit.

℣. Bless we the Lord.

℟. Thanks be to God.

℣. May the souls of the Faithful, through the mercy of God, rest in peace.

℟. Amen.

ON FESTIVALS.

Everything as above on Sundays, till the end of Ps. liv., *Deus in nomine Tuo, (except that instead of* Alleluia, *is begun the Antiphon given in the Proper Services for the Seasons or the Common of Saints.) Then is said* Ps. cxix. *as above, to the 33rd verse: then the Proper Antiphon, the Chapter and the rest as above.*

ON WEEK-DAYS.

℣. O God, make speed, &c.

Hymn, Jam lucis orto sidere, *p.* 166.

Antiphon. Blessed are those that walk.

The Advent Antiphon. Come and deliver.

The Lent Antiphon. As I live.

The Passiontide Antiphon. The ungodly are minded.

Deus, in nomine Tuo. Ps. liv.

1 Save me, O God, for Thy Name's sake : and avenge me in Thy Strength.

2 Hear my prayer, O God : and hearken unto the words of my mouth.

3 For strangers are risen up against me : and tyrants, which have not God before their eyes, seek after my soul.

4 Behold, God is my Helper : the Lord is with them that uphold my soul.

5 He shall reward evil unto mine enemies : destroy Thou them in Thy truth.

6 An offering of a free heart will I give Thee, and praise Thy Name, O Lord : because It is so comfortable.

7 For He hath delivered me out of all my trouble : and mine eye hath seen his desire upon mine enemies.

Glory be to the Father, &c.

On each day of the week, except Saturday, is said one of the following Psalms, but on Saturday is here begun immediately Ps. cxix., *Beati immaculati, as above.*

ON MONDAY.

Domini est terra. Ps. xxiv.

1 The earth is the Lord's and all that therein is : the compass of the world, and they that dwell therein.

2 For He hath founded it upon the seas : and prepared it upon the floods.

3 Who shall Ascend into the hill of the Lord : or who shall Rise up in His holy place?

4 Even he that hath clean hands, and a pure heart : and that hath not lift up his mind unto vanity, nor sworn to deceive his neighbour.

5 He shall receive the blessing from the Lord : and righteousness from the God of his salvation.

6 This is the generation of them that seek Him : even of them that seek thy face, O Jacob.

7 Lift up your heads, O ye gates, and be ye lift up, ye everlasting doors : and the King of Glory shall come in.

8 Who is the King of Glory : it is the Lord strong and mighty, even the Lord mighty in battle.

9 Lift up your heads, O ye gates, and be ye lift up, ye everlasting doors : and the King of Glory shall come in.

10 Who is the King of Glory : even the Lord of hosts, He is the King of Glory.

Glory be to the Father, &c.

ON TUESDAY.

Ad Te, Domine, levavi. Ps. xxv.

1 Unto Thee, O Lord, will I lift up my soul; my God, I have put my trust in Thee : O let me not be confounded, neither let mine enemies triumph over me.

2 For all they that hope in Thee shall not be ashamed : but such as transgress without a cause shall be put to confusion.

3 Show me Thy ways, O Lord : and teach me Thy paths.

4 Lead me forth in Thy truth, and learn me : for Thou art the God of my Salvation; in Thee hath been my hope all the day long.

5 Call to remembrance, O Lord, Thy tender mercies : and Thy lovingkindnesses, which have been ever of old.

6 O remember not the sins and offences of my youth : but according to Thy mercy think Thou upon me, O Lord, for Thy goodness.

7 Gracious and righteous is the Lord : therefore will He teach sinners in the way.

8 Them that are meek shall He guide in judgment : and such as are gentle, them shall He learn His way.

9 All the paths of the Lord are mercy and truth : unto such as keep His covenant, and His testimonies.

10 For Thy Name's sake, O Lord : be merciful unto my sin, for it is great.

11 What man is he, that feareth the Lord : him shall He teach in the way that He shall choose.

12 His soul shall dwell at ease : and his seed shall inherit the land.

13 The secret of the Lord is among them that fear Him : and He will show them His covenant.

14 Mine eyes are ever looking unto the Lord : for He shall pluck my feet out of the net.

15 Turn Thee unto me, and have mercy upon me : for I am desolate and in misery.

16 The sorrows of my heart are enlarged : O bring Thou me out of my troubles.

17 Look upon my adversity and misery : and forgive me all my sin.

18 Consider mine enemies, how

many they are : and they bear a tyrannous hate against me.

19 O keep my soul, and deliver me : let me not be confounded, for I have put my trust in Thee.

20 Let perfectness and righteous dealing wait upon me : for my hope hath been in Thee.

21 Deliver Israel, O God : out of all his troubles.

ON WEDNESDAY.

Judica me, Domine. Ps. xxvi.

1 Be Thou my Judge, O Lord, for I have walked innocently : my trust hath been also in the Lord, therefore shall I not fall.

2 Examine me, O Lord, and prove me : try out my reins and my heart.

3 For Thy Lovingkindness is ever before mine eyes : and I will walk in Thy Truth.

4 I have not dwelt with vain persons : neither will I have fellowship with the deceitful.

5 I have hated the congregation of the wicked : and will not sit among the ungodly.

6 I will wash my hands in innocency, O Lord : and so will I go to Thine Altar ;

7 That I may show the voice of thanksgiving : and tell of all Thy wondrous works.

8 Lord, I have loved the habitation of Thy House : and the Place where Thine Honour dwelleth.

9 O shut not up my soul with the sinners : nor my life with the blood-thirsty ;

10 In whose hands is wickedness : and their right hand is full of gifts.

11 But as for me, I will walk innocently : O deliver me, and be merciful unto me.

12 My foot standeth right : I will praise the Lord in the congregations.

Glory be to the Father, &c.

ON THURSDAY.

Dominus regit me. Ps. xxiii.

1 The Lord is my Shepherd : therefore can I lack nothing.

2 He shall feed me in a green pasture : and lead me forth beside the waters of comfort.

3 He shall convert my soul : and bring me forth in the paths of righteousness, for His Name's sake.

4 Yea, though I walk through the valley of the shadow of death, I will fear no evil : for Thou art with me ; Thy rod and Thy staff comfort me.

5 Thou shalt prepare a Table before me against them that trouble me : Thou hast anointed my head with oil, and my cup shall be full.

6 But Thy Lovingkindness and Mercy shall follow me all the days of my life : and I will dwell in the House of the Lord for ever.

Glory be to the Father, &c.

ON FRIDAY.

Deus, Deus meus. Ps. xxii.

1 My God, My God, look upon Me ; why hast Thou forsaken Me : and art so far from My health, and from the words of My complaint?

2 O My God, I cry in the daytime, but Thou hearest not : and in the night-season also I take no rest.

3 And Thou continuest holy : O Thou worship of Israel.

4 Our fathers hoped in Thee : they trusted in Thee, and Thou didst deliver them.

5 They called upon Thee, and were holpen : they put their trust in Thee, and were not confounded.

6 But as for Me, I am a Worm, and no man : a very scorn of men, and the outcast of the people.

7 All they that see Me laugh Me to scorn : they shoot out their lips, and shake their heads, saying,

8 He trusted in God, that He would deliver Him : let Him deliver Him, if He will have Him.

9 But Thou art He that took Me out of My mother's womb : Thou wast My hope when I hanged yet upon My mother's breasts.

10 I have been left unto Thee ever since I was born : Thou art My God even from My mother's womb.

11 O go not from Me, for trouble is hard at hand : and there is none to help Me.

12 Many oxen are come about Me : fat bulls of Basan close Me in on every side.

13 They gape upon Me with their mouths : as it were a ramping and a roaring lion.

14 I am poured out like water, and all My Bones are out of joint : My Heart also in the midst of My Body is even like melting wax.

15 My strength is dried up like a potsherd, and My tongue cleaveth to My gums : and Thou shalt bring Me into the dust of death.

16 For many dogs are come about Me : and the counsel of the wicked layeth siege against Me.

17 They pierced My Hands and My Feet; I may tell all My Bones : they stand staring and looking upon Me.

18 They part My garments among them : and cast lots upon My vesture.

19 But be not Thou far from Me, O Lord : Thou art My Succour, haste Thee to help Me.

20 Deliver My Soul from the sword : My Darling from the power of the dog.

21 Save Me from the lion's mouth : Thou hast heard Me also from among the horns of the unicorns.

22 I will declare Thy Name unto My brethren : in the midst of the congregation will I praise Thee.

23 O praise the Lord, ye that fear Him : magnify Him, all ye of the seed of Jacob, and fear Him, all ye seed of Israel.

24 For He hath not despised, nor abhorred, the low estate of the poor : He hath not hid His face from him, but when he called unto Him He heard him.

25 My praise is of Thee in the great congregation : my vows will I perform in the sight of them that fear Him.

26 The poor shall eat and be satisfied : they that seek after the Lord shall praise Him; your heart shall live for ever.

27 All the ends of the world shall remember themselves, and be turned unto the Lord : and all the kindreds of the nations shall worship before Him.

28 For the kingdom is the Lord's : and He is the Governor among the people.

29 All such as be fat upon earth : have eaten and worshipped.

30 All they that go down into the dust shall kneel before Him :

and no man hath quickened his own soul.

31 My seed shall serve Him : they shall be counted unto the Lord for a generation.

32 They shall come, and the heavens shall declare His righteousness : unto a people that shall be born, whom the Lord hath made.

Glory be to the Father, &c.

Beati immaculati. Ps. cxix.

1 Blessed are those that are undefiled in the way : and walk in the law of the Lord.

2 Blessed are they that keep His testimonies : and seek Him with their whole heart.

3 For they who do no wickedness : walk in His ways.

4 Thou hast charged : that we shall diligently keep Thy commandments.

5 O that my ways were made so direct : that I might keep Thy statutes!

6 So shall I not be confounded : while I have respect unto all Thy commandments.

7 I will thank Thee with an unfeigned heart : when I shall have learned the judgments of Thy righteousness.

8 I will keep Thy ceremonies : O forsake me not utterly.

9 Wherewithal shall a young man cleanse his way : even by ruling himself after Thy Word.

10 With my whole heart have I sought Thee : O let me not go wrong out of Thy commandments.

11 Thy words have I hid within my heart : that I should not sin against Thee.

12 Blessed art Thou, O Lord : O teach me Thy statutes.

13 With my lips have I been telling : of all the judgments of Thy mouth.

14 I have had as great delight in the way of Thy testimonies : as in all manner of riches.

15 I will talk of Thy commandments : and have respect unto Thy ways.

16 My delight shall be in Thy statutes : and I will not forget Thy Word.

Glory be to the Father, &c.

Retribue servo Tuo.

17 O do well unto Thy servant : that I may live, and keep Thy Word.

18 Open Thou mine eyes : that I may see the wondrous things of Thy law.

19 I am a stranger upon earth : O hide not Thy commandments from me.

20 My soul breaketh out for the very fervent desire : that it hath alway unto Thy judgments.

21 Thou hast rebuked the proud : and cursed are they that do err from Thy commandments.

22 O turn from me shame and rebuke : for I have kept Thy testimonies.

23 Princes also did sit and speak against me : but Thy servant is occupied in Thy statutes.

24 For Thy testimonies are my delight : and my counsellors.

25 My soul cleaveth to the dust : O quicken Thou me, according to Thy Word.

26 I have acknowledged my ways, and Thou heardest me : O teach me Thy statutes.

27 Make me to understand the way of Thy commandments : and so shall I talk of Thy wondrous works.

28 My soul melteth away for

very heaviness : comfort Thou me according unto Thy Word.

29 Take from me the way of lying : and cause Thou me to make much of Thy law.

30 I have chosen the way of truth : and Thy judgments have I laid before me.

31 I have stuck unto Thy testimonies : O Lord, confound me not.

32 I will run the way of Thy commandments : when Thou hast set my heart at liberty.

Glory be to the Father, &c.

Antiphon. Blessed are those that walk : in the law of the Lord.

The Advent Antiphon. Come and deliver : us, O our God.

The Lent Antiphon. As I live : saith the Lord God, I have no pleasure in the death of the wicked; but that the wicked turn from his way, and live.

The Passiontide Antiphon. The ungodly are minded : to do Me some mischief, and My heart is disquieted within Me.

The Chapter, Zech. viii. 16.

Execute the judgment of truth and peace in your gates, saith the Lord.

R. Jesu Christ, Son of the living God, have mercy upon us. ℣. Thou that sittest at the Right Hand of the Father. ℟. Have mercy upon us. ℣. Glory be to the Father, and to the Son : and to the Holy Ghost. ℟. Jesu Christ, Son of the living God, have mercy upon us.

℣. O Lord, arise, help us.

℟. And deliver us for Thy Name's sake.

This ℣., Thou that sittest, is altered on certain days, as marked in the Proper Services.

Lord, have mercy upon us.
Christ, have mercy upon us.
Lord, have mercy upon us.

Our Father, &c.
I believe in God, &c.

℣. Unto Thee have I cried, O Lord.

℟. And early shall my prayer come before Thee.

℣. O let my mouth be filled with Thy praise.

℟. That I may sing of Thy glory and honour all the day long.

℣. Turn Thy Face from my sins.

℟. And put out all my misdeeds.

℣. Make me a clean heart, O God.

℟. And renew a right spirit within me.

℣. Cast me not away from Thy Presence.

℟. And take not Thy Holy Spirit from me.

℣. Give me the comfort of Thy help again.

℟. And stablish me with Thy free Spirit.

℣. Our help is in the Name of the Lord.

℟. Who hath made heaven and earth.

Then is said the following Confession.

We confess to God Almighty, the Father, the Son, and the Holy Ghost, in the sight of the whole company of heaven, that we have sinned exceedingly in thought, word, and deed, of our fault, our own fault, our own great fault; therefore we pray God to have mercy on us.

And those present shall say,

Almighty God have mercy upon us, and bring us to everlasting life. Amen.

[*Or he that sayeth the Office may say,*

I confess to Almighty God in the sight of the whole company of heaven, and to you, that I have sinned exceedingly in thought, word, and deed, of my fault, of my own fault, of my own grievous fault, and calling to mind the communion of Saints, I beseech you, brethren, to pray for me.

And those present shall answer,

Almighty God have mercy upon thee, forgive thy sins, deliver thee from evil, and bring thee to everlasting life. Amen.

Then those present shall say,

We confess to Almighty God in the sight of the whole company of heaven, and to thee, that we have sinned exceedingly in thought, word, and deed, of our fault, of our own fault, of our own grievous fault, and calling to mind the communion of Saints, we beseech thee to pray for us.

And he that sayeth the Office shall answer,

Almighty God have mercy upon you, forgive your sins, deliver you from evil, and bring you to everlasting life. Amen.]

[*And if a Priest be present, let him add,*

The Almighty and merciful Lord grant you Absolution and forgiveness of your sins, time for repentance, amendment of life, and the grace and comfort of His Holy Spirit. Amen.]

℣. Wilt Thou not turn again and quicken us, O Lord?

℟. That Thy people may rejoice in Thee.

℣. Show us Thy mercy, O Lord.

℟. And grant us Thy salvation.

℣. Vouchsafe, O Lord.

℟. To keep us this day without sin.

℣. O Lord, have mercy upon us.

℟. Have mercy upon us.

℣. O Lord, let Thy mercy lighten upon us.

℟. As our trust is in Thee.

[*On ordinary week-days, except after Easter, may here be said*

Miserere mei Deus. Ps. li.

Against Lust.

1 Have mercy upon me, O God, after Thy great goodness : according to the multitude of Thy mercies, do away mine offences.

2 Wash me throughly from my wickedness : and cleanse me from my sin.

3 For I acknowledge my faults : and my sin is ever before me.

4 Against Thee only have I sinned, and done this evil in Thy sight : that Thou mightest be justified in Thy saying, and clear when Thou art judged.

5 Behold, I was shapen in wickedness : and in sin hath my mother conceived me.

6 But lo, Thou requirest truth in the inward parts : and shalt make me to understand wisdom secretly.

7 Thou shalt purge me with hyssop, and I shall be clean : Thou shalt wash me, and I shall be whiter than snow.

8 Thou shalt make me hear of joy and gladness : that the bones which Thou hast broken may rejoice.

9 Turn Thy Face from my sins : and put out all my misdeeds.

10 Make me a clean heart, O God : and renew a right spirit within me.

11 Cast me not away from Thy presence : and take not Thy Holy Spirit from me.

12 O give me the comfort of Thy help again : and stablish me with Thy free Spirit.

13 Then shall I teach Thy ways unto the wicked : and sinners shall be converted unto Thee.

14 Deliver me from blood-guiltiness, O God, Thou that art the God of my health : and my tongue shall sing of Thy righteousness.

15 Thou shalt open my lips, O Lord : and my mouth shall show Thy praise.

16 For Thou desirest no sacrifice, else would I give it Thee : but Thou delightest not in burnt-offerings.

17 The sacrifice of God is a troubled spirit : a broken and contrite heart, O God, shalt Thou not despise.

18 O be favourable and gracious unto Sion : build Thou the walls of Jerusalem.

19 Then shalt Thou be pleased with the sacrifice of righteousness, with the burnt-offerings and oblations : then shall they offer young bullocks upon Thine Altars.

Glory be to the Father, &c.

But this Ps. li. *shall always be said here in Lent, and followed by*

Beati quorum. Ps. xxxii.
Against Pride.

1 Blessed is he whose unrighteousness is forgiven : and whose sin is covered.

2 Blessed is the man unto whom the Lord imputeth no sin : and in whose spirit there is no guile.

3 For while I held my tongue : my bones consumed away through my daily complaining.

4 For Thy hand is heavy upon me day and night : and my moisture is like the drought in summer.

5 I will acknowledge my sin unto Thee : and mine unrighteousness have I not hid.

6 I said, I will confess my sins unto the Lord : and so Thou forgavest the wickedness of my sin.

7 For this shall every one that is godly make his prayer unto Thee, in a time when Thou mayest be found : but in the great water-floods they shall not come nigh him.

8 Thou art a place to hide me in, Thou shalt preserve me from trouble : Thou shalt compass me about with songs of deliverance.

9 I will inform thee, and teach thee in the way wherein thou shalt go : and I will guide thee with Mine eye.

10 Be ye not like to horse and mule, which have no understanding : whose mouths must be held with bit and bridle, lest they fall upon thee.

11 Great plagues remain for the ungodly : but whoso putteth his trust in the Lord, mercy embraceth him on every side.

12 Be glad, O ye righteous, and rejoice in the Lord : and be joyful, all ye that are true of heart.

Glory be to the Father, &c.]

℣. Lord, hear our prayer.

℟. And let our cry come unto Thee.

℣. The Lord be with you.

℟. And with thy spirit.

Let us pray.

O LORD, our heavenly Father, Almighty and Everlasting God, Who hast safely brought us to the beginning of this day; Defend us in the same with Thy mighty Power; and grant that this day we fall into no sin, neither run into any kind of danger; but that all our doings may be ordered by Thy governance, to do always that is righteous in Thy sight; through Jesus Christ our Lord. *Amen.*

℣. The Lord be with you.

℟. And with thy spirit.

℣. Bless we the Lord.

℟. Thanks be to God.

℣. May the souls of the Faithful, through the mercy of God, rest in peace.

℟. Amen.

AT TERCE.

℣. O God, make speed to save us.

℟. O Lord, make haste to help us.

℣. Glory be to the Father, and to the Son: and to the Holy Ghost.

℟. As it was in the beginning, is now, and ever shall be: world without end. Amen.

Alleluia.

But from Septuagesima Sunday to Wednesday in Holy Week, inclusive, is said instead,

Praise to Thee, O Lord, we sing, Of Glory the Eternal King.

Hymn. Nunc Sancte nobis Spiritus.

Come, Holy Ghost, with God the Son,
And God the Father, ever One;
Shed forth Thy grace within our breast,
And dwell with us, a ready guest.

By every power, by heart and tongue,
By act and deed, Thy praise be sung;
Inflame with perfect love each sense,
That others' souls may kindle thence.

O Father, that we ask be done,
Through Jesus Christ, Thine Only Son,
Who, with the Holy Ghost, and Thee,
Shall live and reign eternally. Amen.

Antiphon. O let Thy loving mercies.

Legem pone. Ps. cxix.

33 Teach me, O Lord, the way of Thy statutes: and I shall keep it unto the end.

34 Give me understanding, and I shall keep Thy law: yea, I shall keep it with my whole heart.

35 Make me to go in the path of Thy commandments: for therein is my desire.

36 Incline mine heart unto Thy testimonies: and not to covetousness.

37 O turn away mine eyes, lest they behold vanity: and quicken Thou me in Thy way.

38 O stablish Thy word in Thy servant: that I may fear Thee.

39 Take away the rebuke that I am afraid of: for Thy judgments are good.

40 Behold, my delight is in Thy commandments : O quicken me in Thy righteousness.

41 Let Thy loving Mercy come also unto me, O Lord : even Thy Salvation, according unto Thy word.

42 So shall I make answer unto my blasphemers : for my trust is in Thy Word.

43 O take not the word of Thy truth utterly out of my mouth : for my hope is in Thy judgments.

44 So shall I always keep Thy law : yea, for ever and ever.

45 And I will walk at liberty : for I seek Thy commandments.

46 I will speak of Thy testimonies also, even before kings : and will not be ashamed.

47 And my delight shall be in Thy commandments : which I have loved.

48 My hands also will I lift up unto Thy commandments, which I have loved : and my study shall be in Thy statutes.

Glory be to the Father, &c.

Memor esto servi Tui.

49 O think upon Thy servant, as concerning Thy Word : wherein Thou hast caused me to put my trust.

50 The same is my comfort in my trouble : for Thy Word hath quickened me.

51 The proud have had me exceedingly in derision : yet have I not shrinked from Thy law.

52 For I remembered Thine everlasting judgments, O Lord : and received comfort.

53 I am horribly afraid : for the ungodly that forsake Thy law.

54 Thy statutes have been my songs : in the house of my pilgrimage.

55 I have thought upon Thy Name, O Lord, in the night-season : and have kept Thy law.

56 This I had : because I kept Thy commandments.

57 Thou art my portion, O Lord : I have promised to keep Thy law.

58 I made my humble petition in Thy presence with my whole heart : O be merciful unto me, according to Thy Word.

59 I called mine own ways to remembrance : and turned my feet unto Thy testimonies.

60 I made haste and prolonged not the time : to keep Thy commandments.

61 The congregations of the ungodly have robbed me : but I have not forgotten Thy law.

62 At midnight I will rise to give thanks unto Thee : because of Thy righteous judgments.

63 I am a companion of all them that fear Thee : and keep Thy commandments.

64 The earth, O Lord, is full of Thy mercy : O teach me Thy statutes.

Glory be to the Father, &c.

Bonitatem fecisti.

65 O Lord, Thou hast dealt graciously with Thy servant : according unto Thy Word.

66 O learn me true understanding and knowledge : for I have believed Thy commandments.

67 Before I was troubled, I went wrong : but now have I kept Thy Word.

68 Thou art good and gracious : O teach me Thy statutes.

69 The proud have imagined a lie against me : but I will keep Thy commandments with my whole heart.

70 Their heart is as fat as

brawn: but my delight hath been in Thy law.

71 It is good for me that I have been in trouble: that I may learn Thy statutes.

72 The law of Thy mouth is dearer unto me: than thousands of gold and silver.

73 Thy hands have made me and fashioned me: O give me understanding, that I may learn Thy commandments.

74 They that fear Thee will be glad when they see me: because I have put my trust in Thy Word.

75 I know, O Lord, that Thy judgments are right: and that Thou of very faithfulness hast caused me to be troubled.

76 O let Thy merciful kindness be my comfort: according to Thy Word unto Thy servant.

77 O let Thy loving mercies come unto me, that I may live: for Thy law is my delight.

78 Let the proud be confounded, for they go wickedly about to destroy me: but I will be occupied in Thy commandments.

79 Let such as fear Thee, and have known Thy testimonies: be turned unto me.

80 O let my heart be sound in Thy statutes: that I be not ashamed.

Glory be to the Father, &c.

[ON SUNDAYS.

Antiphon—

To Father, Son, and Holy Ghost,
The God Whom we adore;
Be glory as it was, is now,
And shall be evermore.

The Chapter, 2 Cor. xiii. 44.

The Grace of our Lord Jesus Christ, and the love of God, and the Communion of the Holy Ghost, be with us all. Amen.

R. Incline my heart unto Thy testimonies, and not to covetousness. V. Turn away mine eyes, lest they behold vanity, and quicken Thou me in Thy way. R. And not to covetousness. V. Glory be to the Father, and to the Son: and to the Holy Ghost. R. Incline my heart unto Thy testimonies, and not to covetousness.

V. I said, Lord, be merciful unto me.

R. Heal my soul, for I have sinned against Thee.]

On Sundays, and when the Sunday Psalms are to be said at Lauds, here is said immediately

The Collect.

[ON WEEK-DAYS.

Antiphon. O let Thy loving mercies: come unto me, that I may live.

The Chapter, Jer. xvii. 14.

Heal me, O Lord, and I shall be healed; save me, and I shall be saved; for Thou art my praise.

R. Heal my soul, for I have sinned against Thee. V. I said, Lord, be merciful unto me. R. For I have sinned against Thee. V. Glory be to the Father, and to the Son: and to the Holy Ghost. R. Heal my soul, for I have sinned against Thee.

V. Thou hast been my succour.

R. Leave me not, neither forsake me, O God of my Salvation.]

V. The Lord be with you.

R. And with thy spirit.

On week-days, (except from Easter to Trinity) here follows,

Lord, have mercy, &c.

And the rest of the week-day Prayers, as on Monday at Lauds, p. 150.

[*In Lent shall be said daily at Terce, Miserere mei Deus, Ps. li., followed by*

Domine, ne in furore. Ps. xxxviii.

Against Gluttony.

1 Put me not to rebuke, O Lord, in Thine anger : neither chasten me in Thy heavy displeasure.

2 For Thine arrows stick fast in me : and Thy hand presseth me sore.

3 There is no health in my flesh, because of Thy displeasure : neither is there any rest in my bones, by reason of my sin.

4 For my wickednesses are gone over my head : and are like a sore burden, too heavy for me to bear.

5 My wounds stink, and are corrupt : through my foolishness.

6 I am brought into so great trouble and misery : that I go mourning all the day long.

7 For my loins are filled with a sore disease : and there is no whole part in my body.

8 I am feeble, and sore smitten : I have roared for the very disquietness of my heart.

9 Lord, Thou knowest all my desire : and my groaning is not hid from Thee.

10 My heart panteth, my strength hath failed me : and the sight of mine eyes hath gone from me.

11 My lovers and my neighbours did stand looking upon my trouble : and my kinsmen stood afar off.

12 They also that sought after my life laid snares for me : and they that went about to do me evil talked of wickedness, and imagined deceit all the day long.

13 As for me, I was like a deaf man, and heard not : and as one that is dumb, who doth not open his mouth.

14 I became even as a man that heareth not : and in whose mouth are no reproofs.

15 For in Thee, O Lord, have I put my trust : Thou shalt answer for me, O Lord my God.

16 I have required that they, even mine enemies, should not triumph over me : for when my foot slipped, they rejoiced greatly against me.

17 And I truly, am set in the plague : and my heaviness is ever in my sight.

18 For I will confess my wickedness : and be sorry for my sin.

19 But mine enemies live, and are mighty : and they that hate me wrongfully are many in number.

20 They also that reward evil for good are against me : because I follow the thing that good is.

21 Forsake me not, O Lord my God : be not Thou far from me.

22 Haste Thee to help me : O Lord God of my salvation.

Glory be to the Father, &c.]

After the Collect, which is always that appointed to be said at Lauds,

℣. The Lord be with you.

℟. And with thy spirit.

℣. Bless we the Lord.

℟. Thanks be to God.

℣. May the souls of the Faithful, through the mercy of God, rest in peace.

℟. Amen.

And so shall end Terce, Sext, and None throughout the year, except on the three last days of Holy Week.

AT SEXT.

℣. O God, make speed to save us.

℟. O Lord, make haste to help us.

℣. Glory be to the Father, and to the Son : and to the Holy Ghost;

℟. As it was in the beginning, is now, and ever shall be : world without end. Amen.

Alleluia.

But from Septuagesima Sunday to Wednesday in Holy Week, inclusive, is said instead,

Praise to Thee, O Lord, we sing,
Of Glory the Eternal King.

Hymn. Rector potens verax Deus.

O God of truth, O Lord of might,
Who orderest time and change aright,
And send'st the early morning ray,
And light'st the glow of perfect day :

Extinguish Thou each sinful fire,
And banish every ill desire;
And while Thou keep'st the body whole,
Shed forth Thy peace upon the soul.

O Father, that we ask be done,
Through Jesus Christ, Thine only Son,
Who with the Holy Ghost and Thee,
Shall live and reign eternally. Amen.

Antiphon. Let me not.

Defecit anima mea. Ps. cxix.

81 My soul hath longed for Thy salvation : and I have a good hope because of Thy Word.

82 Mine eyes long sore for Thy Word : saying, O when wilt Thou comfort me?

83 For I am become like a bottle in the smoke : yet do I not forget Thy statutes.

84 How many are the days of Thy servant : when wilt Thou be avenged of them that persecute me?

85 The proud have digged pits for me : which are not after Thy law.

86 All Thy commandments are true : they persecute me falsely; O be Thou my Help.

87 They had almost made an end of me upon earth : but I forsook not Thy commandments.

88 O quicken me after Thy lovingkindness : and so shall I keep the testimonies of Thy mouth.

89 O Lord, Thy Word : endureth for ever in heaven.

90 Thy Truth also remaineth from one generation to another : Thou hast laid the foundation of the earth, and it abideth.

91 They continue this day according to Thine ordinance : for all things serve Thee.

92 If my delight had not been in Thy law : I should have perished in my trouble.

93 I will never forget Thy commandments : for with them Thou hast quickened me.

94 I am Thine, O save me : for I have sought Thy commandments.

95 The ungodly laid wait for me to destroy me : but I will consider Thy testimonies.

96 I see that all things come to an end : but Thy commandment is exceeding broad.

Glory be to the Father, &c.

Quomodo dilexi!

97 Lord, what love have I unto Thy law : all the day long is my study in it.

98 Thou through Thy commandments hast made me wiser than mine enemies : for they are ever with me.

99 I have more understanding than my teachers : for Thy testimonies are my study.

100 I am wiser than the aged : because I keep Thy commandments.

101 I have refrained my feet from every evil way : that I may keep Thy Word.

102 I have not shrunk from Thy judgments : for Thou teachest me.

103 O how sweet are Thy words unto my throat : yea, sweeter than honey unto my mouth.

104 Through Thy commandments I get understanding : therefore I hate all evil ways.

105 Thy Word is a lantern unto my feet : and a light unto my paths.

106 I have sworn, and am steadfastly purposed : to keep Thy righteous judgments.

107 I am troubled above measure : quicken me, O Lord, according to Thy Word.

108 Let the free-will offerings of my mouth please Thee, O Lord : and teach me Thy judgments.

109 My soul is alway in my hand : yet do I not forget Thy law.

110 The ungodly have laid a snare for me : but yet I swerved not from Thy commandments.

111 Thy testimonies have I claimed as mine heritage for ever : and why? they are the very joy of my heart.

112 I have applied my heart to fulfil Thy statutes alway : even unto the end.

Glory be to the Father, &c.

Iniquos odio habui.

113 I hate them that imagine evil things : but Thy law do I love.

114 Thou art my defence and shield : and my trust is in Thy Word.

115 Away from me, ye wicked : I will keep the commandments of my God.

116 O stablish me according to Thy Word, that I may live : and let me not be disappointed of my hope.

117 Hold Thou me up, and I shall be safe : yea, my delight shall be ever in Thy statutes.

118 Thou hast trodden down all them that depart from Thy statutes : for they imagine but deceit.

119 Thou puttest away all the ungodly of the earth like dross : therefore I love Thy testimonies.

120 My flesh trembleth for fear of Thee : and I am afraid of Thy judgments.

121 I deal with the thing that is lawful and right : O give me not over unto mine oppressors.

122 Make Thou Thy servant to delight in that which is good : that the proud do me no wrong.

123 Mine eyes are wasted away with looking for Thy Health : and for the Word of Thy righteousness.

124 O deal with Thy servant according unto Thy loving Mercy : and teach me Thy statutes.

125 I am Thy servant, O grant me understanding : that I may know Thy testimonies.

126 It is time for Thee, Lord, to lay to Thine hand : for they have destroyed Thy law.

127 For I love Thy commandments : above gold and precious stone.

128 Therefore hold I straight all Thy commandments : and all false ways I utterly abhor.

Glory be to the Father, &c.

[ON SUNDAYS.

Antiphon—
> To God the Father, Son,
> And Spirit ever blest,
> Eternal Three in One,
> All glory be addrest.

The Chapter, 1 St. John v. 7.

There are Three that bear record in heaven, the Father, the Word, and the Holy Ghost; and these Three are One.

R. O Lord, Thy Word endureth for ever in heaven. ℣. Thy truth also remaineth from one generation to another. R̠. For ever in heaven. ℣. Glory be to the Father, and to the Son: and to the Holy Ghost. R̠. O Lord, Thy Word endureth for ever in heaven.

℣. The Lord is my Shepherd, therefore can I lack nothing.

R̠. He shall feed me in a green pasture.]

On Sundays, and when the Sunday Psalms are to be said at Lauds, here is said immediately the Collect.

[ON WEEK-DAYS.

Antiphon. Let me not : be disappointed of my hope.

The Chapter, 1 Thess. v. 21, 22.

Prove all things; hold fast that which is good. Abstain from all appearance of evil.

R. I will alway give thanks unto the Lord. ℣. His praise shall ever be in my mouth. R̠. I will alway give thanks. ℣. Glory be to the Father, and to the Son : and to the Holy Ghost. R̠. I will alway give thanks unto the Lord.

℣. The Lord is my Shepherd, therefore can I lack nothing.

R̠. He shall feed me in a green pasture.]

℣. The Lord be with you.

R̠. And with thy spirit.

On week-days, except from Easter to Trinity, here follows,

Lord, have mercy upon us, &c.

And the rest of the week-day Prayers, as on Monday at Lauds, p. 150.

[*In Lent shall be said daily at Sext, Miserere mei Deus,* Ps. li., *preceded by*

Deus misereatur. Ps. lxvii.

1 God be merciful unto us, and bless us : and show us the light of His countenance, and be merciful unto us;

2 That Thy way may be known upon earth : Thy saving health among all nations.

3 Let the people praise Thee, O God : yea, let all the people praise Thee.

4 O let the nations rejoice and be glad : for Thou shalt judge the folk righteously, and govern the nations upon earth.

5 Let the people praise Thee, O God : let all the people praise Thee.

6 Then shall the earth bring forth her increase : and God, even our own God, shall give us His blessing.

7 God shall bless us : and all the ends of the world shall fear Him.

Glory be to the Father, &c.]

After the Collect, which is always that appointed to be said at Lauds, Sext shall end as Terce, p. 182.

AT NONE.

℣. O God, make speed to save us.

℞. O Lord, make haste to help us.

℣. Glory be to the Father, and to the Son : and to the Holy Ghost ;

℞. As it was in the beginning, is now, and ever shall be : world without end. Amen. Alleluia.

But from Septuagesima Sunday to Wednesday in Holy Week, inclusive, is said instead,

Praise to Thee, O Lord, we sing,
Of Glory the Eternal King.

Hymn. Rerum Deus tenax Vigor.

O God, Creation's secret Force,
Thyself unmoved, all motion's source,
Who from the morn till evening's ray,
Through all its changes guid'st the day ;

Grant us when this short life is past,
The glorious evening that shall last :
That by a holy death attained,
Eternal glory may be gained.

O Father, that we ask be done,
Through Jesus Christ, Thine only Son ;
Who with the Holy Ghost and Thee,
Shall live and reign eternally. Amen.

Antiphon. Give me understanding.

Mirabilia. Ps. cxix.

129 Thy testimonies are wonderful : therefore doth my soul keep them.

130 When Thy Word goeth forth : it giveth light and understanding unto the simple.

131 I opened my mouth, and drew in my breath : for my delight was in Thy commandments.

132 O look Thou upon me, and be merciful unto me : as Thou usest to do unto those that love Thy Name.

133 Order my steps in Thy Word : and so shall no wickedness have dominion over me.

134 O deliver me from the wrongful dealings of men : and so shall I keep Thy commandments.

135 Show the light of Thy countenance upon Thy servant : and teach me Thy statutes.

136 Mine eyes gush out with water : because men keep not Thy law.

137 Righteous art Thou, O Lord : and true is Thy judgment.

138 The testimonies that Thou hast commanded : are exceeding righteous and true.

139 My zeal hath even consumed me : because mine enemies have forgotten Thy words.

140 Thy Word is tried to the uttermost : and Thy servant loveth it.

141 I am small, and of no reputation : yet do I not forget Thy commandments.

142 Thy righteousness is an everlasting righteousness : and Thy law is the truth.

143 Trouble and heaviness have taken hold upon me : yet is my delight in Thy commandments.

144 The righteousness of Thy testimonies is everlasting : O grant me understanding, and I shall live.

Glory be to the Father, &c.

Clamavi in toto corde meo.

145 I call with my whole heart : hear me, O Lord, I will keep Thy statutes.

146 Yea, even unto Thee do I

call : help me, and I shall keep Thy testimonies.

147 Early in the morning do I cry unto Thee : for in Thy Word is my trust.

148 Mine eyes prevent the night-watches : that I might be occupied in Thy words.

149 Hear my voice, O Lord, according unto Thy lovingkindness : quicken me, according as Thou art wont.

150 They draw nigh that of malice persecute me : and are far from Thy law.

151 Be Thou nigh at hand, O Lord : for all Thy commandments are true.

152 As concerning Thy testimonies, I have known long since : that Thou hast grounded them for ever.

153 O consider mine adversity, and deliver me : for I do not forget Thy law.

154 Avenge Thou my cause, and deliver me : quicken me, according to Thy Word.

155 Health is far from the ungodly : for they regard not Thy statutes.

156 Great is Thy mercy, O Lord : quicken me, as Thou art wont.

157 Many there are that trouble me, and persecute me : yet do I not swerve from Thy testimonies.

158 It grieveth me when I see the transgressors : because they keep not Thy law.

159 Consider, O Lord, how I love Thy commandments : O quicken me, according to Thy lovingkindness.

160 Thy Word is true from everlasting : all the judgments of Thy righteousness endure for evermore.

Glory be to the Father, &c.

Principes persecuti sunt.

161 Princes have persecuted me without a cause : but my heart standeth in awe of Thy Word.

162 I am as glad of Thy Word : as one that findeth great spoils.

163 As for lies, I hate and abhor them : but Thy law do I love.

164 Seven times a day do I praise Thee : because of Thy righteous judgments.

165 Great is the peace that they have who love Thy law : and they are not offended at it.

166 Lord, I have looked for Thy Saving Health : and done after Thy commandments.

167 My soul hath kept Thy testimonies : and loved them exceedingly.

168 I have kept Thy commandments and testimonies : for all my ways are before Thee.

169 Let my complaint come before Thee, O Lord : give me understanding, according to Thy Word.

170 Let my supplication come before Thee : deliver me, according to Thy Word.

171 My lips shall speak of Thy praise : when Thou hast taught me Thy statutes.

172 Yea, my tongue shall sing of Thy Word : for all Thy commandments are righteous.

173 Let Thine hand help me : for I have chosen Thy commandments.

174 I have longed for Thy Saving Health, O Lord : and in Thy law is my delight.

175 O let my soul live, and it shall praise Thee : and Thy judgments shall help me.

176 I have gone astray like a sheep that is lost : O seek Thy

servant, for I do not forget Thy commandments.

Glory be to the Father, &c.

[ON SUNDAYS.

Antiphon. Of Him, and through Him, and to Him, are all things: to Him be glory for ever.

The Chapter, Eph. iv. 5, 6; Rom. i. 25.

One Lord, one Faith, one Baptism, One God and Father of all, Who is above all, and through all, and in you all, Who is blessed for ever.

R. I call with my whole heart : hear me, O Lord. ℣. I will keep Thy statutes. ℟. Hear me, O Lord. ℣. Glory be to the Father, and to the Son : and to the Holy Ghost. ℟. I call with my whole heart : hear me, O Lord.

℣. O cleanse Thou me from my secret faults.

℟. Keep Thy servant also from presumptuous sins.]

On Sundays, and when the Sunday Psalms are to be said at Lauds, here is said immediately the Collect.

[ON WEEK-DAYS.

Antiphon. Give me understanding : according to Thy Word.

The Chapter, Gal. vi. 2.

Bear ye one another's burdens, and so fulfil the law of Christ.

R. O deliver me, and be merciful unto me. ℣. My foot standeth right : I will praise the Lord in the congregations. ℟. And be merciful unto me. ℣. Glory be to the Father, and to the Son : and to the Holy Ghost. ℟. O deliver me, and be merciful unto me.

℣. O cleanse Thou me from my secret faults.

℟. Keep Thy servant also from presumptuous sins.

℣. The Lord be with you.

℟. And with thy spirit.

On week-days, except from Easter to Trinity, here follows,

Lord, have mercy, &c.

And the rest of the week-day Prayers, as on Monday at Lauds, p. 150.

In Lent shall be said daily at None Miserere mei Deus, Ps. li., *followed by*

Domine, exaudi. Ps. cii.

Against Avarice.

1 Hear my prayer, O Lord : and let my crying come unto Thee.

2 Hide not Thy face from me in the time of my trouble : incline Thine ear unto me when I call ; O hear me, and that right soon.

3 For my days are consumed away like smoke : and my bones are burnt up as it were a firebrand.

4 My heart is smitten down, and withered like grass : so that I forget to eat my bread.

5 For the voice of my groaning : my bones will scarce cleave to my flesh.

6 I am become like a pelican in the wilderness : and like an owl that is in the desert.

7 I have watched, and am even as it were a sparrow : that sitteth alone upon the house-top.

8 Mine enemies revile me all the day long : and they that are

mad upon me are sworn together against me.

9 For I have eaten ashes as it were bread : and mingled my drink with weeping ;

10 And that because of Thine indignation and wrath : for Thou hast taken me up, and cast me down.

11 My days are gone like a shadow : and I am withered like grass.

12 But Thou, O Lord, shalt endure for ever : and Thy remembrance throughout all generations.

13 Thou shalt arise, and have mercy upon Sion : for it is time that Thou have mercy upon her, yea, the time is come.

14 And why? Thy servants think upon her stones : and it pitieth them to see her in the dust.

15 The heathen shall fear Thy Name, O Lord : and all the kings of the earth Thy majesty ;

16 When the Lord shall build up Sion : and when His glory shall appear ;

17 When He turneth Him unto the prayer of the poor destitute : and despiseth not their desire.

18 This shall be written for those that come after : and the people which shall be born shall praise the Lord.

19 For He hath looked down from His sanctuary : out of the heaven did the Lord behold the earth ;

20 That He might hear the mournings of such as are in captivity : and deliver the children appointed unto death ;

21 That they may declare the Name of the Lord in Sion : and His worship at Jerusalem ;

22 When the people are gathered together : and the kingdoms also, to serve the Lord.

23 He brought down my strength in my journey : and shortened my days.

24 But I said, O my God, take me not away in the midst of mine age : as for Thy years, they endure throughout all generations.

25 Thou, Lord, in the beginning hast laid the foundation of the earth : and the heavens are the work of Thy hands.

26 They shall perish, but Thou shalt endure : they all shall wax old as doth a garment ;

27 And as a vesture shalt Thou change them, and they shall be changed : but Thou art the same, and Thy years shall not fail.

28 The children of Thy servants shall continue : and their seed shall stand fast in Thy sight.

Glory be to the Father, &c.]

After the Collect, which is always that appointed to be said at Lauds, None shall end as Terce, p. 182.

SUNDAY AT VESPERS.

℣. O God, make speed to save us.

℟. O Lord, make haste to help us.

℣. Glory be to the Father, and to the Son : and to the Holy Ghost;

℟. As it was in the beginning, is now, and ever shall be : world without end. Amen.

Alleluia.

But from Septuagesima Sunday to Wednesday in Holy Week, inclusive, is said instead,

Praise to Thee, O Lord, we sing,
Of Glory the Eternal King.

Antiphon, when not otherwise ordered. Sit Thou.

Dixit Dominus. Ps. cx.

1 The Lord said unto my Lord : Sit Thou on My right Hand, until I make Thine enemies Thy footstool.

2 The Lord shall send the rod of Thy power out of Sion : be Thou Ruler, even in the midst among Thine enemies.

3 In the day of Thy power shall the people offer Thee free-will offerings with an holy worship : the dew of Thy Birth is of the womb of the morning.

4 The Lord sware, and will not repent : Thou art a Priest for ever after the order of Melchisedek.

5 The Lord upon Thy right Hand : shall wound even kings in the day of His wrath.

6 He shall judge among the heathen; He shall fill the places with the dead bodies : and smite in sunder the heads over divers countries.

7 He shall drink of the brook in the way : therefore shall He lift up His head.

Glory be to the Father, &c.

Antiphon. The Lord said unto my Lord : Sit Thou on My right Hand, until I make Thine enemies Thy footstool.

Antiphon. All His commandments.

Confitebor Tibi. Ps. cxi.

1 I will give thanks unto the Lord with my whole heart : secretly among the faithful, and in the congregation.

2 The works of the Lord are great : sought out of all them that have pleasure therein.

3 His work is worthy to be praised, and had in honour : and His Righteousness endureth for ever.

4 The Merciful and Gracious Lord hath so done His marvellous Works : that they ought to be had in remembrance.

5 He hath given Meat unto them that fear Him : He shall ever be mindful of His covenant.

6 He hath showed His people the power of His Works : that He may give them the heritage of the heathen.

7 The works of His Hands are verity and judgment : all His commandments are true.

8 They stand fast for ever and ever : and are done in truth and equity.

9 He sent Redemption unto His

people : He hath commanded His covenant for ever; Holy and Reverend is His Name.

10 The fear of the Lord is the beginning of wisdom : a good understanding have all they that do thereafter; the praise of it endureth for ever.

Glory be to the Father, &c.

Antiphon. All His commandments : are true; they stand fast for ever and ever.

Antiphon. He hath great delight.

Beatus vir. Ps. cxii.

1 Blessed is the man that feareth the Lord : he hath great delight in His commandments.

2 His seed shall be mighty upon earth : the generation of the faithful shall be blessed.

3 Riches and plenteousness shall be in his house : and his righteousness endureth for ever.

4 Unto the godly there ariseth up light in the darkness : he is merciful, loving, and righteous.

5 A good man is merciful, and lendeth : and will guide his words with discretion.

6 For he shall never be moved : and the righteous shall be had in everlasting remembrance.

7 He will not be afraid of any evil tidings : for his heart standeth fast, and believeth in the Lord.

8 His heart is established, and will not shrink : until he see his desire upon his enemies.

9 He hath dispersed abroad, and given to the poor : and his righteousness remaineth for ever; his horn shall be exalted with honour.

10 The ungodly shall see it, and it shall grieve him : he shall gnash with his teeth, and consume away; the desire of the ungodly shall perish.

Glory be to the Father, &c.

Antiphon. He hath great delight : in His commandments.

Antiphon. Blessed be the Name of the Lord.

Laudate, pueri. Ps. cxiii.

1 Praise the Lord, ye servants : O praise the Name of the Lord.

2 Blessed be the Name of the Lord : from this time forth for evermore.

3 The Lord's Name is praised : from the rising up of the sun unto the going down of the same.

4 The Lord is high above all heathen : and His glory above the heavens.

5 Who is like unto the Lord our God, that hath His dwelling so high : and yet humbleth Himself to behold the things that are in heaven and earth?

6 He taketh up the simple out of the dust : and lifteth the poor out of the mire.

7 That He may set him with the princes : even with the princes of His people.

8 He maketh the barren woman to keep house : and to be a joyful mother of children.

Glory be to the Father, &c.

Antiphon. Blessed be the Name of the Lord : from this time forth for evermore.

Antiphon. But we will praise.

In exitu Israel. Ps. cxiv.

1 When Israel came out of Egypt : and the house of Jacob from among the strange people,

2 Judah was His sanctuary : and Israel His dominion.

3 The sea saw that, and fled : Jordan was driven back.

4 The mountains skipped like rams : and the little hills like young sheep.

5 What aileth thee, O thou sea, that thou fleddest : and thou Jordan, that thou wast driven back?

6 Ye mountains, that ye skipped like rams : and ye little hills, like young sheep?

7 Tremble, thou earth, at the presence of the Lord : at the presence of the God of Jacob :

8 Who turned the hard rock into a standing water : and the flint-stone into a springing well.

Non nobis, Domine. Ps. cxv.

1 Not unto us, O Lord, not unto us, but unto Thy Name give the praise : for Thy loving mercy, and for Thy truth's sake.

2 Wherefore shall the heathen say : Where is now their God?

3 As for our God, He is in heaven : He hath done whatsoever pleased Him.

4 Their idols are silver and gold : even the work of men's hands.

5 They have mouths, and speak not : eyes have they, and see not.

6 They have ears, and hear not : noses have they, and smell not.

7 They have hands, and handle not; feet have they, and walk not : neither speak they through their throat.

8 They that make them are like unto them : and so are all such as put their trust in them.

9 But thou, house of Israel, trust thou in the Lord : He is their succour and defence.

10 Ye house of Aaron, put your trust in the Lord : He is their helper and defender.

11 Ye that fear the Lord, put your trust in the Lord : He is their helper and defender.

12 The Lord hath been mindful of us, and He shall bless us : even He shall bless the house of Israel, He shall bless the house of Aaron.

13 He shall bless them that fear the Lord : both small and great.

14 The Lord shall increase you more and more : you and your children.

15 Ye are the blessed of the Lord : Who made heaven and earth.

16 All the whole heavens are the Lord's : the earth hath He given to the children of men.

17 The dead praise not Thee, O Lord : neither all they that go down into silence.

18 But we will praise the Lord : from this time forth for evermore. Praise the Lord.

Glory be to the Father, &c.

Antiphon. But we will praise : the Lord.

The Chapter, 2 Thess. iii. 5.

The Lord direct your hearts into the Love of God, and into the patient waiting for Christ.

R₂. Thanks be to God.

In the Services of the Season, this Chapter is said at Vespers (1.) *daily from Epiphany to Septuagesima;* (2.) *on all week-days from Septuagesima to the First Sunday in Lent; and* (3.) *daily from Trinity to Advent.*

Hymn. Lucis Creator optime.

O blest Creator of the light,
Who makest the day with radiance bright,
And o'er the forming world didst call
The light from Chaos first of all;

Whose wisdom joined in meet array
The morn and eve, and named them day;
Night comes with all its darkling fears.
Regard Thy People's prayers and tears.

Lest, sunk in sin, and whelmed with strife,
They lose the gift of endless life;
While thinking but the thoughts of time,
They weave new chains of woe and crime.

But grant them grace that they may strain
The heavenly gate and prize to gain;
Each harmful lure aside to cast,
And purge away each error past.

O Father, that we ask be done,
Through Jesus Christ, Thine only Son;
Who, with the Holy Ghost and Thee,
Shall live and reign eternally. Amen.

℣. Lord, let my prayer be set forth.

℟. In Thy sight as the Incense.

In the Services of the Season, this Hymn, ℣. and ℟. are said (1.) *on all Sundays from Epiphany to Lent, and* (2.) *daily from Trinity to Advent.*

Antiphon (as in the Proper Services.)

Magnificat, St. Luke i.

My soul doth magnify the Lord: and my spirit hath rejoiced in God my Saviour.

For He hath regarded: the lowliness of His handmaiden.

For behold, from henceforth: all generations shall call me blessed.

For He that is mighty hath magnified me: and holy is His Name.

And His mercy is on them that

o

fear Him : throughout all generations.

He hath showed strength with His arm : He hath scattered the proud in the imagination of their hearts.

He hath put down the mighty from their seat : and hath exalted the humble and meek.

He hath filled the hungry with good things : and the rich He hath sent empty away.

He remembering His mercy hath holpen His servant Israel : as He promised to our forefathers, Abraham and his seed, for ever.

Glory be to the Father, and to the Son : and to the Holy Ghost ;

As it was in the beginning, is now, and ever shall be : world without end. Amen.

Antiphon (as in the Proper Services.)

℣. The Lord be with you.

℟. And with thy spirit.

Let us pray.

The Collect of the day.

℣. The Lord be with you.

℟. And with thy spirit.

℣. Bless we the Lord.

℟. Thanks be to God.

MEMORIALS AT VESPERS.

Of the Incarnation of our Lord, in Advent.

Antiphon. Fear not, Mary : for thou hast found favour with God, and behold thou shalt bring forth a Son. (*On Sundays and Holy-Days is added* Alleluia.)

℣. There shall come forth a Rod out of the stem of Jesse.

℟. A Branch shall grow out of his roots.

Let us pray.

WE beseech Thee, O Lord, pour Thy grace into our hearts ; that as we have known the Incarnation of Thy Son Jesus Christ by the message of an Angel, so by His Cross and Passion we may be brought unto the glory of His Resurrection ; through the same Jesus Christ our Lord. *Amen.*

At other times, except during the Octave of the Nativity and from Maundy Thursday to Low Sunday, inclusive.

Antiphon. When Thou wast born of a Virgin ineffably, then were the Scriptures fulfilled. As the dew upon the fleece didst Thou descend to save mankind : we praise Thee, O our God. (*On Sundays and Holy-Days is added* Alleluia.)

℣. Blessed be the Lord God of Israel.

℟. For He hath visited and Redeemed His people.

Let us pray.

WE beseech Thee, O Lord, pour Thy grace into our hearts ; that as we have known the Incarnation of Thy Son Jesus Christ by the message of an Angel, so by His Cross and Passion we may be brought unto the glory of His Resurrection : through the same Jesus Christ our Lord. *Amen.*

Memorial of All Saints, to be said throughout the year except on Saints' Days, and from Maundy Thursday to Low Sunday, inclusive.

Antiphon. O how glorious is the Kingdom where all the Saints rejoice with Christ : they are clothed in white robes, and follow the Lamb whithersoever He goeth. (*On Sundays and Holy-Days is added* Alleluia.)

℣. Rejoice in the Lord, O ye Righteous.

℟. Be joyful, all ye that are true of heart.

Let us pray.

O ALMIGHTY God, Who hast knit together Thine elect in one Communion and fellowship, in the mystical Body of Thy Son Christ our Lord; Grant us grace so to follow Thy blessed Saints in all virtuous and godly living, that we may come to those unspeakable Joys, which Thou hast prepared for them that unfeignedly love Thee; through Jesus Christ our Lord. *Amen.*

Memorial of penitent sinners, to be said at Vespers on all weekdays (except Saturdays) from Ash-Wednesday till Wednesday in Holy Week, inclusive.

Antiphon. Who knoweth if the Lord will return and repent, and leave a blessing behind Him?

℣. O Lord, deal not with us after our sins.

℟. Neither reward us after our iniquities.

Let us pray.

O LORD, we beseech Thee, mercifully hear our prayers, and spare all those who confess their sins unto Thee; that they, whose consciences by sin are accused, by Thy merciful pardon may be absolved; through Christ our Lord. *Amen.*

Memorial of the Resurrection, to be said at Vespers on Sundays, from Low Sunday till the Ascension.

Antiphon. And when they looked they saw that the stone was rolled away, for it was very great. Alleluia.

℣. The Lord is Risen.

℟. As He said. Alleluia.

Let us pray.

ALMIGHTY God, Who through Thy Only-begotten Son Jesus Christ hast overcome death, and opened unto us the gate of everlasting Life; We humbly beseech Thee, that, as by Thy special grace preventing us Thou dost put into our minds good desires, so by Thy continual help we may bring the same to good effect; through Jesus Christ our Lord, Who liveth and reigneth with Thee and the Holy Ghost, ever one God, world without end. *Amen.*

Memorial of the Resurrection, to be said at Vespers on week-days from Low Sunday till the Ascension.

Antiphon. Go quickly, and tell His disciples that He is risen from the dead. Alleluia.

℣. The Lord is Risen indeed.

℟. And hath appeared to Simon. Alleluia.

Collect of Easter Day as above.

Memorial of the Passion of our Lord, to be said at Vespers daily from Trinity Sunday till Advent.

Antiphon. We adore Thee, O Christ, and bless Thee, for by Thy Cross Thou hast redeemed the world. (*On Sundays and Holy-Days is added* Alleluia.)

℣. By the power of the Cross.

℞. Deliver us from our enemies, O God.

Let us pray.

O GOD, Who to enlighten the darkness of the world didst vouchsafe to mount upon the Holy Cross, may it please Thee to enlighten our hearts and bodies, Thou Saviour of the world, Who livest and reignest with the Father and the Holy Ghost, ever one God, world without end. *Amen.*

℣. The Lord be with you.

℞. And with thy spirit.

May the souls of the Faithful, through the mercy of God, rest in peace. *Amen.*

MONDAY AT VESPERS.

℣. O God, make speed to save us.

℞. O Lord, make haste to help us.

℣. Glory be to the Father, and to the Son : and to the Holy Ghost ;

℞. As it was in the beginning, is now, and ever shall be : world without end. Amen.
Alleluia.

But from Septuagesima Sunday to Wednesday in Holy Week, inclusive, is said instead,

Praise to Thee, O Lord, we sing,
Of Glory the Eternal King.

Antiphon. The Lord hath inclined.

Dilexi quoniam. Ps. cxvi.

1 I am well pleased : that the Lord hath heard the voice of my prayer;

2 That He hath inclined His ear unto me : therefore will I call upon Him as long as I live.

3 The snares of death compassed me round about : and the pains of hell gat hold upon me.

4 I shall find trouble and heaviness, and I will call upon the Name of the Lord : O Lord, I beseech Thee, deliver my soul.

5 Gracious is the Lord, and righteous : yea, our God is merciful.

6 The Lord preserveth the simple : I was in misery, and He helped me.

7 Turn again then unto thy rest, O my soul : for the Lord hath rewarded thee.

8 And why? Thou hast delivered my soul from death : mine eyes from tears, and my feet from falling.

9 I will walk before the Lord : in the land of the living.

Glory be to the Father, &c.

Antiphon. The Lord hath inclined : His ear unto me.

Antiphon. I believed.

Credidi. Ps. cxvi. 10.

10 I believed, and therefore will I speak; but I was sore troubled : I said in my haste, All men are liars.

11 What reward shall I give unto the Lord : for all the benefits that He hath done unto me?

12 I will receive the Cup of Salvation : and call upon the Name of the Lord.

13 I will pay my vows now in the presence of all His people :

right dear in the sight of the Lord is the death of His saints.

14 Behold, O Lord, how that I am Thy servant : I am Thy servant, and the son of Thine handmaid ; Thou hast broken my bonds in sunder.

15 I will offer to Thee the Sacrifice of Thanksgiving : and will call upon the Name of the Lord.

16 I will pay my vows unto the Lord, in the sight of all His people : in the courts of the Lord's house, even in the midst of thee, O Jerusalem. Praise the Lord.

Glory be to the Father, &c.

Antiphon. I believed : and therefore will I speak.

Antiphon. O praise the Lord.

Laudate Dominum. Ps. cxvii.

1 O praise the Lord, all ye heathen : praise Him, all ye nations.

2 For His merciful kindness is ever more and more towards us : and the truth of the Lord endureth for ever. Praise the Lord.

Glory be to the Father, &c.

Antiphon. O praise the Lord : all ye heathen.

Antiphon. I called.

Ad Dominum. Ps. cxx.

1 When I was in trouble I called upon the Lord : and He heard me.

2 Deliver my soul, O Lord, from lying lips : and from a deceitful tongue.

3 What reward shall be given or done unto thee, thou false tongue : even mighty and sharp arrows, with hot burning coals.

4 Wo is me, that I am constrained to dwell with Mesech : and to have my habitation among the tents of Kedar.

5 My soul hath long dwelt among them : that are enemies unto peace.

6 I labour for peace, but when I speak unto them thereof : they make them ready to battle.

Glory be to the Father, &c.

Antiphon. I called : upon the Lord.

Antiphon. My help.

Levavi oculos. Ps. cxxi.

1 I will lift up mine eyes unto the hills : from whence cometh my help.

2 My help cometh even from the Lord : Who hath made heaven and earth.

3 He will not suffer thy foot to be moved : and He that keepeth thee will not sleep.

4 Behold, He that keepeth Israel : shall neither slumber nor sleep.

5 The Lord Himself is thy Keeper : the Lord is thy Defence upon thy right hand;

6 So that the sun shall not burn thee by day : neither the moon by night.

7 The Lord shall preserve thee from all evil : yea, it is even He that shall keep thy soul.

8 The Lord shall preserve thy going out, and thy coming in : from this time forth for evermore.

Glory be to the Father, &c.

Antiphon. My help : cometh even from the Lord.

The Chapter, 2 Thess. iii. 5.

The Lord direct your hearts into the love of God, and into the patient waiting for Christ.

R̷. Thanks be to God.

In Services of the Season, this Chapter is said at Vespers (1.) *daily from Epiphany to Septuagesima;* (2.) *on all week-days from Septuagesima to the First Sunday in Lent; and* (3.) *daily from Trinity to Advent.*

Hymn for Mondays from Epiphany to Lent.

Immense cœli Conditor.

O great Creator of the sky,
Who wouldest not the floods on high
With earthly waters to confound,
But madest the firmament their bound;

The floods above Thou didst ordain;
The floods below Thou didst restrain:
That moisture might attemper heat,
Lest the parched earth should ruin meet.

Upon our souls, good Lord, bestow
The gift of grace in endless flow:
Lest some renewed deceit or wile
Of former sin should us beguile.

Let Faith discover heavenly light;
So shall its rays direct us right;
And let this Faith each error chase;
And never give to falsehood place.

O Father, that we ask be done,
Through Jesus Christ, Thine only Son;
Who, with the Holy Ghost and Thee,
Shall live and reign eternally. Amen.

℣. Lord, let my prayer be set forth.

℟. In Thy sight as the Incense.

In the Services of the Season, this Hymn, ℣. and ℟., are said on Mondays from Epiphany to Lent.
From Trinity to Advent are said the Hymn, ℣. and ℟., p. 192.

Antiphon. My soul doth magnify.

Magnificat, St. Luke i.

Antiphon. My soul doth magnify: the Lord.

Here follow the week-day Prayers, thus, (*all kneeling.*)

Lord, have mercy upon us.
Christ, have mercy upon us.
Lord, have mercy upon us.
Our Father, &c.

℣. I said, Lord, be merciful unto me.

℟. Heal my soul, for I have sinned against Thee.

℣. Turn Thee again, O Lord, at the last.

℟. And be gracious unto Thy servants.

℣. Let Thy merciful kindness, O Lord, be upon us.

℟. As we do put our trust in Thee.

℣. Let Thy priests be clothed with righteousness.

℟. And Thy saints sing with joyfulness.

℣. O Lord, save the Queen.

℟. And mercifully hear us when we call upon Thee.

℣. O God, save Thy servants and handmaidens.

℟. Which put their trust in Thee.

℣. O Lord, save Thy people.

℟. And bless Thine inheritance.

℣. Peace be within Thy walls.

℟. And plenteousness within Thy palaces.

℣. Let us pray for the dead in Christ.

℟. Grant them, O Lord, eternal rest, and let everlasting light shine upon them.

℣. Hearken unto my voice, O Lord, when I cry unto Thee.

℟. Have mercy upon me, and hear me.

Miserere mei Deus, Ps. li., *p.* 177.

[*This Psalm may be here omitted, except on week-days in Lent, when it shall always be said, and followed by*

De profundis. Ps. cxxx.
Against Envy.

1 Out of the deep have I called unto Thee, O Lord : Lord, hear my voice.

2 O let Thine ears consider well : the voice of my complaint.

3 If Thou, Lord, wilt be extreme to mark what is done amiss : O Lord, who may abide it?

4 For there is mercy with Thee : therefore shalt Thou be feared.

5 I look for the Lord ; my soul doth wait for Him : in His word is my trust.

6 My soul fleeth unto the Lord : before the morning watch, I say, before the morning watch.

7 O Israel, trust in the Lord, for with the Lord there is mercy : and with Him is plenteous Redemption.

8 And He shall redeem Israel : from all his sins.

Glory be to the Father, &c.]

At the end of the Psalm, let the Reader [if a Priest rise from his knees, go to the step of the sanctuary, and] say,

℣. O Lord, arise, help us.

℟. And deliver us for Thy Name's sake.

℣. Turn Thee again, O Lord God of Hosts.

℟. Show the light of Thy Countenance, and we shall be whole.

℣. O Lord, hear my prayer.

℟. And let my cry come unto Thee.

℣. The Lord be with you.

℟. And with thy spirit.

Let us pray.

Collect as in the Proper Services.

℣. The Lord be with you.

℟. And with thy spirit.

℣. Bless we the Lord.

℟. Thanks be to God.

Then follow the Memorials, &c., p. 194.

TUESDAY AT VESPERS.

℣. O God, make speed to save us.

℟. O Lord, make haste to help us.

℣. Glory be to the Father, and to the Son : and to the Holy Ghost ;

℟. As it was in the beginning, is now, and ever shall be : world without end. Amen.

Alleluia.

But from Septuagesima Sunday to Wednesday in Holy Week, inclusive, is said instead,

Praise to Thee, O Lord, we sing,
Of Glory the Eternal King.

Antiphon. We will go.

Lætatus sum. Ps. cxxii.

1 I was glad when they said unto me : We will go into the House of the Lord.

2 Our feet shall stand in thy gates : O Jerusalem.

3 Jerusalem is built as a city : that is at unity in itself.

4 For thither the tribes go up, even the tribes of the Lord : to testify unto Israel, to give thanks unto the Name of the Lord.

5 For there is the seat of judgment : even the seat of the house of David.

6 O pray for the peace of Jerusalem : they shall prosper that love thee.

7 Peace be within thy walls : and plenteousness within thy palaces.

8 For my brethren and com-

panions' sakes : I will wish thee prosperity.

9 Yea, because of the House of the Lord our God : I will seek to do thee good.

Glory be to the Father, &c.

Antiphon. We will go : gladly into the House of the Lord.

Antiphon. O Thou that dwellest.

Ad Te levavi oculos meos. Ps. cxxiii.

1 Unto Thee lift I up mine eyes : O Thou that dwellest in the Heavens.

2 Behold, even as the eyes of servants look unto the hand of their masters, and as the eyes of a maiden unto the hand of her mistress : even so our eyes wait upon the Lord our God, until He have mercy upon us.

3 Have mercy upon us, O Lord, have mercy upon us : for we are utterly despised.

4 Our soul is filled with the scornful reproof of the wealthy : and with the despitefulness of the proud.

Glory be to the Father, &c.

Antiphon. O Thou that dwellest : in the heavens, have mercy upon us.

Antiphon. Our help.

Nisi quia Dominus. Ps. cxxiv.

1 If the Lord Himself had not been on our side, now may Israel say : if the Lord Himself had not been on our side, when men rose up against us;

2 They had swallowed us up quick : when they were so wrathfully displeased at us.

3 Yea, the waters had drowned us : and the stream had gone over our soul.

4 The deep waters of the proud : had gone even over our soul.

5 But praised be the Lord : Who hath not given us over for a prey unto their teeth.

6 Our soul is escaped even as a bird out of the snare of the fowler : the snare is broken, and we are delivered.

7 Our help standeth in the Name of the Lord : Who hath made heaven and earth.

Glory be to the Father, &c.

Antiphon. Our help : standeth in the Name of the Lord.

Antiphon. Do well.

Qui confidunt. Ps. cxxv.

1 They that put their trust in the Lord shall be even as the mount Sion : which may not be removed, but standeth fast for ever.

2 The hills stand about Jerusalem : even so standeth the Lord round about His people, from this time forth for evermore.

3 For the rod of the ungodly cometh not into the lot of the righteous : lest the righteous put their hand unto wickedness.

4 Do well, O Lord : unto those that are good and true of heart.

5 As for such as turn back unto their own wickedness : the Lord shall lead them forth with the evil-doers; but peace shall be upon Israel.

Glory be to the Father, &c.

Antiphon. Do well : O Lord, unto those that are good and true of heart.

Antiphon. Then were we like.

In convertendo. Ps. cxxvi.

1 When the Lord turned again the captivity of Sion : then were we like unto them that dream.

2 Then was our mouth filled with laughter : and our tongue with joy.

3 Then said they among the heathen : The Lord hath done Great Things for them.

4 Yea, the Lord hath done Great Things for us already : whereof we rejoice.

5 Turn our captivity, O Lord : as the rivers in the south.

6 They that sow in tears : shall reap in joy.

7 He that now goeth on his way weeping, and beareth forth good seed : shall doubtless come again with joy, and bring his sheaves with him.

Glory be to the Father, &c.

Antiphon. Then were we like : unto them that dream.

The Chapter, 2 Thess. iii. 5.

The Lord direct your hearts into the love of God, and into the patient waiting for Christ.

R⁄. Thanks be to God.

In Services of the Season, this Chapter is said at Vespers (1.) daily from Epiphany to Septuagesima; (2.) on week-days from Septuagesima to the First Sunday in Lent; and (3.) daily from Trinity to Advent.

Hymn for Tuesdays from Epiphany to Lent.

Telluris ingens Conditor.

Earth's mighty Maker, Whose command
Raised from the sea the solid land ;
And drove each billowy heap away,
And bade the earth stand firm for aye :

That so with flowers of golden hue,
The seeds of each it might renew ;
And fruit-trees bearing fruit might yield,
And pleasant pasture of the field :

Our spirit's rankling wounds efface
With dewy freshness of Thy grace :
That grief may cleanse each deed of ill,
And o'er each lust may triumph still.

Let every soul Thy law obey,
And keep from every evil way ;

Rejoice each promised good to win,
And flee from every mortal sin.

O Father, that we ask be done,
Through Jesus Christ, Thine only Son ;
Who, with the Holy Ghost and Thee,
Shall live and reign eternally.   Amen.

℣. Lord, let my prayer be set forth.

R⁄. In Thy sight as the Incense.

In Services of the Season, this Hymn, ℣. and R⁄., are said on Tuesdays from Epiphany to Lent.

From Trinity to Advent are said the Hymn, ℣. and R⁄., p. 192.

Antiphon. My spirit hath rejoiced.

Magnificat, St. Luke i.

Antiphon. My spirit hath rejoiced in God my Saviour.

The week-day Prayers, p. 198, *with* Miserere, Ps. li., *and the rest.*

The Proper Collect.

℣. The Lord be with you.

R⁄. And with thy spirit.

℣. Bless we the Lord.

R⁄. Thanks be to God.

The Memorials, &c., p. 194.

WEDNESDAY AT VESPERS.

℣. O God, make speed to save us.

R⁄. O Lord, make haste to help us.

℣. Glory be to the Father, and to the Son : and to the Holy Ghost ;

R⁄. As it was in the beginning, is now, and ever shall be : world without end.   Amen.

Alleluia.

But from Septuagesima Sunday to Wednesday in Holy Week, inclusive, is said instead,

Praise to Thee, O Lord, we sing, Of Glory the Eternal King.

Antiphon. Happy is the man.

Nisi Dominus. Ps. cxxvii.

1 Except the Lord build the house : their labour is but lost that build it.

2 Except the Lord keep the city : the watchman waketh but in vain.

3 It is but lost labour that ye haste to rise up early, and so late take rest, and eat the bread of carefulness : for so He giveth His beloved sleep.

4 Lo, children, and the fruit of the womb : are an heritage and gift that cometh of the Lord.

5 Like as the arrows in the hand of the giant : even so are the young children.

6 Happy is the man that hath his quiver full of them : they shall not be ashamed when they speak with their enemies in the gate.

Glory be to the Father, &c.

Antiphon. Happy is the man : that hath his quiver full.

Antiphon. Blessed are all they.

Beati omnes. Ps. cxxviii.

1 Blessed are all they that fear the Lord : and walk in His ways.

2 For thou shalt eat the labours of thine hands : O well is thee, and happy shalt thou be.

3 Thy wife shall be as the fruitful vine : upon the walls of thine house.

4 Thy children like the olive-branches : round about thy table.

5 Lo, thus shall the man be blessed : that feareth the Lord.

6 The Lord from out of Sion shall so bless thee : that thou shalt see Jerusalem in prosperity all thy life long.

7 Yea, that thou shalt see thy children's children : and peace upon Israel.

Glory be to the Father, &c.

Antiphon. Blessed are all they : that fear the Lord.

Antiphon. We wish you good luck.

Sæpe expugnaverunt. Ps. cxxix.

1 Many a time have they fought against me from my youth up : may Israel now say :

2 Yea, many a time have they vexed me from my youth up : but they have not prevailed against me.

3 The plowers plowed upon my back : and made long furrows.

4 But the righteous Lord : hath hewn the snares of the ungodly in pieces.

5 Let them be confounded and turned backward : as many as have evil will at Sion.

6 Let them be even as the grass growing upon the house-tops : which withereth afore it be plucked up ;

7 Whereof the mower filleth not his hand : neither he that bindeth up the sheaves his bosom.

8 So that they who go by say not so much as, The Lord prosper you : we wish you good luck in the Name of the Lord.

Glory be to the Father, &c.

Antiphon. We wish you good luck : in the Name of the Lord.

Antiphon. Out of the deep.

De profundis. Ps. cxxx.

1 Out of the deep have I called unto Thee, O Lord : Lord, hear my voice.

… AT VESPERS.

2 O let Thine ears consider well : the voice of my complaint.
3 If Thou, Lord, wilt be extreme to mark what is done amiss : O Lord, who may abide it?
4 For there is mercy with Thee : therefore shalt Thou be feared.
5 I look for the Lord ; my soul doth wait for Him : in His word is my trust.
6 My soul fleeth unto the Lord : before the morning watch, I say, before the morning watch.
7 O Israel, trust in the Lord, for with the Lord there is mercy : and with Him is plenteous Redemption.
8 And He shall redeem Israel : from all his sins.
Glory be to the Father, &c.

Antiphon. Out of the deep : have I called unto Thee, O Lord.

Antiphon. O Israel.

Domine, non est. Ps. cxxxi.

1 Lord, I am not high-minded : I have no proud looks.
2 I do not exercise myself in great matters : which are too high for me.
3 But I refrain my soul, and keep it low, like as a child that is weaned from his mother : yea, my soul is even as a weaned child.
4 O Israel, trust in the Lord : from this time forth for evermore.
Glory be to the Father, &c.

Antiphon. O Israel : trust in the Lord.

The Chapter, 2 Thess. iii. 5.

The Lord direct your hearts into the love of God, and into the patient waiting for Christ.

R︎. Thanks be to God.

In Services of the Season, this Chapter is said at Vespers (1.) *daily from Epiphany to Septuagesima;* (2.) *on all week-days from Septuagesima to the First Sunday in Lent; and* (3.) *daily from Trinity to Advent.*

Hymn for Wednesdays from Epiphany to First Sunday in Lent.

Cœli Deus sanctissime.

O God, Whose Hand hath spread the sky
And all its shining hosts on high,
And painting it with fiery light,
Made it so beauteous and so bright :

Thou, when the Wednesday was begun,
Didst frame the circle of the Sun,
And set the Moon for ordered change,
And planets for their wider range :

To night and day, by certain line,
Their varying bounds Thou didst assign;
And gav'st a signal, known and meet,
For months begun and months complete.

Enlighten Thou the hearts of men :
Polluted souls make pure again ;
Unloose the bands of guilt within ;
Remove the burden of our sin.

O Father, that we ask be done,
Through Jesus Christ, Thine only Son ;
Who, with the Holy Ghost and Thee,
Shall live and reign eternally. Amen.

℣. Lord, let my prayer be set forth.

℟. In Thy sight as the Incense.

In Services of the Season, this Hymn, ℣. and ℟. are said, on Wednesdays from Epiphany to Lent.

From Trinity to Advent are said the Hymn, ℣. and ℟., p. 192.

Antiphon. O Lord my God.

Magnificat, St. Luke i.

Antiphon. O Lord my God : Thou hast regarded my lowliness.

The week-day Prayers, p. 198, *with Miserere,* Ps. li., *and the rest.*

The Proper Collect.

℣. The Lord be with you.

℟. And with thy spirit.

℣. Bless we the Lord.

℟. Thanks be to God.

The Memorials, &c., p. 194.

THURSDAY AT VESPERS.

℣. O God, make speed to save us.

℟. O Lord, make haste to help us.

℣. Glory be to the Father, and to the Son : and to the Holy Ghost ;

℟. As it was in the beginning, is now, and ever shall be : world without end. Amen.

Alleluia.

But from Septuagesima Sunday to Wednesday in Holy Week, inclusive, is said instead,

Praise to Thee, O Lord, we sing, Of Glory the Eternal King.

Antiphon. And all.

Memento Domine. Ps. cxxxii.

1 Lord, remember David : and all his trouble ;

2 How he sware unto the Lord : and vowed a vow unto the Almighty God of Jacob ;

3 I will not come within the tabernacle of mine house : nor climb up into my bed.

4 I will not suffer mine eyes to sleep, nor mine eyelids to slumber : neither the temples of my head to take any rest.

5 Until I find out a place for the temple of the Lord : an habitation for the mighty God of Jacob.

6 Lo, we heard of the same at Ephrata : and found it in the wood.

7 We will go into His tabernacle : and fall low on our knees before His footstool.

8 Arise, O Lord, into Thy resting-place : Thou, and the ark of Thy strength.

9 Let Thy priests be clothed with righteousness : and let Thy saints sing with joyfulness.

10 For Thy servant David's sake : turn not away the presence of Thine Anointed.

11 The Lord hath made a faithful oath unto David : and He shall not shrink from it.

12 Of the fruit of thy body : shall I set upon thy seat.

13 If thy children will keep My covenant, and My testimonies that I shall learn them : their children also shall sit upon thy seat for evermore.

14 For the Lord hath chosen Sion to be an habitation for Himself : He hath longed for her.

15 This shall be My rest for ever : here will I dwell, for I have a delight therein.

16 I will bless her victuals with increase : and will satisfy her poor with bread.

17 I will deck her priests with health : and her saints shall rejoice and sing.

18 There shall I make the horn of David to flourish : I have ordained a lantern for Mine Anointed.

19 As for His enemies, I shall clothe them with shame : but upon Himself shall His crown flourish.

Glory be to the Father, &c.

Antiphon. And all : his trouble.

Antiphon. Behold, how good.

Ecce, quam bonum! Ps. cxxxiii.

1 Behold, how good and joyful a thing it is : brethren, to dwell together in Unity !

2 It is like the precious ointment upon the head, that ran down unto the beard : even unto Aaron's beard, and went down to the skirts of his clothing.

3 Like as the dew of Hermon : which fell upon the hill of Sion.

4 For there the Lord promised His blessing : and life for evermore.

Glory be to the Father, &c.

Antiphon. Behold, how good : and joyful a thing.

Antiphon. Whatsoever.

Laudate Nomen. Ps. cxxxv.

1 O praise the Lord, laud ye the Name of the Lord : praise it, O ye servants of the Lord!

2 Ye that stand in the house of the Lord : in the courts of the house of our God.

3 O praise the Lord, for the Lord is gracious : O sing praises unto His Name, for it is lovely.

4 For why? the Lord hath chosen Jacob unto Himself : and Israel for His own possession.

5 For I know that the Lord is great : and that our Lord is above all gods.

6 Whatsoever the Lord pleased, that did He in heaven, and in earth : and in the sea, and in all deep places.

7 He bringeth forth the clouds from the ends of the world : and sendeth forth lightnings with the rain, bringing the winds out of His treasures.

8 He smote the first-born of Egypt : both of man and beast.

9 He hath sent tokens and wonders into the midst of thee, O thou land of Egypt : upon Pharaoh, and all his servants.

10 He smote divers nations : and slew mighty kings ;

11 Sehon king of the Amorites, and Og the king of Basan : and all the kingdoms of Canaan ;

12 And gave their land to be an heritage : even an heritage unto Israel His people.

13 Thy Name, O Lord, endureth for ever : so doth Thy memorial, O Lord, from one generation to another.

14 For the Lord will avenge His people : and be gracious unto His servants.

15 As for the images of the heathen, they are but silver and gold : the work of men's hands.

16 They have mouths, and speak not : eyes have they, but they see not.

17 They have ears, and yet they hear not : neither is there any breath in their mouths.

18 They that make them are like unto them : and so are all they that put their trust in them.

19 Praise the Lord, ye house of Israel : praise the Lord, ye house of Aaron.

20 Praise the Lord, ye house of Levi : ye that fear the Lord, praise the Lord.

21 Praised be the Lord out of Sion : Who dwelleth at Jerusalem.

Glory be to the Father, &c.

Antiphon. Whatsoever : the Lord pleased, that did He.

Antiphon. For His Mercy.

Confitemini Domino. Ps. cxxxvi.

1 O give thanks unto the Lord, for He is gracious : and His Mercy endureth for ever.

2 O give thanks unto the God of all gods : for His Mercy endureth for ever.

3 O thank the Lord of all lords : for His Mercy endureth for ever.

4 Who only doeth great won-

ders : for His Mercy endureth for ever.

5 Who by His excellent wisdom made the heavens : for His Mercy endureth for ever.

6 Who laid out the earth above the waters : for His Mercy endureth for ever.

7 Who hath made great lights : for His Mercy endureth for ever ;

8 The sun to rule the day : for His Mercy endureth for ever ;

9 The moon and the stars to govern the night : for His Mercy endureth for ever.

10 Who smote Egypt with their first-born : for His Mercy endureth for ever ;

11 And brought out Israel from among them : for His Mercy endureth for ever.

12 With a mighty hand, and stretched out arm : for His Mercy endureth for ever ;

13 Who divided the Red Sea in two parts : for His Mercy endureth for ever ;

14 And made Israel to go through the midst of it : for His Mercy endureth for ever.

15 But as for Pharaoh and his host, He overthrew them in the Red Sea : for His Mercy endureth for ever.

16 Who led His people through the wilderness : for His Mercy endureth for ever.

17 Who smote great kings : for His Mercy endureth for ever.

18 Yea, and slew mighty kings : for His Mercy endureth for ever ;

19 Sehon king of the Amorites : for His Mercy endureth for ever ;

20 And Og the king of Basan : for His Mercy endureth for ever ;

21 And gave away their land for an heritage : for His Mercy endureth for ever ;

22 Even for an heritage unto Israel His servant : for His Mercy endureth for ever ;

23 Who remembered us when we were in trouble : for His Mercy endureth for ever.

24 And hath delivered us from our enemies : for His Mercy endureth for ever.

25 Who giveth food to all flesh : for His Mercy endureth for ever.

26 O give thanks unto the God of heaven : for His Mercy endureth for ever.

27 O give thanks unto the Lord of lords : for His Mercy endureth for ever.

Glory be to the Father, &c.

Antiphon. For His Mercy : endureth for ever.

Antiphon. Sing us.

Super flumina. Ps. cxxxvii.

1 By the waters of Babylon we sat down and wept : when we remembered thee, O Sion.

2 As for our harps, we hanged them up : upon the trees that are therein.

3 For they that led us away captive required of us then a song, and melody, in our heaviness : Sing us one of the songs of Sion.

4 How shall we sing the Lord's song : in a strange land?

5 If I forget thee, O Jerusalem : let my right hand forget her cunning.

6 If I do not remember thee, let my tongue cleave to the roof of my mouth : yea, if I prefer not Jerusalem in my mirth.

7 Remember the children of Edom, O Lord, in the day of Jerusalem : how they said, Down with it, down with it, even to the ground.

8 O daughter of Babylon, wasted with misery : yea, happy shall he be that rewardeth thee, as thou hast served us.

9 Blessed shall he be that taketh thy children : and throweth them against the stones.

Glory be to the Father, &c.

Antiphon. Sing us : one of the songs of Sion.

The Chapter, 2 Thess. iii. 5.

The Lord direct your hearts into the love of God, and into the patient waiting for Christ.

℟. Thanks be to God.

In Services of the Season this Chapter is said at Vespers (1.) *daily from Epiphany to Septuagesima;* (2.) *on all week-days from Septuagesima to the First Sunday in Lent; and* (3.) *daily from Trinity to Advent.*

Hymn for Thursdays, from Epiphany to the First Sunday in Lent.

Magnæ Deus potentiæ.

Almighty God, Who from the flood
Didst bring to light a twofold brood;
Part in the firmament to fly,
And part in ocean depths to lie :

Appointing fishes in the sea,
And fowls in open air to be;
That each, by origin the same,
Its separate dwelling-place might claim :

Grant that Thy servants, by the tide
Of Blood and Water purified,
No guilty fall from Thee may know,
Nor death eternal undergo.

Let none despair through sin's distress;
Be none puffed up with boastfulness :
That contrite hearts be not dismayed,
Nor haughty souls in ruin laid.

O Father, that we ask be done,
Through Jesus Christ, Thine only Son;
Who, with the Holy Ghost and Thee,
Shall live and reign eternally. Amen.

℣. Lord, let my prayer be set forth.

℟. In Thy sight as the Incense.

From Trinity to Advent is said the Hymn, with the ℣. *and* ℟., *p.* 192.

Antiphon. He hath put down.

Magnificat, St. Luke i.

Antiphon. He hath put down : the mighty from their seat, and hath exalted the humble and meek that confess His Christ.

The week-day Prayers, p. 198, *with Miserere,* Ps. li., *and the rest.*

The Proper Collect.

℣. The Lord be with you.

℟. And with thy spirit.

℣. Bless we the Lord.

℟. Thanks be to God.

The Memorials, &c., p. 194.

FRIDAY AT VESPERS.

℣. O God, make speed to save us.

℟. O Lord, make haste to help us.

℣. Glory be to the Father, and to the Son : and to the Holy Ghost;

℟. As it was in the beginning, is now, and ever shall be : world without end. Amen.

Alleluia.

But from Septuagesima to Wednesday in Holy Week, inclusive, is said instead,

Praise to Thee, O Lord, we sing,
Of Glory the Eternal King.

Antiphon. Before the gods.

Confitebor Tibi. Ps. cxxxviii.

1 I will give thanks unto Thee, O Lord, with my whole heart : even before the gods will I sing praise unto Thee.

2 I will worship toward Thy holy temple, and praise Thy Name, because of Thy lovingkindness and truth : for Thou hast magnified Thy Name, and Thy Word, above all things.

3 When I called upon Thee, Thou heardest me : and enduedst my soul with much strength.

4 All the kings of the earth shall praise Thee, O Lord : for they have heard the words of Thy mouth.

5 Yea, they shall sing in the ways of the Lord : that great is the glory of the Lord.

6 For though the Lord be high, yet hath He respect unto the lowly : as for the proud, He beholdeth them afar off.

7 Though I walk in the midst of trouble, yet shalt Thou refresh me : Thou shalt stretch forth Thy Hand upon the furiousness of mine enemies, and Thy right Hand shall save me.

8 The Lord shall make good His lovingkindness toward me : yea, Thy Mercy, O Lord, endureth for ever ; despise not then the works of Thine own hands.

Glory be to the Father, &c.

Antiphon. Before the gods : will I sing praise unto Thee, my God.

Antiphon. O Lord, Thou hast searched.

Domine, probasti. Ps. cxxxix.

1 O Lord, Thou hast searched me out, and known me : Thou knowest my down-sitting, and mine up-rising ; Thou understandest my thoughts long before.

2 Thou art about my path, and about my bed : and spiest out all my ways.

3 For lo, there is not a word in my tongue : but Thou, O Lord, knowest it altogether.

4 Thou hast fashioned me behind and before : and laid Thine Hand upon me.

5 Such knowledge is too wonderful and excellent for me : I cannot attain unto it.

6 Whither shall I go then from Thy Spirit : or whither shall I go then from Thy Presence?

7 If I climb up into heaven, Thou art there : if I go down to hell, Thou art there also.

8 If I take the wings of the morning : and remain in the uttermost parts of the sea ;

9 Even there also shall Thy Hand lead me : and Thy Right Hand shall hold me.

10 If I say, Peradventure the darkness shall cover me : then shall my night be turned to day.

11 Yea, the darkness is no darkness with Thee, but the night is as clear as the day : the darkness and light to Thee are both alike.

12 For my reins are Thine : Thou hast covered me in my mother's womb.

13 I will give thanks unto Thee, for I am fearfully and wonderfully made : marvellous are Thy works, and that my soul knoweth right well.

14 My bones are not hid from Thee : though I be made secretly, and fashioned beneath in the earth.

15 Thine eyes did see my substance, yet being imperfect : and in Thy book were all my members written ;

16 Which day by day were fashioned : when as yet there was none of them.

17 How dear are Thy counsels unto me, O God : O how great is the sum of them !

18 If I tell them, they are more in number than the sand : when I wake up I am present with Thee.

19 Wilt Thou not slay the wicked, O God : depart from me, ye blood-thirsty men.

20 For they speak unrighteously against Thee : and Thine enemies take Thy Name in vain.

21 Do not I hate them, O Lord, that hate Thee : and am not I grieved with those that rise up against Thee?

22 Yea, I hate them right sore : even as though they were mine enemies.

23 Try me, O God, and seek the ground of my heart : prove me, and examine my thoughts.

24 Look well if there be any way of wickedness in me : and lead me in the way everlasting.

Glory be to the Father, &c.

Antiphon. O Lord, Thou hast searched : me out and known me.

Antiphon. Preserve me.

Eripe me, Domine. Ps. cxl.

1 Deliver me, O Lord, from the evil man : and preserve me from the wicked man.

2 Who imagine mischief in their hearts : and stir up strife all the day long.

3 They have sharpened their tongues like a serpent : adder's poison is under their lips.

4 Keep me, O Lord, from the hands of the ungodly : preserve me from the wicked men, who are purposed to overthrow my goings.

5 The proud have laid a snare for me, and spread a net abroad with cords : yea, and set traps in my way.

6 I said unto the Lord, Thou art my God : hear the voice of my prayers, O Lord.

7 O Lord God, Thou strength of my health : Thou hast covered my head in the day of battle.

8 Let not the ungodly have his desire, O Lord : let not his mischievous imagination prosper, lest they be too proud.

9 Let the mischief of their own lips fall upon the head of them : that compass me about.

10 Let hot burning coals fall upon them : let them be cast into the fire, and into the pit, that they never rise up again.

11 A man full of words shall not prosper upon the earth : evil shall hunt the wicked person to overthrow him.

12 Sure I am that the Lord will avenge the poor : and maintain the cause of the helpless.

13 The righteous also shall give thanks unto Thy Name : and the just shall continue in Thy sight.

Glory be to the Father, &c.

Antiphon. Preserve me : from the wicked man.

Antiphon. Lord, I call.

Domine, clamavi. Ps. cxli.

1 Lord, I call upon Thee, haste Thee unto me : and consider my voice when I cry unto Thee.

2 Let my prayer be set forth in Thy sight as the incense : and let the lifting up of my hands be an evening sacrifice.

3 Set a watch, O Lord, before my mouth : and keep the door of my lips.

4 O let not mine heart be inclined to any evil thing : let me not be occupied in ungodly works with the men that work wickedness, lest I eat of such things as please them.

5 Let the righteous rather smite me friendly : and reprove me.

6 But let not their precious balms break my head : yea, I will pray yet against their wickedness.

7 Let their judges be overthrown in stony places : that they may hear my words, for they are sweet.

8 Our bones lie scattered before

P

the pit : like as when one breaketh and heweth wood upon the earth.

9 But mine eyes look unto Thee, O Lord God : in Thee is my trust, O cast not out my soul.

10 Keep me from the snare that they have laid for me : and from the traps of the wicked doers.

11 Let the ungodly fall into their own nets together : and let me ever escape them.

Glory be to the Father, &c.

Antiphon. Lord, I call : upon Thee, haste Thee unto me.

Antiphon. Thou art my portion.

Voce mea ad Dominum. Ps. cxlii.

1 I cried unto the Lord with my voice : yea, even unto the Lord did I make my supplication.

2 I poured out my complaints before Him : and showed Him of my trouble.

3 When my spirit was in heaviness Thou knewest my path : in the way wherein I walked have they privily laid a snare for me.

4 I looked also upon my right hand : and saw there was no man that would know me.

5 I had no place to flee unto : and no man cared for my soul.

6 I cried unto Thee, O Lord, and said : Thou art my hope, and my portion in the land of the living.

7 Consider my complaint : for I am brought very low.

8 O deliver me from my persecutors : for they are too strong for me.

9 Bring my soul out of prison, that I may give thanks unto Thy Name : which thing if Thou wilt grant me, then shall the righteous resort unto my company.

Glory be to the Father, &c.

Antiphon. Thou art my portion : in the land of the living.

The Chapter, 2 Thess. iii. 5.

The Lord direct your hearts into the love of God, and into the patient waiting for Christ.

℞. Thanks be to God.

In Services of the Season, this Chapter is said at Vespers (1.) *daily from Epiphany to Septuagesima;* (2.) *on all weekdays from Septuagesima to the First Sunday in Lent; and* (3.) *daily from Trinity to Advent.*

Hymn for Fridays from Epiphany to the First Sunday in Lent.

Plasmator hominis Deus.

Maker of men, from Heaven Thy Throne
Who orderest all things, God alone;
By Whose decree the teeming earth
To reptile and to beast gave birth:

The mighty forms that fill the land,
Instinct with life at Thy command,
Thou gav'st subdued to human kind
For service in their rank assigned.

From all Thy servants chase away
Whate'er of thought impure to-day
Hath mingled with the heart's intent,
Or with the actions hath been blent.

In Heaven Thine endless joys bestow,
But grant Thy gifts of grace below:
From chains of strife our souls release;
Bind fast the gentle bands of peace.

O Father, that we ask be done,
Through Jesus Christ, Thine only Son;
Who, with the Holy Ghost and Thee,
Shall live and reign eternally. Amen.

℣. Lord, let my prayer be set forth.

℞. In Thy sight as the Incense.

From Trinity to Advent is said the Hymn, with the ℣. and ℞., p. 192.

Antiphon. God hath holpen.

Magnificat, St. Luke i.

Antiphon. God hath holpen: His servant Israel, as He promised Abraham and his seed; and He hath exalted the humble for ever.

The week-day Prayers, p. 198, *with Miserere,* Ps. li., *and the rest.*

The Proper Collect.

℣. The Lord be with you.

℞. And with thy spirit.

℣. Bless we the Lord.

℞. Thanks be to God.

The Memorials, &c., p. 194.

SATURDAY AT VESPERS; OTHERWISE THE FIRST VESPERS OF SUNDAY.

℣. O God, make speed to save us.

℞. O Lord, make haste to help us.

℣. Glory be to the Father, and to the Son : and to the Holy Ghost;

℞. As it was in the beginning, is now, and ever shall be : world without end. Amen.

Alleluia.

But from Septuagesima to Wednesday in Holy Week, inclusive, is said instead,

Praise to Thee, O Lord, we sing, Of Glory the Eternal King.

Antiphon. Blessed be.

Benedictus Dominus. Ps. cxliv.

1 Blessed be the Lord my Strength : Who teacheth my hands to war, and my fingers to fight;

2 My Hope and my Fortress, my Castle and Deliverer, my Defender in Whom I trust : Who subdueth my people that is under me.

3 Lord, what is man, that Thou hast such respect unto him : or the son of man, that Thou so regardest him?

4 Man is like a thing of nought : his time passeth away like a shadow.

5 Bow Thy heavens, O Lord, and come down : touch the mountains, and they shall smoke.

6 Cast forth Thy lightnings, and tear them : shoot out Thine arrows, and consume them.

7 Send down Thine hand from above : deliver me, and take me out of the great waters, from the hand of strange children;

8 Whose mouth talketh of vanity : and their right hand is a right hand of wickedness.

9 I will sing a new song unto Thee, O God : and sing praises unto Thee upon a ten-stringed lute.

10 Thou hast given victory unto kings : and hast delivered David Thy servant from the peril of the sword.

11 Save me, and deliver me from the hand of strange children : whose mouth talketh of vanity, and their right hand is a right hand of iniquity.

12 That our sons may grow up as the young plants : and that our daughters may be as the polished corners of the temple.

13 That our garners may be full and plenteous with all manner of store : that our sheep may bring forth thousands and ten thousands in our streets.

14 That our oxen may be strong to labour, that there be no decay : no leading into captivity, and no complaining in our streets.

15 Happy are the people that

are in such a case : yea, blessed are the people who have the Lord for their God.

Glory be to the Father, &c.

Antiphon. Blessed be : the Lord my Strength.

Antiphon. For ever.

Exaltabo Te, Deus. Ps. cxlv.

1 I will magnify Thee, O God, my King : and I will praise Thy Name for ever and ever.

2 Every day will I give thanks unto Thee : and praise Thy Name for ever and ever.

3 Great is the Lord, and marvellous, worthy to be praised : there is no end of His greatness.

4 One generation shall praise Thy works unto another : and declare Thy power.

5 As for me, I will be talking of Thy worship : Thy glory, Thy praise, and wondrous works ;

6 So that men shall speak of the might of Thy marvellous acts : and I will also tell of Thy greatness.

7 The memorial of Thine abundant kindness shall be showed : and men shall sing of Thy righteousness.

8 The Lord is gracious and merciful : longsuffering, and of great goodness.

9 The Lord is loving unto every man : and His mercy is over all His works.

10 All Thy works praise Thee, O Lord : and Thy saints give thanks unto Thee.

11 They show the glory of Thy kingdom : and talk of Thy power ;

12 That Thy power, Thy glory, and mightiness of Thy kingdom : might be known unto men.

13 Thy kingdom is an everlasting kingdom : and Thy dominion endureth throughout all ages.

14 The Lord upholdeth all such as fall : and lifteth up all those that are down.

15 The eyes of all wait upon Thee, O Lord : and Thou givest them their meat in due season.

16 Thou openest Thine Hand : and fillest all things living with plenteousness.

17 The Lord is righteous in all His ways : and holy in all His works.

18 The Lord is nigh unto all them that call upon Him : yea, all such as call upon Him faithfully.

19 He will fulfil the desire of them that fear Him : He also will hear their cry, and will help them.

20 The Lord preserveth all them that love Him : but scattereth abroad all the ungodly.

21 My mouth shall speak the praise of the Lord : and let all flesh give thanks unto His holy Name for ever and ever.

Glory be to the Father, &c.

Antiphon. For ever : and ever.

Antiphon. While I live.

Lauda, anima mea. Ps. cxlvi.

1 Praise the Lord, O my soul ; while I live will I praise the Lord : yea, as long as I have any being I will sing praises unto my God.

2 O put not your trust in princes, nor in any child of man : for there is no help in them.

3 For when the breath of man goeth forth he shall turn again to his earth : and then all his thoughts perish.

4 Blessed is he that hath the God of Jacob for his help : and whose hope is in the Lord his God :

5 Who made heaven and earth,

the sea, and all that therein is : Who keepeth His promise for ever;

6 Who helpeth them to right that suffer wrong : Who feedeth the hungry.

7 The Lord looseth men out of prison : the Lord giveth sight to the blind.

8 The Lord helpeth them that are fallen : the Lord careth for the righteous.

9 The Lord careth for the strangers; He defendeth the fatherless and widow : as for the way of the ungodly, He turneth it upside down.

10 The Lord thy God, O Sion, shall be King for evermore : and throughout all generations.

Glory be to the Father, &c.

Antiphon. While I live : will I praise the Lord.

Antiphon. Yea, a joyful and pleasant thing.

Laudate Dominum. Ps. cxlvii. 1—11.

1 O praise the Lord, for it is a good thing to sing praises unto our God : yea, a joyful and pleasant thing it is to be thankful.

2 The Lord doth build up Jerusalem : and gather together the outcasts of Israel.

3 He healeth those that are broken in heart : and giveth medicine to heal their sickness.

4 He telleth the number of the stars : and calleth them all by their names.

5 Great is our Lord, and great is His power : yea, and His wisdom is infinite.

6 The Lord setteth up the meek : and bringeth the ungodly down to the ground.

7 O sing unto the Lord with thanksgiving : sing praises upon the harp unto our God;

8 Who covereth the heaven with clouds, and prepareth rain for the earth : and maketh the grass to grow upon the mountains, and herb for the use of men;

9 Who giveth fodder unto the cattle : and feedeth the young ravens that call upon Him.

10 He hath no pleasure in the strength of an horse : neither delighteth He in any man's legs.

11 But the Lord's delight is in them that fear Him : and put their trust in His mercy.

Glory be to the Father, &c.

Antiphon. Yea, a joyful and pleasant thing : it is to be thankful.

Antiphon. Praise the Lord.

Lauda Hierusalem. Ps. cxlvii. 12.

12 Praise the Lord, O Jerusalem : praise thy God, O Sion.

13 For He hath made fast the bars of thy gates : and hath blessed thy children within thee.

14 He maketh peace in thy borders : and filleth thee with the flour of wheat.

15 He sendeth forth His commandment upon earth : and His word runneth very swiftly.

16 He giveth snow like wool : and scattereth the hoar-frost like ashes.

17 He casteth forth His ice like morsels : who is able to abide His frost?

18 He sendeth out His word, and melteth them : He bloweth with His wind, and the waters flow.

19 He showeth His word unto Jacob : His statutes and ordinances unto Israel.

20 He hath not dealt so with any nation : neither have the heathen knowledge of His laws.

Glory be to the Father, &c.

Antiphon. Praise the Lord : O Jerusalem.

The Chapter, 2 Cor. i. 3, 4.

Blessed be God, even the Father of our Lord Jesus Christ, the Father of Mercies, and the God of all comfort; Who comforteth us in all our tribulation.

R̷. Thanks be to God.

When the Service of the next day is that of the Sunday, this Chapter is said at the Saturday Vespers, (1) from Epiphany to Septuagesima; (2) from Trinity to Advent.

Hymn for Saturdays from Epiphany to First Sunday in Lent.

Deus Creator omnium.

Maker of all things, God most High,
Great Framer of the starry sky;
That rob'st the day in beauteous light,
In sweet repose the quiet night;

May sleep our tired limbs restore,
And fit for toil and use once more;
Relieve our cares, and soothe our breast,
And lull our anxious griefs to rest.

We thank Thee for the day that's gone;
We pray Thee now the night comes on,
Help us poor sinners as we raise
Th' accustomed offering of praise.

To Thee our hearts their music bring;
Thee our united voices sing;
To Thee our pure affections soar,
Thee may our chastened souls adore.

So when the deepening shades prevail,
And night o'er day hath dropp'd her veil,
Faith may no wildering darkness know,
But night with Faith's own radiance glow.

While sleepless Thou dost keep the mind,
Our sins in sleep for ever bind;
Let faith our chastity renew,
And check our sleep's lethargic dew.

From every wrongful passion free,
Our inmost hearts make sleep in Thee,
Nor let the fiend with envious snare
Our rest with sinful terrors scare.

Christ with the Father ever one!
Spirit, of Father and of Son;
God over all, of mighty sway,
Shield us, great Trinity, we pray.
Amen.

V̷. Let our evening prayer come up before Thee, O Lord.

R̷. And let Thy mercy come down on us.

From Trinity to Advent, on Saturdays at Vespers is said the Hymn,

O lux beata Trinitas.

O Trinity of blessed light,
O Unity of princely might,
The fiery sun now goes his way:
Shed Thou within our hearts Thy ray.

To Thee our morning song of praise,
To Thee our evening prayer we raise;
Thy glory suppliant we adore
For ever and for evermore.

All laud to God the Father be;
All laud, Eternal Son, to Thee;
All laud, as is for ever meet,
To God the Holy Paraclete. Amen.

V̷. Let our evening prayer come up before Thee, O Lord.

R̷. And let Thy mercy come down on us.

Antiphon (as in the Proper Services.)

Magnificat, St. Luke i.

Antiphon (as in the Proper Services.)

The week-day Prayers, p. 198, with Miserere, Ps. li., and the rest.

AT COMPLINE.

After the customary Invocation of the Blessed Trinity, &c., let him that sayeth the Office say,

℣. Turn us, O God our Saviour.

℟. And let Thine anger cease from us.

℣. O God, make speed to save us.

℟. O Lord, make haste to help us.

℣. Glory be to the Father, and to the Son : and to the Holy Ghost ;

℟. As it was in the beginning, is now, and ever shall be : world without end. Amen.

Alleluia.

But from the Compline before Septuagesima to Wednesday in Holy Week, inclusive, is said instead of Alleluia,

Praise to Thee, O Lord, we sing,
Of Glory the Eternal King.

COMPLINE I.

Antiphon. Have mercy.

Cum invocarem. Ps. iv.

1 Hear me when I call, O God of my righteousness : Thou hast set me at liberty when I was in trouble ; have mercy upon me, and hearken unto my prayer.

2 O ye sons of men, how long will ye blaspheme Mine Honour : and have such pleasure in vanity, and seek after leasing ?

3 Know this also, that the Lord hath chosen to Himself the man that is godly : when I call upon the Lord, He will hear me.

4 Stand in awe, and sin not : commune with your own heart, and in your chamber, and be still.

5 Offer the sacrifice of righteousness : and put your trust in the Lord.

6 There be many that say : Who will show us any good ?

7 Lord, lift Thou up : the light of Thy countenance upon us.

8 Thou hast put gladness in my heart : since the time that their Corn, and Wine, and Oil increased.

9 I will lay me down in peace, and take my rest : for it is Thou, Lord, only, that makest me dwell in safety.

Glory be to the Father, &c.

In Te Domine, speravi. Ps. xxxi.

1 In Thee, O Lord, have I put my trust : let me never be put to confusion, deliver me in Thy righteousness.

2 Bow down Thine ear to me : make haste to deliver me.

3 And be Thou my strong Rock, and house of defence : that Thou mayest save me.

4 For Thou art my strong Rock, and my Castle : be Thou also my guide, and lead me for Thy Name's sake.

5 Draw me out of the net, that they have laid privily for me : for Thou art my strength.

6 Into Thy hands I commend my spirit : for Thou hast Redeemed me, O Lord, Thou God of truth.

Glory be to the Father, &c.

Qui habitat. Ps. xci.

1 Whoso dwelleth under the defence of the Most High : shall abide under the shadow of the Almighty.

2 I will say unto the Lord, Thou art my Hope, and my strong Hold : my God, in Him will I trust.

3 For He shall deliver thee from the snare of the hunter : and from the noisome pestilence.

4 He shall defend thee under His wings, and thou shalt be safe under His feathers : His faithfulness and truth shall be thy shield and buckler.

5 Thou shalt not be afraid for any terror by night : nor for the arrow that flieth by day;

6 For the pestilence that walketh in darkness : nor for the sickness that destroyeth in the noonday.

7 A thousand shall fall beside thee, and ten thousand at thy right hand : but it shall not come nigh thee.

8 Yea, with thine eyes shalt thou behold : and see the reward of the ungodly.

9 For Thou, Lord, art my hope : Thou hast set Thine house of defence very high.

10 There shall no evil happen unto thee : neither shall any plague come nigh thy dwelling.

11 For He shall give His Angels charge over thee : to keep thee in all thy ways.

12 They shall bear thee in their hands : that thou hurt not thy foot against a stone.

13 Thou shalt go upon the lion and adder : the young lion and the dragon shalt thou tread under thy feet.

14 Because he hath set his love upon Me, therefore will I deliver him : I will set him up, because he hath known My Name.

15 He shall call upon Me, and I will hear him : yea, I am with him in trouble ; I will deliver him, and bring him to honour.

16 With long life will I satisfy him : and show him My salvation.

Glory be to the Father, &c.

Ecce nunc. Ps. cxxxiv.

1 Behold now, praise the Lord : all ye servants of the Lord ;

2 Ye that by night stand in the house of the Lord : even in the courts of the house of our God.

3 Lift up your hands in the sanctuary : and praise the Lord.

4 The Lord that made heaven and earth : give thee blessing out of Sion.

Glory be to the Father, &c.

Antiphon. Have mercy : upon me, and hearken unto my prayer.

This Antiphon is always said, unless some other be appointed.

The Chapter, Jer. xiv. 9.

Thou, O Lord, art in the midst of us, and we are called by Thy Name ; leave us not.

This Chapter is said daily, except from Maundy Thursday to Low Sunday, inclusive.

℟. Thanks be to God.

Hymn. Te lucis ante terminum.
Before the ending of the day,
Creator of the world, we pray
That with Thy wonted favour, Thou
Wouldst be our Guard and Keeper now.

From all ill dreams defend our eyes,
From nightly fears and fantasies ;
Tread under foot our ghostly foe,
That no pollution we may know.

O Father, that we ask be done,
Through Jesus Christ, Thine only Son,
Who with the Holy Ghost and Thee,
Shall live and reign eternally. Amen.

℣. Keep me as the apple of an eye.

℟. Hide me under the shadow of Thy wings.

AT COMPLINE. 217

(handwritten: Save Us)

Antiphon. Come, O Lord.

Nunc dimittis. St. Luke ii. 29.

Lord, now lettest Thou Thy servant depart in peace : according to Thy Word.

For mine eyes have seen : Thy Salvation.

Which Thou hast prepared : before the face of all people ;

To be a Light to lighten the Gentiles : and to be the Glory of Thy people Israel.

Glory be to the Father, &c.

Antiphon. Come, O Lord : and visit us in peace ; that we may rejoice before Thee with a perfect heart.

THE PRAYERS.

All kneeling.

Lord, have mercy upon us.
Christ, have mercy upon us.
Lord, have mercy upon us.

Our Father, &c.

℣. I will lay me down in peace.

℟. And take my rest.

I believe in God, &c.

℣. Let us bless the Father, the Son, and the Holy Ghost.

℟. Let us bless and exalt Him for ever.

℣. Blessed be Thou, O Lord, in the firmament of heaven.

℟. And praised for evermore.

℣. May the Almighty and most merciful God bless us and keep us.

℟. Amen.

Then is said the following Confession.

We confess to God Almighty, the Father, the Son, and the Holy Ghost, in the sight of the whole company of heaven, that we have sinned exceedingly in thought, word, and deed, of our fault, of our own fault, of our own great fault; therefore we pray God to have mercy on us.

And those present shall say,

Almighty God have mercy upon us, and bring us to everlasting life. Amen.

[*Or he that sayeth the Office may say,*

I confess to God Almighty in the sight of the whole company of heaven and to you, that I have sinned exceedingly in thought, word, and deed, of my fault, of my own fault, of my own grievous fault, and calling to mind the Communion of Saints, I beseech you, brethren, to pray for me.

And those present shall answer,

Almighty God have mercy upon thee, forgive thy sins, deliver thee from evil, and bring thee to everlasting life. Amen.

Then those present shall say,

We confess to Almighty God in the sight of the whole company of heaven and to thee, that we have sinned exceedingly in thought, word, and deed, of our fault, of our own fault, of our own grievous fault, and calling to mind the Communion of Saints, we beseech thee to pray for us.

And he that sayeth the Office shall answer,

Almighty God have mercy upon you, forgive you your sins, deliver you from evil, and bring you to everlasting life. Amen.]

[*And if a Priest be present, let him add,*

The Almighty and merciful Lord grant you Absolution and forgiveness of your sins, time for repentance, amendment of life, and the grace and comfort of His Holy Spirit. Amen.]

℣. Wilt Thou not turn again and quicken us, O Lord?

℞. That Thy people may rejoice in Thee.

℣. Show us Thy mercy, O Lord.

℞. And grant us Thy salvation.

℣. Vouchsafe, O Lord.

℞. To keep us this night without sin.

℣. O Lord, have mercy upon us.

℞. Have mercy upon us.

℣. O Lord, let Thy mercy lighten upon us.

℞. As our trust is in Thee.

[*On ordinary week-days is here said,*

℣. Lord, hear my voice, when I cry unto Thee.

℞. Have mercy upon me, and hearken unto me.

Miserere mei Deus. Ps. li.]

℣. Turn us again, Thou God of Hosts.

℞. Show the light of Thy countenance, and we shall be whole.

℣. O Lord, hear our prayer.

℞. And let our cry come unto Thee.

℣. The Lord be with you.

℞. And with thy spirit.

Let us pray.

LIGHTEN our darkness, we beseech Thee, O Lord; and by Thy great mercy defend us from all perils and dangers of this night; for the love of Thy only Son, our Saviour Jesus Christ. Amen.

℣. The Lord be with you.

℞. And with thy spirit.

℣. Bless we the Lord.

℞. Amen.

Here endeth the Service for Compline.

Compline is thus said daily throughout Advent, without change, except that on the Feasts of St. Andrew and St. Thomas, the Hymn, Salvator mundi Domine, *p.* 219, *is said instead of* Te lucis ante terminum.

After Compline is said the following, for the Peace of the Church, every day throughout the year, except on Holy-Days, and from Christmas Eve to the First Sunday after Epiphany, and from Wednesday in Holy Week to Trinity Monday.

Ad Te levavi oculos meos. Ps. cxxiii.

1 Unto Thee lift I up mine eyes : O Thou that dwellest in the heavens.

2 Behold, even as the eyes of servants look unto the hand of their masters, and as the eyes of a maiden unto the hand of her mistress : even so our eyes wait upon the Lord our God, until He have mercy upon us.

3 Have mercy upon us, O Lord, have mercy upon us : for we are utterly despised.

4 Our soul is filled with the scornful reproof of the wealthy : and with the despitefulness of the proud.

Glory be to the Father, &c.

Lord, have mercy upon us.
Christ, have mercy upon us.
Lord, have mercy upon us.

Our Father, Which art in heaven, &c.

℣. O Lord, arise, help us.

℟. And deliver us for Thy Name's sake.

℣. Turn us again, O Lord God of Hosts.

℟. Show the light of Thy countenance, and we shall be whole.

℣. Lord, hear our prayer.

℟. And let our cry come unto Thee.

℣. The Lord be with you.

℟. And with thy spirit.

Let us pray.

O LORD, we beseech Thee, mercifully to hear the prayers of Thy Church, that we, being delivered from all adversities, and serving Thee with a quiet mind, may enjoy Thy peace all the days of our life; through Jesus Christ our Lord, Who liveth and reigneth with Thee and the Holy Ghost, One God, world without end. *Amen.*

℣. May the Souls of the Faithful, through the mercy of God, rest in peace.

℟. Amen.

℣. The Lord be with you.

℟. And with thy spirit.

℣. Bless we the Lord.

℟. Thanks be to God.

COMPLINE II.
On Christmas Eve.
Antiphon to Psalms.

Be ye ready : like unto men that wait for their Lord, when He shall return from the wedding.

The Lesson, Jer. xiv. 9, *as in Compline* i.

Hymn. Salvator mundi Domine.

O Saviour of the world forlorn,
Who, man to save, as man wast Born;
Protect us through this coming night,
And ever save us by Thy might.

Be with us, Lord, in mercy nigh,
And spare Thy servants when they cry;
Our sins blot out, our prayers receive,
Our darkness lighten and forgive.

O let not sleep o'ercome the soul,
Nor Satan with his Spirits foul;
Our flesh keep chaste, that it may be
An holy temple unto Thee.

To Thee, Who makest souls anew,
With heartfelt vows we humbly sue;
That pure in heart, and free from stain,
We from our beds may rise again.

All laud to God the Father be;
All laud, Eternal Son, to Thee;
All laud, as is for ever meet,
To God the Blessed Paraclete. Amen.

℣. Keep me as the apple of an eye.

℟. Hide me under the shadow of Thy wings.

Antiphon, which is said before and after Nunc dimittis.

Watch and pray, for ye know not when the time is. Watch ye therefore, for ye know not when the Lord cometh, at even, or at midnight, or at the cock-crowing, or in the morning; lest coming suddenly He find you sleeping.

Here follow the Prayers, p. 217.

COMPLINE III.
On Christmas Day.
Antiphon to Psalms.

Unto us is Born this day : in the city of David, a Saviour, Which is Christ the Lord.

Hymn, Salvator mundi Domine, *as in Compline* ii.

Antiphon to Nunc dimittis.

Alleluia! THE WORD WAS MADE FLESH, Alleluia; and dwelt among us. Alleluia, Alleluia.

Here follow the Prayers, p. 217.

This Compline is said till the Circumcision of our Lord Jesus Christ.

COMPLINE IV.
On the Circumcision of Christ.
Antiphon to Psalms.

When the Lord was born : the choirs of Angels sang, saying, Salvation to our God, Which sitteth upon the throne, and unto the Lamb.

Hymn, Salvator mundi Domine, *as in Compline* ii., *p.* 219.

Antiphon to Nunc dimittis, *as in Compline* iii.

Here follow the Prayers, p. 217.

This Compline is said daily till the Eve of the Epiphany.

COMPLINE V.
On the Eve and Feast of the Epiphany.
Antiphon to Psalms.

Thou hast appeared, O Christ : Thou Light of Light, to Whom the wise men bring gifts. Alleluia, Alleluia, Alleluia.

Hymn, Salvator mundi Domine, *as in Compline* ii.

Antiphon to Nunc dimittis.

Alleluia. All they from Sheba shall come. Alleluia. They shall bring gold and incense. Alleluia. Alleluia.

Here follow the Prayers, p. 217.

COMPLINE VI.
On the day after the Epiphany.

Everything as in Compline i. *till the Antiphon to* Nunc dimittis.

Save us waking, O Lord, and guard us sleeping : that awake we may be with Christ, and in peace may take our rest.

Here follow the Prayers, p. 217.

This Compline is said (1.) *daily till the First Sunday in Lent, and* (2.) *from Trinity Monday to Advent, except on Feast-days, when Compline* xvi. *is said instead.*

[*On week-days in Lent, Miserere mei Deus,* Ps. li., *is followed by*

Domine exaudi.   Ps. cxliii.
Against Sloth.

1 Hear my prayer, O Lord, and consider my desire : hearken unto me for Thy truth and righteousness' sake.

2 And enter not into judgment with Thy servant : for in Thy sight shall no man living be justified.

3 For the enemy hath persecuted my soul; he hath smitten my life down to the ground : he hath laid me in the darkness, as the men that have been long dead.

4 Therefore is my spirit vexed within me : and my heart within me is desolate.

5 Yet do I remember the time past; I muse upon all Thy works : yea, I exercise myself in the works of Thy hands.

6 I stretch forth my hands unto Thee : my soul gaspeth unto Thee as a thirsty land.

7 Hear me, O Lord, and that soon, for my spirit waxeth faint : hide not Thy face from me, lest I be like unto them that go down into the pit.

8 O let me hear Thy lovingkindness betimes in the morning, for in Thee is my trust : show Thou me the way that I should walk in, for I lift up my soul unto Thee.

9 Deliver me, O Lord, from mine enemies : for I flee unto Thee to hide me.

10 Teach me to do the thing that pleaseth Thee, for Thou art my God : let Thy loving Spirit lead me forth into the land of righteousness.

11 Quicken me, O Lord, for Thy Name's sake : and for Thy righteousness' sake bring my soul out of trouble.

12 And of Thy goodness slay mine enemies : and destroy all them that vex my soul; for I am Thy servant.

Glory be to the Father, &c.]

℣. Turn us again, *as above.*

COMPLINE VII.

On the First Sunday in Lent (i.e. *at Compline after the First Vespers.*)

Antiphon to Psalms.

Lord, lift Thou up : the Light of Thy countenance upon us. Thou hast put gladness in my heart.

The Lesson, Jer. xiv. 9, *as in Compline* i.

R. I will lay me down in peace; and take my rest. ℣. I will not suffer mine eyes to sleep, nor mine eyelids to slumber. ℟. I will take my rest. ℣. Glory be to the Father, and to the Son : and to the Holy Ghost. ℟. I will lay me down in peace, and take my rest.

Hymn. Christe qui Lux es et Dies.
Christ, Thou Who art the Light and Day,
The clouds of night dost drive away;
The very Light of Light art Thou,
Preaching glad tidings here below.

We pray Thee, holy Lord, our Light,
Defend us in this coming night;
O grant us perfect rest in Thee,
A quiet night from perils free.

Let not dull slumber quell the soul,
Nor Satan with his Spirits foul;
Nor let our flesh consent begin
To make us in Thy presence sin.

Grant that our eyes due sleep may take,
Our hearts to Thee be e'er awake;
May Thy Right Hand defend and guide
Thy servants who in Thee confide.

Look down, O Lord, our strong defence,
Repress our foes' proud insolence :
Direct Thy people in all good,
Whom Thou hast purchased with Thy Blood.

Remember us, O Lord, we pray,
Pent in this cumbering frame of clay;
Thou Who dost e'er our souls defend,
Be with Thy servants to the end.

All laud to God the Father be :
All laud, Eternal Son, to Thee :
All laud, as is for ever meet,
To God the Blessed Paraclete. Amen.

℣. Keep me as the apple of an eye.

℟. Hide me under the shadow of Thy wings.

Antiphon to Nunc dimittis.

When thou seest the naked, cover thou him : and hide not thyself from thine own flesh. Then shall thy light break forth as the morning, and the glory of the Lord shall be thy rereward.

Here follow the Prayers, p. 217.

This Compline is said daily till the Third Sunday in Lent.

COMPLINE VIII.

On the Third Sunday in Lent.

Everything as in Compline vii. *till the Antiphon to* Nunc dimittis.

In the midst of life we are in death : of whom may we seek for succour but of Thee, O Lord, Who for our sins art justly displeased? Yet, O Lord God most Holy, O Lord most mighty, O holy and most merciful Saviour, deliver us not into the bitter pains of eternal death.

On Saturdays and Sundays, after Nunc dimittis and its Antiphon, is added,

℣. Cast me not away in the time of age : forsake me not when my strength faileth me.

℞. Yet, O Lord God most Holy, O Lord most mighty, O holy and most merciful Saviour, deliver us not into the bitter pains of eternal death.

℣. Shut not Thy merciful ears to our prayer.

℞. O Lord, most mighty, O holy and most merciful Saviour, deliver us not into the bitter pains of eternal death.

℣. Thou knowest, Lord, the secrets of our hearts ; shut not Thy merciful ears to our prayer.

℞. O holy and most merciful Saviour, deliver us not into the bitter pains of eternal death.

Here follow the Prayers, p. 217.

This Compline is said daily till Passion Sunday, the Fifth in Lent.

COMPLINE IX.

On Passion Sunday.

Antiphon to Psalms.

Have mercy upon me : and hearken unto my prayer.

R. *to Lesson.* Into Thy hands I commend My Spirit. ℣. For Thou hast Redeemed Me, O Lord, Thou God of Truth. Into Thy Hands I commend My Spirit.

Hymn. Cultor Dei memento.
Thou Child of Christ, remember
  The Font's Baptismal dew ;
Remember thy renewal
  In Confirmation too.

And thou, O crafty serpent,
  Who seekest by many an art,
And many a guileful winding,
  To vex the quiet heart ;

Depart, for Christ is present ;
  Since Christ is here, give place ;
And let the sign thou ownest
  Thy ghostly legions chase.

And though awhile the body
  In sleep may lie reclined,
Yet Christ, in very slumber,
  Shall fill the Christian mind.

All laud to God the Father,
  All laud to God the Son ;
To God the Holy Spirit
  Be equal honour done. Amen.

℣. Keep me as the apple of an eye.

℞. Hide me under the shadow of Thy wings.

Antiphon to Nunc dimittis.

O King, Glorious among Thy Saints : Who art ever to be praised, and yet infinitely above us ; Thou, Lord, art in the midst of us, and we are called by Thy Name ; leave us not, O our God ; and in the Day of Judgment vouchsafe to number us among Thy Saints, O King most Blessed.

On Saturday and Palm Sunday is said the following.

℣. O King, most Blessed, govern Thy servants in the right way.

℞. Among Thy Saints, O King most Blessed.

℣. By holy fasts to amend our sinful lives.

℞. O King most Blessed, govern Thy servants in the right way.

℣. To duly keep Thy Paschal Feast.

℞. Among Thy Saints, O King most Blessed.

Here follow the Prayers, p. 217.

This Compline is said daily till Maundy Thursday.

COMPLINE X.
On Maundy Thursday.

Let the Reader begin (after the customary Invocation of the Blessed Trinity, &c., in silence) the

Antiphon. Christ became obedient.

Cum invocarem. Ps. iv.
In Te Domine. Ps. xxxi.
Ecce nunc. Ps. cxxxiv.
Nunc dimittis, &c.

(*All without* Glory be to the Father.)

Antiphon. Christ became obedient: for us unto Death, even the death of the Cross.

After the Antiphon is said the Lord's Prayer *and* Psalm li. *Miserere mei Deus, without* Glory be to the Father, *all kneeling.*

℣. The Lord be with you.
℞. And with thy spirit.

Let us pray.

ALMIGHTY God, we beseech Thee graciously to behold this Thy family, for which our Lord Jesus Christ was contented to be Betrayed, and given up into the hands of wicked men, and to suffer Death upon the Cross; Who now liveth and reigneth with Thee and the Holy Ghost, ever one God, world without end. *Amen.*

℣. The Lord be with you.
℞. And with thy spirit.

℣. Bless we the Lord.
℞. Thanks be to God.

Here endeth Compline x.

COMPLINE XI.
On Good Friday.

Everything as in Compline x. except that at the first words of the Antiphon, Christ became obedient, *all kneel.*

The Lord be with you, &c., *and* Let us pray, *are omitted, and the Compline shall end with the Collect, thus:*

ALMIGHTY God, we beseech Thee graciously to behold this Thy family, for which our Lord Jesus Christ was contented to be Betrayed, and to be given up into the hands of wicked men, and to suffer Death upon the Cross. *Amen.*

Here endeth Compline xi.

COMPLINE XII.
On Easter Eve.

After the usual Invocation of the Blessed Trinity, &c., let the Reader begin thus,

℣. O God, make speed to save us.
℞. O Lord, make haste to help us.
℣. Glory be to the Father, &c. Alleluia.

Antiphon to Psalms.

Alleluia, Alleluia, Alleluia.

Cum invocarem. Ps. iv.
In Te Domine. Ps. xxxi.
Ecce nunc. Ps. cxxxiv.
Nunc dimittis, &c.

Each with Glory be to the Father, &c.

℣. The Lord be with you.
℟. And with thy spirit.

Let us pray.

ALMIGHTY God, Who through Thine Only-begotten Son Jesus Christ, hast overcome death and opened unto us the gate of everlasting life; We humbly beseech Thee, that as by Thy special grace preventing us, Thou dost put into our minds good desires, so by Thy continual help we may bring the same to good effect; through Jesus Christ our Lord, Who liveth and reigneth with Thee and the Holy Ghost, ever One God, world without end. *Amen.*

℣. The Lord be with you.
℟. And with thy spirit.
℣. Bless we the Lord.
℟. Thanks be to God.

This Compline is said daily till Low Sunday, but on and after Easter the following ℣. and ℟. are said immediately after Nunc dimittis *and its Antiphon.*

℣. This is the day which the Lord hath made.
℟. We will rejoice and be glad in it.
℣. In Thy Resurrection, O Christ.
℟. Let heaven and earth rejoice.
℣. The Lord be with you.
℟. And with thy spirit.

Let us pray.
Collect as above.

Here endeth Compline xii.

COMPLINE XIII.

On Low Sunday.
Everything as in Compline i., *except what is here given.*

Antiphon to Psalms.
Alleluia, Alleluia, Alleluia.

Lesson, Jer. xiv. 9, *as in Compline* i.

℟. Thanks be to God.

Hymn. Jesu Salvator seculi.

Jesu, Who brought'st Redemption nigh,
Word of the Father, God most High;
O Light of Light, to man unknown,
And watchful Guardian of Thine Own:

Thy hand Creation made and guides;
Thy wisdom time from time divides:
By this world's cares and toils opprest,
O give our weary bodies rest.

That while in frames of sin and pain,
A little longer we remain,
Our flesh may here in such wise sleep,
That watch with Christ our souls may keep.

O free us, while we dwell below,
From insults from our ghostly foe,
That he may ne'er victorious be
O'er them that are redeemed by Thee.

We pray Thee, King, with glory decked,
In this our Paschal joy, protect,
From all that Death would fain effect,
Thy ransom'd flock, Thine Own elect.

To Thee Who, dead, again dost live,
All glory, Lord, Thy people give;
All glory, as is ever meet,
To Father and to Paraclete. Amen.

℣. Keep me as the apple of an eye.
℟. Hide me under the shadow of Thy wings.

Antiphon to Nunc dimittis.
Alleluia. The Lord is Risen: Alleluia, as He said. Alleluia, Alleluia.

Here follow the Prayers, p. 217.

This Compline is said daily till the Vigil of the Ascension.

COMPLINE XIV.

On the Vigil of The Ascension of our Lord Jesus Christ.

Hymn. Jesu nostra Redemptio.

Jesu, Redemption all divine,
Whom here we love, for Whom we pine,
God, working out creation's plan,
And, in the latter time, made Man;

What love of Thine was that, which led
To take our woes upon Thy Head,
And pangs and cruel death to bear,
To ransom us from death's despair.

To Thee Hell's gate gave ready way,
Demanding there his captive prey:
And now, in pomp and victor's pride,
Thou sittest at the Father's side.

Let very mercy force Thee still
To spare us, conquering all our ill;
And, granting that we ask, on high
With Thine Own Face to satisfy.

Be Thou our Joy and Thou our Guard,
Who art to be our great Reward:
Our glory and our boast in Thee
For ever and for ever be.

All glory, Lord, to Thee we pay,
Ascending o'er the stars to-day;
All glory, as is ever meet,
To Father and to Paraclete. Amen.

℣. Keep me as the apple of an eye.

℟. Hide me under the shadow of Thy wings.

Antiphon to Nunc dimittis.

Alleluia! Christ is gone up: on high! Alleluia! and hath led captivity captive! Alleluia! Alleluia!

Here follow the Prayers, p. 217.

This Compline is said daily till Whitsun Eve.

COMPLINE XV.

On Whitsun Eve.

Antiphon to Psalms.

Alleluia, Alleluia, Alleluia, Alleluia.

Hymn, Salvator mundi Domine, *as in Compline* ii.

But on Whitsun Day, Monday, and Tuesday is said the

Hymn. Veni, Sancte Spiritus.

Come, Thou Holy Paraclete,
And from Thy Celestial seat
 Send Thy light and brilliancy:

Father of the poor, draw near,
Giver of all gifts, be here:
 Come, the soul's true radiancy:

Come, of Comforters the best,
Of the soul the sweetest guest,
 Come in toil refreshingly:

Thou in labour rest most sweet,
Thou art shadow from the heat,
 Comfort in adversity.

O Thou Light, most pure, most blest,
Shine within the inmost breast
 Of Thy faithful company.

Where Thou art not, man hath nought;
Every holy deed and thought
 Comes from Thy Divinity.

What is soiled, make Thou pure;
What is wounded, work its cure;
 What is parched, fructify.

What is rigid, gently bend;
What is frozen, warmly tend;
 Strengthen what goes erringly.

Fill Thy Faithful, who confide
In Thy power to guard and guide,
 With Thy sevenfold Mystery:

Here Thy grace and virtue send;
Grant Salvation in the end,
 And in heav'n felicity.

℣. Keep me as the apple of an eye.

℟. Hide me under the shadow of Thy wings.

Antiphon to Nunc dimittis.

Alleluia! The Comforter, Which is the Holy Ghost; Alleluia! shall teach you all things. Alleluia! Alleluia!

Here follow the Prayers, p. 217.

This Compline is said daily till Trinity Sunday.

COMPLINE XVI.

On Trinity Sunday.
Antiphon to Psalms.

Have mercy upon me : and hearken unto my prayer.

Hymn, Salvator mundi Domine.

Antiphon to Nunc dimittis.

Lord, grant us Thy light; that being rid of the darkness of our hearts, we may come to the true Light, Which is Christ.

Here follow the Prayers, p. 217.

This Compline is also said on the Anniversary of the Dedication of the Church, and on all Holy-Days from Epiphany to Lent, and from Trinity to Advent, except All Saints' Day.

COMPLINE XVII.

On All Saints' Day.
Antiphon to Psalms.

Grant, O Christ : that the Communion of Saints may avail to our ghostly and bodily good.

Everything as in Compline xvi.

COMPLINE XVIII.

On the Feasts of our Lady.
Antiphon to Psalms.

Blessed is the womb that bare Thee, O Christ : and the paps which Thou hast sucked.

Whatever be the last verse of the Hymn, according to the Season, the following is said instead :

All honour, laud, and glory be,
O Jesu, Virgin-born, to Thee!
All glory, as is ever meet,
To Father and to Paraclete. Amen.

Antiphon to Nunc dimittis.

And the Angel came in unto her, and said, Hail! thou that art highly favoured, the Lord is with thee; Blessed art thou among women.

Here follow the Prayers.

THE PENITENTIAL PSALMS.

Against Anger.

To be said at Lauds in Lent.

Domine, ne in furore. Ps. vi.

1 O Lord, rebuke me not in Thine indignation : neither chasten me in Thy displeasure.

2 Have mercy upon me, O Lord, for I am weak : O Lord, heal me, for my bones are vexed.

3 My soul also is sore troubled : but, Lord, how long wilt Thou punish me?

4 Turn Thee, O Lord, and deliver my soul : O save me for Thy mercy's sake.

5 For in death no man remembereth Thee : and who will give Thee thanks in the pit?

6 I am weary of my groaning; every night wash I my bed : and water my couch with my tears.

7 My beauty is gone for very trouble : and worn away because of all mine enemies.

8 Away from me, all ye that work vanity : for the Lord hath heard the voice of my weeping.

9 The Lord hath heard my petition : the Lord will receive my prayer.

10 All mine enemies shall be confounded and sore vexed : they shall be turned back, and put to shame suddenly.

Glory be to the Father, &c.

Against Pride.

To be said at Prime in Lent.

Beati quorum. Ps. xxxii.

1 Blessed is he whose unrighteousness is forgiven : and whose sin is covered.

2 Blessed is the man unto whom the Lord imputeth no sin : and in whose spirit there is no guile.

3 For while I held my tongue : my bones consumed away through my daily complaining.

4 For Thy hand is heavy upon me day and night : and my moisture is like the drought in summer.

5 I will acknowledge my sin unto Thee : and mine unrighteousness have I not hid.

6 I said, I will confess my sins unto the Lord : and so Thou forgavest the wickedness of my sin.

7 For this shall every one that is godly make his prayer unto Thee, in a time when Thou mayest be found : but in the great water-floods they shall not come nigh him.

8 Thou art a place to hide me in, Thou shalt preserve me from trouble : Thou shalt compass me about with songs of deliverance.

9 I will inform thee, and teach thee in the way wherein thou shalt go : and I will guide thee with Mine eye.

10 Be ye not like to horse and mule, which have no understanding : whose mouths must be held with bit and bridle, lest they fall upon thee.

11 Great plagues remain for the ungodly : but whoso putteth his trust in the Lord, mercy embraceth him on every side.

12 Be glad, O ye righteous, and rejoice in the Lord : and be joyful, all ye that are true of heart.

Glory be to the Father, &c.

Against Gluttony.

To be said at Terce in Lent.

Domine, ne in furore. Ps. xxxviii.

1 Put me not to rebuke, O Lord, in Thine anger : neither chasten me in Thy heavy displeasure.

2 For Thine arrows stick fast in me : and Thy hand presseth me sore.

3 There is no health in my flesh, because of Thy displeasure : neither is there any rest in my bones by reason of my sin.

4 For my wickednesses are gone over my head : and are like a sore burden, too heavy for me to bear.

5 My wounds stink and are corrupt : through my foolishness.

6 I am brought into so great trouble and misery : that I go mourning all the day long.

7 For my loins are filled with a sore disease : and there is no whole part in my body.

8 I am feeble, and sore smitten : I have roared for the very disquietness of my heart.

9 Lord, Thou knowest all my desire : and my groaning is not hid from Thee.

10 My heart panteth, my strength hath failed me : and the sight of mine eyes is gone from me.

11 My lovers and my neighbours did stand looking upon my trouble : and my kinsmen stood afar off.

12 They also that sought after my life laid snares for me : and they that went about to do me evil talked of wickedness, and imagined deceit all the day long.

13 As for me, I was like a deaf man, and heard not : and as one that is dumb, who doth not open his mouth.

14 I became even as a man that heareth not : and in whose mouth are no reproofs.

15 For in Thee, O Lord, have I

put my trust : Thou shalt answer for me, O Lord my God.

16 I have required that they, even mine enemies, should not triumph over me : for when my foot slipped, they rejoiced greatly against me.

17 And I, truly, am set in the plague : and my heaviness is ever in my sight.

18 For I will confess my wickedness : and be sorry for my sin.

19 But mine enemies live, and are mighty : and they that hate me wrongfully are many in number.

20 They also that reward evil for good are against me : because I follow the thing that good is.

21 Forsake me not, O Lord my God : be not Thou far from me.

22 Haste Thee to help me : O Lord God of my salvation.

Glory be to the Father, &c.

Against Lust.

To be said at all the Hours in Lent.

Miserere mei Deus. Ps. li.

1 Have mercy upon me, O God, after Thy great goodness : according to the multitude of Thy mercies, do away mine offences.

2 Wash me throughly from my wickedness : and cleanse me from my sin.

3 For I acknowledge my faults : and my sin is ever before me.

4 Against Thee only have I sinned, and done this evil in Thy sight : that Thou mightest be justified in Thy saying, and clear when Thou art judged.

5 Behold, I was shapen in wickedness : and in sin hath my mother conceived me.

6 But lo, Thou requirest truth in the inward parts : and shalt make me to understand wisdom secretly.

7 Thou shalt purge me with hyssop, and I shall be clean : Thou shalt wash me, and I shall be whiter than snow.

8 Thou shalt make me hear of joy and gladness : that the bones which Thou hast broken may rejoice.

9 Turn Thy Face from my sins : and put out all my misdeeds.

10 Make me a clean heart, O God : and renew a right spirit within me.

11 Cast me not away from Thy presence : and take not Thy Holy Spirit from me.

12 O give me the comfort of Thy help again : and stablish me with Thy free Spirit.

13 Then shall I teach Thy ways unto the wicked : and sinners shall be converted unto Thee.

14 Deliver me from blood-guiltiness, O God, Thou that art the God of my health : and my tongue shall sing of Thy righteousness.

15 Thou shalt open my lips, O Lord : and my mouth shall show Thy praise.

16 For Thou desirest no sacrifice, else would I give it Thee : but Thou delightest not in burnt-offerings.

17 The sacrifice of God is a troubled spirit : a broken and contrite heart, O God, shalt Thou not despise.

18 O be favourable and gracious unto Sion : build Thou the walls of Jerusalem.

19 Then shalt Thou be pleased with the sacrifice of righteousness, with the burnt-offerings and oblations : then shall they offer young bullocks upon Thine Altar.

Glory be to the Father, &c.

Against Avarice.

To be said at None in Lent.

Domine, exaudi. Ps. cii.

1 Hear my prayer, O Lord : and let my crying come unto Thee.

2 Hide not Thy face from me in the time of my trouble : incline Thine ear unto me when I call; O hear me, and that right soon.

3 For my days are consumed away like smoke : and my bones are burnt up as it were a firebrand.

4 My heart is smitten down, and withered like grass : so that I forgot to eat my bread.

5 For the voice of my groaning : my bones will scarce cleave to my flesh.

6 I am become like a pelican in the wilderness : and like an owl that is in the desert.

7 I have watched, and am even as it were a sparrow : that sitteth alone upon the house-top.

8 Mine enemies revile me all the day long : and they that are mad upon me are sworn together against me.

9 For I have eaten ashes as it were bread : and mingled my drink with weeping;

10 And that because of Thine indignation and wrath : for Thou hast taken me up, and cast me down.

11 My days are gone like a shadow : and I am withered like grass.

12 But Thou, O Lord, shalt endure for ever : and Thy remembrance throughout all generations.

13 Thou shalt arise, and have mercy upon Sion : for it is time that Thou have mercy upon her, yea, the time is come.

14 And why? Thy servants think upon her stones : and it pitieth them to see her in the dust.

15 The heathen shall fear Thy Name, O Lord : and all the kings of the earth Thy majesty;

16 When the Lord shall build up Sion : and when His glory shall appear:

17 When He turneth Him unto the prayer of the poor destitute : and despiseth not their desire.

18 This shall be written for those that come after : and the people which shall be born shall praise the Lord.

19 For He hath looked down from His sanctuary : out of the heaven did the Lord behold the earth;

20 That He might hear the mournings of such as are in captivity : and deliver the children appointed unto death;

21 That they may declare the Name of the Lord in Sion : and His worship at Jerusalem;

22 When the people are gathered together : and the kingdoms also, to serve the Lord.

23 He brought down my strength in my journey : and shortened my days.

24 But I said, O my God, take me not away in the midst of mine age : as for Thy years, they endure throughout all generations.

25 Thou, Lord, in the beginning hast laid the foundation of the earth : and the heavens are the work of Thy hands.

26 They shall perish, but Thou shalt endure : they all shall wax old as doth a garment;

27 And as a vesture shalt Thou change them, and they shall be changed : but Thou art the same, and Thy years shall not fail.

28 The children of Thy ser-

vants shall continue : and their seed shall stand fast in Thy sight.

Glory be to the Father, &c.

Against Envy.

To be said at Vespers in Lent.

De profundis. Ps. cxxx.

1 Out of the deep have I called unto Thee, O Lord : Lord, hear my voice.

2 O let Thine ears consider well : the voice of my complaint.

3 If Thou, Lord, wilt be extreme to mark what is done amiss : O Lord, who may abide it?

4 For there is mercy with Thee : therefore shalt Thou be feared.

5 I look for the Lord ; my soul doth wait for Him : in His word is my trust.

6 My soul fleeth unto the Lord : before the morning watch, I say, before the morning watch.

7 O Israel, trust in the Lord, for with the Lord there is mercy : and with Him is plenteous Redemption.

8 And He shall redeem Israel : from all his sins.

Glory be to the Father, &c.

Against Sloth.

To be said at Compline in Lent.

Domine exaudi. Ps. cxliii.

1 Hear my prayer, O Lord, and consider my desire : hearken unto me for Thy truth and righteousness' sake.

2 And enter not into judgment with Thy servant : for in Thy sight shall no man living be justified.

3 For the enemy hath persecuted my soul ; he hath smitten my life down to the ground : he hath laid me in the darkness, as the men that have been long dead.

4 Therefore is my spirit vexed within me : and my heart within me is desolate.

5 Yet do I remember the time past ; I muse upon all Thy works : yea, I exercise myself in the works of Thy hands.

6 I stretch forth my hands unto Thee : my soul gaspeth unto Thee as a thirsty land.

7 Hear me, O Lord, and that soon, for my spirit waxeth faint : hide not Thy face from me, lest I be like unto them that go down into the pit.

8 O let me hear Thy lovingkindness betimes in the morning, for in Thee is my trust : show Thou me the way that I should walk in, for I lift up my soul unto Thee.

9 Deliver me, O Lord, from mine enemies : for I flee unto Thee to hide me.

10 Teach me to do the thing that pleaseth Thee, for Thou art my God : let Thy loving Spirit lead me forth into the land of righteousness.

11 Quicken me, O Lord, for Thy Name's sake : and for Thy righteousness' sake bring my soul out of trouble.

12 And of Thy goodness slay mine enemies : and destroy all them that vex my soul ; for I am Thy servant.

Glory be to the Father, &c.

THE SERVICE COMMON OF SAINTS.

For the Feasts of the Blessed Virgin.

AT THE FIRST VESPERS.

Antiphon. A Garden enclosed is My Sister, My Spouse: a Spring shut up, a Fountain sealed. Alleluia!

The Psalms of the week-day.

The Chapter, Ecclus. xxiv. 7, 8.

With all these I sought rest: and in whose inheritance shall I abide? So the Creator of all things gave Me a commandment, and He that made Me caused My tabernacle to rest.

R. My Beloved is Mine, and I am His. ℣. He feedeth among the lilies. ℟. And I am His. ℣. Glory be to the Father, and to the Son: and to the Holy Ghost. ℟. My Beloved is Mine, and I am His.

Hymn. Quem terra, pontus.

The God Whom earth, and sea, and sky
Adore, and laud, and magnify,
Who o'er their threefold fabric reigns,
The Virgin's spotless womb contains.

The God, Whose will by moon and sun
And all things in due course is done,
Is borne upon a Maiden's breast,
By fullest heavenly grace possessed.

How blest that Mother, in whose shrine
The great Artificer Divine,
Whose Hand contains the earth and sky,
Vouchsafed, as in His ark, to lie!

Blest, in the message Gabriel brought;
Blest, by the work the Spirit wrought;
From whom the Great Desire of earth
Took human flesh and human birth.

All honour, laud, and glory be,
O Jesu, Virgin-born, to Thee!
All glory, as is ever meet,
To Father, and to Paraclete. Amen.

This verse is said instead of the last verse of the Hymns at Prime, Terce, Sext, None, and Compline.

℣. Behold, from henceforth.

℟. All generations shall call me blessed.

Antiphon to Magnificat, *as in the Proper Service for Holy-Days.*

The Collect, as in the Proper Service for Holy-Days.

AT LAUDS.

℣. All honour, laud, and glory be.

℟. O Jesu, Virgin-born, to Thee.

℣. O God, make speed, &c.

Antiphons. (1.) This gate shall be shut: it shall not be opened, and no man shall enter in by it; because the Lord, the God of Israel, hath entered in by it, therefore it shall be shut. Alleluia!

Dominus regnavit, Ps. xciii., *and the other Psalms of Sunday, p. 139.*

(2.) As the vine brought I forth pleasant Savour: and I am the mother of Fair Love. Alleluia!

(3.) Who is she that looketh

forth as the morning : fair as the moon, clear as the sun? Alleluia!

(4.) I am the rose of Sharon : and the lily of the valleys. Alleluia!

(5.) Hail, thou that art highly favoured, the Lord is with thee : blessed art thou among women, and blessed is the Fruit of thy womb. Alleluia!

The Chapter, Gen. iii. 14, 15.

And the Lord God said unto the serpent, I will put enmity between thee and the woman, and between thy seed and her Seed; It shall bruise thy head, and thou shalt bruise His heel.

℞. Thanks be to God.

Hymn.

Virgin-born! we bow before Thee!
Blessed was the womb that bore Thee!
Mary, Mother meek and mild,
Blessed was she in her Child!

Blessed was the breast that fed Thee!
Blessed was the hand that led Thee!
Blessed was the parent's eye
That watched Thy slumbering infancy!

Virgin-born! we bow before Thee!
Blessed was the womb that bore Thee!
Mary, Virgin-Mother mild,
Blessed was she in her Child.

Honour, laud, and glory be,
Jesu, Virgin-born, to Thee;
To the Father, as is meet,
And the Blessed Paraclete. Amen.

Or this Hymn.

The Mother of our Glorious King,
The chief of Virgins now we sing,
On whose most holy Maiden Breast
The world's Creator deigned to rest.

For Eden lost by woman's sin
He born of woman, would re-win;
That as from Eve our woe had birth,
Mary might bear the Joy of earth.

All honour, laud, and glory be,
O Jesu, Virgin-born, to Thee,
All glory, as is ever meet,
To Father and to Paraclete. Amen.

℣. And her Child was caught up unto God, and to His Throne.

℞. And the dragon was wroth with the woman.

Antiphon to Benedictus, (*as in the Proper Service of the Season.*)

Collect as in the Proper Service.

AT PRIME.

Antiphon (1.) This gate shall be shut : it shall not be opened, and no man shall enter in by it; because the Lord, the God of Israel, hath entered in by it, therefore it shall be shut. Alleluia!

In the ℞. *to the Chapter, instead of* Thou that sittest, &c., *is said the*

℣. Thou that didst not abhor the Virgin's womb.

AT TERCE.

Antiphon (2.) As the vine brought I forth pleasant Savour : and I am the mother of Fair Love. Alleluia.

The Chapter, Gen. iii. 14, 15.

And the Lord God said unto the serpent, I will put enmity between thee and the woman, and between thy seed and her Seed; It shall bruise thy head, and thou shalt bruise His heel.

R. As in Adam all die, even so in Christ shall all be made alive. ℣. For He must reign till He hath put all enemies under His feet. ℞. In Christ shall all be made alive. ℣. Glory be to the Father, and to the Son : and to the Holy Ghost. ℞. As in Adam all die, even so in Christ shall all be made alive.

℣. Blessed art thou among women.

℞. And blessed is the Fruit of thy womb.

Collect as in the Proper Service.

AT SEXT.

Antiphon (3.) Who is she that looketh forth as the morning : fair as the moon, clear as the sun? Alleluia!

The Chapter, Exod. iii. 2.

And the Angel of the Lord appeared unto Moses in a flame of fire out of the midst of a bush : and he looked, and behold the bush burned with fire, and the bush was not consumed.

R. The Lord shall rehearse it when He writeth up the people. ℣. That He was born there. ℞. When He writeth up the people. ℣. Glory be to the Father, and to the Son : and to the Holy Ghost. ℞. The Lord shall rehearse it when He writeth up the people.

℣. While the King sitteth at His table.

℞. My spikenard sendeth forth the smell thereof.

Collect as in the Proper Service.

AT NONE.

Antiphon (4.) I am the rose of Sharon : and the lily of the valleys. Alleluia!

The Chapter, Isa. vii. 14.

Behold, a Virgin shall conceive and bear a Son, and shall call His Name Immanuel.

R. Rejoice ye with Jerusalem, and be glad with her, all ye that love her. ℣. The Lord hath chosen Sion to be an Habitation for Himself. ℞. And be glad with her, all ye that love her. ℣. Glory be to the Father, and to the Son : and to the Holy Ghost. ℞. Rejoice ye with Jerusalem, and be glad with her, all ye that love her.

℣. Full of grace are thy lips.

℞. Because God hath blessed thee for ever.

Collect as in the Proper Service.

The Second Vespers as the First, except that with the Antiphons of Lauds are said,

Dixit Dominus. Ps. cx.

1 The Lord said unto my Lord : Sit Thou on My right Hand, until I make Thine enemies Thy footstool.

2 The Lord shall send the rod of Thy power out of Sion : be Thou ruler, even in the midst among Thine enemies.

3 In the day of Thy power shall the people offer Thee free-will offerings with an holy worship : the dew of Thy birth is of the womb of the morning.

4 The Lord sware, and will not repent : Thou art a Priest for ever after the order of Melchisedech.

5 The Lord upon Thy right Hand : shall wound even kings in the day of His wrath.

6 He shall judge among the heathen ; He shall fill the places with the dead bodies : and smite in sunder the heads over divers countries.

7 He shall drink of the brook in the way : therefore shall He lift up His Head.

Glory be to the Father, &c.

Laudate pueri. Ps. cxiii.

1 Praise the Lord, ye servants : O praise the Name of the Lord.

2 Blessed be the Name of the Lord : from this time forth for evermore.

3 The Lord's Name is praised : from the rising up of the sun unto the going down of the same.

4 The Lord is high above all heathen : and His glory above the heavens.

5 Who is like unto the Lord our God, that hath His dwelling so high : and yet humbleth Himself to behold the things that are in heaven and earth?

6 He taketh up the simple out of the dust : and lifteth the poor out of the mire;

7 That He may set him with the princes : even with the princes of His people.

8 He maketh the barren woman to keep house : and to be a joyful mother of children.

Glory be to the Father, &c.

Lætatus sum. Ps. cxxii.

1 I was glad when they said unto me : We will go into the house of the Lord.

2 Our feet shall stand in thy gates : O Jerusalem.

3 Jerusalem is built as a city : that is at unity in itself.

4 For thither the tribes go up, even the tribes of the Lord : to testify unto Israel, to give thanks unto the Name of the Lord.

5 For there is the seat of judgment : even the seat of the house of David.

6 O pray for the peace of Jerusalem : they shall prosper that love thee.

7 Peace be within thy walls : and plenteousness within thy palaces.

8 For my brethren and companions' sakes : I will wish thee prosperity.

9 Yea, because of the house of the Lord our God : I will seek to do thee good.

Glory be to the Father, &c.

Nisi Dominus. Ps. cxxvii.

1 Except the Lord build the house : their labour is but lost that build it.

2 Except the Lord keep the city : the watchman waketh but in vain.

3 It is but lost labour that ye haste to rise up early, and so late take rest, and eat the bread of carefulness : for so He giveth His beloved sleep.

4 Lo, children and the fruit of the womb : are an heritage and gift that cometh of the Lord.

5 Like as the arrows in the hand of the giant : even so are the young children.

6 Happy is the man that hath his quiver full of them : they shall not be ashamed when they speak with their enemies in the gate.

Glory be to the Father, &c.

Lauda Hierusalem. Ps. cxlvii. 12.

12 Praise the Lord, O Jerusalem : praise thy God, O Sion.

13 For He hath made fast the bars of thy gates : and hath blessed thy children within thee.

14 He maketh peace in thy borders : and filleth thee with the flour of wheat.

15 He sendeth forth His commandment upon earth : and His word runneth very swiftly.

16 He giveth snow like wool : and scattereth the hoar-frost like ashes.

17 He casteth forth His ice like

morsels : who is able to abide His frost?

18 He sendeth out His word, and melteth them : He bloweth with His wind, and the waters flow.

19 He showeth His word unto Jacob : His statutes and ordinances unto Israel.

20 He hath not dealt so with any nation : neither have the heathen knowledge of His laws.

Glory be to the Father, &c.

For the Feast of an Apostle, or Apostles, except SS. Philip and James.

AT THE FIRST VESPERS.

Antiphon. Be ye strong in battle : and fight with the old serpent; so shall ye receive an eternal kingdom. Alleluia!

The Psalms are said under this one Antiphon.

The Psalms for the day of the week.

The Chapter, Eph. ii. 19, 20.

Now therefore ye are no more strangers and foreigners, but fellow-citizens with the saints, and of the household of God ; and are built upon the Foundation of the Apostles and Prophets.

R. Who are these that fly as a cloud, and as the doves to their windows? ℣. They were purer than snow, they were whiter than milk, they were more ruddy in body than rubies. ℟. And as the doves to their windows. ℣. Glory be to the Father, and to the Son : and to the Holy Ghost. ℟. Who are these that fly as a cloud, and as the doves to their windows?

Hymn. Annue Christe.

O Christ, Thou Lord of worlds!
Thine ear to hear us bow
On this the festival
Of Thine Apostle now :

That all the weary load
Of many a foul offence
May, as we sing his praise,
Be lost in penitence.

Redeemer ! save Thy work,
Thy noble work of grace,
Sealed with the holy light
That beameth from Thy face :
Nor suffer them to fall
To Satan's wiles a prey,
For whom Thou didst on earth
Death's costly ransom pay.

Pity Thy flock, enthralled
By sin's captivity ;
Forgive each guilty soul,
And set the bondmen free :
And those Thou hast redeemed
With Thine own precious Blood,
Grant to rejoice with Thee,
Thou Monarch kind and good.

O Jesu, Saviour blest
And gracious Lord, to Thee,
All glory, virtue, power,
And laud and empire be :
The Father with like praise,
And Spirit we adore;
With Whom Thou reignest God,
For ages evermore. Amen.

℣. Their sound is gone out into all lands.

℟. And their words unto the ends of the world.

Antiphon to Magnificat, (*if not in the Proper Service of the Season.*)

Blessed are ye when men shall hate you : and when they shall separate you from their company, and shall reproach you, and cast out your name as evil for the Son of Man's sake. Rejoice ye in that day, and leap for joy; for behold, your reward is great in heaven.

The Collect from the Proper Service of the Season.

AT LAUDS.

℣. Thou hast given an heritage.

℟. Unto those that fear Thy Name, O Lord.

℣. O God, make speed, &c.

Antiphons. (1.) This is My commandment: that ye love one another, as I have loved you.

Psalms as on Sundays and Feast-days, p. 139.

(2.) Greater love hath no man than this: that a man lay down his life for his friends.

(3.) Ye are My friends: if ye do whatsoever I command you.

(4.) Blessed are the pure in heart: for they shall see God.

(5.) In your patience: possess ye your souls.

The Chapter, Eph. ii. 19, 20.

Now therefore ye are no more strangers and foreigners, but fellow-citizens with the saints, and of the household of God; and are built upon the Foundation of the Apostles and Prophets.

℟. Thanks be to God.

Hymn. Æterna Christi munera.

The Eternal gifts of Christ the King,
The Apostles' glorious deeds, we sing;
And while due hymns of praise we pay,
Our thankful hearts cast grief away.

The Church in these her princes boasts,
These victor-chiefs of warrior hosts;
The soldiers of the heavenly hall,
The lights that rose on earth for all.

'Twas thus the yearning faith of Saints,
The unconquered hope that never faints,
The love of Christ that knows not shame,
The Prince of this world overcame.

In these the Father's glory shone,
In these the will of God the Son;
In these exults the Holy Ghost,
Through these rejoice the Heavenly host.

Redeemer, hear us of Thy love,
That with this glorious band above,
Hereafter, of Thine endless grace,
Thy servants also may have place.
      Amen.

℣. They have declared His honour unto the heathen.

℟. And His wonders unto all people.

Antiphon to Benedictus, (*if there be not one in the Proper Service of the Season.*)

They will deliver you up to the councils, and they will scourge you in their synagogues; and ye shall be brought before governors and kings for My sake, for a testimony against them and the Gentiles.

The Collect from the Proper Service of the Season.

AT PRIME.

Antiphon (1.) This is My commandment: that ye love one another, as I have loved you.

AT TERCE.

Antiphon (2.) Greater love hath no man than this: that a man lay down his life for his friends.

The Chapter, Eph. ii. 19, 20.

Now therefore ye are no more strangers and foreigners, but fellow-citizens with the saints, and of the household of God; and are built upon the foundation of the Apostles and Prophets.

R. Their sound is gone out into all lands. ℣. And their words into the ends of the world. ℟. Into all lands. ℣. Glory be to the Father, and to the Son : and to the Holy Ghost. ℟. Their sound is gone out into all lands.

℣. Thou shalt make them princes in all lands.

℟. They shall remember Thy Name, O Lord.

The Collect from the Proper Service of the Season.

AT SEXT.

Antiphon (3.) Ye are My friends : if ye do whatsoever I command you.

The Chapter, Acts v. 12, 13.

By the hands of the Apostles were many signs and wonders wrought among the people : but the people magnified them.

R. Thou shalt make them princes in all lands. ℣. They shall remember Thy Name, O Lord. ℟. In all lands. ℣. Glory be to the Father, and to the Son : and to the Holy Ghost. ℟. Thou shalt make them princes in all lands.

℣. How dear are Thy friends unto me, O God.

℟. O how great is the sum of them.

The Collect from the Proper Service of the Season.

AT NONE.

Antiphon (5.) In your patience : possess ye your souls.

The Chapter, Acts v. 41.

And they departed from the presence of the council, rejoicing that they were counted worthy to suffer shame for His Name.

R. How dear are Thy friends unto me, O God. ℣. O how great is the sum of them. ℟. Unto me, O God. ℣. Glory be to the Father, and to the Son : and to the Holy Ghost. ℟. How dear are Thy friends unto me, O God.

℣. They have declared His honour unto the heathen.

℟. And His wonders unto all people.

The Collect from the Proper Service of the Season.

AT THE SECOND VESPERS.

Antiphon (1.) The Lord sware and will not repent : Thou art a Priest for ever.

Dixit Dominus. Ps. cx.

1 The Lord said unto my Lord : Sit Thou on My right Hand, until I make Thine enemies Thy footstool.

2 The Lord shall send the rod of Thy power out of Sion : be Thou Ruler, even in the midst among Thine enemies.

3 In the day of Thy power shall the people offer Thee free-will offerings with an holy worship : the dew of Thy Birth is of the womb of the morning.

4 The Lord sware, and will not repent : Thou art a Priest for ever after the order of Melchisedech.

5 The Lord upon Thy right Hand : shall wound even kings in the day of His wrath.

6 He shall judge among the heathen ; He shall fill the places with the dead bodies : and smite in sunder the heads over divers countries.

7 He shall drink of the brook in the way : therefore shall He lift up His head.

Glory be to the Father, &c.

(2.) That He may set Him with the princes, even with the princes of His people.

Laudate pueri. Ps. cxiii.

1 Praise the Lord, ye servants : O praise the Name of the Lord.
2 Blessed be the Name of the Lord : from this time forth for evermore.
3 The Lord's Name is praised : from the rising up of the sun unto the going down of the same.
4 The Lord is high above all heathen : and His glory above the heavens.
5 Who is like unto the Lord our God, that hath His dwelling so high : and yet humbleth Himself to behold the things that are in heaven and earth?
6 He taketh up the simple out of the dust : and lifteth the poor out of the mire;
7 That He may set him with the princes : even with the princes of His people.
8 He maketh the barren woman to keep house : and to be a joyful mother of children.

Glory be to the Father, &c.

(3.) Thou hast broken my bonds in sunder : I will offer to Thee the sacrifice of thanksgiving.

Credidi. Ps. cxvi. 10.

10 I believed, and therefore will I speak ; but I was sore troubled : I said in my haste, All men are liars.
11 What reward shall I give unto the Lord : for all the benefits that He hath done unto me?
12 I will receive the Cup of Salvation : and call upon the Name of the Lord.
13 I will pay my vows now in the presence of all His people : right dear in the sight of the Lord is the death of His saints.
14 Behold, O Lord, how that I am Thy servant : I am Thy servant, and the son of Thine handmaid; Thou hast broken my bonds in sunder.
15 I will offer to Thee the Sacrifice of Thanksgiving : and will call upon the Name of the Lord.
16 I will pay my vows unto the Lord, in the sight of all His people : in the courts of the Lord's house, even in the midst of thee, O Jerusalem. Praise the Lord.

Glory be to the Father, &c.

(4.) He that now goeth on his way weeping : and beareth forth good seed.

In convertendo. Ps. cxxvi.

1 When the Lord turned again the captivity of Sion : then were we like unto them that dream.
2 Then was our mouth filled with laughter : and our tongue with joy.
3 Then said they among the heathen : The Lord hath done Great Things for them.
4 Yea, the Lord hath done Great Things for us already : whereof we rejoice.
5 Turn our captivity, O Lord : as the rivers in the south.
6 They that sow in tears : shall reap in joy.
7 He that now goeth on his way weeping, and beareth forth good seed : shall doubtless come again with joy, and bring his sheaves with him.

Glory be to the Father, &c.

(5.) How dear are Thy friends unto me, O God : O how great is the sum of them.

Domine, probasti. Ps. cxxxix.

1 O Lord, Thou hast searched

me out, and known me : Thou knowest my down-sitting, and mine up-rising ; Thou understandest my thoughts long before.

2 Thou art about my path, and about my bed : and spiest out all my ways.

3 For lo, there is not a word in my tongue : but Thou, O Lord, knowest it altogether.

4 Thou hast fashioned me behind and before : and laid Thine Hand upon me.

5 Such knowledge is too wonderful and excellent for me : I cannot attain unto it.

6 Whither shall I go then from Thy Spirit : or whither shall I go then from Thy Presence?

7 If I climb up into heaven, Thou art there : if I go down to hell, Thou art there also.

8 If I take the wings of the morning : and remain in the uttermost parts of the sea;

9 Even there also shall Thy Hand lead me : and Thy right Hand shall hold me.

10 If I say, Peradventure the darkness shall cover me : then shall my night be turned to day.

11 Yea, the darkness is no darkness with Thee, but the night is as clear as the day : the darkness and light to Thee are both alike.

12 For my reins are Thine : Thou hast covered me in my mother's womb.

13 I will give thanks unto Thee, for I am fearfully and wonderfully made : marvellous are Thy works, and that my soul knoweth right well.

14 My bones are not hid from Thee : though I be made secretly, and fashioned beneath in the earth.

15 Thine Eyes did see my substance, yet being imperfect : and in Thy book were all my members written;

16 Which day by day were fashioned : when as yet there was none of them.

17 How dear are Thy counsels unto me, O God : O how great is the sum of them;

18 If I tell them, they are more in number than the sand : when I wake up I am present with Thee.

19 Wilt Thou not slay the wicked, O God : depart from me, ye blood-thirsty men.

20 For they speak unrighteously against Thee : and Thine enemies take Thy Name in vain.

21 Do not I hate them, O Lord, that hate Thee : and am not I grieved with those that rise up against Thee?

22 Yea, I hate them right sore : even as though they were mine enemies.

23 Try me, O God, and seek the ground of my heart : prove me, and examine my thoughts.

24 Look well if there be any way of wickedness in me : and lead me in the way everlasting.

Glory be to the Father, &c.

The Chapter, Eph. ii. 19.

The Hymn, Annue Christe, *as at the First Vespers, p.* 235.

Antiphon to Magnificat.

In the regeneration, when the Son of Man shall sit in the throne of His glory, ye also shall sit upon twelve thrones, judging the twelve tribes of Israel.

The Collect from the Proper Service of the Season.

THE SERVICE PROPER OF HOLY-DAYS.

NOVEMBER XXX.

St. Andrew, Apostle and Martyr, Holy-Day.

AT THE FIRST VESPERS.

Antiphon. One of the two which heard John speak: and followed Jesus, was Andrew, Simon Peter's brother.

Psalms as of week-days.

The Chapter, Rom. x. 10, 11.

For with the heart man believeth unto righteousness, and with the mouth confession is made unto salvation. For the Scripture saith, Whosoever believeth on Him shall not be ashamed.

R. All day long I have stretched forth My hands to a disobedient and gainsaying people. ℣. O Lord God, to Whom vengeance belongeth, Thou God, to Whom vengeance belongeth, show Thyself. Arise, Thou Judge of the world, and reward the proud after their deserving. ℟. A disobedient and gainsaying people. ℣. Glory be to the Father, and to the Son: and to the Holy Ghost. ℟. All day long I have stretched forth My hands to a disobedient and gainsaying people.

This R. is said at both Vespers.

The Hymn, Annue Christe, *as in the First Vespers of the Common of Apostles, p.* 235.

℣. The Lord loved Andrew.

℟. His sweet savour is before the Most High.

Antiphon to Magnificat.

Jesus, walking by the sea of Galilee, saw two brethren, Simon called Peter, and Andrew his brother, casting a net into the sea, (for they were fishers;) and He saith unto them, Follow Me, and I will make you fishers of men. And they straightway left their nets, and followed Him.

The Collect.

ALMIGHTY God, Who didst give such grace unto Thy holy Apostle Saint Andrew, that he readily obeyed the calling of Thy Son Jesus Christ, and followed Him without delay; Grant unto us all, that we, being called by Thy Holy Word, may forthwith give up ourselves obediently to fulfil Thy holy commandments; through the same Jesus Christ our Lord. *Amen.*

At Lauds and the other Hours, everything as in the Common of Apostles, p. 236, *until the*

Antiphon to Benedictus.

Who for the joy that was set before him endured the cross, despising the shame.

Collect as at the First Vespers.

AT THE SECOND VESPERS.

Antiphon to Magnificat *as at the First Vespers.*

DECEMBER VI.

Memorial of NICOLAS, Bp.

AT LAUDS.

Antiphon. Well done, thou good and faithful servant; thou hast been faithful over a few things, I will make thee ruler over many things; enter thou into the Joy of thy Lord.

℣. The Righteous shall grow as a lily.

℟. He shall flourish for ever before the Lord.

The Collect.

GRANT, we beseech Thee, O Blessed Lord, that we who commemorate Thy holy Confessor and Bishop Nicolas, may increase in faith and love towards Thee, the great Shepherd and Bishop of our souls, Who livest and reignest with the Father and the Holy Ghost, ever One God, world without end. *Amen.*

AT VESPERS.

Antiphon. The glory of this world, with the pleasures thereof, blessed Nicolas set at nought, and thus attained to the Chief Priesthood.

℣. The Lord loved him, and beautified him with comely ornaments.

℟. He clothed him with a robe of glory.

Collect as at Lauds.

DECEMBER VIII.

Memorial of THE CONCEPTION OF THE BLESSED VIRGIN MARY.

AT LAUDS.

Antiphon. With heart and soul sing we glory to Christ on this commemoration of His Blessed Mother.

℣. Blessed art thou among women.

℟. And blessed is the Fruit of thy womb.

The Collect.

O MERCIFUL God, hear the prayers of Thy servants, and grant that we who thus commemorate the Conception of the Mother of our Lord, may hereafter be numbered with her; through the same Thy Son Jesus Christ our Lord, Who liveth and reigneth with Thee and the Holy Ghost, ever One God, world without end. *Amen.*

AT VESPERS.

Antiphon. A Garden enclosed is My Sister, My Spouse; a Spring shut up, a Fountain sealed. Alleluia.

℣. Behold from henceforth.

℟. All generations shall call me Blessed.

Collect as at Lauds.

DECEMBER XIII.

Memorial of LUCY, V. & M.

AT LAUDS.

Antiphon. When the Bridegroom came, they that were ready went in with Him to the marriage.

℣. The Virgins that be her fellows.

℟. Shall bear her company.

The Collect.

HEAR us, O God of our salvation, that as we rejoice in this commemoration of Thy blessed Virgin and Martyr Lucy, we may be filled with devout affections to

Thee; through Jesus Christ our Lord, Who liveth and reigneth with Thee and the Holy Ghost, One God, world without end. *Amen.*

AT VESPERS.

Antiphon. I bless Thee, Father of my Lord Jesus Christ, for by Thy Son Thou hast quenched the flames that torture me.

℣. Full of grace are thy lips.

℞. Because God hath blessed thee for ever.

Collect as at Lauds.

DECEMBER XXI.

St. Thomas, Apostle and Martyr. Holy-Day.

AT THE FIRST VESPERS.

Everything as in the Common of Apostles till the Antiphon to Magnificat, O Oriens, *as in the Proper Service of the Season, p. 12.*

The Collect.

ALMIGHTY and Everliving God, Who for the more confirmation of the faith didst suffer Thy holy Apostle Thomas to be doubtful in Thy Son's Resurrection; Grant us so perfectly and without all doubt, to believe in Thy Son Jesus Christ, that our faith in Thy sight may never be reproved. Hear us, O Lord, through the same Jesus Christ, to Whom, with Thee and the Holy Ghost, be all honour and glory, now and for evermore. *Amen.*

At Lauds and the other Hours, everything as in the Common of Apostles except the Collect, which shall be that said at the First Vespers. The Antiphon to Magnificat *at the Second Vespers is* O Rex gentium, *as in the Proper Service of the Season, p.* 12.

DECEMBER XXXI.

Memorial of SILVESTER, Bp.

AT LAUDS.

Antiphon. Well done, thou good and faithful servant; thou hast been faithful over a few things, I will make thee ruler over many things: enter thou into the Joy of thy Lord.

℣. The Righteous shall grow as a lily.

℞. He shall flourish for ever before the Lord.

The Collect.

GRANT, we beseech Thee, O Blessed Lord, that we who commemorate Thy holy Confessor and Bishop Silvester, may increase in faith and love towards Thee, the great Shepherd and Bishop of our souls, Who livest and reignest with the Father and the Holy Ghost, ever One God, world without end. *Amen.*

AT VESPERS.

Antiphon. A Bishop must be blameless, as the steward of God.

℣. The Lord loved him, and beautified him with comely ornaments.

℞. He clothed him with a robe of glory.

Collect as at Lauds.

JANUARY VIII.

Memorial of LUCIAN, P. & M.

AT LAUDS.

Antiphon. Theirs is the Kingdom of Heaven who have despised the life of this world to gain a reward in the kingdom, and have washed their robes in the Blood of the Lamb.

℣. O God, wonderful art Thou in Thy Saints.

℟. And glorious in Thy Majesty.

The Collect.

ALMIGHTY and Everlasting God, grant unto us so to commemorate Thy holy Martyrs, Lucian and his companions, that we may have our share in the Communion of Saints; through Jesus Christ our Lord, Who liveth and reigneth with Thee and the Holy Ghost, ever One God, world without end. Amen.

AT VESPERS.

Antiphon. The souls of the Saints who followed the Footsteps of Christ rejoice in Heaven, and forasmuch as for love of Him they shed their blood, they shall reign with Him for ever.

℣. Be glad, O ye Righteous, and rejoice in the Lord.

℟. And be joyful, all ye that are true of heart.

Collect as at Lauds.

JANUARY XIII.

Memorial of HILARY, Bp.

AT LAUDS.

Antiphon. Well done, thou good and faithful servant; thou hast been faithful over a few things, I will make thee ruler over many things; enter thou into the Joy of thy Lord.

℣. The Righteous shall grow as a lily.

℟. He shall flourish for ever before the Lord.

The Collect.

GRANT, we beseech Thee, O Blessed Lord, that we who commemorate Thy holy Confessor and Bishop Hilary, may increase in faith and love towards Thee, the great Shepherd and Bishop of our souls, Who livest and reignest with the Father and the Holy Ghost, ever One God, world without end. Amen.

AT VESPERS.

Antiphon. Whosoever shall confess Me before men, him shall the Son of Man also confess before the Angels of God.

℣. The Lord loved him, and beautified him with comely ornaments.

℟. He clothed him with a robe of glory.

Collect as at Lauds.

JANUARY XVIII.

Memorial of PRISCA, V. & M.

AT LAUDS.

Antiphon. When the Bridegroom came, they that were ready went in with Him to the marriage.

℣. The Virgins that be her fellows.

℟. Shall bear her company.

The Collect.

GRANT, O Almighty God, that we who commemorate the martyrdom of Thy blessed Virgin Prisca may profit by the example of her great faith, through our Lord Jesus Christ, Who liveth and reigneth with Thee and the Holy Ghost, ever One God, world without end. Amen.

AT VESPERS.

Antiphon. The kingdom of heaven is like unto a net, that was cast into the sea, and gathered of every kind; which, when it was full, they drew to shore, and sat down, and gathered the good into vessels, but cast the bad away.

℣. Full of grace are thy lips.

℟. Because God hath blessed thee for ever.

Collect as at Lauds.

JANUARY XX.

Memorial of FABIAN, Bp. of Rome.

AT LAUDS.

Antiphon. Except a corn of wheat fall into the ground and die, it abideth alone; but if it die, it bringeth forth much fruit.

℣. The Righteous shall grow as a lily.

℟. He shall flourish for ever before the Lord.

The Collect.

ALMIGHTY and Everlasting God, grant unto us so to commemorate Thy holy Martyr Fabian, that we may have our share in the Communion of Saints; through Jesus Christ our Lord, Who liveth and reigneth with Thee and the Holy Ghost, ever One God, world without end. *Amen.*

AT VESPERS.

Antiphon. Blessed is the man that endureth temptation; for when he is tried, he shall receive the crown of life, which the Lord hath promised to them that love Him.

℣. Thou crownest him with glory and worship.

℟. Thou makest him to have dominion of the works of Thy hands.

Collect as at Lauds.

JANUARY XXI.

Memorial of AGNES, V. & M.

AT LAUDS.

Antiphon. Blessed Agnes standing in the midst of the flames, stretched out her hands and prayed, saying, Almighty, Tremendous, and Worshipful God, I bless Thee, and glorify Thy Name for ever.

℣. The Virgins that be her fellows.

℟. Shall bear her company.

The Collect.

ALMIGHTY and Eternal God, Who hast chosen the weak things of the world to confound the things which are mighty; Grant, we beseech Thee, that we by the commemoration of Thy holy Virgin and Martyr Agnes may glory in Thy power; through Jesus Christ our Lord, Who liveth and reigneth with Thee and the Holy Ghost, ever One God, world without end. *Amen.*

AT VESPERS.

Antiphon. Blessed Agnes standing in the midst of the flames, stretched out her hands and said, I pray to Thee, O Tremendous and Eternal Father, Who by Thy Blessed Son hast saved me from shame; lo! I come to Thee, Whom I have loved, Whom I have sought, Whom I have always desired.

℣. Full of grace are thy lips.

℟. Because God hath blessed thee for ever.

Collect as at Lauds.

JANUARY XXII.

Memorial of VINCENT, Deacon & Martyr.

AT LAUDS.

Antiphon. Let us humbly commemorate this day on which Vincent, the unconquered martyr of Christ, gained the palm of victory, and joyfully entered heaven.

℣. O God, wonderful art Thou in Thy Saints.

℟. And glorious in Thy Majesty.

The Collect.

ALMIGHTY and Everlasting God, grant unto us so to commemorate Thy holy Martyr Vincent, that we may have our share in the Communion of Saints; through Jesus Christ our Lord, Who liveth and reigneth with Thee and the Holy Ghost, ever One God, world without end. *Amen.*

AT VESPERS.

Antiphon. We profess the Christian Religion, and adore One God, Who abideth for ever.

℣. Be glad, O ye Righteous, and rejoice in the Lord.

℟. And be joyful, all ye that are true of heart.

Collect as at Lauds.

JANUARY XXV.

Conversion of St. Paul. Holy-Day.

AT THE FIRST VESPERS.

Antiphon. Suddenly there shined round about him a light from heaven: and he fell to the earth, and heard a Voice saying unto him, Saul, Saul, why persecutest thou Me? And he said, Who art Thou, Lord? And the Lord said, I am Jesus of Nazareth, Whom thou persecutest; it is hard for thee to kick against the pricks.

Psalms of the week-day.

The Chapter, Acts ix. 1—3.

And Saul, yet breathing out threatenings and slaughter against the disciples of the Lord, went unto the high-priest, and desired of him letters to Damascus to the synagogues, that, if he found any of this way, whether they were men or women, he might bring them bound unto Jerusalem. And as he journeyed, he came near Damascus, and suddenly there shined round about him a light from heaven.

R. Because thy rage against Me, and thy tumult is come up into Mine ears, therefore will I put My hook in thy nose, and My bridle in thy lips. ℣. And I will turn thee back. ℟. Therefore will I put My hook in thy nose, and My bridle in thy lips. ℣. Glory be to the Father, and to the Son: and to the Holy Ghost. ℟. Because thy rage against Me, and thy tumult is come up into Mine ears, therefore will I put My hook in thy nose, and My bridle in thy lips.

Hymn, Annue Christe, ℣. *and* ℟. *as in the Common of Apostles,* p. 235.

Antiphon to Magnificat.

The Lord chose one out of the people, and gave him the glory of the Eternal Vision. Let us celebrate the Conversion of Saint Paul.

The Collect.

O GOD, Who, through the preaching of the blessed Apostle Saint Paul, hast caused the light of the Gospel to shine throughout the world; Grant, we beseech Thee, that we, having his wonderful Conversion in remembrance, may show forth our thankfulness unto Thee for the same, by following the holy doctrine which he taught; through Jesus Christ our Lord. *Amen.*

AT LAUDS.

℣. Thou hast given an heritage.

℟. Unto those that fear Thy Name.

℣. O God, make speed, &c.

Antiphons. (1.) Saul (who is also called Paul) mightily convinced the Jews : and that publicly, showing by the Scriptures that Jesus was Christ.

Psalms of Sundays and Holy-Days, p. 139.

(2.) Brother Saul : the Lord, even Jesus, that appeared unto thee in the way as thou camest, hath sent me, that thou mightest receive thy sight, and be filled with the Holy Ghost.

(3.) And Ananias put his hands on him : and straightway there fell from his eyes as it had been scales : and he received sight forthwith and was baptized. And when he had received meat he was strengthened.

(4.) The furious persecutor : fell down, and arose a faithful preacher of the Word.

(5.) He of the Apostles that was last : is by his preaching first.

The Chapter as at the First Vespers. Hymn, Æterna Christi munera, ℣. *and* ℟. *as in the Common of Apostles, p.* 236.

Antiphon to Benedictus.

Let us celebrate the Conversion of Saint Paul the Apostle; for to-day he that had been a persecutor became a chosen vessel. Wherefore Angels and Archangels rejoice and praise in heaven the Son of God.

Collect as at the First Vespers.

AT PRIME.

Antiphon (1.) Saul (who is also called Paul) mightily convinced the Jews : and that publicly, showing by the Scriptures that Jesus was Christ.

AT TERCE.

Antiphon (2.) Brother Saul : the Lord, even Jesus, that appeared unto thee in the way as thou camest, hath sent me, that thou mightest receive thy sight, and be filled with the Holy Ghost.

The Chapter, Acts ix. 1, 2.

And Saul, yet breathing out threatenings and slaughter against the disciples of the Lord, went unto the high priest, and desired of him letters to Damascus to the synagogues, that, if he found any of this way, whether they were men or women, he might bring them bound unto Jerusalem.

R. *as at Terce in the Common of Apostles, p.* 236.

Collect as at the First Vespers.

AT SEXT.

Antiphon (3.) And Ananias put his hands on him: and straightway there fell from his eyes as it had been scales: and he received sight forthwith, and was baptized. And when he had received meat, he was strengthened.

The Chapter, Acts ix. 15.

But the Lord said unto him, Go thy way, for he is a chosen vessel unto Me, to bear My Name before the Gentiles, and kings, and the children of Israel.

℟. *as at Sext in the Common of Apostles, p.* 237.

Collect as at the First Vespers.

AT NONE.

Antiphon (5.) He of the Apostles that was last: is by his preaching first.

The Chapter, Acts ix. 17.

And Ananias went his way, and entered into the house; and putting his hands on him, said, Brother Saul, the Lord, even Jesus, that appeared unto thee in the way as thou camest, hath sent me, that thou mightest receive thy sight, and be filled with the Holy Ghost.

℟. *as at None in the Common of Apostles, p.* 237.

Collect as at the First Vespers.

AT THE SECOND VESPERS.

The Psalms of the Second Vespers of the Common of Apostles are said with the Antiphons of Lauds of this day.

Chapter as at the First Vespers, p. 245.

The Hymn, ℣. *and* ℟., *as in the First Vespers of the Common of Apostles, p.* 235.

Antiphon to Magnificat.

But when it pleased God, Who separated me from my mother's womb, and called me by His grace, to reveal His Son in me, that I might preach Him among the heathen: immediately I conferred not with flesh and blood.

Collect as at the First Vespers.

FEBRUARY II.

The Purification of St. Mary the Blessed Virgin. Holy-Day.

AT THE FIRST VESPERS.

Everything as in the Common of the Blessed Virgin, p. 231, *except the*

Antiphon to Magnificat.

And behold there was a man in Jerusalem whose name was Symeon; and the same man was just and devout, waiting for the consolation of Israel; and the Holy Ghost was upon him.

The Collect.

ALMIGHTY and Everliving God, we humbly beseech Thy Majesty, that, as Thy Only-begotten Son was this day Presented in the temple in substance of our flesh, so we may be presented unto Thee, with pure and clean hearts, by the same Thy Son Jesus Christ our Lord. Amen.

AT LAUDS.

℣. It was revealed unto Symeon by the Holy Ghost.

℟. That he should not see death before he had seen the Lord's Christ.

℣. O God, make speed, &c.

And everything else as at Lauds in the Common of the Blessed Virgin, until the

Antiphon to Benedictus.

The Lord, Whom ye seek, shall suddenly come to His temple; even the Messenger of the covenant, Whom ye delight in; behold, He shall come, saith the Lord of Hosts. But who may abide the day of His Coming? and who shall stand when He appeareth? for He is like a refiner's Fire, and like fullers' Sope. And He shall sit as a refiner and purifier of silver; and He shall purify the sons of Levi.

Collect as at the First Vespers.

At Prime, Terce, Sext, None, Second Vespers, and Compline, everything as in the Common of the Blessed Virgin, p. 232, 233, except

The Collect.

ALMIGHTY and Everliving God, we humbly beseech Thy Majesty, that, as Thy Only-begotten Son was this day Presented in the temple in substance of our flesh, so we may be presented unto Thee, with pure and clean hearts, by the same Thy Son Jesus Christ our Lord. *Amen.*

FEBRUARY III.
Memorial of BLASIUS, Bp.

AT LAUDS.

Antiphon. Theirs is the Kingdom of Heaven who have despised the life of this world to gain a reward in the kingdom, and have washed their robes in the blood of the Lamb.

℣. O God, wonderful art Thou in Thy Saints.

℞. And glorious in Thy Majesty.

The Collect.

ALMIGHTY and Everlasting God, grant unto us so to commemorate Thy holy Martyr Blasius, that we may have our share in the Communion of Saints; through Jesus Christ our Lord, Who liveth and reigneth with Thee and the Holy Ghost, ever One God, world without end. *Amen.*

AT VESPERS.

Antiphon. The souls of the Saints who followed the Footsteps of Christ rejoice in Heaven, and forasmuch as for love of Him they shed their blood, they shall reign with Him for ever.

℣. Be glad, O ye Righteous, and rejoice in the Lord.

℞. And be joyful, all ye that are true of heart.

Collect as at Lauds.

FEBRUARY V.
Memorial of AGATHA, V. & M.

AT LAUDS.

Antiphon. When the Bridegroom came, they that were ready went in with Him to the marriage.

℣. The Virgins that be her fellows.

℞. Shall bear her company.

The Collect.

O GOD, Who amongst other miracles of Thy Power hast granted even to the weakness of women the victory of martyrdom; Mercifully grant that we who commemorate Thy blessed Martyr Agatha, may hereafter be numbered with her; through Jesus Christ our Lord, Who liveth and reigneth with Thee and the Holy Ghost, ever One God, world without end. *Amen.*

AT VESPERS.

Antiphon. Agatha most joyfully and gloriously went to prison, as it were to a banquet, and commended her sufferings to her Lord.

℣. Full of grace are thy lips.

℞. Because God hath blessed thee for ever.

Collect as at Lauds.

FEBRUARY XIV.

Memorial of VALENTINE, Bp.

AT LAUDS.

Antiphon. Theirs is the Kingdom of Heaven who have despised the life of this world to gain a reward in the kingdom, and have washed their robes in the blood of the Lamb.

℣. O God, wonderful art Thou in Thy Saints.

℞. And glorious in Thy Majesty.

The Collect.

ALMIGHTY and Everlasting God, grant unto us so to commemorate Thy holy Martyr Valentine, that we may have our share in the Communion of Saints; through Jesus Christ our Lord, Who liveth and reigneth with Thee and the Holy Ghost, ever One God, world without end. *Amen.*

AT VESPERS.

Antiphon. The souls of the Saints who followed in the Footsteps of Christ rejoice in Heaven, and forasmuch as for love of Him they shed their blood, they shall reign with Him for ever.

℣. Be glad, O ye Righteous, and rejoice in the Lord.

℞. And be joyful, all ye that are true of heart.

Collect as at Lauds.

FEBRUARY XXIV.

St. Matthias, Apostle and Martyr. Holy-Day.

At the First Vespers, and through all the Hours, everything as in the Common of Apostles, p. 235, except

The Collect.

O ALMIGHTY God, Who into the place of the traitor Judas didst choose Thy faithful servant Matthias to be of the number of the Twelve Apostles; Grant that Thy Church, being alway preserved from false Apostles, may be ordered and guided by faithful and true pastors; through Jesus Christ our Lord. *Amen.*

MARCH I.

Memorial of DAVID, Archbishop.

AT LAUDS.

Antiphon. Well done, thou good and faithful servant; thou hast been faithful over a few things, I will make thee ruler over many things; enter thou into the Joy of thy Lord.

℣. The Righteous shall grow as a lily.

℞. He shall flourish for ever before the Lord.

The Collect.

GRANT, we beseech Thee, O Blessed Lord, that we who commemorate Thy holy Confessor and Bishop David, may increase in faith and love towards Thee, the great Shepherd and Bishop of our souls, Who livest and reignest with the Father and the Holy Ghost, ever One God, world without end. *Amen.*

AT VESPERS.

Antiphon. A Bishop must be blameless, as the steward of God.

℣. The Lord loved him, and beautified him with comely ornaments.

℟. He clothed him with a robe of glory.

Collect as at Lauds.

MARCH II.

Memorial of CHAD, Bp.

AT LAUDS.

Antiphon. Well done, thou good and faithful servant; thou hast been faithful over a few things, I will make thee ruler over many things: enter thou into the Joy of thy Lord.

℣. The Righteous shall grow as a lily.

℟. He shall flourish for ever before the Lord.

The Collect.

GRANT, we beseech Thee, O Blessed Lord, that we who commemorate Thy holy Confessor and Bishop Chad, may increase in faith and love towards Thee, the great Shepherd and Bishop of our souls, Who livest and reignest with the Father and the Holy Ghost, ever One God, world without end. *Amen.*

AT VESPERS.

Antiphon. A Bishop must be blameless, as the steward of God.

℣. The Lord loved him, and beautified him with comely ornaments.

℟. He clothed him with a robe of glory.

Collect as at Lauds.

MARCH VII.

Memorial of PERPETUA, M.

AT LAUDS.

Antiphon. The mother was marvellous above all and worthy of honourable mention, because of the hope she had in the Lord.

℣. Whoso loveth son or daughter more than Me.

℟. Is not worthy of Me.

The Collect.

GRANT, O Almighty God, that we who commemorate the martyrdom of the blessed Perpetua, may profit by her example, through our Lord Jesus Christ, Who liveth and reigneth with Thee and the Holy Ghost, ever One God, world without end. *Amen.*

AT VESPERS.

Antiphon. The Kingdom of Heaven is like unto a net, that was cast into the sea, and gathered of every kind; which, when it was full, they drew to shore, and sat down, and gathered the good into vessels, but cast the bad away.

℣. Full of grace are thy lips.

℟. Because God hath blessed thee for ever.

Collect as at Lauds.

MARCH XII.

Memorial of GREGORY, Bp. of Rome.

AT LAUDS.

Antiphon. Well done, thou good and faithful servant; thou hast been faithful over a few things, I will make thee ruler over many things; enter thou into the Joy of thy Lord.

℣. The Righteous shall grow as a lily.

℟. He shall flourish for ever before the Lord.

The Collect.

GRANT, we beseech Thee, O Blessed Lord, that we who commemorate Thy holy Confessor and Bishop Gregory, may increase in faith and love towards Thee, the great Shepherd and Bishop of our souls, Who livest and reignest with the Father and the Holy Ghost, ever One God, world without end. *Amen.*

AT VESPERS.

Antiphon. A Bishop must be blameless, as the steward of God.

℣. The Lord loved him, and beautified him with comely ornaments.

℟. He clothed him with a robe of glory.

Collect as at Lauds.

MARCH XVIII.

Memorial of EDWARD, King of the West Saxons.

AT LAUDS.

Antiphon. Theirs is the Kingdom of Heaven who have despised the life of this world to gain a reward in the kingdom, and have washed their robes in the Blood of the Lamb.

℣. O God, wonderful art Thou in Thy Saints.

℟. And glorious in Thy Majesty.

The Collect.

O GOD, the Conqueror of an Eternal Kingdom; grant unto Thy servants who here commemorate the death of King Edward the Martyr, that as Thou didst vouchsafe to him everlasting glory, so we may be found worthy to have our share in the Communion of Saints, Who livest and reignest with the Father and the Holy Ghost, ever One God, world without end. *Amen.*

AT VESPERS.

Antiphon. The souls of the Saints who followed the Footsteps of Christ rejoice in Heaven, and forasmuch as for love of Him they shed their blood, they shall reign with Him for ever.

℣. Be glad, O ye Righteous, and rejoice in the Lord.

℟. And be joyful, all ye that are true of heart.

Collect as at Lauds.

MARCH XXI.

Memorial of BENEDICT, Abbot.

AT LAUDS.

Antiphon. Well done, thou good and faithful servant; thou hast been faithful over a few things, I will make thee ruler over many things; enter thou into the Joy of thy Lord.

℣. The Righteous shall grow as a lily.

℟. He shall flourish for ever before the Lord.

The Collect.

ALMIGHTY, Everlasting God, Who on this day didst deliver the blessed Benedict from the burden of the flesh; hereafter grant unto us, Thy unworthy servants, to have our share in the company of the Blessed, through Jesus Christ our Lord, Who liveth and reigneth with Thee and the Holy Ghost, ever one God, world without end. Amen.

AT VESPERS.

Antiphon. A Bishop must be blameless, as the steward of God.

℣. The Lord loved him, and beautified him with comely ornaments.

℟. He clothed him with a robe of Glory.

Collect as at Lauds.

MARCH XXV.

𝕿𝖍𝖊 𝕬𝖓𝖓𝖚𝖓𝖈𝖎𝖆𝖙𝖎𝖔𝖓 𝖔𝖋 𝖔𝖚𝖗 𝕷𝖆𝖉𝖞. 𝕳𝖔𝖑𝖞-𝕯𝖆𝖞.

AT THE FIRST VESPERS.

Everything as at the First Vespers of the Common of the Blessed Virgin, page 231, except the

Antiphon to Magnificat.

And the Angel came in unto her, and said, Hail, thou that art highly favoured, the Lord is with thee; Blessed art thou among women.

The Collect.

WE beseech Thee, O Lord, pour Thy grace into our hearts; that, as we have known the Incarnation of Thy Son Jesus Christ by the message of an Angel, so by His Cross and Passion we may be brought unto the glory of His Resurrection; through the same Jesus Christ our Lord. *Amen.*

AT LAUDS.

As at Lauds in the Common of the Blessed Virgin.

Antiphon to Benedictus.

The Holy Ghost shall come upon thee, and the power of the Highest shall overshadow thee; therefore also that Holy Thing Which shall be born of thee shall be called the Son of God.

Collect as at the First Vespers.

Prime, Terce, Sext, None, Second Vespers, and Compline, as in the Common of the Blessed Virgin.

APRIL III.

Memorial of RICHARD, Bp.

AT LAUDS.

Antiphon. Well done, thou good and faithful servant; thou hast been faithful over a few things, I will make thee ruler over many things; enter thou into the Joy of thy Lord.

℣. The Righteous shall grow as a lily.

℟. He shall flourish for ever before the Lord.

The Collect.

GRANT, we beseech Thee, O Blessed Lord, that we who commemorate Thy holy Confessor and Bishop Richard may increase in faith and love towards Thee, the great Shepherd and Bishop of our souls, Who livest and reignest with the Father and the Holy Ghost, ever One God, world without end. *Amen.*

AT VESPERS.

Antiphon. A Bishop must be blameless, as the steward of God.

℣. The Lord loved him, and beautified him with comely ornaments.

℟. He clothed him with a robe of glory.

Collect as at Lauds.

APRIL IV.

Memorial of AMBROSE, Bp.

AT LAUDS.

Antiphon. Well done, thou good and faithful servant; thou hast been faithful over a few things, I will make thee ruler over many things; enter thou into the Joy of thy Lord.

℣. The Righteous shall grow as a lily.

℟. He shall flourish for ever before the Lord.

The Collect.

O GOD, Who gavest Ambrose to Thy people to be a minister of eternal life; Grant that we may follow his holy teaching; through Jesus Christ our Lord, Who liveth and reigneth with Thee and the Holy Ghost, ever One God, world without end. *Amen.*

AT VESPERS.

Antiphon. A Bishop must be blameless, as the steward of God.

℣. The Lord loved him, and beautified him with comely ornaments.

℞. He clothed him with a robe of glory.

Collect as at Lauds.

APRIL XIX.

Memorial of ALPHEGE, Abp. of Canterbury.

AT LAUDS.

Antiphon. Theirs is the Kingdom of Heaven who have despised the life of this world to gain a reward in the kingdom, and have washed their robes in the Blood of the Lamb.

℣. O God, wonderful art Thou in Thy Saints.

℞. And glorious in Thy Majesty.

The Collect.

O GOD, Who crownedst the blessed Alphege, Archbishop of Canterbury, with the glory of martyrdom; Grant unto his successors and the Church under their guidance still to glorify Thee; through Jesus Christ our Lord, Who liveth and reigneth with Thee and the Holy Ghost, ever One God, world without end. *Amen.*

AT VESPERS.

Antiphon. The souls of the Saints who followed the Footsteps of Christ rejoice in Heaven, and forasmuch as for love of Him they shed their blood, they shall reign with Him for ever.

℣. Be glad, O ye Righteous, and rejoice in the Lord.

℞. And be joyful, all ye that are true of heart.

Collect as at Lauds.

APRIL XXIII.

Memorial of ST. GEORGE.

AT LAUDS.

Antiphon. Theirs is the Kingdom of Heaven who have despised the life of this world to gain a reward in the kingdom, and have washed their robes in the Blood of the Lamb.

℣. O God, wonderful art Thou in Thy Saints.

℞. And glorious in Thy Majesty.

The Collect.

ALMIGHTY and Everlasting God, grant unto us so to commemorate Thy holy Martyr Saint George, that we may have our share in the Communion of Saints; through Jesus Christ our Lord, Who liveth and reigneth with Thee and the Holy Ghost, ever One God, world without end. *Amen.*

AT VESPERS.

Antiphon. The souls of the Saints who followed the footsteps of Christ rejoice in Heaven, and forasmuch as for love of Him they shed their blood, they shall reign with Him for ever.

℣. Be glad, O ye Righteous, and rejoice in the Lord.

℞. And be joyful, all ye that are true of heart.

Collect as at Lauds.

APRIL XXV.
St. Mark, Evangelist and Martyr. Holy-Day.

AT THE FIRST VESPERS.

Antiphon. Light Eternal : shall shine on Thy Saints, O Lord, and length of days. Alleluia.

Psalms of the week-day.

The Chapter, Eph. iv. 7, 8.

Unto every one of us is given grace, according to the measure of the gift of Christ. Wherefore He saith, When He ascended up on high, He led captivity captive, and gave gifts unto men.

℟. Her Nazarites were purer than snow, they were whiter than milk. Alleluia! Alleluia! ℣. Their sound is gone out into all lands, and their words into the ends of the world. ℟. Alleluia! Alleluia! ℣. Glory be to the Father, and to the Son : and to the Holy Ghost. ℟. Her Nazarites were purer than snow, they were whiter than milk. Alleluia! Alleluia!

Hymn. Tristes erant Apostoli.

If in Ascension-tide, the Proper Doxology is said instead of the last verse.

The Apostles' hearts are full of pain,
For their dear Lord so lately slain,
That Lord His servants' wicked train
With bitter scorn had dared arraign.

We pray Thee, King with glory deck'd,
In this our Paschal joy protect,
From all that Death would fain effect,
Thy ransomed flock, Thine own elect.

To Thee Who, dead, again dost live,
All glory, Lord, Thy people give;
All glory, as is ever meet,
To Father and to Paraclete. Amen.

℣. Then were the disciples glad.

℟. When they saw the Lord. Alleluia.

Antiphon to Magnificat.

Go forth, O ye daughters of Zion ; and behold the Martyr with the Crown, wherewith the Lord crowned him in the day of the gladness of his heart.

The Collect.

O ALMIGHTY God, Who hast instructed Thy Holy Church with the heavenly doctrine of Thy Evangelist Saint Mark; Give us grace, that, being not like children, carried away with every blast of vain doctrine, we may be established in the truth of Thy Holy Gospel; through Jesus Christ our Lord. *Amen.*

AT LAUDS.

℣. The voice of joy and health.

℟. Is in the dwelling of the righteous.

℣. O God, make speed, &c.

Antiphons. (1.) Thy Saints, O Lord : shall flourish as a lily, Alleluia! and they shall be as a sweet smelling savour unto Thee. Alleluia.

Psalms as on Sundays and Feast-days, p. 139.

(2.) Blessed are the Folk : that He hath chosen to Him to be His inheritance. Alleluia.

(3.) Blessed is the People, O Lord, that can rejoice in Thee : they shall walk in the Light of Thy Countenance. Alleluia.

(4.) O ye Spirits and Souls of the Righteous : bless ye the Lord. Alleluia.

(5.) There remaineth a rest : for the People of God. Alleluia.

The Chapter, Eph. iv. 7, 8.

Unto every one of us is given grace, according to the measure of the gift of Christ. Wherefore He saith, When He Ascended up on high, He led captivity captive, and gave gifts unto men.

Hymn. Claro Paschali gaudio.

If in Ascension-tide, the Proper Doxology is said instead of the last verse.

In this our bright and Paschal day
The sun shines out with purer ray;
When Christ to earthly sight made plain,
The glad Apostles see again.

The Wounds, the riven Wounds He shows
In that His Flesh with light that glows,
With public voice both far and nigh
The Lord's arising testify.

O Christ, the King, Who lov'st to bless,
Do Thou our hearts and souls possess;
To Thee our praise that we may pay,
To Whom our laud is due for aye.

We pray Thee, King with glory deck'd,
In this our Paschal joy protect,
From all that Death would fain effect,
Thy ransomed flock, Thine own elect.

To Thee Who, dead, again dost live,
All glory, Lord, Thy people give:
All glory, as is ever meet,
To Father and to Paraclete. Amen.

℣. Rejoice in the Lord, ye Righteous.

℟. For it becometh well the Just to be thankful. Alleluia.

Antiphon to Benedictus.

Light Eternal shall shine on Thy Saints, O Lord, and length of days. Alleluia.

Collect as at the First Vespers.

AT PRIME.

Antiphon (1.) Thy Saints, O Lord : shall flourish as a lily, Alleluia! and they shall be as a sweet smelling savour unto Thee. Alleluia.

AT TERCE.

Antiphon (2.) Blessed are the Folk : that He hath chosen to Him to be His inheritance. Alleluia.

The Chapter, Eph. iv. 7, 8.

Unto every one of us is given grace, according to the measure of the gift of Christ. Wherefore He saith, When He Ascended up on high, He led captivity captive, and gave gifts unto men.

℟. Your sorrow. Alleluia, Alleluia. ℣. Shall be turned into joy. ℟. Alleluia, Alleluia. ℣. Glory be to the Father, and to the Son : and to the Holy Ghost. ℟. Your sorrow shall be turned into joy. Alleluia, Alleluia.

℣. Right dear in the sight of the Lord.

℟. Is the death of His Saints. Alleluia.

Collect as at the First Vespers.

AT SEXT.

Antiphon (3.) Blessed is the People, O Lord, that can rejoice in Thee : they shall walk in the Light of Thy Countenance. Alleluia.

The Chapter, Ephes. iv. 10.

He that descended is the Same also that Ascended up far above all heavens, that He might fill all things.

℟. Right dear in the sight of the Lord. Alleluia, Alleluia. ℣. Is the death of His Saints. ℟. Alleluia, Alleluia. ℣. Glory be to the Father, and to the Son : and to the Holy Ghost. ℟. Right dear in the sight of the Lord is the death of His Saints. Alleluia, Alleluia.

℣. Rejoice in the Lord, ye Righteous.

℟. For it becometh well the Just to be thankful. Alleluia.

Collect as at the First Vespers.

AT NONE.

Antiphon (5.) There remaineth a rest : for the People of God. Alleluia.

The Chapter, Ephes. iv. 11, 12.

And He gave some Apostles, and some Prophets, and some Evangelists, and some Pastors and Teachers; for the perfecting of the Saints.

℟. Rejoice in the Lord, ye Righteous. Alleluia, Alleluia. ℣. For it becometh well the Just to be thankful. ℟. Alleluia, Alleluia. ℣. Glory be to the Father, and to the Son : and to the Holy Ghost. ℟. Rejoice in the Lord, ye Righteous. Alleluia, Alleluia.

℣. The voice of joy and health.

℟. Is in the dwellings of the Righteous. Alleluia.

Collect as at the First Vespers.

AT THE SECOND VESPERS.

The Antiphons of Lauds, Thy Saints, *and the rest, are said to the Psalms of the Second Vespers of the Common of Apostles, p.* 237.

The Chapter, **℟**., *Hymn,* ℣. *and* ℟., *Antiphon to Magnificat, and Collect, as at the First Vespers, p.* 255.

MAY I.

SS. Philip and James, Apostles and Martyrs. Holy-Day.

AT THE FIRST VESPERS.

Antiphon. I go to prepare a place for you ; but I will see you again, Alleluia ! and your heart shall rejoice. Alleluia, Alleluia.

Psalms of the week-day.

The Chapter, Wisd. v. 1.

Then shall the Righteous man stand in great boldness before the face of such as have afflicted him, and made no account of his labours.

℟., *Hymn,* Tristes erant Apostoli, ℣. *and* ℟., *as at the First Vespers of St. Mark, p.* 255.

Antiphon to Magnificat.

Have I been so long time with you ; and yet hast thou not known Me, Philip ? He that hath seen Me hath seen the Father. Alleluia.

The Collect.

O ALMIGHTY God, Whom truly to know is Everlasting Life ; Grant us perfectly to know Thy Son Jesus Christ to be the Way, the Truth, and the Life ; that, following the steps of Thy holy Apostles, Saint Philip and Saint James, we may steadfastly walk in the Way that leadeth to eternal life ; through the same Thy Son Jesus Christ our Lord. *Amen.*

AT LAUDS.

℣. He was known of them.

℞. In Breaking of Bread. Alleluia.

℣. O God, make speed, &c.

Antiphons. (1.) Lord, show us the Father : and it sufficeth us. Alleluia.

Psalms as on Sundays and Feast-days.

(2.) He that hath seen Me : hath seen the Father. Alleluia.

(3.) I am the Way, the Truth, and the Life : no man cometh to the Father, but by Me. Alleluia.

(4.) O ye Spirits and Souls of the Righteous : bless ye the Lord. Alleluia.

(5.) If ye abide in Me, and My words abide in you : ye shall ask what ye will, and it shall be done unto you. Alleluia.

The Chapter, Wisd. v. 1.

Then shall the Righteous man stand in great boldness before the face of such as have afflicted him, and made no account of his labours.

℞. Thanks be to God.

Hymn, Claro Paschali gaudio, ℣. and ℞., *as in the Lauds of St. Mark, p.* 256.

Antiphon to Benedictus.

Let not your heart be troubled ; ye believe in God, believe also in Me. In My Father's House are many mansions. Alleluia.

Collect as at the First Vespers.

AT PRIME.

Antiphon (1.) Lord, show us the Father : and it sufficeth us. Alleluia.

AT TERCE.

Antiphon (2.) He that hath seen Me : hath seen the Father. Alleluia.

The Chapter, Wisd. v. 1.

Then shall the Righteous man stand in great boldness before the face of such as have afflicted him, and made no account of his labours.

R. *as at Terce on St. Mark, p.* 256.

Collect as at the First Vespers.

AT SEXT.

Antiphon (3.) I am the Way, the Truth, and the Life : no man cometh to the Father, but by Me. Alleluia.

The Chapter, Acts iv. 33.

And with great power gave the Apostles witness of the Resurrection of the Lord Jesus : and great grace was upon them all.

R. *as at Sext on St. Mark, p.* 256.

Collect as at the First Vespers.

AT NONE.

Antiphon (5.) If ye abide in Me, and My words abide in you : ye shall ask what ye will, and it shall be done unto you. Alleluia.

The Chapter, Acts v. 41.

And they departed from the presence of the council, rejoicing that they were counted worthy to suffer shame for His Name.

R. *as at None on St. Mark, p.* 257.

Collect as at the First Vespers.

AT THE SECOND VESPERS.

The Antiphons of Lauds, Lord, show us, *and the rest, are said to the Psalms of the Second Vespers of the Common of Apostles, p.* 237.

The Chapter, Wisd. v. 1.

Then shall the Righteous man stand in great boldness before the face of such as have afflicted him, and made no account of his labours.

Hymn, Tristes erant Apostoli, ℣. *and* ℟., *as on the First Vespers of St. Mark, p.* 255.

Antiphon to Magnificat.

If ye had known Me, ye should have known My Father also; and from henceforth ye know Him, and have seen Him. Alleluia.

Collect as at the First Vespers.

MAY III.

Memorial of THE INVENTION OF THE CROSS.

AT LAUDS.

Antiphon. The Kingdom of Heaven is like unto a treasure hid in a field. Alleluia.

℣. We adore Thee, O Christ, and bless Thee.

℟. For by Thy Holy Cross Thou hast redeemed the world. Alleluia.

The Collect.

O SAVIOUR of the world, Who by Thy Cross and precious Blood hast redeemed us; Save us and help us, we humbly beseech Thee, O Lord. *Amen.*

AT VESPERS.

Antiphon. The Tree of Life, which bare twelve manner of fruits, and yielded her fruits every month; and the Leaves of the Tree were for the Healing of the nations. Alleluia.

℣. Tell it out among the heathen.

℟. That the Lord reigneth from the Tree.

Collect as at Lauds.

MAY VI.

Memorial of ST. JOHN THE EVANGELIST at the Latin gate.

AT LAUDS.

Antiphon. The Apostle John, being plunged into a vessel of boiling oil; by Divine mercy came forth unharmed. Alleluia.

℣. Greatly is blessed John to be had in honour.

℟. For he leant on Jesus' bosom at the Last Supper. Alleluia.

The Collect.

MERCIFUL Lord, we beseech Thee to cast Thy bright beams of light upon Thy Church, that it, being enlightened by the doctrine of Thy Blessed Apostle and Evangelist Saint John, may so walk in the light of Thy Truth that it may at length attain to the light of everlasting life; through Jesus Christ our Lord. *Amen.*

AT VESPERS.

Antiphon. When blessed John returned from exile, much people of men and women went out to meet him, crying, Blessed is he that cometh in the Name of the Lord. Alleluia.

℣. Rejoice in the Lord, ye Righteous.

℟. For it becometh well the Just to be thankful. Alleluia.

Collect as at Lauds.

If either of the three Memorials next following happen after Trinity Sunday, it shall be said altogether as for Silvester, Bp., *Dec. xxxi., with change of name.*

MAY XIX.

Memorial of DUNSTAN, Abp. of Canterbury.

AT LAUDS.

Antiphon. Light Eternal shall shine on Thy Saints, O Lord, and length of days. Alleluia.

℣. Rejoice in the Lord, ye Righteous.

℟. For it becometh well the Just to be thankful. Alleluia.

The Collect.

GRANT, we beseech Thee, O Blessed Lord, that we who commemorate Thy holy Confessor and Bishop Dunstan may increase in faith and love towards Thee, the great Shepherd and Bishop of our souls, Who livest and reignest with the Father and the Holy Ghost, ever One God, world without end. *Amen.*

AT VESPERS.

Antiphon. Go forth, O ye daughters of Zion, and behold the Righteous Man with the Crown wherewith the Lord hath crowned Him in the day of His Espousals, and in the day of the gladness of His heart.

℣. Then were the disciples glad.

℟. When they saw the Lord. Alleluia.

Collect as at Lauds.

MAY XXVI.

Memorial of AUGUSTIN, Abp. of Canterbury.

AT LAUDS.

Antiphon. Light Eternal shall shine on Thy Saints, O Lord, and length of days. Alleluia.

℣. Rejoice in the Lord, ye Righteous.

℟. For it becometh well the Just to be thankful. Alleluia.

The Collect.

GRANT, we beseech Thee, O Blessed Lord, that we who commemorate Thy holy Confessor and Bishop Augustin, may increase in faith and love towards Thee, the great Shepherd and Bishop of our souls, Who livest and reignest with the Father and the Holy Ghost, ever One God, world without end. *Amen.*

AT VESPERS.

Antiphon. Go forth, O ye daughters of Zion, and behold the Righteous Man with the Crown wherewith the Lord hath crowned Him in the day of His Espousals, and in the day of the gladness of His heart.

℣. Then were the disciples glad.

℟. When they saw the Lord. Alleluia.

Collect as at Lauds.

MAY XXVII.

Memorial of VENERABLE BEDE.

AT LAUDS.

Antiphon. Light Eternal shall

shine on Thy Saints, O Lord, and length of days. Alleluia.

℣. Rejoice in the Lord, ye Righteous.

℟. For it becometh well the Just to be thankful. Alleluia.

The Collect.

GRANT, we beseech Thee, O Blessed Lord, that we who commemorate Thy holy Confessor and Priest Venerable Bede, may increase in faith and love towards Thee, the great Shepherd and Bishop of our souls, Who livest and reignest with the Father and the Holy Ghost, ever One God, world without end. *Amen.*

AT VESPERS.

Antiphon. Go forth, O ye daughters of Zion, and behold the Righteous Man with the Crown wherewith the Lord hath crowned Him in the day of His Espousals, and in the day of the gladness of His heart.

℣. Then were the disciples glad.

℟. When they saw the Lord. Alleluia.

Collect as at Lauds.

If either of the two following Memorials happen after Trinity Sunday, it shall be said altogether as for Lucian, P. and M., Jan. viii., *with change of name.*

JUNE I.

Memorial of NICOMEDE, P. & M.

AT LAUDS.

Antiphon. Light Eternal shall shine on Thy Saints, O Lord, and length of days. Alleluia.

℣. Rejoice in the Lord, ye Righteous.

℟. For it becometh well the Just to be thankful. Alleluia.

The Collect.

ALMIGHTY and Everlasting God, grant unto us so to commemorate Thy holy Martyr Nicomede, that we may have our share in the Communion of Saints; through Jesus Christ our Lord, Who liveth and reigneth with Thee and the Holy Ghost, ever One God, world without end. *Amen.*

AT VESPERS.

Antiphon. Go forth, O ye daughters of Zion, and behold the Righteous Man with the Crown wherewith the Lord hath crowned Him in the day of His Espousals, and in the day of the gladness of His heart.

℣. Then were the disciples glad.

℟. When they saw the Lord. Alleluia.

Collect as at Lauds.

JUNE V.

Memorial of BONIFACE, Bp. & M.

AT LAUDS.

Antiphon. Light Eternal shall shine on Thy Saints, O Lord, and length of days. Alleluia.

℣. Rejoice in the Lord, ye Righteous.

℟. For it becometh well the Just to be thankful. Alleluia.

The Collect.

ALMIGHTY and Everlasting God, grant unto us so to commemorate Thy holy Martyr Boniface, that we may have our share in the Communion of Saints; through Jesus Christ our Lord, Who liveth and reigneth with Thee and the Holy Ghost, ever One God, world without end. *Amen.*

AT VESPERS.

Antiphon. Go forth, O ye daughters of Zion, and behold the Righteous Man with the Crown wherewith the Lord hath crowned Him in the day of His Espousals, and in the day of the gladness of His heart.

℣. Then were the disciples glad.

℟. When they saw the Lord. Alleluia.

Collect as at Lauds.

JUNE XI.

St. Barnabas, Apostle and Martyr. Holy=Day.

If before Trinity Sunday, everything as of St. Mark, p. 255, with the Collect of St. Barnabas.

If after Trinity Sunday, everything as in the Common of Apostles, p. 235, with the Collect of St. Barnabas.

The Collect.

O LORD God Almighty, Who didst endue Thy holy Apostle Barnabas with singular gifts of the Holy Ghost; Leave us not, we beseech Thee, destitute of Thy manifold gifts, nor yet of grace to use them alway to Thy honour and glory; through Jesus Christ our Lord. *Amen.*

JUNE XVII.

Memorial of ST. ALBAN.

AT LAUDS.

Antiphon. Theirs is the Kingdom of Heaven who have despised the life of this world to gain a reward in the kingdom; and have washed their robes in the Blood of the Lamb.

℣. O God, wonderful art Thou in Thy Saints.

℟. And glorious in Thy Majesty.

The Collect.

ALMIGHTY and Everlasting God, grant unto us so to commemorate Thy holy Martyr Alban, that we may have our share in the Communion of Saints; through Jesus Christ our Lord, Who liveth and reigneth with Thee and the Holy Ghost, ever One God, world without end. *Amen.*

AT VESPERS.

Antiphon. The souls of the Saints who followed the Footsteps of Christ rejoice in Heaven; and forasmuch as for love of Him they shed their blood, they shall reign with Him for ever.

℣. Be glad, O ye Righteous, and rejoice in the Lord.

℟. And be joyful, all ye that are true of heart.

Collect as at Lauds.

JUNE XX.

Memorial of THE TRANSLATION OF EDWARD, King of the West Saxons.

AT LAUDS.

Antiphon. Theirs is the Kingdom of Heaven who have despised the life of this world to gain a reward in the kingdom; and have washed their robes in the Blood of the Lamb.

℣. O God, wonderful art Thou in Thy Saints.

℟. And glorious in Thy Majesty.

The Collect.

ALMIGHTY and Everlasting God, grant unto us so to commemorate Thy holy Martyr Edward, that we may have our share in the Communion of Saints; through Jesus Christ our Lord, Who liveth and reigneth with Thee and the Holy Ghost, ever One God, world without end. *Amen.*

AT VESPERS.

Antiphon. The souls of the Saints who followed the Footsteps of Christ rejoice in Heaven; and forasmuch as for love of Him they shed their blood, they shall reign with Him for ever.

℣. Be glad, O ye Righteous, and rejoice in the Lord.

℟. And be joyful, all ye that are true of heart.

Collect as at Lauds.

JUNE XXIV.
Nativity of St. John Baptist.
Holy-Day.

AT THE FIRST VESPERS.

Antiphon. But the Angel said unto him, Fear not, Zacharias: for thy prayer is heard, and thy wife Elisabeth shall bear thee a son, and thou shalt call his name John.

Psalms of the week-day.

The Chapter, Jer. i. 5.

Before I formed thee in the belly I knew thee: and before thou camest forth out of the womb I sanctified thee, and ordained thee a prophet unto the nations.

℟. Among those that are born of women there is not a greater prophet than John the Baptist. ℣. The voice of one crying in the wilderness, Prepare ye the way of the Lord. ℟. There is not a greater prophet than John the Baptist. ℣. Glory be to the Father, and to the Son : and to the Holy Ghost. ℟. Among those that are born of women there is not a greater prophet than John the Baptist.

Hymn. Ut queant laxis.

Greatest of Prophets, Messenger appointed
Paths for thy Lord and Saviour to prepare,
Oh! for a tongue unsoiled, thy praise and wonders
    Meet to declare!

From highest heaven Gabriel descending,
Gave to thy father promise of thy birth,
Gave thee thy name, and for thy life predicted
    Deeds of great worth.

Yet did that father falter at the promise,
Dumb was he struck for doubting of the same,
Till at thy birth his voice again returning,
    Uttered thy name.

Pent in the closet of the womb, thy Saviour
Thou didst adore within His Chamber shrined;
Thus did each parent in their unborn offspring
    Mysteries find.

Praise we our God, Who dwelleth in the
highest,
Father, and Son, and Spirit ever blest,
And may He grant us, while on earth,
forgiveness,
   In heaven rest. Amen.

℣. There was a man sent from God.

℟. Whose name was John.

Antiphon to Magnificat.

When Zacharias went into the temple : of the Lord, there appeared unto him an Angel of the Lord standing on the right side of the Altar of Incense.

The Collect.

ALMIGHTY God, by Whose Providence Thy servant John Baptist was wonderfully Born, and sent to prepare the way of Thy Son our Saviour, by preaching of repentance ; Make us so to follow his doctrine and holy life, that we may truly repent according to his preaching ; and after his example constantly speak the truth, boldly rebuke vice, and patiently suffer for the Truth's sake; through Jesus Christ our Lord. *Amen.*

AT LAUDS.

℣. There was a man sent from God.

℟. Whose name was John.

℣. O God, make speed, &c.

Antiphons. (1.) Elisabeth's full time came that she should be delivered : and she brought forth a son, John Baptist, the Forerunner of the Lord.

(2.) They made signs to his father, how he would have him called : and he asked for a writing table, and wrote, saying, His name is John.

(3.) Thou shalt call his name John : and thou shalt have joy and gladness, and many shall rejoice at his birth.

(4.) He shall be great in the sight of the Lord : and shall drink neither wine nor strong drink ; and he shall be filled with the Holy Ghost, even from his mother's womb.

(5.) He shall go before Him in the spirit and power of Elias : to turn the hearts of the fathers to the children, and the disobedient to the wisdom of the just ; to make ready a people prepared for the Lord.

The Chapter, Isa. xlix. 1.

Listen, O isles, unto me ; and hearken, ye people from far : the Lord hath called me from the womb ; from the bowels of my mother hath He made mention of my name.

℟. Thanks be to God.

Hymn. O nimis felix.

O blessed Saint of high renown and honour,
Called in thy mother's womb, by God ordained,
Mightiest Martyr, dweller in the desert,
  Virgin unstained.

Saints with their crowns shall glitter, some with increase
Thirty-fold, some with double wreaths shall shine,
Yet shall no other diadem of glory
  Glitter like thine.

Come thou again, the crooked highways straighten,
Break the hard rocks that in our bosoms rest,
Meet for our Lord, Who ever cometh onwards
  With footsteps blest.

Praise we our God, Who dwelleth in the highest,
Father, and Son, and Spirit ever blest,
And may He grant us, while on earth, forgiveness,
  In heaven rest. Amen.

℣. Amongst those born of woman.

℟. There is not a greater prophet than John the Baptist.

Antiphon to Benedictus.

And his father Zacharias was filled with the Holy Ghost, and prophesied, saying, Blessed be the Lord God of Israel.

AT PRIME.

Antiphon (1.) Elisabeth's full time came that she should be delivered : and she brought forth a son, John Baptist, the Forerunner of the Lord.

AT TERCE.

Antiphon (2.) They made signs to his father, how he would have him called : and he asked for a writing table, and wrote, saying, His name is John.

The Chapter, Isa. xlix. 1.

Listen, O isles, unto me; and hearken, ye people from far : the Lord hath called me from the womb; from the bowels of my mother hath He made mention of my name.

R. Thou hast crowned Him with glory and worship. ℣. Thou makest Him to have dominion of the works of Thy hands. ℟. With glory and worship. ℣. Glory be to the Father, and to the Son : and to the Holy Ghost. ℟. Thou hast crowned Him with glory and worship.

℣. Thou hast set upon His head, O Lord.

℟. A crown of pure gold.

Collect as at the First Vespers.

AT SEXT.

Antiphon (3.) Thou shalt call his name John : and thou shalt have joy and gladness, and many shall rejoice at his birth.

The Chapter, Isa. xlix. 5, 6.

And now saith the Lord, that formed Me from the womb to be His servant : I will also give Thee for a light to the Gentiles, that Thou mayest be My Salvation to the ends of the earth.

R. Thou hast set upon His head, O Lord. ℣. A crown of pure gold. ℟. Upon His head, O Lord. ℣. Glory be to the Father, and to the Son : and to the Holy Ghost. ℟. Thou hast set upon His head, O Lord, a crown of pure gold.

℣. The Righteous shall flourish like a palm-tree.

℟. And shall spread abroad like a cedar in Libanus.

Collect as at the First Vespers.

AT NONE.

Antiphon (5.) He shall go before Him in the spirit and power of Elias : to turn the hearts of the fathers to the children, and the disobedient to the wisdom of the just; to make ready a people prepared for the Lord.

The Chapter, Isa. xlix. 7.

Kings shall see and arise, princes also shall worship, because of the Lord that is faithful, and the Holy One of Israel, and He shall choose thee.

R. The Righteous shall flourish like a palm-tree. ℣. And spread abroad like a cedar in Libanus.

℟. Like a palm-tree. ℣. Glory be to the Father, and to the Son: and to the Holy Ghost. ℟. The Righteous shall flourish like a palm-tree.

℣. The Righteous shall grow as a lily.

℟. He shall flourish for ever before the Lord.

Collect as at the First Vespers.

AT THE SECOND VESPERS.

The Antiphons of Lauds are said to the Psalms of the week-day.

The Chapter, R., *Hymn,* ℣. *and* ℟., *as at the First Vespers, p.* 263.

Antiphon to Magnificat.

And thou, Child, shalt be called the Prophet of the Highest: for thou shalt go before the Face of the Lord, to prepare His ways.

Collect as at the First Vespers.

JUNE XXIX.

St. Peter, Apostle and Martyr. Holy-Day.

AT THE FIRST VESPERS.

Antiphon. Jesus saith unto them, But Whom say ye that I am? And Simon Peter answered: and said, Thou art the Christ, the Son of the Living God. And Jesus answered and said unto him, Blessed art thou, Simon Bar-Jona. And I say unto thee, That thou art Peter, and upon this Rock I will build My Church.

Psalms of the week-day.

The Chapter, Acts xii. 4.

Peter therefore was kept in prison; but prayer was made without ceasing of the Church to God for him.

R. Cornelius the centurion, a devout man, and one that feared God, saw in a vision evidently an Angel of God coming in to him, and saying, Cornelius, send men to Joppa, and call for one Simon, whose surname is Peter: he shall tell thee what thou oughtest to do. ℣. When Cornelius, as yet unregenerate in Christ, prayed, an Angel appeared unto him, saying. ℟. Cornelius, send men to Joppa, and call for one Simon, whose surname is Peter: he shall tell thee what thou oughtest to do. ℣. Glory be to the Father, and to the Son: and to the Holy Ghost. ℟. Cornelius the centurion, a devout man, and one that feared God, saw in a vision evidently an Angel of God coming in to him, and saying, Cornelius, send men to Joppa, and call for one Simon, whose surname is Peter: he shall tell thee what thou oughtest to do.

Hymn, Annue Christe, ℣. *and* ℟., *as in the Common of Apostles, p.* 235.

Antiphon to Magnificat.

Blessed Peter, the Apostle, saw Christ coming to meet him: he worshipped Him, and said, Lord, whither goest Thou? I go unto Rome, to be there crucified afresh.

The Collect.

O ALMIGHTY God, Who by Thy Son Jesus Christ didst give to Thy Apostle Saint Peter many excellent gifts, and commandedst him earnestly to Feed Thy flock; Make, we beseech Thee, all Bishops and Pastors diligently to preach Thy

Holy Word, and the people obediently to follow the same, that they may receive the crown of everlasting glory; through Jesus Christ our Lord. *Amen.*

AT LAUDS.

℣. Thou art Peter.

℟. And upon this Rock I will build My Church.

℣. O God, make speed, &c.

Antiphons. (1.) Now Peter and John went up together into the temple at the hour of prayer: being the ninth hour.

Psalms as on Sundays and Holy-Days.

(2.) Silver and gold have I none: but such as I have give I thee.

(3.) And the Angel saith unto Peter: Cast thy garment about thee, and follow me.

(4.) Simon, son of Jonas, lovest thou Me? Lord, Thou knowest all things: Thou knowest that I love Thee. Feed My sheep.

(5.) Thou art Peter: and upon this Rock I will build My Church.

The Chapter, Acts xii. 5.

Peter therefore was kept in prison: but prayer was made without ceasing of the Church unto God for him.

℟. Thanks be to God.

Hymn, Æterna Christi munera, ℣. *and* ℟., *as in the Common of Apostles, p.* 236.

Antiphon to Benedictus.

Whatsoever thou shalt bind on earth, shall be bound in heaven; and whatsoever thou shalt loose on earth, shall be loosed in heaven.

Collect as at the First Vespers.

AT PRIME.

Antiphon (1.) Now Peter and John went up together into the temple at the hour of prayer: being the ninth hour.

AT TERCE.

Antiphon (2.) Silver and gold have I none: but such as I have give I thee.

The Chapter, Acts xii. 5.

Peter therefore was kept in prison: but prayer was made without ceasing of the Church unto God for him.

℟. *as at Terce in the Common of Apostles, p.* 236.

Collect as at the First Vespers.

AT SEXT.

Antiphon (3.) And the Angel saith unto Peter: Cast thy garment about thee, and follow me.

The Chapter, Acts xii. 7.

And behold, the Angel of the Lord came upon him, and a light shined in the prison; and he smote Peter on the side, and raised him up, saying, Arise up quickly. And his chains fell off from his hands.

℟. *as at Sext in the Common of Apostles, p.* 237.

Collect as at the First Vespers.

AT NONE.

Antiphon (5.) Thou art Peter, and upon this Rock I will build My Church.

The Chapter, Acts xii. 9.

And he went out and followed him; and wist not that it was true which was done by the Angel; but thought he saw a vision.

R. *as at None in the Common of Apostles, p. 237.*

Collect as at the First Vespers.

AT THE SECOND VESPERS.

Everything as at the Second Vespers of the Common of Apostles, p. 237, till

Collect as at the First Vespers.

JULY II.

Memorial of THE VISITATION OF THE BLESSED VIRGIN MARY.

AT LAUDS.

Antiphon. Rise up, my love, my fair one, and come away; for, lo, the winter is past, the rain is over and gone; the flowers appear on the earth.

℣. Blessed art thou among women.

℟. And blessed is the Fruit of thy womb.

The Collect.

O GOD, Who didst move the most holy Virgin Mary, the Mother of Thy Only-begotten Son, our Lord God, for the sake of mutual consolation to Visit the blessed Elisabeth; Grant that He may so visit our hearts, that we may be defended from all dangers; through the same Jesus Christ our Lord, Who with Thee and the Holy Ghost liveth and reigneth, ever One God, world without end. Amen.

AT VESPERS.

Antiphon. Let me see thy countenance, let me hear thy voice; for sweet is thy voice, and thy countenance is comely.

℣. Behold, from henceforth.

℟. All generations shall call Me Blessed.

Collect as at Lauds.

JULY IV.

Memorial of THE TRANSLATION OF MARTIN, Bp.

AT LAUDS.

Antiphon. Well done, thou good and faithful servant; thou hast been faithful over a few things, I will make thee ruler over many things; enter thou into the Joy of thy Lord.

℣. The Righteous shall grow as a lily.

℟. He shall flourish for ever before the Lord.

The Collect.

GRANT, we beseech Thee, O Blessed Lord, that we who commemorate Thy holy Confessor and Bishop Martin, may increase in faith and love towards Thee, the great Shepherd and Bishop of our souls, Who livest and reignest with the Father and the Holy Ghost, ever One God, world without end. Amen.

AT VESPERS.

Antiphon. A Bishop must be blameless, as the steward of God.

℣. The Lord loved him, and beautified him with comely ornaments.

℟. He clothed him with a robe of glory.

Collect as at Lauds.

JULY XV.

Memorial of SWITHUN, Bp.

AT LAUDS.

Antiphon. Well done, thou good and faithful servant; thou hast been faithful over a few things, I will make thee ruler over many things; enter thou into the Joy of thy Lord.

℣. The Righteous shall grow as a lily.

℟. He shall flourish for ever before the Lord.

The Collect.

GRANT, we beseech Thee, O Blessed Lord, that we who commemorate Thy holy Confessor and Bishop Swithun, may increase in faith and love towards Thee, the great Shepherd and Bishop of our souls, Who livest and reignest with the Father and the Holy Ghost, ever One God, world without end. Amen.

AT VESPERS.

Antiphon. A Bishop must be blameless, as the steward of God.

℣. The Lord loved him, and beautified him with comely ornaments.

℟. He clothed him with a robe of glory.

Collect as at Lauds.

JULY XX.

Memorial of MARGARET, V. & M.

AT LAUDS.

Antiphon. When the Bridegroom came, they that were ready went in with Him to the marriage.

℣. The Virgins that be her fellows.

℟. Shall bear her company.

The Collect.

GRANT, O Almighty God, that we who commemorate the martyrdom of Thy blessed Virgin Margaret may profit by the example of her great faith, through our Lord Jesus Christ, Who liveth and reigneth with Thee and the Holy Ghost, ever One God, world without end. Amen.

AT VESPERS.

Antiphon. The kingdom of heaven is like unto a net; that was cast into the sea, and gathered of every kind; which, when it was full, they drew to shore, and sat down, and gathered the good into vessels, but cast the bad away.

℣. Full of grace are thy lips.

℟. Because God hath blessed thee for ever.

Collect as at Lauds.

JULY XXII.

Memorial of ST. MARY MAGDALENE.

AT LAUDS.

Antiphon. Instead of the thorn shall come up the fir-tree, and instead of the brier shall come up the myrtle-tree; and it shall be to the Lord for a name, for an everlasting sign that shall not be cut off.

℣. Her sins, which are many, are forgiven.

℟. For she loved much.

The Collect.

MERCIFUL Father, give us grace that we never presume to sin through the example of any creature; but if it shall chance us at any time to offend Thy Divine Majesty, that then we may truly repent and lament the same, after the example of Mary Magdalene, and by lively faith obtain remission of all our sins; through the only merits of Thy Son, our Saviour Christ. *Amen.*

AT VESPERS.

Antiphon. When Jesus was in Bethany, in the house of Simon the leper; there came unto Him a woman having an alabaster box of very precious ointment.

℣. Mary hath chosen that good part.

℟. Which shall not be taken away from her.

Collect as at Lauds.

JULY XXV.

St. James, Apostle and Martyr. Holy-Day.

Everything as in the Common of Apostles, p. 235, except

The Collect.

GRANT, O Merciful God, that as Thine holy Apostle Saint James, leaving his father and all that he had, without delay was obedient unto the Calling of Thy Son Jesus Christ, and followed Him; so we, forsaking all worldly and carnal affections, may be evermore ready to follow Thy holy commandments; through Jesus Christ our Lord. *Amen.*

JULY XXVI.

Memorial of St. ANNE, Mother of the Blessed Virgin Mary.

AT LAUDS.

Antiphon. Who can find a virtuous woman? for her price is far above rubies.

℣. Full of grace are thy lips.

℟. Because God hath blessed thee for ever.

The Collect.

O GOD, Who on this day didst take to Thyself the Holy Anne, mother of the Blessed Virgin; Grant that we who thus commemorate her may have our share in the Communion of Saints; through Him Who did not abhor the Virgin's Womb, and now liveth and reigneth with Thee and the Holy Ghost, ever One God, world without end. *Amen.*

AT VESPERS.

Antiphon. A woman that feareth the Lord, she shall be praised.

℣. Lord, I have loved the Habitation of Thy House.

℟. And the Place where Thine Honour dwelleth.

Collect as at Lauds.

AUGUST I.

Memorial of St. PETER'S CHAINS.

AT LAUDS.

Antiphon. The same night Peter was sleeping; between two soldiers bound with two chains.

℣. Thou art Peter.

℟. And upon this Rock I will build My Church.

The Collect.

O ALMIGHTY God, Who by Thy Son Jesus Christ didst give to Thy Apostle Saint Peter many excellent gifts, and commandedst him earnestly to Feed Thy flock; Make, we beseech Thee, all Bishops and Pastors diligently to preach Thy holy Word, and the people obediently to follow the same, that they may receive the crown of everlasting glory; through Jesus Christ our Lord. *Amen.*

AT VESPERS.

Antiphon. And behold, the Angel of the Lord came upon him, and a light shined in the prison; and he smote Peter on the side, and raised him up, saying, Arise up quickly. And his chains fell off from his hands.

℣. I am Thy servant, and the son of Thine handmaid.

℟. Thou hast broken my bonds in sunder.

Collect as at Lauds.

AUGUST VI.

Memorial of THE TRANSFIGURATION.

AT LAUDS.

Antiphon. Jesus taketh Peter, James and John his brother, and bringeth them up into a high mountain apart, and was transfigured before them; and His Face did shine as the sun, and His raiment was white as the light.

℣. Behold, a Voice out of the cloud.

℟. This is My Beloved Son.

The Collect.

O GOD, Who didst on this day Transfigure Thy Only-begotten Son in the sight of Fathers of the Old and New Covenant; Grant us, we beseech Thee, so to please Thee, that we may hereafter obtain the sight of His Glory in Whom Thou wert well pleased; through the same our Lord Jesus Christ, Who liveth and reigneth with Thee and the Holy Ghost, ever One God, world without end. *Amen.*

AT VESPERS.

Antiphon. And behold, there talked with Him two men, Moses and Elias; who appeared in glory, and spake of His decease, which He should accomplish at Jerusalem.

℣. We look for the Saviour, the Lord Jesus Christ.

℟. Who shall change our vile body, that it may be fashioned like unto His glorious body.

Collect as at Lauds.

AUGUST VII.

Memorial of THE NAME OF JESUS.

AT LAUDS.

Antiphon. God also hath highly

exalted Him, and given Him a Name which is above every name; that at the Name of JESUS every knee should bow, of things in heaven, and things in earth, and things under the earth.

℣. Our help standeth in the Name of the Lord.

℟. Who hath made heaven and earth.

The Collect.

O GOD, Who hast made the most sweet Name of Jesus a source of joy to Thy faithful people, and a cause of terror to evil spirits; Grant that we who venerate this Holy Name, may in this life obtain comfort, and in the life to come everlasting happiness; through the same Thy Son our Lord Jesus Christ, Who liveth and reigneth with Thee and the Holy Ghost, ever One God, world without end. *Amen.*

AT VESPERS.

Antiphon. Whatsoever ye do in word or deed; do all in the Name of the Lord Jesus.

℣. Blessed be the Name of the Lord.

℟. From this time forth for evermore.

Collect as at Lauds.

AUGUST X.

Memorial of ST. LAWRENCE.

AT LAUDS.

Antiphon. Gold is tried in the fire; and acceptable men in the furnace of adversity.

℣. The Righteous shall grow as a lily.

℟. He shall flourish for ever before the Lord.

The Collect.

O GOD, Who didst give to Blessed Lawrence grace to withstand his fiery torture; Grant to us, we beseech Thee, to quench the flames of our sins, through Jesus Christ our Lord, Who liveth and reigneth with Thee and the Holy Ghost, ever One God, world without end. *Amen.*

AT VESPERS.

Antiphon. Blessed Lawrence when lying on the gridiron; cried out from the midst of the flames, I worship my God, and Him only do I serve.

℣. O ye Fire and Heat, bless ye the Lord.

℟. Out of the midst of the fire hath He delivered them.

Collect as at Lauds.

AUGUST XXIV.

St. Bartholomew, Apostle and Martyr. Holy=Day.

Everything as in the Common of Apostles, p. 235.

The Collect.

O ALMIGHTY and Everlasting God, Who didst give to Thine Apostle Bartholomew grace truly to believe and to preach Thy Word; Grant, we beseech Thee, unto Thy Church, to love that Word which he believed, and both to preach and receive the same; through Jesus Christ our Lord. *Amen.*

AUGUST XXVIII.

Memorial of AUGUSTINE, Bp. of Hippo.

AT LAUDS.

Antiphon. Well done, thou good and faithful servant; thou hast been faithful over a few things, I will make thee ruler over many things; enter thou into the Joy of thy Lord.

℣. The Righteous shall grow as a lily.

℞. He shall flourish for ever before the Lord.

The Collect.

O GOD, Who madest the blessed Augustine a doctor and a teacher of Thy Church; Grant us to follow the Holy Doctrines that he taught, through Jesus Christ our Lord, Who liveth and reigneth with Thee and the Holy Ghost, ever One God, world without end. *Amen.*

AT VESPERS.

Antiphon. A Bishop must be blameless, as the steward of God.

℣. The Lord loved him, and beautified him with comely ornaments.

℞. He clothed him with a robe of glory.

Collect as at Lauds.

AUGUST XXIX.

Memorial of THE BEHEADING OF ST. JOHN BAPTIST.

AT LAUDS.

Antiphon. Herod himself had sent forth and laid hold upon John, and bound him in prison for Herodias' sake, his brother Philip's wife; for John had said unto Herod, It is not lawful for thee to have her.

℣. The Righteous shall grow as a lily.

℞. He shall flourish for ever before the Lord.

The Collect.

ALMIGHTY God, by Whose providence Thy servant John Baptist was wonderfully Born, and sent to prepare the way of Thy Son our Saviour, by preaching of repentance; Make us so to follow his doctrine and holy life, that we may truly repent according to his preaching; and after his example constantly speak the truth, boldly rebuke vice, and patiently suffer for the Truth's sake; through Jesus Christ our Lord. *Amen.*

AT VESPERS.

Antiphon. The king sent an executioner, and commanded his head to be brought; and he went and beheaded him in the prison. And when his disciples heard of it, they came and took up his corpse, and laid it in a tomb.

℣. Thou hast crowned him with glory and worship.

℞. Thou makest him to have dominion over the works of Thy Hands.

Collect as at Lauds.

SEPTEMBER I.

Memorial of GILES, Abbot.

AT LAUDS.

Antiphon. Well done, thou good and faithful servant; thou hast been faithful over a few things, I will make thee ruler over many things; enter thou into the Joy of thy Lord.

℣. The Righteous shall grow as a lily.

℞. He shall flourish for ever before the Lord.

The Collect.

GRANT, we beseech Thee, O Blessed Lord, that we who commemorate Thy holy Confessor and Abbot Giles, may increase in faith and love towards Thee, the great Shepherd and Bishop of our souls, Who livest and reignest with the Father and the Holy Ghost, ever One God, world without end. *Amen.*

AT VESPERS.

Antiphon. A Bishop must be blameless, as the steward of God.

℣. The Lord loved him, and beautified him with comely ornaments.

℟. He clothed him with a robe of glory.

Collect as at Lauds.

SEPTEMBER VII.

Memorial of ENURCHUS, Bp.

AT LAUDS.

Antiphon. Well done, thou good and faithful servant; thou hast been faithful over a few things, I will make thee ruler over many things; enter thou into the Joy of thy Lord.

℣. The Righteous shall grow as a lily.

℟. He shall flourish for ever before the Lord.

The Collect.

GRANT, we beseech Thee, O Blessed Lord, that we who commemorate Thy holy Confessor and Bishop Enurchus, may increase in faith and love towards Thee, the great Shepherd and Bishop of our souls, Who livest and reignest with the Father and the Holy Ghost, ever One God, world without end. *Amen.*

AT VESPERS.

Antiphon. A Bishop must be blameless, as the steward of God.

℣. The Lord loved him, and beautified him with comely ornaments.

℟. He clothed him with a robe of glory.

Collect as at Lauds.

SEPTEMBER VIII.

Memorial of THE NATIVITY OF THE BLESSED VIRGIN MARY.

AT LAUDS.

Antiphon. A little fountain became a river.

℣. All honour, laud, and glory be.

℟. O Jesu, Virgin-born, to Thee.

The Collect.

MERCIFUL Lord, hear the prayers of Thy servants who commemorate the Nativity of the Mother of God; and grant that by the Incarnation of Thy dear Son, we may be indeed made nigh unto Him, Who liveth and reigneth with Thee and the Holy Ghost, ever One God, world without end. *Amen.*

AT VESPERS.

Antiphon. With heart and soul let us praise Christ our King on the Nativity of Mary His Mother.

℣. Blessed art thou among women.

℟. And blessed is the Fruit of thy womb.

Collect as at Lauds.

SEPTEMBER XIV.

Memorial of THE EXALTATION OF THE HOLY CROSS.

AT LAUDS.

Antiphon. The Kingdom of Heaven is like unto treasure hid in a field. Alleluia.

℣. We adore Thee, O Christ, and bless Thee.

℞. For by Thy Holy Cross Thou hast redeemed the world. Alleluia.

The Collect.

O SAVIOUR of the world, Who by Thy Cross and precious Blood hast redeemed us: Save us and help us, we humbly beseech Thee, O Lord. *Amen.*

AT VESPERS.

Antiphon. The Tree of Life, which bare twelve manner of fruits, and yielded her fruits every month; and the leaves of the Tree were for the Healing of the nations. Alleluia.

℣. Tell it out among the heathen.

℞. That the Lord reigneth from the Tree.

Collect as at Lauds.

SEPTEMBER XVII.

Memorial of LAMBERT, Bp. & M.

AT LAUDS.

Antiphon. Theirs is the Kingdom of Heaven who have despised the life of this world to gain a reward in the kingdom, and have washed their robes in the Blood of the Lamb.

℣. O God, wonderful art Thou in Thy Saints.

℞. And glorious in Thy Majesty.

The Collect.

ALMIGHTY and Everlasting God, grant unto us so to commemorate Thy holy Martyr Lambert, that we may have our share in the Communion of Saints; through Jesus Christ our Lord, Who liveth and reigneth with Thee and the Holy Ghost, ever One God, world without end. *Amen.*

AT VESPERS.

Antiphon. The souls of the Saints who followed the Footsteps of Christ rejoice in Heaven, and forasmuch as for love of Him they shed their blood, they shall reign with Him for ever.

℣. Be glad, O ye Righteous, and rejoice in the Lord.

℞. And be joyful, all ye that are true of heart.

Collect as at Lauds.

SEPTEMBER XXI.

St. Matthew, Apostle, Evangelist, and Martyr. Holy-Day.

AT THE FIRST VESPERS.

Everything as in the Common of Apostles, p. 235.

Antiphon to Magnificat.

In the midst of the Throne : and round about the Throne, were four Beasts full of eyes before and behind.

The Collect.

O ALMIGHTY God, Who by Thy blessed Son didst call Matthew from the receipt of custom to be an Apostle and Evangelist; Grant us grace to forsake all covetous desires, and inordinate love of riches, and to follow the same Thy Son Jesus Christ, Who liveth and reigneth with Thee and the Holy Ghost, One God, world without end. *Amen.*

AT LAUDS.
Antiphon to Benedictus.

And the four Beasts had each of them six wings about him; and they were full of eyes within; and they rest not day and night, saying, Holy, Holy, Holy, Lord God Almighty, Which was, and Is, and is to Come. Alleluia.

Collect as at the First Vespers.

AT THE SECOND VESPERS.
Antiphon to Magnificat.

And the first Beast was like a lion, and the second Beast like a calf, and the third Beast had a face as a man, and the fourth Beast was like a flying eagle. Alleluia.

Collect as at the First Vespers.

SEPTEMBER XXVI.
Memorial of ST. CYPRIAN.

AT LAUDS.
Antiphon. Theirs is the Kingdom of Heaven who have despised the life of this world to gain a reward in the kingdom, and have washed their robes in the Blood of the Lamb.

℣. O God, wonderful art Thou in Thy Saints.

℞. And glorious in Thy Majesty.

The Collect.

ALMIGHTY and Everlasting God, grant unto us so to commemorate Thy holy Martyr, Cyprian, that we may have our share in the Communion of Saints; through Jesus Christ our Lord, Who liveth and reigneth with Thee and the Holy Ghost, ever One God, world without end. *Amen.*

AT VESPERS.
Antiphon. The souls of the Saints who followed the Footsteps of Christ rejoice in Heaven, and forasmuch as for love of Him they shed their blood, they shall reign with Him for ever.

℣. Be glad, O ye Righteous, and rejoice in the Lord.

℞. And be joyful, all ye that are true of heart.

Collect as at Lauds.

SEPTEMBER XXIX.
St. Michael and all Angels.
Holy-Day.

AT THE FIRST VESPERS.
Antiphon to the Psalms.

The Heavenly Host adore the Son of the Great King: Cherubim and Seraphim proclaim Him Holy.

Psalms of the week-day.

The Chapter, Rev. xii. 7.

There was war in Heaven: Michael and his Angels fought against the Dragon, and the Dragon fought and his angels; and prevailed not, neither was their place found any more in Heaven.

℞. And I heard the voice of many Angels round the Throne, saying with a loud voice, Worthy is the Lamb that was slain. ℣. To receive power, and riches, and wisdom, and strength, and honour, and glory, and blessing. ℞. Worthy is the Lamb that was slain. ℣. Glory be to the Father, and to the Son: and to the Holy

Ghost. ℟. And I heard the voice of many Angels round the Throne, saying with a loud voice, Worthy is the Lamb that was slain.

Hymn. Tibi Christe splendor Patris.
Thee, O Christ, the Father's Splendour,
   Life and virtue of the heart,
In the presence of the Angels
   Sing we now with tuneful art :
Meetly in alternate chorus
   Bearing our responsive part.

Thus we praise with veneration
   All the armies of the sky ;
Chiefly him, the warrior Primate
   Of celestial chivalry :
Michael, who in princely virtue
   Cast Abaddon from on high.

By whose watchful care, repelling,
   King of Everlasting grace !
Every ghostly adversary,
   All things evil, all things base ;
Grant us of Thine only goodness
   In Thy Paradise a place.

Laud and honour to the Father,
   Laud and honour to the Son,
Laud and honour to the Spirit,
   Ever Three and ever One :
Consubstantial, Co-eternal,
   While unending ages run. Amen.

℣. He maketh His Angels spirits.

℟. And His Ministers a flaming fire.

Antiphon to Magnificat.

At that time shall Michael stand up : the Great Prince, that standeth for the children of thy people.

The Collect.

O EVERLASTING God, Who hast ordained and constituted the services of Angels and men in a wonderful order ; Mercifully grant that, as Thy Holy Angels alway do Thee service in Heaven, so by Thy appointment they may succour and defend us on earth ; through Jesus Christ our Lord. Amen.

AT LAUDS.

℣. The smoke of the incense, which came with the prayers of the saints.

℟. Ascended up before God, out of the Angel's hand.

℣. O God, make speed, &c.

Antiphons. (1.) To Thee all Angels cry aloud : the heavens and all the Powers therein.

Psalms of Sundays and Holy-Days.

(2.) I am Raphael : one of the seven holy Angels which present the prayers of the Saints.

(3.) And I saw the Seven Angels which stood before God : and to them were given seven trumpets.

(4.) O ye Angels of the Lord, bless ye the Lord : praise Him and magnify Him for ever.

(5.) With Angels and Archangels, and with all the company of Heaven : we laud and magnify Thy glorious Name.

The Chapter, Rev. xii. 7.

There was war in Heaven : Michael and his Angels fought against the Dragon, and the Dragon fought and his angels ; and prevailed not, neither was their place found any more in Heaven.

℟. Thanks be to God.

Hymn. Christe sanctorum decus Angelorum.

Christ, of the Holy Angels Light and Gladness,
Maker and Saviour of the human race,
O may we reach the world unknown to sadness,
   And see Thy Face.

Angel of peace, may Michael to our dwelling
Down from high heaven in mighty calmness come,
Breathing all peace, and hideous war dispelling
   To hell's dark gloom.

Angel of might, may Gabriel swift descending
Far from our gates our ancient foe repel,
And, as of old o'er Zacharias bending,
    In temples dwell.

Angel of health, may Raphael lighten o'er us,
To every sick bed speed his healing flight,
In deeds of doubt direct the way before us,
    Guide us aright.

Mary, the harbinger of peace supernal,
Mother of God, with all the Angel train,
All Saints be with us, till the bliss Eternal
    In Christ we gain.

Be this by Thy thrice Holy Godhead granted,
Father, and Son, and Spirit ever blest;
Whose glory by the Angel Host is chanted,
    By all confessed. Amen.

℣. Praise Him, all ye Angels of His.

℟. Praise Him, all His Host.

Antiphon to Benedictus.

Take heed that ye despise not one of these little ones; for I say unto you, That in heaven their Angels do always behold the Face of My Father Which is in Heaven.

Collect as at the First Vespers.

AT PRIME.

Antiphon (1.) To Thee all Angels cry aloud: the Heavens and all the Powers therein.

AT TERCE.

Antiphon (2.) I am Raphael: one of the seven holy Angels which present the prayers of the Saints.

The Chapter, Rev. xii. 7.

There was war in Heaven: Michael and his Angels fought against the Dragon, and the Dragon fought and his angels; and prevailed not, neither was their place found any more in Heaven.

℟. He shall give His Angels charge over thee; to keep thee in all thy ways. ℣. They shall bear thee in their hands. ℟. To keep thee in all thy ways. ℣. Glory be to the Father, and to the Son: and to the Holy Ghost. ℟. He shall give His Angels charge over thee; to keep thee in all thy ways.

℣. Thou shalt go upon the lion and adder.

℟. The young lion and the Dragon shalt thou tread under thy feet.

Collect as at the First Vespers.

AT SEXT.

Antiphon (3.) And I saw the Seven Angels which stood before God: and to them were given seven trumpets.

The Chapter, Dan. vii. 9, 10.

I beheld till the thrones were cast down, and the Ancient of days did sit, Whose garment was white as snow, and the hair of His Head like the pure wool: His throne was like the fiery flame, and His wheels as burning fire. A fiery stream issued and came forth from before Him: thousand thousands ministered unto Him, and ten thousand times ten thousand stood before Him: the Judgment was set, and the books were opened.

℟. Thou shalt go upon the lion and adder; the young lion and the Dragon shalt thou tread under thy feet. ℣. Resist the Devil, and he will flee from you. ℟. And the Dragon shalt thou tread under thy feet. ℣. Glory be to the Father, and to the Son : and to the Holy Ghost. ℟. Thou shalt go upon the lion and adder; the young lion and the Dragon shalt thou tread under thy feet.

℣. The smoke of the incense, which came with the prayers of the saints.

℟. Ascended up before God out of the Angel's hand.

AT NONE.

Antiphon (5.) With Angels and Archangels, and all the company of heaven : we laud and magnify Thy glorious Name.

The Chapter, Rev. viii. 3.

There was given unto another Angel much incense, that he should offer it with the prayers of all Saints upon the golden Altar, which was before the Throne.

R. In the time of Harvest I will say to the Reapers, Gather ye together first the tares, and bind them in bundles to burn them. ℣. But gather the Wheat into My Barn. ℟. And bind the tares in bundles to burn them. ℣. Glory be to the Father, and to the Son : and to the Holy Ghost. ℟. In the time of Harvest I will say to the Reapers, Gather ye together first the tares, and bind them in bundles to burn them.

℣. The Harvest is the end of the world.

℟. The Reapers are the Angels.

Collect as at the First Vespers.

AT THE SECOND VESPERS.

The Antiphons of Lauds, with the Psalms of Sunday. Everything else as in the First Vespers, except the

Antiphon to Magnificat.

I am Gabriel, that stand in the presence of God; and am sent to speak unto thee, and to show thee these glad tidings.

SEPTEMBER XXX.
Memorial of ST. JEROME.

AT LAUDS.

Antiphon. Well done, thou good and faithful servant ; thou hast been faithful over a few things, I will make thee ruler over many things ; enter thou into the Joy of thy Lord.

℣. The Righteous shall grow as a lily.

℟. He shall flourish for ever before the Lord.

The Collect.

O GOD, Who madest the blessed Jerome a doctor and teacher of Thy Church ; Grant us to follow the Holy Doctrines that he taught, through Jesus Christ our Lord, Who liveth and reigneth with Thee and the Holy Ghost, ever One God, world without end. *Amen.*

AT VESPERS.

Antiphon. God hath set some in the Church, first Apostles, secondarily Prophets, thirdly Teachers.

℣. The Lord loved him, and beautified him with comely ornaments.

℟. He clothed him with a robe of glory.

Collect as at Lauds.

OCTOBER I.

Memorial of REMIGIUS, Bp.

AT LAUDS.

Antiphon. Well done, thou good and faithful servant; thou hast been faithful over a few things, I will make thee ruler over many things; enter thou into the Joy of thy Lord.

℣. The Righteous shall grow as a lily.

℞. He shall flourish for ever before the Lord.

The Collect.

GRANT, we beseech Thee, O Blessed Lord, that we who commemorate Thy holy Confessor and Bishop Remigius, may increase in faith and love towards Thee, the great Shepherd and Bishop of our souls, Who livest and reignest with the Father and the Holy Ghost, ever One God, world without end. *Amen.*

AT VESPERS.

Antiphon. A Bishop must be blameless, as the steward of God.

℣. The Lord loved him, and beautified him with comely ornaments.

℞. He clothed him with a robe of glory.

Collect as at Lauds.

OCTOBER VI.

Memorial of FAITH, V. & M.

AT LAUDS.

Antiphon. When the Bridegroom came, they that were ready went in with Him to the marriage.

℣. The Virgins that be her fellows.

℞. Shall bear her company.

The Collect.

GRANT, O Almighty God, that we who commemorate the martyrdom of Thy blessed Virgin Faith, may profit by her example, through our Lord Jesus Christ, Who liveth and reigneth with Thee and the Holy Ghost, ever One God, world without end. *Amen.*

AT VESPERS.

Antiphon. The kingdom of heaven is like unto a net, that was cast into the sea, and gathered of every kind; which, when it was full, they drew to shore, and sat down, and gathered the good into vessels, but cast the bad away.

℣. Full of grace are thy lips.

℞. Because God hath blessed thee for ever.

Collect as at Lauds.

OCTOBER IX.

Memorial of ST. DENYS, the Areopagite.

AT LAUDS.

Antiphon. Theirs is the Kingdom of Heaven who have despised the life of this world to gain a reward in the kingdom, and have washed their robes in the Blood of the Lamb.

℣. O God, wonderful art Thou in Thy Saints.

℞. And glorious in Thy Majesty.

The Collect.

ALMIGHTY and Everlasting God, grant unto us so to commemorate Thy holy Martyr Denys, that we may have our share in the Communion of Saints; through Jesus Christ our Lord, Who liveth and reigneth with Thee and the Holy Ghost, ever One God, world without end. *Amen.*

AT VESPERS.

Antiphon. The souls of the Saints who followed the Footsteps of Christ rejoice in Heaven, and forasmuch as for love of Him they shed their blood, they shall reign with Him for ever.

℣. Be glad, O ye Righteous, and rejoice in the Lord.

℟. And be joyful, all ye that are true of heart.

Collect as at Lauds.

OCTOBER XIII.

Memorial of THE TRANSLATION OF KING EDWARD THE CONFESSOR.

AT LAUDS.

Antiphon. Well done, thou good and faithful servant; thou hast been faithful over a few things, I will make thee ruler over many things; enter thou into the Joy of thy Lord.

℣. The Righteous shall grow as a lily.

℟. He shall flourish for ever before the Lord.

The Collect.

O GOD, Who hast vouchsafed unto the blessed King Edward Thy Confessor a crown of heavenly glory; Grant that we who commemorate him on earth may hereafter reign with him in Heaven; through Jesus Christ our Lord, Who liveth and reigneth with Thee and the Holy Ghost, ever One God, world without end. *Amen.*

AT VESPERS.

Antiphon. I will liken him unto a wise man which built his house upon a rock.

℣. The Lord loved him, and beautified him with comely ornaments.

℟. He clothed him with a robe of glory.

Collect as at Lauds.

OCTOBER XVII.

Memorial of ETHELDREDA, Virgin.

AT LAUDS.

Antiphon. The Bridegroom came, and they that were ready went in with Him to the Marriage.

℣. The Virgins that be her fellows.

℟. Shall bear her company.

The Collect.

O LORD Jesu Christ, the Bridegroom against Whose coming chaste Virgins do watch and trim their lamps; Grant that we who commemorate Thy holy Virgin Etheldreda may have our share in the Communion of Saints, Who livest and reignest with the Father and the Holy Ghost, ever One God, world without end. *Amen.*

AT VESPERS.

Antiphon. The kingdom of heaven is like unto a net, that was cast into the sea, and gathered of every kind; which, when it was full, they drew to shore, and sat down, and gathered the good into vessels, but cast the bad away.

℣. Full of grace are thy lips.

℟. Because God hath blessed thee for ever.

Collect as at Lauds.

OCTOBER XVIII.

St. Luke, Evangelist. Holy-Day.

AT THE FIRST VESPERS.

Everything as on St. Matthew's Day, p. 275, except

The Collect.

ALMIGHTY God, Who calledst Luke the Physician, whose praise is in the Gospel, to be an Evangelist, and Physician of the soul; May it please Thee, that, by the wholesome medicines of the doctrine delivered by him, all the diseases of our souls may be healed; through the Merits of Thy Son Jesus Christ our Lord. Amen.

OCTOBER XXV.

Memorial of CRISPIN, *Martyr.*

AT LAUDS.

Antiphon. Theirs is the Kingdom of Heaven who have despised the life of this world to gain a reward in the kingdom, and have washed their robes in the Blood of the Lamb.

℣. O God, wonderful art Thou in Thy Saints.

℟. And glorious in Thy Majesty.

The Collect.

ALMIGHTY and Everlasting God, grant unto us so to commemorate Thy holy Martyr Crispin, that we may have our share in the Communion of Saints; through Jesus Christ our Lord, Who liveth and reigneth with Thee and the Holy Ghost, ever One God, world without end. Amen.

AT VESPERS.

Antiphon. The souls of the Saints who followed the Footsteps of Christ rejoice in Heaven, and forasmuch as for love of Him they shed their blood, they shall reign with Him for ever.

℣. Be glad, O ye Righteous, and rejoice in the Lord.

℟. And be joyful, all ye that are true of heart.

Collect as at Lauds.

OCTOBER XXVIII.

SS. Simon and Jude, Apostles and Martyrs. Holy-Day.

Everything as in the Common of Apostles, p. 235, except this Chapter, which shall be said at both Vespers, at Lauds, and at Terce.

The Chapter, Rom. viii. 28.

We know that all things work together for good to them that love God, to them that are the called according to His purpose.

The Collect.

O ALMIGHTY God, Who hast built Thy Church upon the foundation of the Apostles and Prophets, Jesus Christ Himself being the head Corner-Stone; Grant us so to be joined together in unity of spirit by their doctrine, that we may be made an Holy Temple acceptable unto Thee; through Jesus Christ our Lord. Amen.

O praise the Name of the Lord.

2 Blessed be the Name of the Lord : from this time forth for evermore.

3 The Lord's Name is praised : from the rising up of the sun unto the going down of the same.

4 The Lord is high above all heathen : and His glory above the heavens.

5 Who is like unto the Lord our God, that hath His dwelling so high : and yet humbleth Himself to behold the things that are in heaven and earth ?

6 He taketh up the simple out of the dust : and lifteth the poor out of the mire ;

7 That He may set him with the princes : even with the princes of His people.

8 He maketh the barren woman to keep house : and to be a joyful mother of children.

Glory be to the Father, &c.

NOVEMBER I.

All Saints' Day. Holy-Day.

AT THE FIRST VESPERS.

Antiphons. (1.) The Souls of the Righteous are in the Hand of God : and there shall no torment touch them.

Laudate pueri. Ps. cxiii.

1 Praise the Lord, ye servants :

(2.) O how glorious is the kingdom where All the Saints rejoice with Christ : they are arrayed in white robes, and follow the Lamb whithersoever He goeth.

Laudate Dominum. Ps. cxvii.

1 O praise the Lord, all ye heathen : praise Him, all ye nations.

2 For His merciful kindness is ever more and more towards us : and the truth of the Lord endureth for ever. Praise the Lord.

Glory be to the Father, &c.

(3.) The Righteous shall shine, and run to and fro like sparks among the stubble : they shall judge the nations, and have dominion over the people.

Lauda anima mea. Ps. cxlvi.

1 Praise the Lord, O my soul : while I live will I praise the Lord : yea, as long as I have any being, I will sing praises unto my God.

2 O put not your trust in princes, nor in any child of man : for there is no help in them.

3 For when the breath of man goeth forth he shall turn again to his earth : and then all his thoughts perish.

4 Blessed is he that hath the God of Jacob for his help : and whose hope is in the Lord his God ;

5 Who made heaven and earth, the sea, and all that therein is : Who keepeth His promise for ever ;

6 Who helpeth them to right that suffer wrong : Who feedeth the hungry.

7 The Lord looseth men out of prison : the Lord giveth sight to the blind.

8 The Lord helpeth them that are fallen : the Lord careth for the righteous.

9 The Lord careth for the strangers ; He defendeth the fatherless and widow : as for the way of the ungodly, He turneth it upside down.

10 The Lord thy God, O Sion, shall be King for evermore : and throughout all generations.

Glory be to the Father, &c.

(4.) At the commandment of the Holy One they will stand in their order : and never faint in their watches.

Laudate Dominum. Ps. cxlvii.

1 O praise the Lord, for it is a good thing to sing praises unto our God : yea, a joyful and pleasant thing it is to be thankful.

2 The Lord doth build up Jerusalem : and gather together the outcasts of Israel.

3 He healeth those that are broken in heart : and giveth medicine to heal their sickness.

4 He telleth the number of the stars : and calleth them all by their names.

5 Great is our Lord, and great is His power : yea, and His wisdom is infinite.

6 The Lord setteth up the meek : and bringeth the ungodly down to the ground.

7 O sing unto the Lord with thanksgiving : sing praises upon the harp unto our God ;

8 Who covereth the heaven with clouds, and prepareth rain for the earth : and maketh the grass to grow upon the mountains, and herb for the use of men ;

9 Who giveth fodder unto the cattle : and feedeth the young ravens that call upon Him.

10 He hath no pleasure in the strength of an horse : neither delighteth He in any man's legs.

11 But the Lord's delight is in them that fear Him : and put their trust in His mercy.

Glory be to the Father, &c.

(5.) Blessed are they that dwell in Thy House : they will be alway praising Thee.

Lauda Hierusalem. Ps. cxlvii. 12.

12 Praise the Lord, O Jerusalem : praise thy God, O Sion.

13 For He hath made fast the bars of thy gates : and hath blessed thy children within thee.

14 He maketh peace in thy borders : and filleth thee with the flour of wheat.

15 He sendeth forth His commandment upon earth : and His word runneth very swiftly.

16 He giveth snow like wool : and scattereth the hoar-frost like ashes.

17 He casteth forth His ice like morsels : who is able to abide His frost?

18 He sendeth out His Word, and melteth them : He bloweth with His wind, and the waters flow.

19 He showeth His Word unto Jacob : His statutes and ordinances unto Israel.

20 He hath not dealt so with any nation : neither have the heathen knowledge of His laws.

The Chapter, Rev. vii. 2, 3.

And I saw another Angel ascending from the east, having the seal of the living God: and he cried with a loud voice to the four Angels, to whom it was given to hurt the earth, and the sea, saying, Hurt not the earth, neither the sea, nor the trees, till we have sealed the Servants of our God in their foreheads.

R. Praise our God, all ye His Servants, and ye that fear Him, both small and great. V. For the Lord God Omnipotent reigneth. R. Praise Him, both small and great. V. Glory be to the Father, and to the Son : and to the Holy Ghost. R. Praise our God, all ye His Servants, and ye that fear Him, both small and great.

Hymn. Si quis valet numerare.

If there be that skills to reckon
  All the numbers of the Blest,
He, perchance, can weigh the gladness
  Of the everlasting rest
Which, their earthly warfare finished,
  They through suffering have possessed.

Through the vale of lamentation
  Happily and safely past,
Now the years of their affliction
  In their memory they recast,
And the end of all perfection
  They can contemplate at last.

While their cruel Tempter duly
  Suffers torments evermore :
To the Saviour that redeemed them
  Those redeemed ones praises pour ;
And the Monarch that rewards them
  Those rewarded saints adore.

In a glass, through types and riddles,
  Dwelling here, we see alone ;
Then serenely, purely, clearly,
  We shall know as we are known ;
Fixing our enlightened vision
  On the glory of the Throne.

There the Trinity of Persons
  Unbeclouded shall we see ;
There the Unity of Essence
  Shall revealed in glory be ;
While we hail the Threefold Godhead
  And the simple Unity.

Wherefore, man, take heart and courage,
  Whatsoe'er thy present pain ;
Such untold reward through suffering
  Thou hereafter mayst attain ;
And for ever in His glory
  With the Light of Light to reign.

Laud and honour to the Father ;
  Laud and honour to the Son ;

Laud and honour to the Spirit;
 Ever Three and ever One;
Consubstantial, Co-eternal,
 While unending ages run.

℣. Be glad, O ye Righteous, and rejoice in the Lord.

℟. Be thankful, all ye that are true of heart.

Antiphon to Magnificat.

Lo, a Lamb stood on the Mount Sion, and with Him an hundred and forty and four thousand having His Father's Name on their foreheads.

The Collect.

O ALMIGHTY God, Who hast knit together Thine elect in one Communion and fellowship, in the mystical Body of Thy Son Christ our Lord; Grant us grace so to follow Thy blessed Saints in all virtuous and godly living, that we may come to those unspeakable Joys, which Thou hast prepared for them that unfeignedly love Thee; through Jesus Christ our Lord. *Amen.*

AT LAUDS.

℣. The Righteous live for evermore.

℟. Their reward also is with the Lord.

℣. O God, make speed, &c.

Antiphons. (1.) I beheld, and lo, a great Multitude: which no man could number, of all nations, and kindreds, and people, and tongues, stood before the Throne.

Psalms of Sundays and Holy-Days.

(2.) And all the Angels stood round about the Throne: and about the elders, and the four beasts, and fell before the Throne on their faces, and worshipped.

(3.) Thou hast Redeemed us to God by Thy Blood: out of every kindred, and tongue, and people, and nation.

(4.) O ye Angels of the Lord, bless ye the Lord: praise Him and magnify Him for ever.

(5.) All His Saints shall praise Him: even the Children of Israel, even the People that serveth Him. Such honour have All His Saints.

The Chapter, Rev. vii. 2, 3.

And I saw another Angel ascending from the east, having the seal of the living God: and he cried with a loud voice to the four Angels, to whom it was given to hurt the earth, and the sea, saying, Hurt not the earth, neither the sea, nor the trees, till we have sealed the Servants of our God in their foreheads.

℟. Thanks be to God.

Hymn. Harum laudum præconia.

The praises that the Blessed know
The Church shall imitate below,
Whene'er she greets, in yearly strain,
The birthdays of her Saints again.

Now, all their battles past and gone,
The Crown of Glory is set on;
For Chastity, as lily white,
For Martyrdom, as ruby bright.

This cannot human fancy know,
Nor tongue of Men nor Angels show,
Till endless life the victory brings
That gives for earthly, heavenly things.

One day of those most glorious rays
Is better than ten thousand days;
Refulgent with celestial light,
And with God's fullest knowledge bright.

That we the Saints' blest lives may reach,
That we their blessed faith may teach,
May join above, and love below,
The Spirit of All Grace bestow! Amen.

℣. The Righteous shall receive a glorious Kingdom.

℞. And a beautiful crown from the Lord's Hand.

Antiphon to Benedictus.

The glorious company of the Apostles; the goodly Fellowship of the Prophets; the noble Army of Martyrs; the Holy Church throughout all the world doth acknowledge Thee, O Holy, Blessed, and Glorious Trinity.

Collect as at the First Vespers.

AT PRIME.

Antiphon (1.) I beheld, and lo, a great Multitude: which no man could number, of all nations, and kindreds, and people, and tongues, stood before the Throne.

AT TERCE.

Antiphon (2.) And all the Angels stood round about the Throne: and about the elders, and the four beasts, and fell down before the Throne on their faces, and worshipped.

The Chapter, Rev. vii. 2, 3.

And I saw another Angel ascending from the east, having the seal of the living God: and he cried with a loud voice to the four Angels, to whom it was given to hurt the earth and the sea, saying, Hurt not the earth, neither the sea, nor the trees, till we have sealed the Servants of our God in their foreheads.

R. Be glad, O ye Righteous, and rejoice in the Lord. ℣. And be joyful, all ye that are true of heart. ℞. And rejoice in the Lord. ℣. Glory be to the Father, and to the Son: and to the Holy Ghost. ℞. Be glad, O ye Righteous, and rejoice in the Lord.

℣. Let the Righteous be glad, and rejoice before God.

℞. Let them also be merry and joyful.

Collect as at the First Vespers.

AT SEXT.

Antiphon (3.) Thou hast Redeemed us to God, by Thy Blood: out of every kindred, and tongue, and people, and nation.

The Chapter, Rev. vii. 4.

I heard the number of them which were Sealed; and there were Sealed an hundred and forty and four thousand, of all the tribes of the children of Israel.

R. Let the Righteous be glad and rejoice before God. ℣. Let them also be merry and joyful. ℞. And rejoice before God. ℣. Glory be to the Father, and to the Son: and to the Holy Ghost. ℞. Let the Righteous be glad and rejoice before God.

℣. The Souls of the Righteous are in the Hands of God.

℞. And there shall no torment touch them.

Collect as at the First Vespers.

AT NONE.

Antiphon (5.) All His Saints shall praise Him: even the Children of Israel, even the People that serveth Him. Such honour have All His Saints.

The Chapter, Rev. vii. 9, 10.

I beheld, and lo, a great Multitude, which no man could number, of all nations, and kindreds, and people, and tongues, stood before the Throne, and before the Lamb, clothed with white robes, and palms in their hands; and cried with a loud voice, saying, Salvation to our God Which sitteth upon the throne, and unto the Lamb.

R. The Souls of the Righteous are in the Hands of God. ℣. And there shall no torment touch them. ℟. In the Hands of God. ℣. Glory be to the Father, and to the Son : and to the Holy Ghost. ℟. The Souls of the Righteous are in the Hands of God.

℣. The Righteous Lord loveth Righteousness.

℟. His Countenance will behold the thing that is just.

Collect as at the First Vespers.

AT THE SECOND VESPERS.

The Antiphons of Lauds, with these five Psalms.

Confitebor Tibi. Ps. cxi.

1 I will give thanks unto the Lord with my whole heart : secretly among the faithful, and in the congregation.

2 The works of the Lord are great : sought out of all them that have pleasure therein.

3 His work is worthy to be praised, and had in honour : and His Righteousness endureth for ever.

4 The Merciful and Gracious Lord hath so done His marvellous works : that they ought to be had in remembrance.

5 He hath given Meat unto them that fear Him : He shall ever be mindful of His covenant.

6 He hath showed His people the power of His works : that He may give them the heritage of the heathen.

7 The works of His Hands are verity and judgment : all His commandments are true.

8 They stand fast for ever and ever : and are done in truth and equity.

9 He sent Redemption unto His people : He hath commanded His covenant for ever; Holy and Reverend is His Name.

10 The fear of the Lord is the beginning of wisdom : a good understanding have all they that do thereafter; the praise of it endureth for ever.

Glory be to the Father, &c.

Credidi. Ps. cxvi. 10.

10 I believed, and therefore will I speak ; but I was sore troubled : I said in my haste, All men are liars.

11 What reward shall I give unto the Lord : for all the benefits that He hath done unto me?

12 I will receive the Cup of Salvation : and call upon the Name of the Lord.

13 I will pay my vows now in the presence of all His people : right dear in the sight of the Lord is the death of His saints.

14 Behold, O Lord, how that I am Thy servant : I am Thy servant, and the son of Thine handmaid ; Thou hast broken my bonds in sunder.

15 I will offer to Thee the Sacrifice of Thanksgiving : and will call upon the Name of the Lord.

16 I will pay my vows unto the Lord, in the sight of all His people : in the courts of the Lord's house, even in the midst of thee, O Jerusalem. Praise the Lord.

Glory be to the Father, &c.

In convertendo. Ps. cxxvi.

1 When the Lord turned again the captivity of Sion : then were we like unto them that dream.
2 Then was our mouth filled with laughter : and our tongue with joy.
3 Then said they among the heathen : The Lord hath done Great Things for them.
4 Yea, the Lord hath done Great Things for us already : whereof we rejoice.
5 Turn our captivity, O Lord : as the rivers in the south.
6 They that sow in tears : shall reap in joy.
7 He that now goeth on his way weeping, and beareth forth good seed : shall doubtless come again with Joy, and bring his Sheaves with him.

Glory be to the Father, &c.

Eripe me, Domine. Ps. cxl.

1 Deliver me, O Lord, from the evil man : and preserve me from the wicked man.
2 Who imagine mischief in their hearts : and stir up strife all the day long.
3 They have sharpened their tongues like a serpent : adder's poison is under their lips.
4 Keep me, O Lord, from the hands of the ungodly : preserve me from the wicked men, who are purposed to overthrow my goings.
5 The proud have laid a snare for me, and spread a net abroad with cords : yea, and set traps in my way.
6 I said unto the Lord, Thou art my God : hear the voice of my prayers, O Lord.
7 O Lord God, Thou strength of my health : Thou hast covered my head in the day of battle.

8 Let not the ungodly have his desire, O Lord : let not his mischievous imagination prosper, lest they be too proud.
9 Let the mischief of their own lips fall upon the head of them : that compass me about.
10 Let hot burning coals fall upon them : let them be cast into the fire, and into the pit, that they never rise up again.
11 A man full of words shall not prosper upon the earth : evil shall hunt the wicked person to overthrow him.
12 Sure I am that the Lord will avenge the poor : and maintain the cause of the helpless.
13 The righteous also shall give thanks unto Thy Name : and the just shall continue in Thy sight.

Glory be to the Father, &c.

Lauda Hierusalem. Ps. cxlvii. 12.

12 Praise the Lord, O Jerusalem : praise thy God, O Sion.
13 For He hath made fast the bars of thy gates : and hath blessed thy children within thee.
14 He maketh peace in thy borders : and filleth thee with the flour of wheat.
15 He sendeth forth His commandment upon earth : and His Word runneth very swiftly.
16 He giveth snow like wool : and scattereth the hoar-frost like ashes.
17 He casteth forth His ice like morsels : who is able to abide His frost?
18 He sendeth out His Word, and melteth them : He bloweth with His wind, and the waters flow.
19 He showeth His Word unto Jacob : His statutes and ordinances unto Israel.

20 He hath not dealt so with any nation: neither have the heathen knowledge of His laws.

Glory be to the Father, &c.

The Chapter, ℟., *Hymn*, Si quis valet numerare, ℣. *and* ℟., *as at the First Vespers, p.* 285.

Antiphon to Magnificat.

God shall wipe away all tears from their eyes; and there shall be no more death, neither sorrow, nor crying, neither shall there be any more pain; for the former things are passed away.

Collect as at the First Vespers.

NOVEMBER VI.
Memorial of LEONARD, Conf.

AT LAUDS.

Antiphon. O ye holy and humble men of heart, bless ye the Lord; praise Him and magnify Him for ever.

℣. The Righteous shall grow as a lily.

℟. He shall flourish for ever before the Lord.

The Collect.

ALMIGHTY, Everlasting God, Who on this day didst deliver the blessed Leonard from the burden of the flesh; Hereafter grant unto us, Thy unworthy servants, to have our share in the company of the Blessed; through Jesus Christ our Lord, Who liveth and reigneth with Thee and the Holy Ghost, ever One God, world without end. *Amen.*

AT VESPERS.

Antiphon. Whosoever will confess Me before men, him will I confess also before My Father.

℣. The Lord loved him and beautified him with comely ornaments.

℟. He clothed him with a robe of glory.

Collect as at Lauds.

NOVEMBER XI.
Memorial of MARTIN, Bp.

AT LAUDS.

Antiphon. Well done, thou good and faithful servant; thou hast been faithful over a few things, I will make thee ruler over many things; enter thou into the Joy of thy Lord.

℣. The Righteous shall grow as a lily.

℟. He shall flourish for ever before the Lord.

The Collect.

GRANT, we beseech Thee, O Blessed Lord, that we who commemorate Thy holy Confessor and Bishop Martin, may increase in faith and love towards Thee, the great Shepherd and Bishop of our souls, Who livest and reignest with the Father and the Holy Ghost, ever One God, world without end. *Amen.*

AT VESPERS.

Antiphon. A Bishop must be blameless, as the steward of God.

℣. The Lord loved him, and beautified him with comely ornaments.

℟. He clothed him with a robe of glory.

Collect as at Lauds.

NOVEMBER XIII.
Memorial of BRITIUS, Bp.

AT LAUDS.

Antiphon. Well done, thou good

and faithful servant; thou hast been faithful over a few things, I will make thee ruler over many things; enter thou into the Joy of thy Lord.

℣. The Righteous shall grow as a lily.

℟. He shall flourish for ever before the Lord.

The Collect.

GRANT, we beseech Thee, O Blessed Lord, that we who commemorate Thy holy Confessor and Bishop Britius, may increase in faith and love towards Thee, the great Shepherd and Bishop of our souls, Who livest and reignest with the Father and the Holy Ghost, ever One God, world without end. Amen.

AT VESPERS.

Antiphon. A Bishop must be blameless, as the steward of God.

℣. The Lord loved him, and beautified him with comely ornaments.

℟. He clothed him with a robe of glory.

Collect as at Lauds.

NOVEMBER XV.

Memorial of MACHUTUS, Bp.

AT LAUDS.

Antiphon. Well done, thou good and faithful servant; thou hast been faithful over a few things, I will make thee ruler over many things; enter thou into the Joy of thy Lord.

℣. The Righteous shall grow as a lily.

℟. He shall flourish for ever before the Lord.

The Collect.

GRANT, we beseech Thee, O Blessed Lord, that we who commemorate Thy holy Confessor and Bishop Machutus, may increase in faith and love towards Thee, the great Shepherd and Bishop of our souls, Who livest and reignest with the Father and the Holy Ghost, ever One God, world without end. Amen.

AT VESPERS.

Antiphon. A Bishop must be blameless, as the steward of God.

℣. The Lord loved him, and beautified him with comely ornaments.

℟. He clothed him with a robe of glory.

Collect as at Lauds.

NOVEMBER XVII.

Memorial of HUGH, Bp.

AT LAUDS.

Antiphon. Well done, thou good and faithful servant: thou hast been faithful over a few things, I will make thee ruler over many things; enter thou into the Joy of thy Lord.

℣. The Righteous shall grow as a lily.

℟. He shall flourish for ever before the Lord.

The Collect.

O GOD, Who didst adorn Thy blessed Confessor and Bishop Hugh with excellent gifts; Grant unto us to follow his example in all Godly virtue; through Jesus Christ our Lord, Who liveth and reigneth with Thee and the Holy Ghost, ever One God, world without end. *Amen.*

AT VESPERS.

Antiphon. A Bishop must be blameless, as the steward of God.

℣. The Lord loved him, and beautified him with comely ornaments.

℞. He clothed him with a robe of glory.

Collect as at Lauds.

NOVEMBER XX.

Memorial of EDMUND, King & M.

AT LAUDS.

Antiphon. Theirs is the Kingdom of Heaven who have despised the life of this world to gain a reward in the kingdom, and have washed their robes in the Blood of the Lamb.

℣. O God, wonderful art Thou in Thy Saints.

℞. And glorious in Thy Majesty.

The Collect.

ALMIGHTY and Everlasting God, grant unto us so to commemorate Thy holy Martyr Edmund, that we may have our share in the Communion of Saints; through Jesus Christ our Lord, Who liveth and reigneth with Thee and the Holy Ghost, ever One God, world without end. *Amen.*

AT VESPERS.

Antiphon. The souls of the Saints who followed the Footsteps of Christ rejoice in Heaven, and forasmuch as for love of Him they shed their blood, they shall reign with Him for ever.

℣. Be glad, O ye Righteous, and rejoice in the Lord.

℞. And be joyful, all ye that are true of heart.

Collect as at Lauds.

NOVEMBER XXII.

Memorial of CECILIA, V. & M.

AT LAUDS.

Antiphon. When the Bridegroom came, they that were ready went in with Him to the marriage.

℣. The Virgins that be her fellows.

℞. Shall bear her company.

The Collect.

GRANT, O Almighty God, that we who commemorate the martyrdom of Thy blessed Virgin Cecilia, may profit by the example of her great faith; through our Lord Jesus Christ, Who liveth and reigneth with Thee and the Holy Ghost, ever One God, world without end. *Amen.*

AT VESPERS.

Antiphon. The kingdom of heaven is like unto a net, that was cast into the sea, and gathered of every kind; which, when it was full, they drew to shore, and sat down, and gathered the good into vessels, but cast the bad away.

℣. Full of grace are thy lips.

℞. Because God hath blessed thee for ever.

Collect as at Lauds.

NOVEMBER XXIII.

Memorial of CLEMENT, Bp.

AT LAUDS.

Antiphon. Theirs is the Kingdom of Heaven who have despised the life of this world to gain a reward in the kingdom, and have washed their robes in the Blood of the Lamb.

℣. O God, wonderful art Thou in Thy Saints.

℟. And glorious in Thy Majesty.

The Collect.

ALMIGHTY and Everlasting God, grant unto us so to commemorate Thy holy Martyr Clement, that we may have our share in the Communion of Saints; through Jesus Christ our Lord, Who liveth and reigneth with Thee and the Holy Ghost, ever One God, world without end. *Amen.*

AT VESPERS.

Antiphon. The souls of the Saints who followed the Footsteps of Christ rejoice in Heaven, and forasmuch as for love of Him they shed their blood, they shall reign with Him for ever.

℣. Be glad, O ye Righteous, and rejoice in the Lord.

℟. And be joyful, all ye that are true of heart.

Collect as at Lauds.

NOVEMBER XXV.
Memorial of CATHERINE, V. & M.

AT LAUDS.

Antiphon. When the Bridegroom came, they that were ready went in with Him to the marriage.

℣. The Virgins that be her fellows.

℟. Shall bear her company.

The Collect.

O EVERLASTING God, Who hast ordained and constituted the services of Angels and men in a wonderful order; Mercifully grant that as Thy Holy Angels alway do Thee service in heaven, so by Thy appointment they may succour and defend us on earth; through Jesus Christ our Lord. *Amen.*

AT VESPERS.

Antiphon. The kingdom of heaven is like unto a net, that was cast into the sea, and gathered of every kind; which, when it was full, they drew to shore, and sat down, and gathered the good into vessels, but cast the bad away.

℣. Full of grace are thy lips.

℟. Because God hath blessed thee for ever.

Collect as at Lauds.

APPENDIX TO THE SERVICE PROPER OF HOLY-DAYS.[1]

NOVEMBER XXVII.
Memorial of ODE, Virgin.

AT LAUDS.

Antiphon. When the Bridegroom came, they that were ready went in with Him to the marriage.

℣. The Virgins that be her fellows.

℟. Shall bear her company.

The Collect.

GRANT, O Almighty God, that we, who remember before Thee

---

[1] The Saints here commemorated are found in the Kalendar of the Scotch Prayer Book put forth by the late Patrick Torry, D.D., Bishop of St. Andrew's. In the Kalendar of this book they stand in Italics.

the triumph of Thy holy Virgin Ode, may gain grace by the example of her purity; through Jesus Christ our Lord, Who liveth and reigneth with Thee and the Holy Ghost, ever One God, world without end. *Amen.*

AT VESPERS.

Antiphon. They shall walk with Me in white, for they are worthy.

℣. Full of grace are thy lips.

℟. Because God hath blessed thee for ever.

Collect as at Lauds.

DECEMBER IV.

Memorial of DROSTANE, Abbot.

AT LAUDS.

Antiphon. Well done, thou good and faithful servant; thou hast been faithful over a few things, I will make thee ruler over many things; enter thou into the Joy of thy Lord.

℣. The Lord led His righteous servant through straight paths.

℟. And showed him the Kingdom of God.

The Collect.

O ALMIGHTY and Everlasting God, by Whose manifold gifts Thy servant Drostane was mercifully strengthened to extend and increase Thy kingdom; Give us grace to follow his example, and hereafter share his joys; through Jesus Christ our Lord, Who liveth and reigneth with Thee and the Holy Ghost, ever one God, world without end. *Amen.*

AT VESPERS.

Antiphon. Holy Drostane, setting at nought the earthly things of this world, sought for the Pearl of great price, and now hath joy for evermore.

℣. *and* ℟. *and Collect as at Lauds.*

JANUARY XI.

Memorial of DAVID, King.

AT LAUDS.

Antiphon. Theirs is the Kingdom of Heaven who have despised the life of this world to gain a reward in the kingdom, and have washed their robes in the Blood of the Lamb.

℣. O God, wonderful art Thou in Thy Saints.

℟. And glorious in Thy Majesty.

The Collect.

ALMIGHTY and Everlasting God, grant unto us so to commemorate Thy servant King David, that we may have our share in the Communion of Saints; through Jesus Christ our Lord, Who liveth and reigneth with Thee and the Holy Ghost, ever One God, world without end. *Amen.*

AT VESPERS.

Antiphon. They who follow the Footsteps of Christ rejoice in the Lord alway.

℣. Be glad, O ye Righteous, and rejoice in the Lord.

℟. And be joyful, all ye that are true of heart.

Collect as at Lauds.

JANUARY XVIII.
Memorial of MUNGO, Bp.

AT LAUDS.

Antiphon. Well done, thou good and faithful servant; thou hast been faithful over a few things, I will make thee ruler over many things; enter thou into the Joy of thy Lord.

℣. The Righteous shall grow as a lily.

℟. He shall flourish for ever before the Lord.

The Collect.

GRANT, we beseech Thee, O Blessed Lord, that we who commemorate Thy holy Confessor and Bishop Mungo, may increase in faith and love towards Thee, the great Shepherd and Bishop of our souls, Who livest and reignest with the Father and the Holy Ghost, ever One God, world without end. *Amen.*

AT VESPERS.

Antiphon. A Bishop must be blameless, as the steward of God.

℣. The Lord loved him, and beautified him with comely ornaments.

℟. He clothed him with a robe of glory.

Collect as at Lauds.

FEBRUARY XVIII.
Memorial of COLMAN, Bp. & Confessor.

AT LAUDS.

Antiphon. Well done, thou good and faithful servant; thou hast been faithful over a few things, I will make thee ruler over many things; enter thou into the Joy of thy Lord.

℣. The Righteous shall grow as a lily.

℟. He shall flourish for ever before the Lord.

The Collect.

GRANT, we beseech Thee, O Blessed Lord, that we who commemorate Thy holy Confessor and Bishop Colman, may increase in faith and love towards Thee, the great Shepherd and Bishop of our souls, Who livest and reignest with the Father and the Holy Ghost, ever One God, world without end. *Amen.*

AT VESPERS.

Antiphon. A Bishop must be blameless, as the steward of God.

℣. The Lord loved him, and beautified him with comely ornaments.

℟. He clothed him with a robe of glory.

Collect as at Lauds.

MARCH XI.
Memorial of CONSTANTINE, King.

AT LAUDS.

Antiphon. Theirs is the Kingdom of Heaven who have despised the life of this world to gain a reward in the kingdom, and have washed their robes in the Blood of the Lamb.

℣. O God, wonderful art Thou in Thy Saints.

℟. And glorious in Thy Majesty.

The Collect.

ALMIGHTY and Everlasting God, grant unto us so to commemorate Thy servant King Constantine, that we may have our share in the Communion of Saints; through Jesus Christ our Lord, Who liveth and reigneth with Thee and the Holy Ghost, ever One God, world without end. *Amen.*

AT VESPERS.

Antiphon. They who followed the Footsteps of Christ rejoice in the Lord alway.

℣. Be glad, O ye Righteous, and rejoice in the Lord.

℟. And be joyful, all ye that are true of heart.

Collect as at Lauds.

MARCH XVII.

Memorial of PATRICK, Bp. & Confessor.

AT LAUDS.

Antiphon. Thou, O Lord, art my glory and my joy; Thou hast exalted me to Thy Holy Hill and to Thy dwelling.

℣. I have found David My servant.

℟. With My holy oil have I anointed him.

The Collect.

O ALMIGHTY God, Who by the preaching of Thy blessed Confessor and Bishop, Saint Patrick, didst cause the light of Thy Gospel to shine amongst the heathen; Grant that we who set forth his memory may have our share with him in the Communion of Saints; through Jesus Christ our Lord, Who liveth and reigneth with Thee and the Holy Ghost, ever One God, world without end. *Amen.*

AT VESPERS.

Antiphon. A Bishop must be blameless, as the steward of God.

℣. The Lord loved him, and beautified him with comely ornaments.

℟. He clothed him with a robe of glory.

Collect as at Lauds.

MARCH XVIII.

Memorial of CYRIL, Bp.

AT LAUDS.

Antiphon. Well done, thou good and faithful servant; thou hast been faithful over a few things, I will make thee ruler over many things; enter thou into the Joy of thy Lord.

℣. The Righteous shall grow as a lily.

℟. He shall flourish for ever before the Lord.

The Collect.

GRANT, we beseech Thee, O Blessed Lord, that we who commemorate Thy holy Confessor and Bishop Cyril, may increase in faith and love towards Thee, the great Shepherd and Bishop of our souls, Who livest and reignest with the Father and the Holy Ghost, ever One God, world without end. *Amen.*

AT VESPERS.

Antiphon. A Bishop must be blameless, as the steward of God.

℣. The Lord loved him, and

beautified him with comely ornaments.

℟. He clothed him with a robe of glory.

Collect as at Lauds.

MARCH XX.

Memorial of CUTHBERT, Bp. & Confessor.

AT LAUDS.

Antiphon. Well done, thou good and faithful servant; thou hast been faithful over a few things, I will make thee ruler over many things; enter thou into the Joy of thy Lord.

℣. The Righteous shall grow as a lily.

℟. He shall flourish for ever before the Lord.

The Collect.

O GOD, Who hast wonderfully endowed Thy Saints with glory everlasting; Grant unto us, who on earth remember before Thee Thy holy Confessor and Bishop Cuthbert, that we may have our share in his heavenly joy hereafter; through Jesus Christ our Lord, Who liveth and reigneth with the Father and the Holy Ghost, ever One God, world without end. *Amen.*

AT VESPERS.

Antiphon. A Bishop must be blameless, as the steward of God.

℣. The Lord loved him, and beautified him with comely ornaments.

℟. He clothed him with a robe of glory.

Collect as at Lauds.

APRIL XX.

Memorial of SERF, Bp.

AT LAUDS.

Antiphon. Well done, thou good and faithful servant; thou hast been faithful over a few things, I will make thee ruler over many things; enter thou into the Joy of thy Lord.

℣. The Righteous shall grow as a lily.

℟. He shall flourish for ever before the Lord.

The Collect.

GRANT, we beseech Thee, O Blessed Lord, that we who commemorate Thy holy Confessor and Bishop Serf, may increase in faith and love towards Thee, the great Shepherd and Bishop of our souls, Who livest and reignest with the Father and the Holy Ghost, ever One God, world without end. *Amen.*

AT VESPERS.

Antiphon. A Bishop must be blameless, as the steward of God.

℣. The Lord loved him, and beautified him with comely ornaments.

℟. He clothed him with a robe of glory.

Collect as at Lauds.

JUNE IX.

Memorial of COLUMBA, Abbot.

AT LAUDS.

Antiphon. Well done, thou good and faithful servant; thou hast been faithful over a few things, I will make thee ruler over many things; enter thou into the Joy of thy Lord.

℣. The Righteous shall grow as a lily.

℟. He shall flourish for ever before the Lord.

The Collect.

O ALMIGHTY and Everlasting God, Who by the preaching of Columba, didst vouchsafe to manifest Thy love towards our nation; Mercifully grant that we who remember his virtue may hereafter share his glory; through Jesus Christ our Lord, Who liveth and reigneth, ever One God, world without end. *Amen.*

AT VESPERS.

Antiphon. Break forth into joy, sing together, ye waste places; for the Lord hath comforted His people, and redeemed them.

℣. The dry places shall be full of springs of water.

℟. And the wilderness shall blossom as a rose.

Collect as at Lauds.

JULY VI.

Memorial of PALLADIUS, Bp.

AT LAUDS.

Antiphon. Well done, thou good and faithful servant; thou hast been faithful over a few things, I will make thee ruler over many things; enter thou into the Joy of thy Lord.

℣. The Righteous shall grow as a lily.

℟. He shall flourish for ever before the Lord.

The Collect.

GRANT, we beseech Thee, O Blessed Lord, that we who commemorate Thy holy Confessor and Bishop Palladius, may increase in faith and love towards Thee, the great Shepherd and Bishop of our souls, Who livest and reignest with the Father and the Holy Ghost, ever One God, world without end. *Amen.*

AT VESPERS.

Antiphon. A Bishop must be blameless, as the steward of God.

℣. The Lord loved him, and beautified him with comely ornaments.

℟. He clothed him with a robe of glory.

Collect as at Lauds.

SEPTEMBER XVI.

Memorial of NINIAN, Bp.

AT LAUDS.

Antiphon. Well done, thou good and faithful servant; thou hast been faithful over a few things, I will make thee ruler over many things; enter thou into the Joy of thy Lord.

℣. The Righteous shall grow as a lily.

℟. He shall flourish for ever before the Lord.

The Collect.

GRANT, O Almighty God, that we who here commemorate Thy holy Confessor and Bishop Ninian, may have grace so to follow his example, that hereafter we may share his joys; through Jesus Christ our Lord, Who with Thee and the Holy Ghost, liveth and reigneth, ever One God, world without end. *Amen.*

AT VESPERS.

Antiphon. A Bishop must be blameless, as the steward of God.

℣. The Lord loved him, and beautified him with comely ornaments.

℟. He clothed him with a robe of glory.

Collect as at Lauds.

SEPTEMBER XXIII.

Memorial of ADAMNAN, Bp.

AT LAUDS.

Antiphon. Well done, thou good and faithful servant; thou hast been faithful over a few things, I will make thee ruler over many things; enter thou into the Joy of thy Lord.

℣. The Righteous shall grow as a lily.

℟. He shall flourish for ever before the Lord.

The Collect.

O ALMIGHTY and Everlasting God, Who by the preaching of Thy servant Adamnan didst vouchsafe to manifest Thy love towards our nation; Mercifully grant that we who remember his virtue may hereafter share his glory; through Jesus Christ our Lord, Who with Thee and the Holy Ghost liveth and reigneth, ever One God, world without end. *Amen.*

AT VESPERS.

Antiphon. Break forth into joy, sing together, ye waste places; for the Lord hath comforted His people, and redeemed them.

℣. The dry places shall be full of springs of water.

℟. And the wilderness shall blossom as a rose.

Collect as at Lauds.

NOVEMBER XVI.

Memorial of MARGARET, Queen.

AT LAUDS.

Antiphon. Kings' daughters were amongst thy honourable women.

℣. Kings shall be thy nursing fathers.

℟. And their queens thy nursing mothers.

The Collect.

O LORD Jesu Christ, King Eternal, grant that we may follow the example of Thy faithful servant Margaret, and be found fruitful in good works, Who livest and reignest with the Father and the Holy Ghost, ever One God, world without end. *Amen.*

AT VESPERS.

Antiphon. The daughters saw her and blessed her; yea the queens and the concubines, and they praised her. Her renown went forth among the heathen for her beauty; for it was perfect through My comeliness, which I had put upon her, saith the Lord God.

℣. The Lord is my refuge.

℟. And my God is the strength of my confidence.

Collect as at Lauds.

A TABLE OF PSALMS.

	PAGE		PAGE
Ad Dominum, cxx.	90	Dominus regnavit, xciii.	139
Ad Te, Domine, levavi, xxv.	172	Ecce nunc benedicite, cxxxiv.	216
Ad Te levavi oculos meos, cxxiii.	200	Ecce quam bonum, cxxxiii.	204
Beati immaculati, cxix.	168	Eripe me, Domine, cxl.	90
Beati omnes, cxxviii.	202	Exaltabo Te, Deus, cxlv.	212
Beati quorum, xxxii.	178	In convertendo, cxxvi.	200
Beatus vir, cxii.	25	In exitu Israel, cxiv.	191
Benedictus Dominus, cxliv.	211	In Te, Domine, speravi, xxxi.	215
Bonum est confiteri, xcii.	162	Jubilate Deo, c.	139
Cantate Domino, cxlix.	50	Judica me, Deus, xliii.	151
Confitebor Tibi, cxi.	25	Judica me, Domine, xxvi.	173
Confitebor Tibi quoniam, cxxxviii.	207	Lætatus sum, cxxii.	199
Confitemini Domino quoniam, cxviii.	47	Lauda anima mea, cxlvi.	20
Confitemini Domino quoniam, cxxxvi.	205	Lauda Hierusalem, cxlvii. (v. 12)	21
Credidi, cxvi. (v. 10)	89	Laudate Dominum de cœlis, cxlviii.	50
Cum invocarem, iv.	215	Laudate Dominum in sanctis, cl.	51
De profundis, cxxx.	26	Laudate Dominum omnes gentes, cxvii.	20
Deus, Deus meus, xxii.	173	Laudate Dominum quoniam, cxlvii.	20
Deus, Deus meus, lxiii.	48	Laudate Nomen Domini, cxxxv.	205
Deus, in nomine, liv.	166	Laudate, pueri, cxiii.	19
Deus misereatur, lxvii.	49	Levavi oculos, cxxi.	197
Dilexi quoniam, cxvi.	196	Memento, Domine, cxxxii.	26
Dixit Dominus, cx.	24	Miserere mei, Deus, li.	46
Domine, clamavi, cxli.	90	Nisi Dominus, cxxvii.	202
Domine, exaudi, cii.	188	Nisi quia Dominus, cxxiv.	200
Domine, exaudi, cxliii.	159	Non nobis, Domine, cxv.	192
Domine, ne in furore, vi.	150	Qui confidunt, cxxv.	200
Domine, ne in furore, xxxviii.	182	Qui habitat, xci.	215
Domine, non est, cxxxi.	203	Sæpe expugnaverunt, cxxix.	202
Domine, probasti, cxxxix.	208	Super flumina, cxxxvii.	206
Domine, Refugium, xc.	156	Te decet hymnus, lxv.	154
Domini est terra, xxiv.	171	Verba mea auribus, v.	148
Dominus regit me, xxiii.	173	Voce mea ad Dominum, cxlii.	91

A TABLE OF CANTICLES.

	PAGE		PAGE
Audite cœli (Song of Moses, Deut. xxxii.)	163	Ego dixi (Song of Hezekiah, Isa. xxxviii.)	152
Benedicite, omnia opera (Song of the Three Children)	49	Exultavit cor meum (Song of Hannah, 1 Sam. ii.)	155
Benedictus (Song of Zachariah, St. Luke i.)	143	Magnificat (Song of our Lady, St. Luke i.)	193
Cantemus Domino (Song of Moses, Exod. xv.)	157	Nunc dimittis (Song of Simeon, St. Luke ii.)	217
Confitebor Tibi (Song of Isaiah, Isa. xii.)	149	Quicunque vult (Creed of St. Athanasius)	169
Domine, audivi (Song of Habakkuk, Hab. iii.)	160		

A TABLE OF LATIN HYMNS.

	PAGE
Ad Cœnam Agni providi	102
Adesto Sancta Trinitas	126
Æterna Christi munera	236
Æterna cœli gloria	161
Æterne rerum Conditor	51
Æterne Rex Altissime	111
Ales diei nuntius	153
Annue Christe	235
A Patre Unigenitus	40
A solis ortus cardine	22
Audi, benigne Conditor	60
Aurora jam spargit polum	165
Ave colenda Trinitas	127
Beata nobis gaudia	121
Chorus novæ Hierusalem	99
Christe, qui Lux es et Dies	221
Christe sanctorum decus Angelorum	277
Claro Paschali gaudio	256
Cœli Deus sanctissime	203
Conditor alme siderum	2
Cultor Dei memento	222
Deus, Creator omnium	214
Ecce jam noctis	143
Ecce tempus idoneum	68
Ex more docti mystico	59
Harum laudum præconia	286
Hostis Herodes impie	39
Hymnum canamus gloriæ	112
Immense cœli Conditor	198
Jam Christus astra ascenderat	119
Jam lucis orto sidere	166
Jesu, nostra Redemptio	225
Jesu, quadragenariæ	69
Jesu, Salvator seculi	224
Lucis Creator optime	192
Lustra sex qui jam peregit	78
Lux ecce surgit aurea	158
Magnæ Deus potentiæ	207
Nox et tenebræ et nubila	155
Nunc Sancte nobis Spiritus	179
O Lux beata Trinitas	214
O nimis felix	264
Pange lingua gloriosi	77
Plasmator hominis Deus	210
Quem terra, pontus	231
Rector potens, verax Deus	183
Rerum Deus tenax vigor	186
Rex gloriose martyrum	33
Salvator mundi Domine	219
Sancte Dei pretiose	28
Sermone blando Angelus	100
Si quis valet numerare	285
Splendor Paternæ gloriæ	149
Telluris ingens Conditor	201
Te lucis ante terminum	216
Tibi Christe splendor Patris	277
Tristes erant Apostoli	255
Ut queant laxis resonare fibris	263
Veni Creator Spiritus	119
Veni Redemptor gentium	21
Veni Sancte Spiritus	225
Vexilla Regis prodeunt	76
Vox clara ecce intonat	3

A TABLE OF ENGLISH TRANSLATIONS OF LATIN HYMNS.

Hymn	PAGE
All-glorious King of Martyrs Thou	33
All hail! adorèd Trinity	127
Almighty God, Who from the flood	207
Before the ending of the day	216
Behold the golden dawn arise	158
Be present, Holy Trinity	126
Blest joys for mighty wonders wrought	121
Christ, of the holy Angels Light and gladness	277
Christ, Thou Who art the Light	221
Come, Holy Ghost, our souls inspire	119
Come, Holy Ghost, with God the Son	179
Come, Thou Holy Paraclete	225
Come, Thou Redeemer of the earth	21
Creator blest, Eternal King	51
Creator of the stars of night	2
Dawn sprinkles all the East with light	165
Earth's mighty Maker, Whose command	201
Eternal glory of the sky	161
Eternal Monarch, King most High	111
From God the Father, Virgin-born	40
From lands that see the sun arise	22
Greatest of Prophets	263
Hence, night and clouds that night-time brings	155
If there be that skills to reckon	285
In this our bright and Paschal day	256
Jesu, Redemption all divine	225
Jesu, the Law and Pattern whence	69
Jesu, Who brought'st Redemption nigh	224
Lo! now a thrilling voice sounds forth	3
Lo! now is our accepted day	68
Lo! now the melting shades of night are rending	143
Maker of all things, God most High	214
Maker of men, from Heaven	210
Now Christ, ascending whence He came	119
Now that the daylight fills the sky	166
O blessed Saint of high renown	264
O blest Creator of the Light	192
O Christ, Thou Lord of worlds	235
O God, Creation's secret Force	186
O God of Truth, O Lord of might	183
O God, Whose hand hath spread the sky	203
O Great Creator of the sky	198
O Maker of the world, give ear	60
O Saviour of the world forlorn	219
O Trinity of blessed light	214
Saint of God, elect and precious	28
Sing, my tongue, the glorious battle	77
Sing we triumphant hymns of praise	112
The Apostles' hearts are full of pain	255
Thee, O Christ, the Father's Splendour	277
The fast, as taught by holy lore	59
The God, Whom earth, and sea, and sky	231
The Lamb's high banquet we await	102
The Mother of our Glorious King	232
The praises that the Blessed know	286
The Royal Banners forward go	76
The Eternal gifts of Christ the King	236
The wingèd herald of the day	153
Thirty years among us dwelling	78
Thou Brightness of the Father's ray	149
Thou Child of Christ, remember	222
Virgin-born! we bow before Thee	232
Why, impious Herod, vainly fear	39
With gentle voice the Angel gave	100
Ye Choirs of New Jerusalem	99

FINIS.

March, 1891.

THEOLOGICAL AND DEVOTIONAL WORKS

PUBLISHED BY

J. MASTERS & Co., 78, NEW BOND ST.

BOOKS FOR THE USE OF THE CLERGY.

Now ready, Seventh Edition, much enlarged.

THE PRIEST'S PRAYER BOOK, with a brief Pontifical. Containing Private Prayers and Intercessions; Offices, Readings, Prayers, Litanies, and Hymns, for the Visitation of the Sick; Offices for Bible and Confirmation Classes, Cottage Lectures, &c.; Notes on Confession, Direction, Missions, and Retreats; Remedies for Sin; Anglican Orders; Bibliotheca Sacerdotalis, &c., &c.

 One Vol. cloth . . . 6s. 6d.   Two Vols. cloth . . . . 7s. 6d.
 One Vol. calf or morocco 10s. 6d.

 Reprinted from "The Priest's Prayer Book,"

RESPONSAL TO THE OFFICES OF THE SICK. For the Use of Attendants. Cloth, 1s.
PAROCHIAL OFFICES. 1d.   SCHOOL OFFICES. 1d.
OFFICE FOR A RURIDECANAL SYNOD OR CLERICAL MEETING. 1d.
ANGLICAN ORDERS. A Summary of Historical Evidence. 1d.
ITINERARY. Devotions for those who are about to journey. ½d., or 3s. 6d. per 100.

EMBER HOURS. By the Rev. W. E. HEYGATE, M.A., Rector of Brighstone, Isle of Wight. Third Edition Revised, with an Essay on RELIGION IN RELATION TO SCIENCE, by the Rev. T. S. ACKLAND, M.A., Vicar of Newton Wold, author of "Story of Creation," &c. Fcap. 8vo., cloth, 3s.

MEMORIALE VITÆ SACERDOTALIS; or, Solemn Warnings of the Great Shepherd, JESUS CHRIST, to the Clergy of His Holy Church. From the Latin of Arvisenet. Adapted to the Use of the Anglican Church by A. P. FORBES, D.C.L., Bishop of Brechin. Third edition, Fcap. 8vo., cloth, 3s. 6d.; calf, 8s.

THE CHURCHMAN'S DIARY: an Almanack and Directory for the Celebration of the Services of the Church. 4d.; cloth, 10d.; interleaved, 6d.; cloth interleaved, 1s.; roan tuck, 2s.

SERMONS REGISTER, for Ten Years, by which an account may be kept of Sermons, the number, subject, and when preached. Post 4to., 1s.

REGISTER OF SERMONS, PREACHERS, NUMBER OF COMMUNICANTS, AND AMOUNT OF OFFERTORY. Fcap. 4to., bound, 4s. 6d. (The Book of Strange Preachers as ordered by the 52nd Canon.)

REGISTER OF PERSONS CONFIRMED AND ADMITTED TO HOLY COMMUNION. For 500 names, 4s. 6d. For 1000 names, 7s. 6d. half-bound.

THE BOOK OF COMMON PRAYER OF 1662, according to the *Sealed Copy* in the Tower, and containing the Acts of Uniformity of 1st Elizabeth and 14th Charles II. Printed in red and black, fcap. 8vo., cloth, 2s. 6d., published at 12s. 6d.

 The above work, originally published in 1847, is an exact reprint, is very much reduced in price, and contains 600 pages.

ALTAR SERVICES, with Ornamental Initial Letters and Red Rubrics. Imp. 8vo. This fine Edition, printed at the Chiswick Press, is kept bound in morocco plain, 25s.; morocco antique, 30s.; also in various other bindings.

THE LITANY, TOGETHER WITH THE LATTER PART OF THE COMMINATION SERVICE NOTED. Edited by RICHARD REDHEAD. Handsomely printed in red and black. Demy 4to., wrapper, 7s. 6d.; plain morocco, 20s.; morocco panelled, &c., 30s.

THE LITTLE HOURS OF THE DAY, according to the Kalendar of the Church of England. Complete Edition, crown 8vo., cloth, 3s. 6d.; wrapper, 2s. 6d.

HORARIUM; seu Libellus Precationum, Latinè editus. 18mo., cl. 8d.

THE CLERGYMAN'S MANUAL OF PRIVATE PRAYERS. Collected and Compiled from Various Sources. A Companion Book to "The Priest's Prayer Book." Cloth, 1s.

THE PRIEST IN HIS INNER LIFE. By the late CANON LIDDON. Fcap. 8vo., cloth, 1s.

THE PARISH AND THE PRIEST. Colloquies on the Pastoral Care, and Parochial Institutions, of a Country Village. By the Rev. F. E. PAGET, Rector of Elford. Fcap. 8vo., 2s. 6d.
This work was originally published anonymously, but the author's name is now allowed to be added.

MEMORANDA PAROCHIALIA, or the Parish Priest's Pocket Book. By the Rev. F. E. PAGET, M.A., Rector of Elford. 3s. 6d., double size 5s.

FELIX DUPANLOUP, Bishop of Orleans. By the author of "Charles Lowder." Post 8vo., cloth, 1s. 6d.

THE BUILDERS OF THE CHURCH IN NORTHUMBRIA. Being a History of the Twelve Saints to whom the Stalls in Wakefield Cathedral are dedicated: S. Edwin, S. Paulinus, S. Oswald, S. Hilda, S. Chad, S. Cuthbert, S. Wilfrid, S. John of Beverley, S. Beda, S. Willibrord, S. Alcuin, S. Aelred. By M. H. HALL. Dedicated by permission to the Right Rev. the LORD BISHOP OF WAKEFIELD. Crown 8vo., 2s., cloth.

MOTHER'S EVENING TALKS. By FRANCES MACLEAN. Edited, with Preface, by the Ven. J. G. SCOTT, Archdeacon of Dublin. Royal 16mo., cloth, 1s. 6d.

MEMENTO. A Perpetual Calendar, or Hints to Awaken Memory. Suggested by A. L. J. G. 4to. Printed on handmade paper. Cloth, elegant, 4s. 6d.

HOLY WEEK AND EASTER. Daily Services—Mattins, Holy Communion, and Evensong—from Palm Sunday to Easter Tuesday inclusive. With TENEBRÆ (from the Rouen Use) for the three last days of Holy Week. The Psalms and Lessons in full, together with Hymns, Antiphons, and other Devotional matter. 18mo., about 250 pp., limp cloth, 2s.

HINTS ON CONFIRMATION TEACHING. In Question and Answer. With a Preface by the Rev. GEORGE BODY, M.A., Canon of Durham. Paper cover, 1s.; cloth, 1s. 6d.

LAY BAPTISM. An Inquiry into the Spiritual Value and Validity of that Ceremony. With an Appendix containing some Remarks upon a Charge lately delivered by the Lord Bishop of Edinburgh relating to Lay Baptism. By F. NUTCOMBE OXENHAM, M.A. Dedicated by permission to the Lord Bishop of Argyll and the Isles. Second edition, enlarged. Crown 8vo., cloth, 2s.

WHAT IS MODERN ROMANISM? By the Right Rev. the BISHOP OF SPRINGFIELD. Crown 8vo., cloth, 4s.

NOTES FOR MEDITATIONS ON THE COLLECTS FOR SUNDAYS AND HOLY DAYS. By the Rev. ARTHUR C. A. HALL, M.A. Part I. Advent to Trinity. 12mo., cloth, 3s. Part II. Trinity to Advent. 3s. 6d.

EPISODES IN CLERICAL AND PARISH LIFE, with other Sketches on Church Subjects contributory to Christian Unity. By WILLIAM STAUNTON, D.D. Imperial 16mo., cloth, price 4s. 6d.

THE DAY OFFICE OF THE CHURCH, according to the Kalendar of the Church of England; consisting of Lauds, Vespers, Prime, Terce, Sext, None, and Compline, throughout the Year. To which are added, the Order for the Administration of the Reserved Eucharist, Penance, and Unction; together with the Office of the Dead, Commendation of a Soul, divers Benedictions and Offices, and full Rubrical Directions. A complete Edition, especially for Sisterhoods and Religious Houses. By the Editor of "The Little Hours of the Day." In small 8vo., with considerable alterations and additions, cloth, red edges, 5s.; paper, 4s. 6d.

THE LOVE OF THE ATONEMENT, a Devotional Exposition of the Fifty-third chapter of Isaiah. By the Right Rev. R. MILMAN, D.D., Bishop of Calcutta. Sixth Edition. Fcap. 8vo., cloth, 3s. 6d.; calf, 8s.

THE SEVEN LAMPS OF FIRE COMPARED WITH THE SEVEN WORDS FROM THE CROSS, being Addresses delivered (with some alterations) at S. Columba's, Haggerston, on Good Friday, 1887. By the Rev. J. B. JOHNSON, Assistant Priest. 6d.

MYSTERIES OF PSALM CX. Four Sermons preached (in a simplified form) at S. Columba's, Haggerston, in Advent, 1888. By the Rev. J. B. JOHNSON, Assistant Priest. Fcap. 8vo., paper wrapper, 92 pp. 1s.

WORDS IN SEASON TO WORKING WOMEN, being Readings and Stories on the chief Seasons of the Church. By AUSTIN CLARE. 16mo., cl. 1s. 3d.

A STANDARD WORK ON RITUAL.

THE POLITY OF THE CHRISTIAN CHURCH OF EARLY, MEDIÆVAL, AND MODERN TIMES. By ALEXIUS AURELIUS PELLICCIA. Translated from the original Latin by the Rev. J. C. BELLETT, M.A. 8vo., cloth, 15s.

GOD'S WITNESS IN PROPHECY AND HISTORY. Bible Studies on the Historical Fulfilments of the Prophetic Blessings on the Twelve Tribes contained in Gen. xlix. With a Supplementary Inquiry into the History of the Lost Tribes. By the Rev. J. C. BELLETT, M.A. Crown 8vo., cloth, 6s.

MERCY AND TRUTH. Lent Sermons on the Conditions of the Workings of Grace. By the Rev. GEORGE A. COBBOLD, B.A. Crown 8vo., cloth, 2s.

SELECT SERMONS OF S. LEO THE GREAT ON THE INCARNATION, WITH THE TWENTY-EIGHTH EPISTLE, CALLED THE "TOME." Translated, with Notes, by the Rev. W. BRIGHT, D.D., Regius Professor of Ecclesiastical History, Canon of Christ Church, Oxford, and Examining Chaplain to the Lord Bishop of Ely. Second edition. Crown 8vo., 5s.

BROUGHT TO BOOK. Dr. R. W. DALE on the characteristic Conceptions of the Anglican Bishops and Clergy, and an Answer thereto on each several Matter of Gainsaying. Three Sermons by H. W. HOLDEN, Curate, Whitchurch, Salop. Crown 8vo., paper, 6d.; cloth, 1s.

HOLY WEEK AND OTHER SERMONS preached in S. Andrew's Church, Pau. By the Rev. R. H. D. ACLAND-TROYTE, M.A., Chaplain. Published by request. Fcap. 8vo., 1s. 6d., paper cover.

FOOTSTEPS TO CALVARY: Meditations on the Passion. With a Preface by the Right Rev. the Lord Bishop of Lichfield. Fcap. 8vo., 2s. 6d.

THE DOOM OF SACRILEGE AND THE RESULTS OF CHURCH SPOLIATION. Dedicated, by permission, to the Rt. Hon. VISCOUNT CRANBROOK, G.C.S.I. By JAMES WAYLAND JOYCE, M.A., Late Student of Ch. Ch., Rector of Burford (Third portion) Co. Salop, and Prebendary of Hereford. Crown 8vo., 4s.

This work is based to a considerable extent on Sir Henry Spelman's "History and Fate of Sacrilege," (1853,) which is out of print.

PSYCHOLOGUS: The Story of a Soul. A Poem. By JULIA GODDARD. Second edition. Fcap. 8vo., 1s.

OUTLINES OF CHURCH TEACHING. A Series of Instructions for the Sundays and Chief Holy Days of the Christian Year. By C. C. G. With Preface by the Rev. FRANCIS PAGET, D.D., Regius Professor of Pastoral Theology in the University of Oxford, and Canon of Christ Church. Second edit. Cr. 8vo., cl. 3s. 6d.

OUTLINES OF PLAIN INSTRUCTIONS FOR BIBLE CLASSES. Edited by the Rev. J. R. WEST, M.A., Canon of Lincoln, and Vicar of Wrawby. Fcap. 8vo., 8d.

LOOKING FOR THE CHURCH. An Abridgment of "A Presbyterian Looking for the Church." New edition, revised and edited by the Rev. FRANCIS KITCHIN. Crown 8vo., cloth limp, 2s.; cloth boards, red edges, 3s.

THE CHURCH IN ENGLAND CATHOLIC DEFENCE TRACTS.
1. The Church of England the Catholic Church in England. ½d.
2. Protestantism not English but Foreign. ½d.

THE "S. PAUL'S SERIES." MANUALS OF CHRISTIAN DOCTRINE.
A Complete Scheme of Graduated Instruction for Sunday Schools, by the Rev. WALKER GWYNNE. Approved by the Most Rev. the METROPOLITAN OF CANADA. Introduction by the Rev. R. W. CHURCH, M.A., D.C.L., Dean of S. Paul's.—Prayers for Children, in Four Grades: Primary, 4d. Junior, 6d. Middle, 10d. Senior for Teachers and older Scholars, 1s. 6d.

NOTES ON THE ANGELS. Based on the Writings of S. Thomas Aquinas. Edited by a Priest, and dedicated by permission to the Rev. A. D. Wagner, M.A. Compiled for School Teaching by the Lady in Charge of S. Mary's School for the Daughters of the Clergy and others, Queen Square, Brighton, and inscribed also to the Pupils who have attended this School for the last thirty years. 2nd edition. Cloth, 1s. 6d.

ANGELS. A few Remarks on their office as Ministering Spirits. By Mrs. STONE, author of "A Handbook to the Christian Year." Square 16mo., 3d.

ANCIENT EPITAPHS, From 1250 to 1800. Arranged in Chronological order. By T. F. RAVENSHAW, M.A., F.S.A. In Demy 8vo., cloth, reduced from 7s. 6d. to 2s. 6d.
This volume, containing nearly 500 epitaphs, will prove a valuable collection to those interested in the search after brasses and other monuments of the past. A very large number were copied by the author from tablets, headstones, and brasses, the remainder being supplied by his friends or taken from county histories.

THE CHRISTIAN SANCTIFIED BY THE LORD'S PRAYER. By the Author of "The Hidden Life of the Soul," &c. 16mo., cloth, 1s. 6d.

THE LIFE OF PEACE. By the Rev. R. C. LUNDIN BROWN, M.A., late Vicar of Rhodes, Manchester. Fcap. 8vo., cloth, 2s. 6d.

CONFIRMATION LECTURES delivered to a Village Congregation in the Diocese of Oxford. By the Ven. ARCHDEACON POTT. Fifth edition. 2s.

IS IT RIGHT TO PRAY FOR THE DEAD? By A. J. ANDERSON, Assistant Curate of Mattishall Bergh. With a Preface by H. MORTIMER LUCKOCK, D.D., Canon of Ely, author of "After Death," &c. Royal 16mo., leatherette, 8d.

PRAYERS FOR THE DEAD AND THE COMMUNION OF SAINTS. By WILLIAM RATHBONE SUFFLE, B.D. Second Edition. Square 32mo., cloth, 1s.

KALENDAR OF THE IMITATION: Sentences for every day of the year from the "Imitatio Christi." Translated from the edition of 1630. Edited by the late Rev. J. M. NEALE, D.D. New edition, royal 32mo., cloth, 1s.

VILLAGE CONFERENCES ON THE CREED. By the Rev. S. BARING-GOULD, M.A., Vicar of Lew Trenchard, Devon; author of "Origin and Development of Religious Belief," &c. Third Edition. Crown 8vo., cloth, 3s. 6d.

ONE HUNDRED SKETCHES OF SERMONS FOR EXTEMPORE PREACHERS. By the Rev. S. BARING-GOULD, M.A., author of "Origin and Development of Religious Belief," &c. Fourth Edition. Crown 8vo., cloth, 6s.

CHRIST IN THE LAW; or, the Gospel foreshadowed in the Pentateuch. Compiled from various sources. By a Priest of the Church of England. Third Edition. Fcap. 8vo., cloth, 3s. 6d.

GENESIS AND MODERN SCIENCE. By the Author of "CHRIST in the Law," &c. An Explanation of the First Chapter of the Bible in accordance with observed facts. Fcap. 8vo., 1s. 6d.

THE PLAIN GUIDE. By the Rev. J. S. POLLOCK, M.A. New and recent edition, revised, 3d.; limp cloth, 6d.; cloth boards, red edges, 9d.; French mor. 1s. 3d.

THE FIGHT OF FAITH. Words for Christian Soldiers. A Manual for Confirmation. By the Rev. J. S. POLLOCK, M.A. Super-royal 32mo., wrapper, 3d.; cloth or leatherette, 6d.

THE HELIOTROPIUM. By DREXELIUS. 12mo., cloth, 2s. 6d.

FAST AND FESTIVAL. By M. W. Super-royal 32mo., 6d.

PLAIN CHURCH TEACHING FOR WEEKDAYS THROUGHOUT THE YEAR; or, Readings from the Collect, Epistle, and Gospel of each Sunday and Holyday. Third edition. Cloth limp, 3s.; cloth boards, red edges, 4s.

THE COPTIC MORNING SERVICE FOR THE LORD'S DAY. Translated into English by JOHN, MARQUESS OF BUTE, K.T. With the Original Coptic of those parts said aloud. Crown 8vo., cloth, 6s.

ALL THE DAYS OF OUR LIFE. Short Readings for Daily Life and for the Church Seasons. By C. H. B. Second edition. 32mo., cloth, 1s. 6d.

HELPS TO MEDITATION FOR BEGINNERS. By a Priest of the Church of England. Edited by the Rev. CANON BODY. 18mo., 3d.

SUGGESTIONS ON THE METHOD OF MEDITATION. By the Rev. W. B. TREVELYAN. With a Preface by the LORD BISHOP OF ELY. 2d.

AN ACT OF SPIRITUAL COMMUNION. By the Rev. JAMES SKINNER, M.A. With Notice by the Rev. T. T. CARTER, M.A., Superior General of the Confraternity of the Blessed Sacrament. Royal 32mo., cloth, 6d.

TWELVE MEDITATIONS ON THE CHARACTER AND MIND OF OUR LORD JESUS CHRIST. By M. T. 18mo., wrapper, 6d.

THE QUIET LIFE. Readings for the Six Sundays in Lent. By M. T. 18mo., wrapper, 6d.

A CATECHISM OF THEOLOGY. 18mo., cloth, 1s. 6d.; paper, 1s.
"Very carefully put together, and containing a large mass of trustworthy information in brief compass."—*Church Times.*

HEROES OF THE CROSS. A Series of Biographical Studies of Saints, Martyrs, and Christian Pioneers. By W. H. DAVENPORT ADAMS. Crown 8vo., 488 pp., cloth, 7s. 6d.

CURIOSITIES OF SUPERSTITION AND SKETCHES OF SOME UNREVEALED RELIGIONS. By W. H. DAVENPORT ADAMS, author of "Heroes of the Cross," &c. Crown 8vo., cloth, reduced from 5s. to 2s. 6d.

THOUGHTS ON HOLINESS, Doctrinal and Practical. By W. A. COPINGER. Fcap. 8vo., cloth, reduced from 2s. 6d. to 1s.

A STUDENT PENITENT OF 1695. Diary, Correspondence, &c., of a Student, illustrating Academical Life at Oxford. By the Rev. F. E. PAGET, M.A., Rector of Elford. Crown 8vo., cloth, 4s. 6d.

SIX PLAIN SERMONS ON THE LOVE OF GOD. Founded on the Treatise of S. Francis de Sales. By the Rev. A. J. W. McNEILE. Fcap. 8vo., cloth, red edges, 1s. 6d.

FIVE PLAIN SERMONS ON THE SACRAMENT OF THE ALTAR. By the Rev. W. H. CLEAVER, M.A. Fifth Edition. Fcap. 8vo., 1s.

SIX PLAIN SERMONS ON PENITENCE. By the Rev. W. H. CLEAVER, M.A. Fourth Edition. Fcap. 8vo., 1s.

CHURCH CHOIRS; containing a Brief History of the Changes in Church Music during the last Forty or Fifty Years, with Directions for the Formation, Management, and Instruction of Cathedral, Collegiate, and Parochial Choirs; being the result of thirty-six years' experience in Choir Training. By FREDERICK HELMORE. Fourth Edition, Crown 8vo., 1s.

SPEAKERS, SINGERS, AND STAMMERERS. With Illustrations. By FREDERICK HELMORE, author of "Church Choirs," "The Chorister's Instruction Book," &c. Crown 8vo., cloth, 4s. 6d.

THE ITALIAN REGISTERS. Voce di Petto. Voce di Gola. Voce di Testa. By FREDERICK HELMORE, author of "Speakers, Singers, and Stammerers," &c., &c. Dedicated to Sir Arthur Sullivan. Crown 8vo., price 6d.

THE CLERGYMAN'S AND CHOIRMASTER'S VADE MECUM, in selecting from Hymns Ancient and Modern, complete edition. Compiled by the Rev. JAMES LEONARD FRANCIS, M.A. Royal oblong 16mo., wrapper, 1s.
The object aimed at in these Tables is to show, almost at a glance, what Hymns there are in the book in harmony with the various parts of the service, in order that from these a choice may be made suitable for the particular occasion upon which they are to be sung.

Published by J. Masters and Co.,

With 12 Photographs, extra cloth, gilt edges, 5s.; morocco, 10s.
HYMNS FOR LITTLE CHILDREN. By Mrs. C. F. ALEXANDER. Sixty-eighth Edition, handsomely printed on thick toned paper, with red border lines, 16mo., 2s. 6d.

With 85 Engravings, small 4to., cloth extra, reduced from 6s. to 3s. 6d.
CHEAP EDITION, IN PAPER COVER, 2s.
MORAL SONGS. By Mrs. C. F. ALEXANDER. The Illustrations have been arranged and engraved by James D. Cooper.

FOR THE SICK, AFFLICTED, &c.

LIGHT IN DARKNESS. Thoughts for the Suffering. By S. M. C. With a Notice by H. L. SIDNEY LEAR. 32mo., cloth, 6d.

IN TIME OF NEED, or, Words in Season for the Use of District Visitors and others. By JESSIE E. CARTER. Edited by the Rev. CHARLES BODINGTON, Vicar of Christ Church, Lichfield. Super-royal 32mo., 1s. 6d.; roan, 2s. 6d.

CHRISTUS CONSOLATOR. Short Meditations for Invalids, from the Writings of Dr. PUSEY, selected by a Lady. With a Preface by GEORGE E. JELF, M.A., Canon of Rochester. 2s.; roan, 3s.

THE EVENING OF LIFE; or, Meditations and Devotions for the Aged. By the Rev. W. E. HEYGATE, M.A., Rector of Brighstone, Isle of Wight. Third Edition. Crown 8vo., cloth, 4s.

HOMEWARD BOUND. The Voyage and the Voyagers; the Pilot and the Port. By the Rev. F. E. PAGET, M.A., Rector of Elford. Third edition. Crown 8vo., cloth, 4s.

POCKET BOOK OF DEVOTIONS AND EXTRACTS FOR IN-VALIDS. By C. L. Edited by the Ven. ALFRED POTT, B.D., Archdeacon of Berks; Rector of Sonning; Chaplain to the Bp. of Oxford. Super-royal 32mo., cloth, 1s. 6d.

THE DEAD IN CHRIST. A Word of Consolation for Mourners. By the Rev. R. C. LUNDIN BROWN, M.A., late Vicar of Rhodes, Manchester. Third Edition, super-royal 32mo., cloth boards, 1s. 6d.; cloth limp, 1s.

THOUGHTS FOR THE SICK. By M. W. With a Preface by the Rev. H. MONTAGU VILLIERS. Super-royal 32mo., 6d.

A SHORT MANUAL FOR NURSES, intended for those engaged in Nursing the Sick. Compiled by the Author of "Meditations for the Christian Year," &c. Edited by the Very Rev. W. J. BUTLER, M.A., Dean of Lincoln. 32mo., cloth, 6d.

IN MEMORIAM. Thoughts Selected and Arranged by J. F. ELTON and L. BOURDILLON. For use as a book of daily remembrance for departed friends. Royal 32mo., 2s.

PRAYERS AND MAXIMS FOR THE SICK AND AGED. In large type. Fourth Edition. Crown 8vo., cloth, 2s. 6d.

DEVOTIONS FOR THE SICK ROOM, PRAYERS IN SICKNESS, &c. By R. BRETT. Cloth, 2s. 6d.

COMPANION FOR THE SICK ROOM: being a Compendium of Christian Doctrine. By R. BRETT. 2s. 6d.

OFFICES FOR THE SICK AND DYING. Reprinted from "The Churchman's Guide to Faith and Piety." By R. BRETT. 1s.

LEAFLETS FOR THE SICK AND DYING; supplementary to the Offices for the same in "The Churchman's Guide to Faith and Piety." By R. BRETT. Price per set of eight, 6d.; cardboard, 9d.

Publications of the Confraternity of the Blessed Sacrament.

THE MANUAL OF THE CONFRATERNITY. Eighth edition, revised and enlarged. 4d.; cloth, red edges, 6d.

AN ALTAR BOOK FOR YOUNG PERSONS. Suitable also for Choristers. 28th Thousand. Cloth, with a picture of the Crucifixion, 8d.; with nine pictures, 1s. 3d.; with red edges, gold lettered, 1s. 6d.

SPRING BUDS: Counsels for the Young. From the French. By the Translator of "Gold Dust." With a Preface by CHARLOTTE M. YONGE. Imp. 32mo., cloth, 2s.; limp cloth, 1s. 6d.; roan, 3s. 6d.; calf or morocco, 6s.

GOLD DUST SERIES.

GOLD DUST: a Collection of Golden Counsels for the Sanctification of Daily Life. Translated from the French. Edited by C. M. YONGE. In Two Parts. Price of each Part, cloth gilt, 1s.; wrapper, 6d.; roan, 1s. 6d.; limp calf, 2s. 6d.
    The Two Parts, in case, cloth gilt, 2s. 6d.; limp calf, 6s.
    In one Volume, cloth, 1s. 6d.; limp roan, 2s. 6d.; limp calf, 3s. 6d.

GOLD DUST. (In larger type.) Translated from the French. Edited by C. M. YONGE. Complete in 1 Vol., Imp. 32mo., cloth, full gilt sides, 2s. 6d.; roan, 3s. 6d.; calf or morocco, 6s.

GOLDEN TREASURES. Counsels for the Happiness of Daily Life. Translated and abridged from the French. Edited by F. M. F. SKENE, Author of "The Divine Master." Uniform with "Gold Dust," cloth gilt, 1s.; roan, 1s. 6d.; calf, 2s. 6d.

"This little book has been drawn from the same source as 'Gold Dust,' and will be found to possess all the rare qualities which won so favourable a reception for its predecessor."

SPARKS OF LIGHT FOR EVERY DAY. Collected by Madame GUIZOT DE WITT; done into English by the Translator of "Gold Dust." Edited by CHARLOTTE M. YONGE. Cloth gilt, 1s.; wrapper, 6d.; limp roan, 1s. 6d.; limp calf, 2s. 6d.

LIGHT. A Devotional Reading on the Twenty-seventh Psalm. With Preface by the Rev. R. W. RANDALL, Vicar of All Saints, Clifton, Bristol. Cloth gilt, red edges, 1s., uniform with "Gold Dust."

DIVINE BREATHINGS; or, a Pious Soul's Thirstings after CHRIST. With a Preface by W. J. LOFTIE. Cloth gilt, 1s., uniform with "Gold Dust."

BY THE RIGHT REV. J. R. WOODFORD, D.D.,
Late Lord Bishop of Ely.

ORDINATION SERMONS preached in the Dioceses of Oxford and Winchester, 1860—72. 8vo., 5s.

SERMONS PREACHED IN VARIOUS CHURCHES OF BRISTOL. Second Edition. 8vo., 5s.

OCCASIONAL SERMONS. Vol. 2. Second Edition. 8vo., 5s.

BY THE REV. A. G. MORTIMER,
Rector of S. Mary's, Castleton, New York.

LEARN OF JESUS CHRIST TO DIE. Addresses on the Words of our LORD from the Cross, taken as teaching the Way of Preparation for Death. 16mo., cloth, 2s.

NOTES ON THE SEVEN PENITENTIAL PSALMS, chiefly from Patristic Sources. 3s. 6d.

HELPS TO MEDITATION. Sketches for every Day in the Year. With Introduction by the Bishop of Springfield. Vol. I. Advent to Trinity, 220 Meditations. 8vo., cloth, 7s. 6d. Vol. II. Trinity. 7s. 6d. The object of this work is to supply Material for Meditation and Outlines of Sermons.

LAWS OF PENITENCE. Addresses on the Words of our LORD from the Cross. 18mo., cloth, 1s. 6d.

THE LAWS OF HAPPINESS. Addresses on the Beatitudes. 2s.

FORTY HYMN TUNES TO POPULAR HYMNS. 4to., wrapper, 1s. 6d.; cloth, 2s.

BY THE RT. REV. E. T. CHURTON, D.D.,
Bishop of Nassau.

THE MISSIONARY'S FOUNDATION OF DOCTRINE, with Practical Reflections. Crown 8vo., 344 pp., 5s.

THE ISLAND MISSIONARY. A Manual of Instruction and Routine. In Ten Practical Addresses. Crown 8vo., 136 pp., 3s. Second edition, enlarged.

BY THE REV. J. R. WEST.

THE DIVINELY SANCTIONED USE OF SYMBOLISM. Fcp. 8vo.

THE DIVINE CONSTITUTION OF THE CHURCH ON EARTH. Fcap. 8vo., cloth limp, 8d.; wrapper, 4d.

WRESTED TEXTS. Third Edition, complete, revised and enlarged. Paper, 1s.; cloth limp, 1s. 6d.

ON THE FIGURES AND TYPES OF THE OLD TESTAMENT. Second Edition, revised, cloth limp, 1s. 6d.

ON THE NATURE AND CONSTITUTION OF THE PRESENT KINGDOM OF HEAVEN UPON EARTH. Fcap. 8vo., 2s. 6d.

A SHORT TREATISE ON THE HOLY EUCHARIST. Fcap. 8vo., 2s. 6d.

PARISH SERMONS ON THE HOLY EUCHARIST. Fcap. 8vo., cloth, 4s. 6d.

PARISH SERMONS ON THE ASCENSION OF OUR LORD. Fcap. 8vo., 3s. 6d.

PARISH SERMONS FOR THE ADVENT AND CHRISTMAS SEASONS. Fcap. 8vo., 3s.

THE MEMORIAL BEFORE GOD. Crown 8vo., 9d.

"WHAT MEAN YE BY THIS SERVICE?" Exodus xii. 26. Some Account of the Meaning of the Chief Service of the Christian Religion. 4d.

BY THE REV. G. S. HOLLINGS.

JESUS IN THE MIDST, or Penitent Thoughts and Prayers on the Passion of the Divine Redeemer, and on the Seven Words of our Lord. Royal 32mo., cloth, 1s.

ONE BORN OF THE SPIRIT, OR THE UNIFICATION OF OUR LIFE IN GOD. Crown 8vo., 3s. 6d.

PARADOXES OF THE LOVE OF GOD, especially as shown in the way of the Evangelical Counsels. Crown 8vo., 4s.

MEDITATIONS ON THE DIVINE LIFE AND THE BLESSED SACRAMENT, together with Considerations on the Transfiguration. Crown 8vo., cloth, 3s. 6d.

CONSIDERATIONS ON THE SPIRITUAL LIFE. Suggested by Passages in the Collects for the Sundays in Lent. Crown 8vo., cloth, 2s. 6d.

CONSIDERATIONS ON THE WISDOM OF GOD. Crown 8vo., cloth, 4s.

BY H. L. SIDNEY LEAR.

READINGS FROM HOLY SCRIPTURE. First and Second Series in one vol., reduced from 3s. 6d. to 2s.

LIFE OF SISTER ROSALIE. Second Edition. Cloth, 8d.

THE HOLY CHILDHOOD OF OUR BLESSED LORD. Meditations for a Month. 32mo., 6d.

BY THE REV. T. T. CARTER, M.A.,
Late Rector of Clewer, Hon. Can. of Ch. Ch., Oxford, Warden of the House of Mercy, Clewer.

HARRIET MONSELL. A Memoir. With Portrait from steel engraving by Stodart. Third and Cheap Edition. Crown 8vo., cloth, 2s. 6d.

THE ROMAN QUESTION. In Letters to a Friend. Second Edit., revised and enlarged. Crown 8vo., 3s. 6d.

A REASON FOR DISTRUSTING THE REV. LUKE RIVINGTON'S APPEAL TO THE FATHERS. Crown 8vo., 6d.

PARISH TEACHINGS. The Apostles' Creed and Sacraments. Crown 8vo., cloth, 4s. 6d. New Edition in the Press.

PARISH TEACHINGS. Second Series. The LORD's Prayer, and other Sermons. Crown 8vo., cloth, 4s. 6d.

SERMONS. Third Edition. 8vo., 9s.

SPIRITUAL INSTRUCTIONS. Crown 8vo., cloth.
1. THE HOLY EUCHARIST. Fifth Edition. 3s. 6d.
2. THE DIVINE DISPENSATIONS. Second Edition. 3s. 6d.
3. THE RELIGIOUS LIFE. 3s. 6d.
4. THE LIFE OF GRACE. Second Edition. 3s. 6d.
5. OUR LORD'S EARLY LIFE. 3s. 6d.
6. OUR LORD'S ENTRANCE ON HIS MINISTRY. 3s. 6d. *New Vol. now ready.*

LENT LECTURES. Four Series in 1 Vol. Crown 8vo., cloth, 6s.

THE IMITATION OF OUR LORD. Fifth edit. Demy 8vo., 2s. 6d.

THE DOCTRINE OF THE PRIESTHOOD IN THE CHURCH OF ENGLAND. Third Edition. 4s.

THE DOCTRINE OF CONFESSION IN THE CHURCH OF ENGLAND. Third Edition. Crown 8vo., 5s.

THE DOCTRINE OF THE HOLY EUCHARIST, drawn from the Holy Scriptures and the Records of the Church of England. 4th Edit. Fcp. 8vo., 9d.

VOWS AND THE RELIGIOUS STATE. Crown 8vo., 2s.

FAMILY PRAYERS. Seventh Edition. 18mo., cloth, 1s.

EDITED BY THE REV. T. T. CARTER.

A BOOK OF PRIVATE PRAYER FOR MORNING, MID-DAY, NIGHT, AND OTHER TIMES, with Rules for those who would live to GOD amid the business of daily life. Twelfth Edition. Limp cloth, 1s.; cl., red edges, 1s. 3d.; roan, 1s. 6d.; French morocco, 2s.; limp calf, 3s. 6d.

THE DAY OF PRAYER. Short Prayers for every Hour of the Day. Second Edition. 3d.

LITANIES, and other Devotions. Second Edition. 1s. 6d.

MEMORIALS FOR USE IN A RELIGIOUS HOUSE. Second Edition Enlarged. 6d.

NIGHT OFFICE FOR CHRISTMAS. 6d.

THE FOOTPRINTS OF THE LORD ON THE KING'S HIGHWAY OF THE CROSS. Devotional Aids for Holy Week. Fcap. 8vo., cloth, 1s.

FOOTSTEPS OF THE HOLY CHILD, being Readings on the Incarnation. Part I., 1s. Part II., 2s. 6d. In One Vol., 3s. 6d. cloth.

MANUAL OF DEVOTION FOR SISTERS OF MERCY. In Eight Parts, or Two Vols., cloth, 10s.; calf or morocco, 17s.

COLLECTS, EPISTLES, AND GOSPELS, suggested for use on certain special occasions and Holy-Days. Crown 8vo., 1s. 6d.

SIMPLE LESSONS; or, Words Easy to be Understood. A Manual of Teaching. Three Parts in one Volume. Third Edition. 18mo., cloth, 3s.
I. On the Creed. II. On the Ten Commandments. III. On the Sacraments.

Published by J. Masters and Co.,

MANUALS OF PRAYER.

THE DAY HOURS OF THE CHURCH OF ENGLAND, newly Translated and Arranged according to the Prayer Book and the Authorised Translation of the Bible. 15th thousand. Crown 8vo., wrapper, 1s.; cl., 1s. 6d.; calf or mor., 7s. A new Edition, with Illustrations, in the Press.

THE SERVICE FOR CERTAIN HOLYDAYS. Being a Supplement to "The Day Hours of the Church of England." New Edition. Crown 8vo., 2s.

THE DAY HOURS, SUPPLEMENT, MEMORIALS, AND LITANIES. 1 Vol., roan, 9s.; calf or morocco, 13s.

THE DAY OFFICE OF THE CHURCH. New Edition. Small 8vo., cloth, red edges, 5s.; paper, 4s. 6d.

THE CHURCHMAN'S GUIDE TO FAITH AND PIETY. A Manual of Instruction and Devotions. Compiled by ROBERT BRETT. Fifth Edition. Cloth, 3s. 6d.; antique calf or plain morocco, 8s. 6d. Two Vols., cloth, 4s.; limp calf, 11s.; limp morocco, 12s.

THE PRIMER, set forth at large with many Godly and Devout Prayers. Edited, from the Post-Reformation Recension, by the Rev. GERARD MOULTRIE, M.A., Vicar of South Leigh. Fourth Thousand. 18mo., cloth, reduced from 3s. to 2s.

"The Primer is the authorized Book of Family and Private Prayer for the laity of the Church. Its sources are of antiquity equal with that of the Book of Common Prayer; and it was revised and published by the Bishops at the Reformation at the same time with that Book. It is the only book of Private Devotion which has received the sanction of the English Church."—*Preface.*

THE HOURS OF THE PRIMER. Published separately for the use of individual members of a household in Family Prayer. 18mo., cloth, reduced from 1s. to 8d.

MANUAL OF DEVOTION FOR SISTERS OF MERCY. Edited by the Rev. T. T. CARTER, M.A. In Eight Parts. Two Vols. cloth, 10s.; calf or mor. 17s.

A BOOK OF PRIVATE PRAYER FOR MORNING, MID-DAY, NIGHT, AND OTHER TIMES, with Rules for those who would live to GOD amid the business of Daily Life. Edited by the Rev. T. T. CARTER. 12th edit. Limp cloth, 1s.; cloth, red edges, 1s. 3d.; roan, 1s. 6d.; French mor., 2s.; limp calf, 3s. 6d.

THE MANUAL: a Book of Devotion. By the Rev. W. E. HEYGATE. Twenty-first Edition. Cloth limp, 1s.; boards, 1s. 3d.; leather, 1s. 6d.; French mor. 2s.; limp calf, 3s. 6d. Cheap Edition, 6d. A Superior Edition, 12mo., cloth, 1s. 6d.

SURSUM CORDA: Aids to Private Devotion. Collected from the Writings of English Churchmen. Compiled by the Rev. F. E. PAGET. 2s. 6d. cloth.

THE MANTLE OF PRAYER; a Book of Devotions, compiled chiefly from those of Bishop Andrewes. By A. N. With a Preface by the Very Rev. W. J. BUTLER, D.D., Dean of Lincoln. Fcap. 8vo., cloth, 1s. 6d.; roan, 2s. 6d.

POCKET MANUAL OF PRAYERS FOR THE HOURS, &c., with the Collects from the Prayer Book. New Edition. Royal 32mo., cloth, 1s.; limp roan, 2s.; calf, 3s.

This popular Manual has been revised by several clergymen, and important additions have been made for the purpose of rendering it more suitable for private use, and especially for Retreats.

SHORT DAILY PRAYERS. 4th edition. Toned paper, same size as "Gold Dust." 48 pages, cloth, 1s.; padded calf, 2s.—An Edition in large type, demy 32mo., cloth, 1s.; calf, 2s. 6d.

"I think this little Book of Prayers is calculated to be very useful to many, and may tend to encourage the habit of prayer at all times of need."—Rev. T. T. CARTER.

THE POCKET BOOK OF DAILY PRAYERS. Translated from Eastern Originals. By the Rev. S. C. MALAN, M.A. Suited for the Waistcoat Pocket. Cloth, 6d.; roan, 1s.

DEVOTIONS FOR DAILY USE. With Preface by the Hon. and Rev. Canon COURTENAY. Royal 32mo., cloth extra, 1s.

SHORT DEVOTIONS FOR THE SEASONS. By F. H. M. Cloth, 9d.

A MANUAL OF PRIVATE DEVOTIONS, containing Prayers for each Day in the Week, Devotions for the Holy Communion, and for the Sick. By BISHOP ANDREWES. 6d.

A COLLECTION OF PRIVATE DEVOTIONS FOR THE HOURS OF PRAYER. By BISHOP COSIN. 1s.

THE CHRISTIAN'S PLAIN GUIDE. By the Rev. WALTER A. GRAY, M.A., Vicar of Arksey. 32mo., cloth boards, 1s. Cheap Edition, wrapper, 6d.

THE DEVOUT CHORISTER. Thoughts on his Vocation, and a Manual of Devotions for his use. By THOMAS F. SMITH, B.D. 32mo., cloth, 1s.

A MANUAL OF DEVOTIONS FOR SCHOOL-BOYS. Compiled from various sources. By R. BRETT. 6d.

PRAYERS FOR LITTLE CHILDREN AND YOUNG PERSONS. By R. BRETT. 6d.; cloth, 8d. Part I. 2d.; cloth, 4d.; Part II. 4d.; cloth, 6d.

THE YOUNG CHURCHMAN'S MANUAL. Second Edition. 6d.

FAMILY PRAYERS.

FAMILY PRAYERS. By the Rev. CANON CARTER. Sixth Edition. 18mo., cloth, 1s.

BOOK OF FAMILY PRAYERS, collected from the Public Liturgy of the Church of England. By E. G., Minor Canon of Durham. 2s.

FAMILY PRAYERS adapted to the course of the Ecclesiastical Year. By the late Rev. R. A. SUCKLING. Sixth Edition. 6d.; cloth, 1s.

PRAYERS FOR FAMILY USE. From Ancient Sources. With Preface by the Archdeacon of S. Alban's. Fcap. 8vo., cloth, 1s.

PRAYERS FOR A CHRISTIAN HOUSEHOLD, chiefly taken from the Scriptures, from the Ancient Liturgies, and the Book of Common Prayer. By the Rev. T. BOWDLER. Fcap. 8vo., cloth, 2s. 6d.

FAMILY DEVOTIONS FOR A FORTNIGHT. Compiled from the Works of BISHOP ANDREWES, KEN, WILSON, KETTLEWELL, NELSON, SPINCKES, &c. (Suited also for private use.) New Edition. Fcap. 8vo., cloth, 1s. 6d.

PRAYERS AND LITANIES, taken from Holy Scripture, together with a Calendar and Table of Lessons. Arranged by the Rev. J. S. B. MONSELL, LL.D. 16mo., cloth, 1s.

FAMILY PRAYERS FOR THE CHILDREN OF THE CHURCH. 4d., cloth, 8d.

MORNING AND EVENING PRAYERS FOR A FAMILY OR HOUSEHOLD. Wrapper, 2d. These Prayers were approved and sanctioned by the Right Rev. SAMUEL WILBERFORCE, Lord Bishop of Oxford.

A SHORT OFFICE OF EVENING AND MORNING PRAYER FOR FAMILIES. 6d.

SHORT SERVICES FOR DAILY USE IN FAMILIES. Cloth, 1s.

DEVOTIONAL BOOKS.

BENEATH THE CROSS. Readings for Children on our LORD'S Seven Sayings. By FLORENCE WILFORD. Edited by CHARLOTTE M. YONGE. 18mo., cloth boards, 1s. 6d.; limp cloth, 1s.

MEDITATIONS ON THE SUFFERING LIFE OF OUR LORD. Translated from Pinart. Adapted to the use of the Anglican Church by A. P. FORBES, D.C.L., Bishop of Brechin. Seventh Edition. Fcap. 8vo., cloth, 5s.; calf, 10s.

NOURISHMENT OF THE CHRISTIAN SOUL. Translated from Pinart. Adapted to the use of the Anglican Church by A. P. FORBES, D.C.L., Bishop of Brechin. Fifth Edition. Fcap. 8vo., cloth, 5s.; calf, 10s.

THE MIRROR OF YOUNG CHRISTIANS. Translated from the French. Edited by A. P. FORBES, D.C.L., Bishop of Brechin. With Engravings, 2s. 6d.; morocco antique, 7s.

THE DIVINE MASTER: a Devotional Manual illustrating the Way of the Cross. By F. M. F. SKENE, author of "Hidden Depths," &c. With Ten steel Engravings. Eleventh Edit. 2s. 6d.; morocco, 5s. Cheap Edition, in wrapper, 1s.

THE SHADOW OF THE HOLY WEEK. By F. M. F. SKENE. 18mo., cloth, 1s.

THE PSALTER, or Seven Ordinary Hours of Prayer, according to the Use of the Church of Sarum. Beautifully printed and illustrated. Fcap. 4to., antique binding. Reduced to 15s.

THE DIVINE LITURGY: a Manual of Devotions for the Sacrament of the Altar. For those who communicate. FOURTH EDITION, revised, with additional Prayers and Hymns, limp cloth, 1s. 6d. A superior edition printed on toned paper, cloth boards, red edges, 2s. 6d.; calf, 6s.

A FEW DEVOTIONAL HELPS FOR THE CHRISTIAN SEASONS. Edited by Two Clergymen. Two Vols., cloth, 5s. 6d.

THE GREAT TRUTHS OF THE CHRISTIAN RELIGION. Edited by the Rev. W. U. RICHARDS, M.A. 8th edition. Fcp. 8vo. cloth, 3s.; calf, 8s. Five Parts, in packet, 2s. 6d.

MEDITATIONS ON THE MOST PRECIOUS BLOOD AND EXAMPLE OF CHRIST. By the Rev. J. S. TUTE, M.A., Vicar of Markington, Yorkshire. Fcap. 8vo., cloth, 1s.

SPIRITUAL VOICES FROM THE MIDDLE AGES. Price 3s. 6d.

PRAYERS AND MAXIMS. In large type. Fourth Edition. Crown 8vo. cloth, 2s. 6d.

THE HOUR OF DEATH. A Manual of Prayers and Meditations intended chiefly for those who are in Sorrow or in Sickness. By the Rev. J. B. WILKINSON. Royal 32mo., 2s.

MEDITATIONS ON OUR LORD'S PASSION. Translated from the Armenian of Matthew, Vartabed. By the Rev. S. C. MALAN, M.A. 2s. 6d.

TWELVE SHORT AND SIMPLE MEDITATIONS ON THE SUFFERINGS OF OUR LORD JESUS CHRIST. Edited by the Very Rev. DEAN BUTLER. 2s. 6d.

THE FOOTPRINTS OF THE LORD ON THE KING'S HIGHWAY OF THE CROSS. Devotional Aids for Holy Week. Edited by the Rev. T. T. CARTER. Fcap. 8vo., cloth, 1s.

SELECTIONS, NEW AND OLD. With a Preface by Bishop WILBERFORCE. Fcap. 8vo., reduced from 2s. 6d. to 1s. 6d.

FOOTSTEPS OF THE HOLY CHILD, being Readings on the Incarnation. Edited by the Rev. T. T. CARTER. Part I., fcap. 8vo., 1s. Part II., 2s. 6d. In One Vol. cloth, 3s. 6d.

THE HIDDEN LIFE. Translated from Nepveu's Pensées Chrétiennes. Fourth Edition, enlarged. 18mo., 2s.

COMPANION FOR LENT. Being an Exhortation to Repentance, from the Syriac of S. Ephraem; and Thoughts for Every Day in Lent, gathered from other Eastern Fathers and Divines. By the Rev. S. C. MALAN, M.A. 1s. 3d.

THE CHRISTIAN'S DAY. By the Rev. F. E. PAGET, M.A. Royal 32mo., 2s. cloth.

MEDITATIONS FOR EVERY WEEK IN THE CHRISTIAN YEAR. By the Compiler of "Plain Prayers," with an Introduction by the Very Rev. W. J. BUTLER, D.D., Dean of Lincoln. Second Edition. 18mo., cloth, 1s. 6d.

THE SEVEN WORDS FROM THE CROSS. A Devotional Commentary. By BELLARMINE. Second Edition. 1s. 6d.

THE THREE HOURS AGONY: Meditations, Prayers, and Hymns on the Seven Words from the Cross of our Most Holy Redeemer, together with Additional Devotions on the Passion. 4d.
Sanctioned by the Right Rev. the Bishops of Winchester and Bath and Wells.

THE THREE HOURS SERVICE; in Commemoration of our Blessed LORD's Agony. A Form of Prayer which may be used in Churches on Good Friday during the time of the Three Hours Darkness. By the Rev. ALFRED CHILD, M.A. 2d.

OUR NEW LIFE IN CHRIST. Edited by a Parish Priest. Fifth edition. Royal 32mo., 6d.

By the same Author.

THE PRESENCE OF JESUS ON THE ALTAR: a Sequel to "Our New Life in CHRIST." With a Few Simple Ways of Worshipping Him at the Celebration of the Blessed Sacrament. To which are added, Devotions and Hymns. 18mo., limp cloth, 1s.

HOW TO COME TO CHRIST. Instructions on Repentance, Holy Communion, and Union with CHRIST. Second edition. Royal 32mo., 4d.

PLAIN WORDS ABOUT OUR LORD'S LIFE; or, How to Follow CHRIST. Fcap. 8vo., 6s. 6d., or in 12 Parts separately.
These two works were originally written for reading at some Mothers' Meetings in connection with Mission work in a very neglected and populous district in London.

SQUARE PRESENT BOOKS.

New Edition, square 32mo., thick toned paper, cloth, 1s.; mor., red edges, 3s.; calf, round corners, red and gold edges, 3s. 6d.—Cheap Edit., Roy. 32mo., 4d.; cl., 6d.; mor., 1s. 6d.

Brother Lawrence's Conversations and Letters.

THE PRACTICE OF THE PRESENCE OF GOD THE BEST RULE OF A HOLY LIFE, being Conversations and Letters of Brother Lawrence.
The present Archbishop of Canterbury, in his work entitled "Singleheart," speaks in commendation of "Brother Lawrence."

QUAINT CHARMS, KNOTS, AND VERSES. Selected from the Works of GEORGE HERBERT, 1593—1635, by A. L. J. G. Second edition. Square 32mo., white leatherette, 1s.

CHIPS FROM THE ROYAL IMAGE, being Fragments of the Eikon Basiliké, the Pourtraicture of his Sacred Majesty (Charles I.) in his Solitudes and Sufferings. Arranged by A. E. M. ANDERSON MORSHEAD. Edited by C. M. YONGE. Thick toned paper, square 32mo., 1s.

THE PRESENT STATE OF THE FAITHFUL DEPARTED. A Sermon. By the Rev. CANON BODY. Ninth edition, in square 32mo., on thick toned paper, 1s. cloth.—The usual fcap. 8vo. edition, in paper, price 6d.

LIGHT. A Devotional Reading on the Twenty-seventh Psalm. With Preface by the Rev. R. W. RANDALL, Vicar of All Saints, Clifton, Bristol. Cloth gilt, red edges, 1s., uniform with "Gold Dust."

DIVINE BREATHINGS; or, a Pious Soul's Thirstings after CHRIST. With a Preface by W. J. LOFTIE. Cloth gilt, 1s., uniform with "Gold Dust."

JOYFUL YEARS. Translated from the Latin of Lohner, by the Author of "CHARLES LOWDER," &c. Imperial 32mo., cloth, 1s. 6d.

Published by J. Masters and Co., 78, New Bond Street.

MANUALS FOR HOLY COMMUNION.

THE SIXTY-EIGHTH EDITION.

STEPS TO THE ALTAR: A Manual of Devotions for the Blessed Eucharist. By the Rev. W. E. SCUDAMORE, M.A., Rector of Ditchingham.

    1. SIXPENCE . . . . IMPERIAL 32mo., cloth, 6d.; French morocco, 1s. 6d.
    2. ONE SHILLING . . DEMY 18mo., cloth, 1s.; Persian calf, 2s.; limp calf or morocco, 3s. 6d.
    3. ONE SHILLING AND THREEPENCE . . DEMY 18mo., (large type,) cloth boards, 1s. 3d.; limp calf, 4s.
    4. TWO SHILLINGS . . ROYAL 32mo., printed on toned paper, with red border lines and rubrics, cloth, 2s.; French morocco, 3s.; limp calf or morocco, 4s. 6d.; German calf, 5s. 6d.; russia, 6s.

The ROYAL 32mo. Edition and the COLLECTS, EPISTLES, AND GOSPELS, can be had bound together, price 2s. 6d., cloth; French morocco, 4s.; morocco, round corners, red and gold edges, 6s. 6d.; German calf or russia, ditto, 7s.

INCENSE FOR THE ALTAR. A Series of Devotions for the Use of earnest Communicants, whether they receive frequently or at longer intervals. By the Rev. W. E. SCUDAMORE, Rector of Ditchingham. Royal 32mo., cl., 2s. 6d.; calf, 5s.

EUCHARISTIC MANUAL, consisting of Instructions and Devotions for the Holy Sacrament of the Altar. From various sources. By the Rev. G. R. PRYNNE, M.A., Vicar of S. Peter's, Plymouth. Nineteenth edition. 1s. 6d.; cloth; calf or morocco, 4s. 6d.; German calf, round corners, 5s. Cheap edition, limp cloth, 1s.; roan, 2s.; Persian calf, 3s.; calf or morocco boards, 4s.

THE MANUAL: a Book of Devotions, containing Prayers for every necessity, and Instructions for a Devout Life. By the Rev. W. E. HEYGATE, M.A. 23rd edition. Royal 32mo., cloth limp, 1s.; boards, 1s. 3d.; roan, 1s. 6d.; French mor. 2s.; calf, 3s. 6d.; cheap edition, 6d.
An edition in larger type, Fcap. 8vo., cloth, 1s. 6d.

THE PATHWAY OF FAITH; or, a Manual of Instructions and Prayers, for those who desire to serve GOD in the station of life in which He has placed them. Limp cloth, 1s.; cloth boards, 1s. 3d.

SHORT DEVOTIONS FOR THE SACRAMENT OF THE ALTAR. By the Rev. W. H. CLEAVER. Third edition. 4d.

DIVINE SERVICE. A Complete Manual of Worship for Assisting and Communicating at the Holy Sacrifice. 654 pages, cloth boards, red edges, fcap. 8vo., 7s. 6d.

THE DIVINE LITURGY. A Manual of Devotions for the Sacrament of the Altar. Fourth Edition, revised and enlarged. Imp. 32mo., 1s. 6d. A Superior Edition printed on toned paper. Cloth boards, red edges, 2s. 6d.; calf, 6s.

DEVOTIONS FOR HOLY COMMUNION. Edited by the Rev. W. U. RICHARDS. 32mo., cloth, 1s.

GUIDE TO THE EUCHARIST. Containing Instructions and Directions, with Forms of Preparation and Self-Examination. 4d.

MANUAL FOR COMMUNICANTS; being an Assistant to a Devout and worthy reception of the LORD'S Supper. Paper cover, 6d. Large type, 6d.

MANUAL ON THE HOLY COMMUNION. Part IV. of Manuals of Devotion for Sisters of Mercy. Edited by the Rev. T. T. CARTER. 2s.

THE CHURCHMAN'S ASSISTANT AT HOLY COMMUNION. By the Rev. ROBERT F. LAURENCE, M.A. Fcap. 8vo., cloth, 2s.

THE CHURCHMAN'S GUIDE TO FAITH AND PIETY. A Manual of Instruction and Devotion. Compiled by ROBERT BRETT. Fifth Edition, revised. In 1 vol., cloth, 3s. 6d.; calf or morocco, 8s. 6d. In 2 vols., cloth, 4s.; calf, 11s.; morocco, 12s.

LONDON: J. MASTERS & CO., 78, NEW BOND STREET.

www.ingramcontent.com/pod-product-compliance
Lightning Source LLC
Chambersburg PA
CBHW031855220426
43663CB00006B/638